Managing the Human Side of Information Technology: Challenges and Solutions

Edward J. Szewczak and Coral R. Snodgrass
Canisius College, USA

IRM Press
Publisher of innovative scholarly and professional
information technology titles in the cyberage

Hershey • London • Melbourne • Singapore • Beijing

Acquisition Editor:	Mehdi Khosrow-Pour
Senior Managing Editor:	Jan Travers
Managing Editor:	Amanda Appicello
Development Editor:	Michele Rossi
Copy Editor:	Jane Conley
Typesetter:	LeAnn Whitcomb
Cover Design:	Tedi Wingard
Printed at:	Integrated Book Technology

Published in the United States of America by
  IRM Press (an imprint of Idea Group Inc.)
  701 E. Chocolate Avenue, Suite 200
  Hershey PA 17033-1240
  Tel: 717-533-8845
  Fax: 717-533-8661
  E-mail: cust@idea-group.com
  Web site: http://www.idea-group.com

and in the United Kingdom by
  IRM Press (an imprint of Idea Group Inc.)
  3 Henrietta Street
  Covent Garden
  London WC2E 8LU
  Tel: 44 20 7240 0856
  Fax: 44 20 7379 3313
  Web site: http://www.eurospan.co.uk

Library of Congress Cataloging-in-Publication Data

Managing the human side of information technology : challenges and solutions / [edited by]
  Edward J. Szewczak and Coral R. Snodgrass.
    p. cm.
  Includes bibliographical references and index.
  ISBN 1-931777-74-8 (paper)
  1. Information resources management. I. Szewczak, Edward. II. Snodgrass, Coral.

T58.64.M3595 2003
658.4'038--dc21

2003040623

eISBN 1-59140-021-X

Previously published in a hard cover version by Idea Group Publishing.

British Cataloguing in Publication Data
A Cataloguing in Publication record for this book is available from the British Library.

New Releases from IRM Press

- **Multimedia and Interactive Digital TV: Managing the Opportunities Created by Digital Convergence**/Margherita Pagani
  ISBN: 1-931777-38-1; eISBN: 1-931777-54-3 / US$59.95 / © 2003
- **Virtual Education: Cases in Learning & Teaching Technologies**/ Fawzi Albalooshi (Ed.)
  ISBN: 1-931777-39-X; eISBN: 1-931777-55-1 / US$59.95 / © 2003
- **Managing IT in Government, Business & Communities**/Gerry Gingrich (Ed.)
  ISBN: 1-931777-40-3; eISBN: 1-931777-56-X / US$59.95 / © 2003
- **Information Management: Support Systems & Multimedia Technology**/ George Ditsa (Ed.)
  ISBN: 1-931777-41-1; eISBN: 1-931777-57-8 / US$59.95 / © 2003
- **Managing Globally with Information Technology**/Sherif Kamel (Ed.)
  ISBN: 42-X; eISBN: 1-931777-58-6 / US$59.95 / © 2003
- **Current Security Management & Ethical Issues of Information Technology**/Rasool Azari (Ed.)
  ISBN: 1-931777-43-8; eISBN: 1-931777-59-4 / US$59.95 / © 2003
- **UML and the Unified Process**/Liliana Favre (Ed.)
  ISBN: 1-931777-44-6; eISBN: 1-931777-60-8 / US$59.95 / © 2003
- **Business Strategies for Information Technology Management**/Kalle Kangas (Ed.)
  ISBN: 1-931777-45-4; eISBN: 1-931777-61-6 / US$59.95 / © 2003
- **Managing E-Commerce and Mobile Computing Technologies**/Julie Mariga (Ed.)
  ISBN: 1-931777-46-2; eISBN: 1-931777-62-4 / US$59.95 / © 2003
- **Effective Databases for Text & Document Management**/Shirley A. Becker (Ed.)
  ISBN: 1-931777-47-0; eISBN: 1-931777-63-2 / US$59.95 / © 2003
- **Technologies & Methodologies for Evaluating Information Technology in Business**/ Charles K. Davis (Ed.)
  ISBN: 1-931777-48-9; eISBN: 1-931777-64-0 / US$59.95 / © 2003
- **ERP & Data Warehousing in Organizations: Issues and Challenges**/Gerald Grant (Ed.)
  ISBN: 1-931777-49-7; eISBN: 1-931777-65-9 / US$59.95 / © 2003
- **Practicing Software Engineering in the 21ˢᵗ Century**/Joan Peckham (Ed.)
  ISBN: 1-931777-50-0; eISBN: 1-931777-66-7 / US$59.95 / © 2003
- **Knowledge Management: Current Issues and Challenges**/Elayne Coakes (Ed.)
  ISBN: 1-931777-51-9; eISBN: 1-931777-67-5 / US$59.95 / © 2003
- **Computing Information Technology: The Human Side**/Steven Gordon (Ed.)
  ISBN: 1-931777-52-7; eISBN: 1-931777-68-3 / US$59.95 / © 2003
- **Current Issues in IT Education**/Tanya McGill (Ed.)
  ISBN: 1-931777-53-5; eISBN: 1-931777-69-1 / US$59.95 / © 2003

Excellent additions to your institution's library!
Recommend these titles to your Librarian!

*To receive a copy of the IRM Press catalog, please contact
(toll free) 1/800-345-4332, fax 1/717-533-8661,
or visit the IRM Press Online Bookstore at: [http://www.irm-press.com]!*

Note: All IRM Press books are also available as ebooks on netlibrary.com as well as other ebook sources. Contact Ms. Carrie Skovrinskie at [cskovrinskie@idea-group.com] to receive a complete list of sources where you can obtain ebook information or IRM Press titles.

Managing the Human Side of Information Technology: Challenges and Solutions

Table of Contents

Preface

This book is the second in the Series in Managing the Human Side of Information Technology sponsored by Idea Group Publishing. This Series was created to address the influence of information technology (IT) in modern organizations and its effect on individuals, focusing on managing the human side of this technology for competitive advantage and organizational prosperity. As the co-editors of the first Series book, *Managing the Human Side of Information Technology: Challenges and Solutions*, noted:

> Organizations must understand that there are a vast number of information resources, particularly human resources, while recognizing the potential of [IT] in support of managerial activities. The days of identifying computer-based information systems as only a collection of hardware and software are gone. In order to be able to achieve greater utilization of this technology, there must be much more emphasis given to the value of individuals who handle and use information resources (Szewczak & Khosrowpour, p. i).

Technologies continue to change and evolve at a rapid pace. The dazzling growth of the Internet as a provider of a host of information resources is perhaps the most significant example of this technological change and evolution. How this technology has impacted people and how people have responded to it in turn have provided students of the human side of IT a fertile ground for study and research.

The chapters of this book are organized into parts that correspond to four broad categories of interest: 1) leadership, risk, spirit and IT; 2) organizational communication and IT; 3) organizational groups and IT; and 4) culture and IT.

Within the leadership, risk and IT category (Part I), Walter O. Einstein and John H. Humphreys present a new leader behavior model in "The Changing Face of Leadership: The Influence of Information Technology." This new model is needed in light of the degree to which emerging instances of IT have changed both the organizational context and the traditional leader-follower power relationship. When used with effective diagnosis, the new model provides guidance to leaders in situations where they have power, as well as situations where power is lacking.

In "The Social Antecedents of Business Process Planning Effectiveness," Sofiane Sahraoui departs from earlier studies that view the organization as made up of distinct IT and business functions. Instead the organization is viewed holistically, i.e., information systems form the skeleton of business processes, and business processes cannot be disentangled from information systems. A model of business process planning effectiveness is presented that identifies information-enabled leadership, planning culture, knowledge worker management and strategic alignment as key social antecedents.

Various human side risk factors must be considered if IT is to be used successfully to restructure more traditional jobs at the operational and managerial levels of organizations. In "Assessing the Risks of IT-Enabled Jobs," Laura Lally appeals to Normal Accident Theory and the Theory of High Reliability Organizations to examine the issues related to reengineering jobs with IT. Key questions are raised that must be answered if managerial jobs are to be designed that will be more efficient and realistic for a given organizational environment: Are the demands of the new job realistic for the organization's workforce? Do the new jobs consider the issues of separation of duties and redundancy? Do the new jobs require greater degrees of autonomy and responsibility?

Huub J.M. Ruël offers an interesting look at the human side of office IT in the broadest sense in "The Non-Technical Side of Office Technology: Managing the Clarity of the Spirit and the Appropriation of Office Technology." He argues that the management of office IT projects would be more effective if systems developers were more focused on the concepts of spirit and appropriation as developed in Adaptive Structuration Theory, which starts from the assumption that the effects of advanced IT are not a function of the technology itself but of the way the IT is used. His study has implications for changes in internal organizational environment as well as job design characteristics.

Within the organizational communication and IT category (Part II), Dianne Willis examines "Computer Mediated Communication – The Power of Email as a Driver for Changing the Communication Paradigm." Using her own institution as the focus, Willis reports on a survey of people's feelings about the use of email and how they see future patterns of communication developing within the institution. The issues of overload and of alternate forms of communication are examined and discussed.

The Internet is a technology that is used to communicate vast quantities of data and information throughout the world. In the chapter, "Personal Information Privacy and the Internet: Issues, Challenges and Solutions," Edward J. Szewczak looks at the technological, social and legal dimensions of the personal information privacy issue and the problems that the Internet presents to those who value their personal privacy.

Knowledge communication is the focus of "E-communication of Interdepartmental Knowledge: An Action Research Study of Process Improvement Groups" by Ned Kock and Robert J. McQueen. The authors report on an action research project whose results suggest that email conferencing support has a positive impact on knowledge dissemination in organizations when combined with a group methodology (here, MetaProi) for process improvement. One of the main effects was an increase or decrease in individual learning in process improvement groups, depending on the complexity of the issues being discussed and the clarity of electronic contributions by group members.

The Jet Propulsion Laboratory (JPL) at the California Institute of Technology is the site at which research was conducted by Olivia Ernst Neece on the topics of organizational learning and knowledge management. In "A Strategic Systems Perspective of Organizational Learning: Development of a Process Model Linking Theory and Practice," she details how the process model enabled the growth and development of organizational learning at JPL and helped provide the basis for future creative efforts.

Within the organizational groups and IT category (Part III), two chapters by Pak Yoong and Brent Gallupe focus on group support systems (GSS). The first focuses on "reflective practice" to facilitate face-to-face electronic meetings. The authors propose a model of active reflection, which is the attribute of having insight and of giving meaning to data, among other things. The second chapter describes the use of "action learning" to facilitate GSS training. Action learning is a group learning and problem-solving process wherein group members work on real issues and problems with an emphasis on self-development and learning by doing. One of the main emphases for these ideas is to improve the adoption rate of technologies that support electronic face-to-face meetings in organizations.

The third chapter in this part by Thekla Rura-Polley and Ellen Baker considers remote innovation, i.e., innovation organized through electronic collaboration. In "Extending Collaboration Support Systems: Making Sense in Remote Innovation," the authors look at the importance of sensemaking in collaborations with the support of computer-based support tools. They describe a Web-based system called LiveNet that provides members with various tools to effectively accomplish innovation across regions and industries, and consider how this technology can promote the building of relationships among participants.

Within the culture and IT category (Part IV), Andrew Targowski and Ali Metwalli present "The Framework for a Cross-Cultural Communication Process, Efficiency, and Cost in the Global Economy." The framework is intended to produce successful communication among different cultures from different civilizations, thereby promoting global peace through trade. Their research method is based on the quantitative analysis of a cross-cultural communication process and system rather than the more usual qualitative analysis.

Robert W. Gerulat brings a fresh perspective to the issue of outsourcing in the chapter on "Cultural Characteristics of IT Professionals: An Ethnographic Perspective." Drawing on the discipline of anthropology, he considers two underlying research questions: 1) What are the common cultural norms, values, beliefs, and assumptions that describe the culture of IT professionals? and 2) How are cultural norms, values, and beliefs transmitted to and reinforced by the IT community? His study points to important differences between IT professionals who are managerially oriented and those who are technically oriented.

Acknowledgments

Many people have contributed to the production of this book. Their dedication to the writing of high quality chapters and their commitment to submitting them to the publisher on time have made it possible to complete work within the publisher's production schedule. For their efforts we are very thankful. Our college also deserves thanks for its support. In particular, we would like to thank Richard A. Shick, Dean of the Wehle School of Business at Canisius College, for his gracious support throughout this project, and Carol Michalski for her efficient secretarial support. Also, we thank Jan Travers and Michele Rossi of Idea Group Publishing for their hard work, dedication and understanding during the production of this high quality book.

Edward J. Szewczak & Coral R. Snodgrass
Canisius College

Part I

Leadership, Risk, Spirit and Information Technology

Chapter I

The Changing Face of Leadership: The Influence of Information Technology

Walter O. Einstein
University of Massachusetts–Dartmouth, USA

John H. Humphreys
Eastern New Mexico University, USA

Leadership, as a concept, has been with us ever since people have fashioned themselves into groups. Although the definition of leadership depends upon one's theoretical perspective, "few of us would dispute the point that leaders exercise influence, taking actions that, in one way or another, shape the behavior of others" (Mumford, Zaccaro, Harding, Jacobs, & Fleishman, 2000, p. 11). Effective leadership, however, is somewhat dependent upon the current context and environment. In this regard, it is readily apparent that advancing information technologies have forever changed the management landscape (Hitt, 2000). "As we enter the post-industrial information age, ... a premium is placed on the organization's ability to rapidly adapt to changing competitive environments and new technologies" (Mumford, Zaccaro, Connelly, & Marks, 2000, p. 167). Organizations will operate in a state of continual transformation, leaving managers to struggle in a changing environment of ambiguity and uncertainty (Hitt, 2000). Indeed, many prominent university programs are beginning to offer courses that attempt to "explore and analyze dynamic, practical solutions for breaking the shackles of traditional management techniques to develop the leadership organizations need to succeed in the fast-changing business environment" (Clerk, 2000, p. 16). To further compound the confusion, it is obvious that emerging technology is also changing the leader-follower context and that traditional leadership constructs are simply not adequate during such a period of escalating technological advancement (Fulmer, Gibbs, & Goldsmith, 2000). What is clear is that emerging technologies have forced many organizations to alter their hierarchical management designs (Dervitsiotis, 1998) and diminished the traditional power base of many managers (Sawhney & Prandelli, 2000). No longer is it common for a manager to possess the information monopoly necessary to sustain such formal position power (Wang, 1997). As technologies emerge and advance, it is simply a business imperative that organizational leadership evolves as well. There is much agreement that an organization's IT human capital must be effectively managed for both organizational and individual success (Mata, Fuerst, & Barney, 1995; Ross, Beath, & Goodhue, 1996). There is a growing consensus that in the new world of advancing technology, human capital may well be the preeminent strategic capability (Stewart, 1997) and the primary asset by which organizational change and effectiveness can be achieved (Roepke, 2000). Many IT leaders understand that the greatest challenges to organizational success are more often associated with people rather than information technology itself (Roepke, 2000) and that a new type of leadership will be needed to effectively develop this human capital (Hitt, 2000).

In this Chapter's beginning, we introduce the degree to which emerging information technologies have changed both the organizational context and the traditional leader-follower power relationship, and the significant challenges that have arisen from this evolution. In addition, we examine the emergence of leadership substitutes, such as teams, that are common to many information technology work groups and discuss the kind of leader influence that appears to be warranted. Most importantly, however, we present a leader behavior model tied closely to the situational leadership paradigm. In this model, we seek to show that unique actions and behaviors are associated with four specific leadership styles. Further, the model shows leaders' behavioral differences based upon whether they do or do not possess rational legal authority, commonly referred to as "position power." Most leadership discussions are limited to the descriptive nature of leadership and fail to offer specific guidance in identifying which leadership style is situational appropriate. We seek to remedy that shortcoming and take the critical next step of identifying leader behaviors that are appropriate for enhancing followers' effort toward successful goal-directed behavior.

THE NEW LEADERSHIP LANDSCAPE

From the very dawn of business enterprise, organizational success has resided within the ability of individual leaders to obtain an acceptable performance level from their subordinate followers. Leadership, however, became a serious topic of interest within the business community with the expansion of industrialization. The concept of leadership was very basic. Whether leading the entire organization, or a few production workers, leadership entailed the issuance of specific rewards in exchange for conformance to the standards set by the leader. Burns (1978) labeled this exchange relationship as transactional leadership. He suggested that, within this bargaining process, both leader and followers are aware of the power resources and attitudes of the other party. Although leader and follower share a related purpose, the relationship does not transcend the exchange process. Therefore, the leader and followers are not bound together in a mutual and continuing quest of higher purpose (Burns, 1978). This form of leadership was effective during an era of marketplace expansion and nonexistent competition (Tichy & DeVanna, 1986). Much of what we consider standard management thinking was developed during a time of relative environmental stability (Hitt, 2000).

Today, however, we find a much different environment. The competitive landscape of the 21st Century will be characterized by ever-increasing complexity and continual transformation. Authors are beginning to assert that transformational innovation will be the key to organizational survival (Foster, 2000) and that firms must begin to communicate a transformational IT vision (Armstrong & Sambamurthy, 1999). Appropriately, many believe that advancing information technologies will continue to drive this state of constant transformation (Mumford, Zaccaro, Connelly, & Marks, 2000; Wang, 1997). Hitt (2000) declares, "As we enter this new business frontier, new forms of managerial thinking along with new organizational structures will be required" (p. 13). Clearly, these new organizational structures have begun to emerge and management thinking is racing to keep up.

Organizational Structure: The Movement From Hierarchy To Teams

Today, we see a shift away from the old-style management pyramid as a direct result of the escalation of information technology (Vroman, 1994). The literature details a "proliferation of new organizational designs–virtual, boundaryless, horizontal, shamrock, lattice, collateral, and network organizations, all of which share a flattening of the traditional hierarchy, that is, the vertically integrated bureaucracy" (Klenke, 1997, p. 149). The growth of work teams has certainly emerged from these new designs as a means to encourage collaboration, fluidity, innovation, and creativity. These teams often create very complex relationships and can become smaller organizations unto themselves, with members drawn from within and outside the parent firm (Handy, 1995; Jarvenpaa & Leidner, 1999; Slowinski, Oliva, & Lowenstein, 1995). This complexity, along with the diminished management control that accompanies it, raises serious questions about effective leadership of such teams. Of particular importance, what are the specific behavioral roles of leaders of such teams in relation to team members?

This concern is particularly relevant for leaders of high performance teams. Larson and LaFasto (1989) suggest that high performance teams are characterized by the following components: 1) a shared commitment; 2) unambiguous goals that are perceived by team members as crucial; 3) a results-driven structure that emphasizes participation and collaboration; 4) skilled and competent team members; 5) an environment that is conducive to trust, camaraderie, and communication; 6) standards of excellence; and 7) systems of support and recognition. These features certainly mirror those found in many teams made up of IT professionals. These teams "are unique and different from both traditional work groups and other organizational teams because of the nature of their work which depends not only on individual and collective performance and mutual accountability, but it is also governed by reciprocal interactions between organizational and technological process" (Klenke, 1997, p. 161). Klenke (1997) shows that information technology teams are different from other teams in three important aspects: 1) they possess a unique set of knowledge, skills, and abilities; 2) they are knowledge workers; and 3) they are engaged in continuous learning.

Achieving true teamwork is difficult because it necessitates merging individual accomplishment and satisfaction with team maintenance (McGrath, 1990). Moreover, there are additional complications with IT teams as they are often confronted with greater ambiguities, more information, and directives from multiple perspectives (Klenke, 1997). In this climate, team success is reliant upon matching the knowledge and skill set of the team members with specific project requirements. High performance IT teams are often composed of information technology professionals who are highly trained and typically hold strong beliefs, not only about technology, but about teamwork and leadership as well. In addition, they often carry out responsibilities once reserved for management. As such, they are often referred to as self-managing teams. High performance IT teams are typically more likely to be cross-functional, cross-disciplinary, multifunctional, high involvement, and self-managing than other types of teams (Klenke, 1997) and are often comprised of individuals who excel in regulating their own behavior (Goodman, Devadas, & Hughson, 1988). Because of this self-regulation, there is the belief that leadership of high performance technology teams is potentially governed by the presence of leadership substitutes (Howell & Bowen, 1990; Klenke, 1997).

Leadership Substitutes

Leadership substitutes theory suggests that the need for hierarchical leadership is diminished when certain attributes of followers, tasks, and organizations are present (Kerr & Jermier, 1978; Howell & Dorfman, 1986). Howell and Bowen (1990) offer eight individual/organizational attributes they believe have the potential to replace ineffective leadership:

1) Closely-knit teams of highly trained individuals–experience and continuous training, along with significant group cohesion, can substitute for formal leadership.
2) Intrinsic satisfaction–intrinsic satisfaction of followers, created by producing high quality work, alleviates the need for formal leadership.
3) Computer technology–when followers have access to organizational data, and to other workers to help them solve problems, they become less dependent upon formal leadership.
4) Extensive professional education–employees with a great deal of formal education can perform most assignments without supervision and may actually rebel against direction provided by a formal leader.
5) Team approaches–followers' professional norms and standards, and feedback from competent team peers, can substitute for formal leadership.
6) High-ability independent workers–even when followers don't have extensive formal education, ability combined with experience can serve as a substitute for formal leadership.
7) Distributed feedback–feedback from peers, clients, and even the work itself, can replace hierarchical feedback and substitute for feedback from formal leadership.
8) Procedures–specific work rules, guidelines, and policies can provide task guidance to a certain extent, thereby diminishing the need for guidance from a formal leader.

Highly experienced, formally educated, well-trained professionals pursuing intrinsically satisfying work personify what we think of when we envision a cohesive IT work team. It is obvious that in many high performance IT teams, these potential leader substitutes are commonplace. So, can we assume that a high performance IT team doesn't need effective leadership? Our position is absolutely not. First of all, leader substitutes are thought to be helpful when ineffective or weak leadership is present; they're certainly not the ideal. Also, many of the early empirical examinations of this theory were not very supportive (Howell & Dorfman, 1981, 1986; Podsakoff, Dorfman, Howell, & Todor, 1986) and more recent studies have not proven to be any more supportive than earlier ones (Podsakoff & MacKenzie, 1997). Moreover, leadership substitutes theory does not suggest the abolition of leadership: rather, it is in itself an act of leadership (Howell & Bowen, 1990). Even in high performance teams, the demand for leadership does not vanish (Klenke, 1997). In fact, several studies show that although more demanding, leadership in such teams is even more critical than in other work groups (Hackman, 1986; Katzenbach & Smith, 1993; Manz & Sims, 1993).

So the question remains, "What leadership styles would be appropriate for leading a high performance team of professionals in an advancing technological environment?" A review of the literature offers some rather consistent answers from which a couple of particular leadership theories can be inferred. In continuing with the leadership substitutes theme, Pool (1997) suggests managers may need to alter their leadership style when a leadership substitute is present or to simply increase workers' motivation. DeVries, Roe, and Taillieu (1998) "assume that situational characteristics have an effect on subordinates' need for supervision, whereas need for supervision in its turn influences the opportunity the leader has to influence subordinate behavior by means of his or her leadership style" (p. 486). Motivating followers by altering one's leadership style to accommodate a follower's need for supervision is a textbook description of Hersey and Blanchard's Situational Leadership Theory.

SITUATIONAL LEADERSHIP THEORY

Situational Leadership Theory (SLT) is primarily based on the interaction among the degree of leader task behavior, relationship behavior, and the followers' readiness to perform (Hersey & Blanchard, 1993). SLT views the readiness of followers as a primary factor in any leadership event (Fernandez & Vecchio, 1997). The primary premise is that an effective leader should vary his/her leadership style based upon the readiness, or maturity level, of the follower (readiness is determined by the follower's need for achievement, willingness to accept responsibility, ability, and education/experience). SLT states that followers with very low readiness should be given a telling style, low readiness would suggest a selling style, high readiness would suggest a participating style, and very high readiness would elicit a delegating style.

Again, the notion is that one leadership style will not work for all followers. If you have a new team member with little experience, precise directives and close supervision would likely be in order. If you have a direct report with many years of experience, who is willing to take on the task, and who wants to succeed, the leader should simply delegate what needs to be accomplished. One would assume that participatory and delegation leadership would be the norm among many professional IT teams. This model also moves away from the notion that a leader is either task oriented or people oriented. Situational leadership proponents advise that to be effective across a spectrum, leaders must be able to be both and know when one or the other is appropriate.

A discussion of SLT, however, must also include the fact that empirical studies have produced a very mixed record of support, at best (Fernandez & Vecchio, 1997). Although criticized by many in academia (Blank, Weitzel, & Green, 1986, 1990; Graeff, 1983; Norris & Vecchio, 1992), Hersey and Blanchard's Situational Leadership Theory has been widely adopted by practitioners (Butler & Reese, 1991). SLT has been a major component of leader training in such Fortune 500 companies as IBM, MobilOil, and Xerox and is accepted in all branches of the military (Robbins, 1989). University Associates (1986) suggests that SLT has become the most widely accepted managerial philosophy in the United States, Canada, Mexico, Europe, Africa, and the Far East.

In addition, some have speculated that followers may actually self-select themselves into teams and/or jobs that require a particular level of employee readiness. Indeed, it should come as no surprise that IT professionals often self-select themselves not only into the profession, but into organizations and/ or teams where opportunities for education and learning are valued (Klenke, 1997). Fernandez & Vecchio (1997) support the view that this dynamic would possibly help to account for the findings that are supportive of the theory but it would not negate the theory's basic principles.

Situational Leadership Theory does have a number of strengths (Caskey, 1988). It is straightforward and easy to learn, it functions at the most basic level of leader-follower interaction, and focuses primarily on follower performance. However, Hersey and Blanchard's theory may offer the greatest benefit to the extent that it reminds us that it is crucial to treat individual followers differently (Fernandez & Vecchio, 1997). This idea of individualized consideration is a hallmark of Bass' (1985) conceptualization of transformational leadership.

TRANSFORMATIONAL AND TRANSACTIONAL LEADERSHIP: THE FULL RANGE OF LEADER BEHAVIOR

In reviewing the literature concerning organizational change, structure, and leadership in the information age, it is apparent that many are also sending the siren's call for transformational leadership as a model for effective influence. Roepke (2000) asserts that the traditional, hierarchical management style will not be effective with today's workers, particularly those involved with emerging information technologies. These, and other, autonomous workers are sending out a signal that organizations must move to a more collaborative philosophy where value is placed on people and participation. Hitt (2000) declares that " as we move into what will be a century of unprecedented challenges, successful leaders will rely even more intently on ... flexibility, capable delegation, teamwork, the ability to build for the long-term while meeting short-term needs, and vision" (p. 17). Dervitsiotis (1998), while discussing the management of organizational change and the new learning organization, states that today's leaders must bind people together around a shared identity and sense of destiny and offer a common vision that propels an organization to focused action. Wang (1997), when discussing the impact of information technology on organizational leadership, suggests the leader's role is that of a coach due to the dynamic nature of cooperative work team networks. In examining high performance teams in particular, Gardiner (1988) concluded that commitment, not authority, produced the greatest results. Klenke (1997) describes effective IT leaders as facilitators who are not dependent upon legitimate authority based on position power. Waldman (1994) points out that these leaders "move team members to higher levels of self-control so that competent team members are empowered to control their own responsibilities, to lead their own components of the project in coordination with other team members whose coordination efforts are assisted by the leader" (p. 97). We believe that these writers are united in the belief that transformational leaders are needed in this period of turbulence created by emerging high-technology innovations.

Bass proclaims that in such a volatile environment, transactional leadership can be a prescription for mediocrity. He asserts that to achieve long-term superior performance, a new type of leader must emerge. These leaders will "broaden and elevate the interests of their employees, generate awareness and acceptance of the purposes and missions of the organization, and stir the employees to look beyond their own self-interests for the good of the overall entity" (Bass, 1990, p. 19). Transforming leadership occurs when leader and followers are involved in such a manner that they elevate the motivation and morality of one another. The related purposes of leader and followers are joined together as one. Therefore, by inspiration, heightened success criteria, and the application of alternative problem-solving methods, transformational leaders are able to get their followers to accomplish maximum performance.

In recent years, management theorists have given considerable, and well-deserved, attention to the testing of transformational leadership as a viable model. In fact, during the five-year period from 1990 to 1995 alone, over 100 theses and dissertations investigated the concept and behaviors of transforming leadership (Avolio, Bass, & Jung, 1995). Bass (1990) suggests that by applying the behavioral characteristics of transformational leadership, leaders can guide their followers toward extra effort and extraordinary performance.

The historian James MacGregor Burns, in his book *Leadership* (1978), was the first to coin the terms transactional and transformational leadership. His interest was primarily political leadership, but the terms quickly caught on in organizational management circles.

Transactional Leadership

The key to the transactional style of leadership is the exchange between the leader and follower. They influence each other in a way that both parties receive something of value. In other words, the leaders give subordinates something that they want (for example, a salary increase) in exchange for something that the leaders desire (for example, greater productivity, conformity to standards, etc.). The parties are mutually dependent upon one another and the contributions of each side are understood and rewarded (Burns, 1978). In this transaction, leader influence is based on the premise that it is in the best interest of the subordinates to follow.

Transactional leadership is usually characterized by the leader behaviors of contingent reward and management-by-exception (Avolio, Bass, & Jung, 1995; Bass, 1985). A more active transactional leader typically employs a style of contingent reward (reward is contingent upon the follower meeting an agreed upon, and mutually understood, goal), whereas a more passive transactional leader tends to practice the avoidance of corrective actions as long as goals are met. This type of leader behavior is characterized by the old adage, "if it ain't broke, don't fix it" (Bass, 1990).

Transactional leader behavior is the style of leadership that is most often exhibited in industry today (Yammarino & Bass, 1990). Moreover, active transactional leader behavior (contingent reward) has been positively correlated to follower attitudes and performance (Avolio, Waldman, & Einstein, 1988; Bass & Avolio, 1990; Dubinsky, Yammarino, Jolson, & Spangler, 1995; Waldman, Bass, & Yammarino, 1990). The published literature indicates that this is not the case with contingent punishment or management-by-exception leader behavior (Avolio, Waldman, & Einstein, 1988; Bass, 1985; Howell & Avolio, 1993; Kessler, 1993; Kirby, Paradise, & King, 1992; Podsakoff, Todor, & Skov, 1982).

Transformational Leader Behavior

Transformational leader behavior does not depend upon an exchange of commodities between leader and follower (Bass, 1985). Transformational leaders operate out of deeply held personal value systems that cannot be negotiated or exchanged between individuals. By expressing these personal standards, transformational leaders unite their followers but, more importantly, they can change their followers' goals and beliefs. Because of Bass' influence, it is commonly assumed that transformational leaders achieve this in four distinctive ways by demonstrating: 1) individual consideration, 2) intellectual stimulation, 3) inspirational motivation, and 4) charisma.

Individual Consideration. Transformational leaders tend to pay close attention to the interindividual differences among their followers. They often act as mentors to their subordinates. Coaching and advising followers with individual personal attention characterize this behavior. These leaders are intent on removing obstacles that might inhibit both the development and performance of their followers. A primary component of individual consideration is the understanding that each follower has different needs and that those needs would change over time. Therefore, transformational leaders must accurately diagnose the needs of individual followers in order to optimize each follower's individual potential (Avolio, Waldman, & Yammarino, 1991).

Intellectual Stimulation. Transformational leaders also provide ways and reasons for followers to alter their perceptions of problems and even their own attitudes and values (Avolio, Waldman, & Yammarino, 1991). This is characterized by promoting intelligence, rationality, logical thinking, and careful problem solving. An intellectually stimulating leader is intent on showing subordinates new ways of looking at old problems (Avolio, Waldman, & Einstein, 1988). They tend to emphasize teaching their followers to search for sensible solutions. They develop followers who see difficulties as problems to be solved (Bass, 1990).

Inspirational Motivation. Transformational leaders inspire their followers to accomplish great feats. This dimension of transformational leadership is characterized by the communication of high expectations, using symbols to focus efforts, and expressing important purposes in simple ways. The potential to inspire followers is partially realized by the synergy created by demonstrating individual consideration and intellectual stimulation (Avolio,

Waldman, & Yammarino, 1991). Such behavior increases the leader's appeal as it increases the confidence and self-worth of followers. Inspirational leaders often provide encouragement and optimism during difficult times and set the group standard as far as work ethic is concerned.

Charisma. Attaining charisma in the eyes of followers is a critical step in becoming a transformational leader (Bass, 1990). Charismatic leaders exert an enormous amount of influence (Conger & Kanungo, 1988; Howell & Frost, 1989). They are people that followers want to trust and show commitment. Followers consistently place an inordinate amount of confidence and trust in charismatic leaders (Howell & Avolio, 1992). This charismatic dimension of transformational leadership is characterized by providing vision and a sense of mission, instilling pride in and among the group, and gaining respect and trust. A recent study by Waldman, Ramirez, House, and Puranam (2001) has provided evidence that leader charisma is a significant predictor of organizational performance under conditions of uncertainty.

More recent iterations of Bass' conceptualization of transformational leadership have divided this charismatic dimension into behavioral and attributed idealized influence. Idealized influence can be considered a culmination of the other three I's (individual consideration, intellectual stimulation, and inspirational motivation) coupled with a strong emotional bond with the leader (Avolio, Waldman, & Yammarino, 1991). Leaders who demonstrate idealized influence develop much personal power and influence with followers and are, therefore, often labeled as charismatic.

These leadership factors define the constructs associated with the leadership style and behaviors that constitute what Avolio and Bass (1991) have termed the "full range" of leadership styles and behaviors. This full range includes leader styles and behaviors that are extremely transformational at one end to those that are highly avoidant at the other end (Avolio, Bass, & Jung, 1995).

Benefits of Transformational Leader Behavior

There is a preponderance of literature indicating that transformational leadership can lead to substantial organizational rewards (Bass, 1990; Deluga, 1988; Yammarino, Spangler, & Bass, 1993), and that transformational leader behavior delivers an augmentation effect, that is, performance, effort, and satisfaction, that rises above that derived by contingent reward leader behavior alone (Avolio, Waldman, & Einstein, 1988; Geyer & Steyrer, 1998; Waldman, Bass, & Yammarino, 1990; Yammarino & Bass, 1990; Yammarino, Spangler, & Bass, 1993).

Transformational leadership has been positively correlated to leader effectiveness ratings, leader and follower satisfaction, follower efforts, and overall organizational performance (Avolio, Waldman, & Einstein, 1988; Bass, Avolio, & Goodheim, 1987; Hater & Bass, 1988; Howell & Avolio, 1993; Kessler, 1993; Lowe, Kroeck, & Sivasubramaniam, 1996; Seltzer & Bass, 1990; Waldman, Bass, & Einstein, 1987; Yammarino, Spangler, & Bass, 1993). In addition, findings have been reported that suggest that transformational leader behavior is associated with employee commitment to the organization, trust in the leader, and positive organizational citizenship behaviors (Bycio, Hackett, & Allen, 1995; Podsakoff, MacKenzie, Moorman, & Fetter, 1990). Further, there is evidence to indicate that transformational leadership is particularly effective during periods of turbulence (Humphreys & Parise, 2000) and has produced empirical support in a high-technology context (Ehrlich, Meindl, & Viellieu, 1990). Recent research has also suggested that leaders who support emerging information technologies exhibit more transformational leader behaviors than those leaders who offer no such support (Humphreys, 2001).

Personal Characteristics Of Transformational Leaders

The personal characteristics of transformational leaders have also been the topic of research (Dubinsky, Yammarino, & Jolson, 1995; Kirby, Paradise, & King, 1992; Ross & Offerman, 1997). Tichy and DeVanna (1986) conducted face-to-face interviews with some of America's best-known transformational leaders (for example, Lee Iacocca, Jack Sparks, and Robert Stemple). Their observations led them to suggest seven common characteristics that these leaders seemed to possess that differentiated them from transactional managers.

First, they identified themselves as change agents. Their professional and personal image was to make a difference and change the organization for which they had assumed responsibility. They were compared to athletic coaches who took over a troubled program with the intent of making its athletes champions. They embraced the accountability of transforming the organization. Transactional managers tend to manage what they find and leave things pretty much the way they found them (Tichy & DeVanna, 1986). Transformational leadership is about change and innovation.

In addition, each of these leaders demonstrated courage. They exhibited the willingness to take risks and challenge the status quo in the larger interest of the organization. They demonstrated the emotional courage to reveal truths that others did not want to hear.

A third characteristic was a strong belief in people. These leaders were very powerful but tended to avoid an autocratic style. They were sensitive to the needs of their followers and worked to empower their subordinates. Each played the multiple roles of cheerleader, coach, counselor, and leader as they attempted to unite different personalities into a singular organizational mission.

These transformational leaders were also value driven. Each person interviewed could articulate a set of core values and exhibited behaviors that were consistent with those beliefs.

Another characteristic shared by these leaders was their quest for knowledge. They were all dedicated life-long learners. They viewed past mistakes as learning experiences. Even at their lofty status, this group remained adaptable in their attitudes and approaches.

A sixth common characteristic was their ability to deal with ambiguity and uncertainty. They had little difficulty coping with an ever-changing environment. They were able to gracefully balance the emotional and cognitive aspects of problem solving.

Finally, each of these leaders was a visionary. Not only were they able to dream, they could translate those dreams into images and symbols that allowed their followers to share them. The ability to draw others into the vision is a critical component of transforming leadership. Bass (1990) asserts that effective leaders must have this ability to influence the attitudes and behaviors of their followers.

It is extraordinary how closely these characteristics match the types of leadership previously suggested by those examining the leader-follower dyad in high performance IT teams. Clearly, in this new management landscape of technological change and innovation, organizations need transformational leadership (Tichy & Ulrich, 1984). When discussing the initiative to align the human side of IT with proper leadership at 3M, Roepke (2000) speaks to the organization's desire to have its employees move from a transactional psychological contract (i.e., short-term exchange of benefits) to a relational psychological contract (i.e., long-term, mutually satisfying relationship). It is obvious that he is advocating transformational leadership. Klenke (1997) believes that in IT teams, transactional leadership is "likely to be limited by a technical perspective which sees technological change as needing primarily technical problem-solving skills, with little attention to interpersonal skills and organizational consequences" (p. 160). Transformational leadership, on the other hand, requires considerable people and conceptual skills to overcome resistance to change and facilitate greater benefits from the investment in IT (Beatty & Lee, 1992). Klenke (1997) goes on to say that depending upon the task and the development stage of an IT team, the leader(s) should exercise the full range of leadership styles ranging from autocratic to transformational leadership. This full range of leader behavior is an integral component of our new model for influence in the current high performance IT context.

A NEW MODEL

With the call for both situational and transformational leadership, we believe it is time for a new model. In their review of Situational Leadership Theory (SLT), Fernandez & Vecchio (1997), based upon the mixed empirical support, suggest, "It may be useful to expand on the original logic contained in SLT to incorporate evidence that relatively more effective leaders employ a greater range of tactics that manifest a variety of styles, and that such leaders are better able to identify tactics that are most appropriate for a given target person" (p. 76).

In addition, although Bass and colleagues' notion of the full range of leader behavior has enjoyed exceptional empirical support, critics of transformational leadership theory have questioned Bass' (1985) construct as to its practical implementation for everyday, frontline leaders and managers. Therefore, we propose a new, practical model for matching situational diagnostics with appropriate leader behaviors. We expand on Hersey and Blanchard's situational model and relate it to the leadership work of Bass, and others, providing guidance for leaders holding no position power (e.g., leading a cross-functional team), as well as those with such power. The model describes what behaviors a leader might effectively employ, after careful diagnosis, and how those behaviors might be employed in four key leadership situations.In the last three decades, the work of Hersey and Blanchard (1969 through 1996), Burns (1978), and Bass, with his colleagues (1985 through 1997), have evoked much scholarly activity aimed at elucidating the work and empirically testing its efficacy (Avolio, Waldman, & Einstein, 1988; Avolio, Waldman, & Yammarino, 1991; Bass, 1985, 1996, 1997; Bass & Avolio, 1989, 1990, 1994; Bass, Waldman, Avolio, & Bebb, 1987; Einstein, 1995; Graeff, 1983; Howell & Avolio, 1993; Lowe, Kroeck, & Sivasubramaniam, 1996; Vecchio, 1987; Waldman, Bass, & Einstein, 1987; Yammarino, Spangler, & Bass, 1993). To date, however, there have been few attempts to explicitly combine the leadership model of Hersey and Blanchard with the transactional-transformational leadership ideas of Burns and Bass, et. al., in such a way as to provide behavioral guidance for leader-managers in practical situations. Certainly in the 21st Century workplace, with the emphasis on cross-functional teams and participative environments, adaptation of these important works to such contexts is warranted.

Therefore, it is our purpose to: (1) present a diagnostic model that integrates Hersey and Blanchard's situational model with the leadership work of Bass; and (2) propose a new model that outlines specific leadership behaviors that, flowing from the diagnostic model, might be employed by leader-managers in situations involving formal leaders with position power and informal leaders without such power.

We will propose particular leadership behaviors as they apply to situations where:

- The leader has position power (formal authority) and, after diagnosis, chooses to exert control over followers;
- The leader has position power and, after diagnosis, chooses not to exert control over followers;
- The leader does not have position power (e.g., is "project leader" in a team environment) and, after diagnosis, chooses to exert control over others (we intentionally avoid the use of "followers" in this instance as the term follower implies that the leader does in fact have position power); and
- The leader does not have position power and, after diagnosis, chooses not to exert control over others.

Leadership is about influence, which is often defined as the ability to change another's behavior. Effective leadership, however, requires that leaders not only exercise influence, but they must determine when, where, and how to exercise it (House & Howell, 1992; Winter, 1991). The goal of leadership is to exert influence with the involvement of others; e.g., they willingly agree to change; leadership involves the use of power and influence to affect a person or group whether the person wielding the influence has the ultimate authority (position power) to do so or not. Therefore, effective leaders should be consciously focused on the analysis of power relationships.

Transformational leaders analyze these relationships by diagnosing leader-follower relations, understanding the job demands, and then matching the maturity level (readiness) of followers to the situation (Bass, 1985). Thus, they are in control of the situation and can identify successful ways of dealing with people by selecting a style of leadership called "contingent reward." Einstein (1995) recognized that in the early stages of the leader-follower relationship, the leader is in control and, as in parenting, is "responsible for" the success of followers. As times goes on, the leader begins transferring control and moving toward an interdependent state called "responsible to." This movement from contingent reward leader behavior to the mutual state of "responsible to" is the basis for the augmentation effect described by a plethora of previous research examining transforming leadership (Avolio, Waldman, & Einstein, 1988; Geyer & Steyrer, 1998; Yammarino, Spangler, & Bass, 1993). Transformational leaders begin the leader-follower relationship with a sense of "responsibility for" the growth and development of followers. They seek to enhance the relationship by arousing and maintaining trust, confidence, and desire, even in the transactional role. The goal is to transform followers toward a relationship that shifts the dependent "responsibility for" into a relationship that is interdependent, and people are "responsible to" each other. A transformational leader's bottom line goal is to bring followers up to the level where they can succeed in accomplishing organizational tasks without direct leader intervention. Unfortunately, many traditional leaders entrap themselves and their followers by making themselves indispensable. They do this by remaining in a relationship that relies on contingent reward. They rely on position power to control the relationship. Transforming leadership requires the leader to develop and maintain trust, by being consistent and authentic in behavior toward followers (and others), build confidence by sharing in the success of goal achievement(s), and heighten desire by raising the level of individual need. Transformational leaders exercise their skill by way of a three-step process involving:

- Diagnosing the leadership situation with respect to the power dynamics, the priorities of the situation (task or people), and follower willingness (motivation);
- Maintaining control while transacting the basic contingent reward relationship between leader and follower(s); and,
- Transferring control while transforming followers into interdependent, effective, mature people who perform beyond normal expectations and have self-control (i.e., control is transferred as followers' job capacity increases).

DIAGNOSING THE LEADERSHIP SITUATION

The first step in employing effective transformational leadership involves diagnosing the situation in terms of three critical issues: power, priorities, and people (Einstein, 1995). In the diagnostic model of leadership styles (Figure 1), these alliterated symbols refer to the current power relationship, the leader's role in priorities, and the followers' readiness.

Leader-Follower Power Relationships

Position Power. Position power, coming from the organization, gives the leader the organizational right (authority) to demand compliance from others. Typically, the leader has the formal position power to hire, fire, impose decisions, and veto the proposals of followers. With position power the leader controls people by allocating rewards (contingent reward) or by dishing out

Figure 1: A diagnostic model of leadership styles

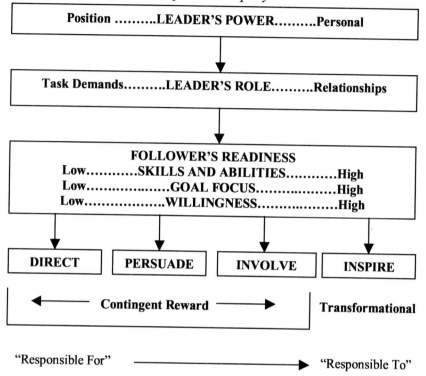

Source: Einstein, W. O. (1995). The challenge of leadership: A diagnostic model of transformational leadership. The Journal of Applied Management and Entrepreneurship, 1(2), 120-133.

retribution (contingent punishment). Position power is a finite resource; e.g., the more one must use it, the less powerful it is, because people don't like to be intimidated and will at some point start to rebel.

Personal Power. Personal power is different from position power, as it rests with the individual regardless of formal bureaucratic position. Its basis is some combination of expertise on the part of the leader in doing the work of the organization and willingness on the part of the follower to be influenced. It also stems from the extent to which a leader can use followers' internalized values or beliefs that he or she has the political skill and/or expertise to find paths leading to valued rewards. Managers usually overlook personal power because they have position power to rely upon as their primary control mechanism. While people do not generally like others to hold power over them, their resistance is less likely when the power is perceived to be based on legitimate organizational expertise. A further thought follows from considering power, to the degree that power determines the range of choice the leader has to exercise control. The bottom line of power is simply that if one has some combination of position power as well as personal power, that person can influence people more easily and to a greater degree. Therefore, effective leaders must consider personal power as a tool.

Using personal power is essential because leaders are often not given enough position power (authority) to do their jobs. If a manager has an employee who is not performing and whose performance cannot be improved, can the manager fire the employee? Or more importantly to this discussion, if the leader is a project leader with team members who are not subordinates, on what basis does the leader exert influence? Most leaders know that they don't possess the authority they would like to have so they fill the gap by using personal power. Power gaps differ from job to job, of course, but most managers know that they have a power gap in their work. It is one of the frustrating aspects of being a manager. Imagine then, the difficulty in effectively leading a team of professionals in a context where position power is at best very limited or, at worst, completely absent. Although there are several potential personal power characteristics, we believe that relationship power offers the greatest benefits in the current environment.

No personal power resource is better known than relationship power. We hear of "old boy networks" or the saying, "It's not so much what you know as who you know." Such comments reflect an important political reality. It is easier (and more rewarding) to work with people who are liked, respected, and admired than those who are not liked or known. Additionally, most people find that work conflicts are much easier to work through with friends than within the context of formal relationships. Who you know, and more importantly whom you can work with harmoniously, is important. Many successful people could not get anything done if they did not have coworkers, bosses, and subordinates with whom they had solid relationships.

There are situations that require leaders to rely on relationship power to succeed. First of all, managers can experience a power gap in dealing with their subordinates. In certain circumstances, some subordinates may even have more power than their managers. Consider these subordinates:

- experts in a particular part of the work;
- employees who are so popular with others that if they were disciplined; it would have serious repercussions;
- individuals who are almost impossible to replace; and
- key people in the workflow.

Such individuals may be difficult to confront without some political maneuvering and effectively using personal power. In today's high-tech world, this scenario is becoming quite commonplace.

In addition, most people have a host of others in key work groups on whom they rely. These others, often called "internal suppliers," provide them with the raw materials or support they need in order to perform well. If these other groups do not cooperate, managers cannot order them to do so. Many professional IT project teams certainly operate in this manner. The manager, or project leader, may have no recourse but to use effective personal power as other methods of influence would be ineffectual.

Given the diagnosis model (Figure 1), it seems clear that the successful leader must build personal power to expand the range of styles available and move the follower(s) toward a "responsible to" relationship, since the less personal power one has the more one must rely on position power.

Leader's Role Issues

The leader's mission is to balance priorities between accomplishing tasks central to the organization's existence and making people responsive to those job demands. For a leader to approach priorities in this way is particularly important because it focuses the leader's thinking on where leadership control should be directed. The mission of the leader is to make decisions about tasks, take care of people, and set priorities between these two. As the leader proves successful in task accomplishment, the priority for tasks shifts to the follower(s), and effective use of contingent reward enables the leader to shift to a persuasive style. As personal power builds, a bond begins to form between the leader and the follower(s).

Follower's Job Capacity

The third element of the leader's diagnosis has to do with an analysis of the follower's capacity to accomplish the assigned task(s). This area of diagnosis is where the least research has been done under the heading of transformational leadership. The leading work on the concept of readiness has been accomplished by Hersey and Blanchard (1969 through 1996), who state that readiness, in relation to one's job consists of two combined factors: (1) the readiness factor (innate ability, education, training, and experience), which reflects a person's capability for performing the job; and (2) the psychological maturity factor, which is associated with an individual's self-confidence, desire for achievement, and willingness to accept responsibility.

We believe there is one other critical factor; the degree of understanding and commitment followers and/or team members show toward organizational goals. When a person possesses high capability, high desire for achievement, high commitment, high responsibility, and understands and accepts organizational goals, that person possesses high job capacity.

Having diagnosed the appropriate leadership style, the second step for the effective transformational leader is to help the followers answer the contingent reward question: "What's in it for me?" The leadership style with which the leader accomplishes this step is dependent upon the diagnosis just discussed. For example, if the diagnosis shows that job demands are ambiguous, the follower's capacity to perform is low, and the leader has sufficient position power, then a high degree of direction and leader control may be necessary. By directing followers toward what must be done, there is a greater chance that tasks will be successfully completed and rewards will follow. The leader may consequently use a directive, telling style of leadership. As job demands become relatively straightforward and followers begin to develop clearer "responsible to" behaviors (as determined by effective diagnoses), the leader may employ a more persuasive, involving, or inspiring style.

At its best, the leader is able to diagnose which style will get the best results given the power, priorities, and people with which the leader has to work. Effective leaders shift from directing to persuading, and then make the control shift of being involved but no longer in control, and finally to an inspiring style where transformations can take place.

MATCHING BEHAVIORS AND STYLE

Thus far we have discussed the concepts of Hersey/Blanchard and Bass, as seen through a model proposed by Einstein (1995), as they relate to the selection and employment of leadership styles which match a leader's diagnosis of a given situation (Figure 1).

Figure 2 provides an overview of an expansion of the material just discussed, which can be used to help leaders manage their leadership responsibilities not only within their supervisory group, but outside this group as well. Three concepts are presented: (1) leadership behaviors demonstrated within the group when the leader has position power at his/her disposal (upper half of the model) versus those behaviors outside the group, where the leader does not have position power (lower half of the model); (2) behavioral styles, presented on a continuum from Directive to Inspirational, with a mid-point, between Persuading and Involving that signals a shift in control from "responsible for" toward "responsible to" behaviors; and (3) a notation indicating the point at which Contingent Reward style leadership moves from Transactional to a Transformational style.

Based on the model represented in Figure 2, we believe that transformational leaders have the opportunity to use any and all leadership styles, as the situation requires. Transactional leaders, on the other hand, stop short. That is, they can move left to right within this model but they only go as far as "involve" and never get to "inspire." You will notice that the behaviors on the left side of the model are quite different from top to bottom. As the leadership styles shift right, however, the behavioral differences are less pronounced because of the "responsibility to" relationship that is emerging.

Figure 2: Leader behavior matching leader styles within and outside supervisory group

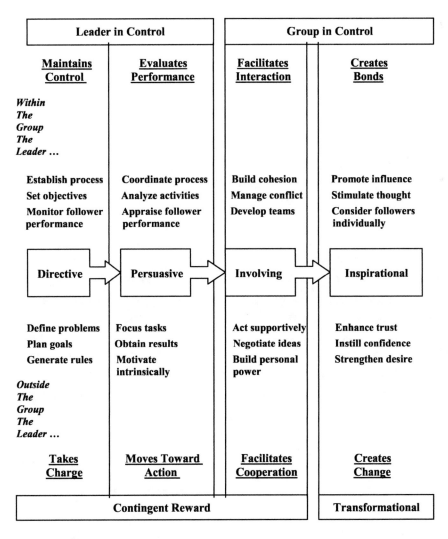

Leader in Control: Within the Group

If a diagnosis determines the necessity for a leader to employ a Directive style, certain behaviors will be more successful than others. Specifically, as a Directive leader, one should maintain control since the priority is to accomplish required tasks with people who lack certain aspects of job capacity. It is therefore necessary to help members establish an orderly process to accomplish organizational tasks, while simultaneously seeking ways to improve the diagnosed deficiencies in their capacities. Leaders in such situations:

Establish process. Provide direct supervision, set up rules to make repeated actions more routine, and provide a forum for people to suggest alterations or improvements to the rules.

Set job objectives. Assign specific tasks; assure the objectives are measurable; provide mechanisms for ensuring feedback that will compare performance with past and expected future accomplishment; and provide the necessary direct support to make sure that the objectives are attainable, realistic, and timely. As the leader-follower relationship moves toward a "responsible to" relationship, the leader implements a more shared process.

Monitor performance. It is well understood that people desire and require feedback in order to regulate their own performance. Feedback is an essential ingredient in any situation where the leader wishes to maintain control while simultaneously fostering personal growth in followers.

Careful diagnosis may indicate that leader control is necessary but, because of the perceived job capacities of the followers, the appropriate behaviors should be persuasive and evaluative rather than directive and controlling. In such situations, leaders will:

Coordinate process. This style affords more flexible interpretation of rules and more informal talk among followers about accomplishing tasks. In this environment, the leader can spend more time as a coach and less time as boss. Feedback is still an important commodity, with the primary source of data coming from co-workers.

Analyze activities. Setting objectives becomes a shared process as followers take on a greater role. As job capacity increases, so does the personal stake in setting objectives. The leader is building an environment where capable people support the activities they help create.

Appraise performance. In this context, the leader is not so much concerned with formal appraisals but, rather, being on hand to understand what is going on and what intrinsic rewards might be appropriate for each of the followers.

Group in Control: Within the Group

When diagnoses indicate that the group being supervised might be willing and able to exert more control over situations, the leader may choose to employ an involving style and attempt to facilitate their interaction. In such situations, the leader will:

Build cohesion. Cohesion is developed in collaborative organizational climates, which are grounded in trust (Larson & LaFasto, 1989). Trust flows from a climate that includes: (1) honesty, no lies, no exaggerations; (2) openness–a willingness to share, and a receptivity to information, perceptions, ideas; (3) consistency–predictable behavior and responses; and (4) respect– treating people with dignity and fairness (Larson & LaFasto, 1989).

Manage conflict. In 1981, Fisher and Ury saw conflict as a growth industry. Today, with more emphasis on collaborative climate building, the ability to manage conflict is tantamount to being an effective leader when one's diagnosis indicates the need for an Involving Leadership Style. Larson et al. (1996) outline effective strategy for reducing conflict: reduce tension by injecting humor (when appropriate), by separating the parties, or by facilitating a tension reduction interaction during which each person in conflict makes small, usually public, concession and invites the other party to reciprocate.

Develop teams. Larson and LaFasto (1989) provide a succinct overview of team development issues empirically based. Leaders working with these elements will strive toward developing and maintaining clear, elevating goals, results-driven structures, competent team members, unified commitment, and principled leadership.

When the diagnoses indicate that the group can handle it, a leader might engage in inspirational behaviors aimed at creating bonds. Such behaviors would include promoting follower influence, stimulating intellectual inspiration, and being individually considerate (clearly and specifically equitable as opposed to equal). This material is covered at length in the works of Avolio, Waldman, and Einstein (1988), Avolio, Waldman, and Yammarino (1991), Bass (1985), Bass and Avolio (1990), and Einstein (1995). We obviously believe in the ideas to be of great importance, but space constraints and our focus in this chapter do not allow for extrapolation here.

Leading Groups Outside the Chain of Command

Much of a leader's time is spent in activities outside the group over which she/ he has legitimate hierarchical authority (position power). Whereas, in previous discussions, the leader has had both personal and position power at her/his disposal, in these circumstances the leader must evoke power on the basis of personal characteristics outside the realm of organizational authority (personal power).

The diagnostic process is essentially the same with the exception that the leader has no position power. For example, a leader may see it necessary to apply directive control with a group with low job capability, but must do so using different behaviors. However, the process is exactly the same: diagnosis is crucial. The use of contingent rewards is still important, but in these instances, the leader must rely almost exclusively on intrinsic rewards offered to followers. Leaders, consistent with diagnoses, should still move from Directive to Persuasive to Involving to Inspirational styles of leadership (along with the corresponding shift from a "responsible for" towards a "responsible to" relationship). The differences in leader behaviors may be subtle, but are nonetheless of great importance (see Figure 2, at the bottom, under the heading "Outside the group the leader").

Leader in Control: Outside the Chain of Command

The leader of a project team (or other such group outside his/her "chain of command") is in charge of a project that is strictly time-bound, the success of which is often crucial to the survival of an organization. After diagnosis of the project team members, the leader determines that it is necessary to exert some control. This leader has two styles available, depending upon the diagnosis of the team members and the preferred style: Directive or Persuasive. If the leader sees a directive style as being most appropriate, the focus will be on providing the group with a definition of the problems or mission, planning the goals related to the problem solution or mission accomplishment, and generating the ground rules for successful completion of the project. In other words, the leader, using personal power, takes charge of the group. The success or failure of the mission will depend upon the correct diagnosis of the situation and the amount of personal power attributed to the leader by the followers in the situation.

If, given the same situation, a determination is made through diagnosis that a Persuasive style is better suited, the leader will, after defining the problems and developing the goals and ground rules, win acceptance from the group of these rules and goals, help the group focus on the task, and, using personal power and intrinsic rewards (superordinate goals, sense of accomplishment, etc.) as motivators, win support from the group as leader and move them toward action.

Group in Control: Outside the Chain of Command

Where diagnosis of the situation, the organizational climate, and leader-follower relations warrant, leaders may determine that the best style mandates more intensive group involvement. In such situations, the leader will attempt to facilitate cooperation by: acting supportively, employing communication skills such as active listening (Rogers, 1957) and "principled leadership" behaviors (Larson & LaFasto, 1988); negotiating ideas, using the strategic skills outlined in Lewicki, et al. (1996); and, through the development and use of such skills, building personal power. Unlike position power, personal power is given to leaders by followers and, when used appropriately, becomes stronger with use.

In situations where change initiation and management is a primary issue and where diagnosis of leader-follower relationships, climate, and personal style preferences warrant, the leader may attempt a Transformational style of leadership. Previous research has indicated causal relationships between transformational leadership and innovation/change (Bass, 1985; Conger & Kanungo, 1987; House, 1977; Howell & Avolio, 1993; Howell & Higgins, 1990; Oberg, 1972). Treating people as individuals and providing opportunities and support for intellectual stimulation are at the heart of Bass' (1985) transformational leadership model, and instill confidence and strengthen desires of followers to do their best. We believe that in the current high technology context, effective influence dictates that leaders employ the full range of leader behaviors from contingent reward to truly transformational, and that the models provided will assist leaders (formal and informal) in determining which behaviors are appropriate.

FUTURE TRENDS

It is clear that information technology has forever changed the structure of many organizations, and that this restructuring has created significant leadership challenges. We've attempted to provide solutions to some of those challenges in this chapter. This being said, however, the future will likely exacerbate the current issues and create new ones. We believe that one such area will be providing effective leadership to virtual teams. Firms are already beginning to establish virtual project teams where members tend to only interact via information technology (Grenier & Metes, 1995; Lipnack & Stamps, 1997). Although virtual teams offer tremendous flexibility and the ability to rapidly serve the needs of a dynamic environment, "a dark side to the new form also exists: such dysfunctions as low individual commitment, role overload, role ambiguity, absenteeism, and social loafing may be exaggerated in a virtual context" (Jarvenpaa & Leidner, 1999, p. 792). Clearly, future research should further investigate the leader-follower relationship within the virtual team context.

CONCLUSION

Rapid technological advancements, especially those associated with information technologies, are forcing organizations to rethink how they operate and accept that many approaches that worked well in the past are simply no longer effective. There is little question that many organizations are becoming less structured and that a premium is being placed upon the firm's ability to adapt to ever-changing environments often created by new technologies. More than ever, today's organizations must focus on the development of leaders who can not only cope, but also thrive in this complex and dynamic world.

Bass asserts that for organizations to achieve long-term superior performance, especially in a changing environment, a new type of leader must emerge. We believe it is crucial that as management thinking moves into the 21st Century, effective leadership (both contingent reward and transformational) must be developed at all levels of the organization. We believe that this is particularly true when discussing leadership and high performance teams of technology professionals. How practicing managers determine and deliver the appropriate transforming leader behaviors has been the focus of this chapter.

In this chapter, we have provided a diagnostic model of leadership styles. In addition, a new model was proposed that outlines specific leadership behaviors that, when used with the diagnostic model, can provide specific behavioral guidance to leaders. Using the diagnostic model, leaders can evaluate the leader-follower relationship (power), the job demands versus relationship building (priorities), and the readiness of the followers (people) in order to select an appropriate style of leadership that fits the situation. Then leading the group toward interdependence with the leader to a shared "responsibility to," the leader can move beyond contingent reward to leadership behaviors that are truly transforming. By gaining skill in selecting appropriate leader behaviors and applying the characteristics of transformational leadership, leaders can guide their followers toward extra effort and performance beyond expectations.

Further, the new model, when used in conjunction with effective diagnosis, provides guidance to leaders in situations where they have position power as well as those where such power is lacking. We believe that this issue, where the leader has no position power and is charged with effecting and/or managing change, is both common to many current team environments and rich in research possibilities. Research in organizations should now begin to test the efficacy of the model and, perhaps more importantly, examine the informal leadership behaviors necessary to create and manage change in environments where innovation is simply a business imperative. How do such leaders enhance trust, instill confidence, and strengthen desires in their "followers"? To what extent can organizations that have been successful at managing change attribute their success to such informal leaders? What specific behaviors do such leaders exhibit, particularly those attempting to influence a cohesive IT team? There are many questions yet to be answered.

ACKNOWLEDGMENTS

We gratefully acknowledge Ms. Molly Zettel for her comments and editing in the preparation of this manuscript.

REFERENCES

Armstrong, C. P., & Sambamurthy, V. (1999). Information technology assimilation in firms: The influence of senior leadership and IT infrastructures. *Information Systems Research*, 10(4), 304-327.

Avolio, B. J., & Bass, B. M. (1991). *The Full Range of Leadership Development*. Binghamton, NY: Center for Leadership Studies.

Avolio, B. J., Bass, B. M., & Jung, D. I. (1995). *Multifactor Leadership Questionnaire Technical Report*. Redwood City, CA: Mind Garden.

Avolio, B. J., Waldman, D. A., & Einstein, W. O. (1988). Transformational leadership in a management game simulation: Impacting the bottom line. *Journal of Group and Organizational Studies*, 13(1), 58-80.

Avolio, B. J., Waldman, D. A., & Yammarino, F. J. (1991). The four I's of transformational leadership. *Journal of European Industrial Training*, 15(4), 9-16.

Bass, B. M. (1985). *Leadership and Performance Beyond Expectations*. New York: The Free Press.

Bass, B. M. (1990). From transactional to transformational leadership: Learning to share the vision. *Organizational Dynamics*, 18(3), 19-31.

Bass, B. M. (1996). Is there universality in the full range model of leadership? *International Journal of Public Administration*, 19(6), 731-762.

Bass, B. M. (1997). Does the transactional–transformational leadership paradigm transcend organizational and national boundaries? *American Psychologist*, 52(2), 130-139.

Bass, B. M., & Avolio, B. J. (1989). *Manual for the Multifactor Leadership Questionnaire Profile*. New York: Free Press.

Bass, B. M., & Avolio, B. J. (1990). Developing transformational leadership: 1992 and beyond. *Journal of European Industrial Training*, 14(5), 21-27.

Bass, B. M., & Avolio, B. J. (Eds.) (1994). *Improving Organizational Effectiveness Through Transformational Leadership*. Thousand Oaks, CA: Sage.

Bass, B. M., Avolio, B. J., & Goodheim, L. (1987). Quantitative description of world-class industrial, political, and military leaders. *Journal of Management*, 13, 7-19.

Bass, B. M., Waldman, D. A., Avolio, B. J., & Bebb, M. (1987). Transformational leadership: The falling dominoes effect. *Group and Organization Studies*, 24, 73-87.

Beatty, L., & Lee, G. (1992). Leadership among middle managers: An exploration in the context of technological change. *Human Relations*, 45(9), 957-989.

Blank, W., Weitzel, J. R., & Green, S. G. (1986). Situational leadership theory: A test of underlying assumptions. Paper presented at the *National Academy of Management Conference*, Chicago.

Blank, W., Weitzel, J. R., & Green, S. G. (1990). A test of situational leadership theory. *Personnel Psychology*, 43(3), 579-597.

Burns, J. M. (1978). *Leadership*. New York: Harper & Row.

Butler, J. K., & Reese, R. M. (1991). Leadership style and sales performance: A test of the situational leadership model. *Journal of Personal Selling and Sales Management*, 11(3), 37-46.

Bycio, P., Hackett, R. D., & Allen, J. S. (1995). Further assessments of Bass's (1985) conceptualization of transactional and transformational leadership. *Journal of Applied Psychology*, 80(4), 468-478.

Caskey, F. (1988). *Leadership Style and Team Process: A Comparison of the Managerial Grid and Situational Leadership* (Project No. 25). St. Paul, MN: University of Minnesota, Department of Vocational and Technical Education (ERIC Document Reproduction Service No. ED 296 162).

Clerk, J. (2000). For U.S. MBAs, it's about vision and risk. *International Herald Tribune*, March, 16.

Cohen, A., & Bradford, D. (1989). *Influence Without Authority*. New York: Wiley.

Conger, J. A., & Kanungo, R. N. (1987). Toward a behavioral theory of charismatic leadership in organizational settings. *Academy of Management Review*, 12, 637-647.

Conger, J. A., & Kanungo, R. N. (1988). *Charismatic Leadership: The Elusive Factor in Organizational Effectiveness*. San Francisco, CA: Jossey-Bass.

Deluga, R. J. (1988). Relationship of transformational and transactional leadership with employee influencing strategies. *Group and Organization Studies*, 13(4), 456-467.

Dervitsiotis, K. N. (1998). The challenge of managing organizational change: Exploring the relationship of reengineering, developing learning organizations and total quality management. *Total Quality Management*, 9(1), 109-123.

DeVries, R. E., Roe, R. A., & Taillieu, T. C. B. (1998). Need for supervision. *Journal of Applied Behavioral Science*, 34(4), 486-502.

Dubinsky, A. J., Yammarino, F. J., & Jolson, M. A. (1995). An examination of linkages between personal characteristics and dimensions of transformational leadership. *Journal of Business and Psychology*, 9(3), 315-335.

Dubinsky, A. J., Yammarino, F. J., Jolson, M. A., & Spangler, W. D. (1995). Transformational leadership: An initial investigation in sales management. *Journal of Personal Selling and Sales Management*, 15(2), 17-29.

Ehrlich, S., Meindl, J., & Viellieu, B. (1990). The charismatic appeal of a transformational leader: An empirical case study of a small, high technology contractor. *Leadership Quarterly*, 1(4), 229-248.

Einstein, W. O. (1995). The challenge of leadership: A diagnostic model of transformational leadership. *The Journal of Applied Management and Entrepreneurship*, 1(2), 120-133.

Fernandez, C. F., & Vecchio, R. P. (1997). Situational leadership theory revisited: A test of an across-jobs perspective. *Leadership Quarterly*, 8(1), 67-85.

Fisher, R., & Ury, W. (1981). *Getting to Yes: Negotiating Agreement Without Giving In*. New York: Penguin Books.

Foster, R. N. (2000). Managing technological innovation for the next 25 years. *Research Technology Management*, 43(1), 29-31.

Fulmer, R. M., Gibbs, P. A. and Goldsmith, M. (2000). Developing leaders: How winning companies keep on winning. *Sloan Management Review*, 42(1), 49-60.

Gardiner, J. (1988). Building leadership teams. In Green, M. M. (Ed.), *Leaders For a New Era*. New York: Macmillan Publishing Company.

Geyer, A. L. J., & Steyrer, J. M. (1998). Transformational leadership and objective performance in banks. *Applied Psychology: An International Review*, 47(3), 397-420.

Goodman, P., Devadas, S., & Hughson, T. (1988). Groups and productivity: Analyzing effectiveness of self-managing teams. In Campbell, J., Campbell, R. & Associates (Eds.), *Productivity in Organizations*. San Francisco: Jossey-Bass.

Graeff, C. L. (1983). The situational leadership theory: A critical view. *Academy of Management Review*, 8, 285-291.

Grenier, R., & Metes, G. (1995). *Going Virtual*. Upper Saddle River, NJ: Prentice Hall.

Hackman, R. (1986). The psychology of self-management in organizations. In Pollack, M. and Perloft, R. (Eds.), *Psychology and Work: Productivity, Change, and Employment*. Washington, DC: American Psychological Association.

Handy, C. (1995). Trust and the virtual organization. *Harvard Business Review*, 73(3), 40-48.

Hater, J. J., & Bass, B. M. (1988). Superiors' evaluations and subordinates' perceptions of transformational and transactional leadership. *Journal of Applied Psychology*, 73(4), 695-702.

Hersey, P., & Blanchard, K. H. (1969). *Management of Organizational Behavior*. Englewood Cliffs, NJ: Prentice Hall.

Hersey, P., & Blanchard, K. H. (1993). *Management of Organizational Behavior: Utilizing Human Resources* (6th ed.). Englewood Cliffs, NJ: Prentice Hall.

Hersey, P., Blanchard, K. H., & Johnson, D. E. (1996). *Management of Organizational Behavior* (7th ed.). Englewood Cliffs, NJ: Prentice Hall.

Hitt, M. A. (2000). The new frontier: Transformation of management for the new millennium. *Organizational Dynamics*, 28(3), 7-17.

House, R. J. (1977). A 1976 theory of charismatic leadership. In Hunt, J. G. and Larson, L. L. (Eds.), *Leadership: The Cutting Edge*, 189-207. Carbondale, IL: Southern Illinois University Press.

House, R. J., & Howell, J. M. (1992). Personality and charismatic leadership. *Leadership Quarterly*, 3, 81-108.

Howell, J. M., & Avolio, B. J. (1992). The ethics of charismatic leadership: Submission or liberation? *Academy of Management Executive*, 6(2), 43-54.

Howell, J. M., & Avolio, B. J. (1993). Transformational leadership, transactional leadership, locus of control, and support for innovation: Key predictors of consolidated business-unit performance. *Journal of Applied Psychology*, 78(6), 891-902.

Howell, J. P., & Bowen, D. E. (1990). Substitutes for leadership: Effective alternatives to ineffective leadership. *Organizational Dynamics*, 19(1), 20-39.

Howell, J., & Dorfman, P. (1981). Substitutes for leadership: Test of a construct. *Academy of Management Journal*, 24, 714-728.

Howell, J., & Dorfman, P. (1986). Leadership and leadership substitutes among professional and nonprofessional workers. *Journal of Applied Behavioral Science*, 22(1), 29-46.

Howell, J. M., & Frost, P. J. (1989). A laboratory study of charismatic leadership. *Organizational Behavior and Human Decision Processes*, 43, 243-269.

Howell, J. M., & Higgins, C. A. (1990). Champions of technological innovation. *Administrative Science Quarterly*, 35, 317-341.

Humphreys, J. H. (2001). Transformational and transactional leader behavior: The relationship with support for e-commerce and emerging technology. In *Proceedings of the International Applied Business Research Conference*, Cancun, Mexico.

Humphreys, J. H., & Parise, P. A. (2000). Shifting culture: The relationship between transformational leadership and sales productivity during a period of organizational turbulence. Interactive session presented at the *41st meeting of the Western Academy of Management*, Hawaii, April.

Jarvenpaa, S. L., & Leidner, D. E. (1999). Communication and trust in global virtual teams. *Organization Science*, 10(6), 791-816.

Katzenbach, J., & Smith, D. (1993). *The Wisdom of Teams*. New York: Harper Business.

Kerr, S., & Jermier, J. M. (1978). Substitutes for leadership: Their meaning and measurement. *Organizational Behavior and Human Performance*, 22, 375-403.

Kessler, T. G. (1993). *The Relationship Between Transformational, Transactional, and Laissez-faire Leadership Behaviors and Job Satisfaction in a Research Environment*. Unpublished doctoral dissertation, Nova University, Ft. Lauderdale.

Kirby, P. C., Paradise, L. V., & King, M. I. (1992). Extraordinary leaders in education: Understanding transformational leadership. *Journal of Educational Research*, 85(5), 303-311.

Klenke, K. (1997). Leadership dispersion as a function of performance in information systems teams. *Journal of High Technology Management Research*, 97(8), 149-170.

Larson, C., & LaFasto, F. M. J. (1989). *Teamwork: What Must Go Right/What Can Go Wrong*. Beverly Hills, CA: Sage.

Larson, C., LaFasto, F. M., Lewicki, R. J., Hiam, A., & Olander, K. W. (1996). *Think Before You Speak: A Complete Guide to Strategic Negotiation*. New York: John Wiley & Sons.

Lipnack, J., & Stamps, J. (1997). *Virtual Teams: Reaching Across Space, Time, and Organizations with Technology*. New York: John Wiley & Sons.

Lowe, K. B., Kroeck, K. G., & Sivasubramaniam, N. (1996). Effectiveness correlates of transformational and transactional leadership: A meta-analytic review of the MLQ literature. *Leadership Quarterly*, 7, 385-425.

Manz, C., & Sims, H. (1993). *Business Without Bosses*. New York: John Wiley.

Mata, F. J., Fuerst, W. L., & Barney, J. B. (1995). Information technology and sustained competitive advantage: A resource based analysis. *MIS Quarterly*, 19(4), 487-505.

McGrath, J. (1990). Time matters in groups. In Galegher, J., Kraut, R. and Edigo, C. (Eds.), *Intellectual Teamwork: The Social and Technological Bases of Cooperative Work*. Hillsdale, NJ: Erlbaum.

Mumford, M. D., Zaccaro, S. J., Connelly, M. S., & Marks, M. A. (2000). Leadership skills: Conclusions and future directions. *Leadership Quarterly*, 11(1), 155-171.

Mumford, M. D., Zaccaro, S. J., Harding, F. D., Jacobs, T. O., & Fleishman, E. A. (2000). Leadership skills for a changing world: Solving complex social problems. *Leadership Quarterly*, 11(1), 11-36.

Norris, W. R., & Vecchio, R. P. (1992). Situational leadership theory: A replication. *Group and Organization Management*, 17(3), 331-342.

Oberg, W. (1972). Charisma, commitment, and contemporary organization theory. *M.S.U. Business Topics*, 20, 18-32.

Podsakoff, P. M., Dorfman, P. W., Howell, J. P., & Todor, W. D. (1986). Leader reward and punishment behaviors: A preliminary test of a culture-free style of leadership effectiveness. In Farmer, R. N. (Ed.), *Advances in International Comparative Management*, 2, 95-138. Greenwich, CT: JAI Press.

Podsakoff, P. M., & MacKenzie, S. B. (1997). Kerr and Jermier's substitutes for leadership model: Background, empirical assessment, and suggestions for future research. *Leadership Quarterly*, 8(2), 117-133.

Podsakoff, P. M., MacKenzie, S. B., Moorman, R. H., & Fetter, R. (1990). Transformational leader behaviors and their effect on followers' trust in leader, satisfaction, and organizational citizenship behaviors. *Leadership Quarterly*, 1(2), 107-142.

Podsakoff, P. M., Todor, W. D., & Skov, R. (1982). Effects of leader contingent and noncontingent reward and punishment behaviors on subordinate performance and satisfaction. *Academy of Management Journal*, 25(4), 810-821.

Pool, S. W. (1997). The relationship of job satisfaction with substitutes of leadership, leadership behavior, and work motivation. *Journal of Psychology Interdisciplinary & Applied*, 131(3), 271-284.

Robbins, S.P. (1989). *Organizational Behavior: Concepts, Controversies, and Applications*. Englewood Cliffs, NJ: Prentice-Hall.

Roepke, R. (2000). Aligning the IT human resource with business vision: The leadership initiative at 3M. *MIS Quarterly*, 24(2), 327-354.

Rogers, C.R. (1957). *Active Listening*. Chicago: University of Chicago Press.

Ross, J. W., Beath, C. M., & Goodhue, D. L. (1996). Building long-term competitiveness through IT assets. *Sloan Management Review*, 38(1), 31-42.

Ross, S. M., & Offerman, L. R. (1997). Transformational leaders: Measurement of personality attributes and work group performance. *Personality and Social Science Bulletin*, 23(10), 1078-1086.

Sawhney, M., & Prandelli, E. (2000). Communities of creation: Managing distributed innovation in turbulent markets. *California Management Review*, 42(4), 24-55.

Seltzer, J., & Bass, B. M. (1990). Transformational leadership: Beyond initiation and consideration. *Journal of Management*, 16(4), 693-703.

Slowinski, G., Oliva, E., & Lowenstein, L. (1995). Medusa alliances: Managing complex interorganizational relationships. *Business Horizons*, 48-52.

Smith, P. B., & Peterson, M. F. (1988). *Leadership, Organizations, and Culture: An Event Management Model*. London: Sage Publications.

Stewart, T.A. (1997). *Intellectual Capital: The New Wealth of Organizations*. New York: Currency.

Tichy, N. M., & DeVanna, M. A. (1986). *The Transformational Leader*. New York: Wiley.

Tichy, N. M., & Ulrich, D. O. (1984). The leadership challenge–A call for the transformational leader. *Sloan Management Review*, 59-68.

University Associates. (1986). *Situational Leadership Resource Guide*. San Diego, CA: University Associates.

Vecchio, R. P. (1987). Situational leadership theory: An examination of a prescriptive theory. *Journal of Applied Psychology*, 72, 444-451.

Vroman, W. (1994). Workplace by design: Mapping the high performance workscape. *Academy of Management Executive*, 8(4), 83-86.

Waldman, D. (1994). Transformational leadership in multifunctional teams. In Bass, B. and Avolio, B. (Eds.), *Improving Organizational Effectiveness Through Transformational Leadership*. Newbury Park, CA: Sage.

Waldman, D. A., Bass, B. M., & Einstein, W. O. (1987). Leadership and outcomes of performance appraisal. *Journal of Occupational Psychology*, 60, 177-186.

Waldman, D. A., Bass, B. M., & Yammarino, F. J. (1990). Adding to contingent reward behavior: The augmenting effect of charismatic leadership. *Group and Organization Studies*, 15(4), 381-394.

Waldman, D. A., Ramirez, G. G., House, R. J., & Puranam, P. (2001). Does leadership matter? CEO leadership attributes and profitability under conditions of perceived environmental uncertainty. *Academy of Management Journal*, 44(1), 134-143.

Wang, S. (1997). Impact of information technology on organizations. *Human Systems Management*, 16(2), 83-91.

Winter, D. G. (1991). A motivational model of leadership: Predicting long-term management success from TAT measures of power motivation and responsibility. *Leadership Quarterly*, 2(2), 67-80.

Yammarino, F. J., & Bass, B. M. (1990). Transformational leadership and multiple levels of analysis. *Human Relations*, 43(10), 975-995.

Yammarino, F. J., Spangler, W. D., & Bass, B. M. (1993). Transformational leadership and performance: A longitudinal investigation. *Leadership Quarterly*, 4(1), 81-102.

Chapter II

The Social Antecedents of Business Process Planning Effectiveness

Sofiane Sahraoui
American University of Sharjah, United Arab Emirates

INTRODUCTION

Although there has been a wide coverage in the IS literature of the alignment of IT plans with organizational plans, most studies focused on the mechanics of this alignment rather than its antecedents (Brancheau, Janz, & Wetherbe, 1996; Rodgers, 1997). Therefore, emphasis was put on the strategies, structures, and planning methodologies used to attain alignment (Henderson & Sifonis, 1988; Tallon & Kraemer, 1998). A minor line of research that focused on the people involved in the creation of alignment (Nelson & Cooprider, 1996; Subramani, Henderson, & Cooprider, 1999) dealt with the state in which business and IT executives within an organizational unit understand and are committed to the business and IT mission, objectives, and plans (Reich & Benbasat, 2000). While this chapter would partially fit within studies examining the social antecedents of alignment, it departs sharply from earlier studies in the sense that it does not consider the organization as made up of distinct IT and business functions. Instead it adopts a holistic view whereby information systems form the skeleton of business processes and neither can be disentangled from the other. This peculiar perspective on the role of IT in the organization makes it essential to consider antecedents to alignment that go beyond the dichotomy between IT and business. The key concepts that will be introduced throughout this study derive from this logic. Information-enabled leadership, the planning culture, knowledge worker management, and strategic alignment are key constructs that form the backbone of our model of business process planning. The latter is the outcome of integrating IT and business planning. Planning effectiveness that is posited as the outcome variable of the previous variables is itself re-conceptualized within the proposed perspective.

CONCEPTUAL MODEL

The information systems literature provides a wide range of models for undertaking IT planning but lacks research into the catalytic effect of information-enabled leaders to ensure that business planning and IT planning are fully aligned, knowledge workers are fully involved, and the planning culture is conducive to planning effectiveness. In many cases, the best strategic planning efforts fail to yield desired results because of the absence of an effective, enabled leader to guide planning efforts and oversee their proper implementation.

Strategic alignment implies that enterprise outcomes are a result of the mix of a human resource strategy, a business strategy, and an information technology strategy coated within a supportive planning culture. The achievement of the proper mix requires an action-oriented framework, which goes beyond awareness of the issues and problems and focuses on a structured process of directed change (Wysocki & DeMichiel, 1996). Information-enabled leaders are capable of developing human resource strategies centered on the empowerment of knowledge workers through formal mechanisms like delegation of decision-making power or through informal mechanisms like a planning culture. They are imbued by a process paradigm in planning process-based (cross-functional) IT applications. Subsequently, the IT strategy is expected to fall in place through harnessing the enabling role of IT on one hand and the knowledge and skills of an empowered knowledge workforce on the other hand, with the objective of reengineering business processes in line with the business process strategy devised.

This chapter will assess the role of information-enabled leaders in achieving this strategic alignment between human resources, strategic planning, and IT planning within the framework of a planning culture. A literature review on leadership, information systems planning, and corporate cultures will provide the conceptual framework for analyzing information-enabled leadership in the context of this strategic alignment. Conceptual material will draw on a series of interviews with senior IT planners in several commercial and off-shore banks in the State of Bahrain, to sort out the information-enabled dimension of IT planner's role and assess its impact on the quality of the planning process. Rather than a classical empirical paper with distinct theoretical and empirical components, the material will be mostly advocating theoretical concepts supported by sparse narratives from the interviews. Therefore, it will not be based on systematic testing either quantitative or qualitative.

Given the paucity of findings in the literature regarding the specific leadership role of leaders in creating an organizational environment conducive to planning effectiveness, we will highlight such a role through a set of artifacts that can be directly related to IT planning effectiveness. In other words, the beliefs, attitudes, and behaviors of information-enabled leaders translate into planning-related artifacts that are conducive to effectiveness. Artifacts include strategic alignment, the establishment of a planning culture, and empowerment of knowledge workers. These artifacts or mediating variables translate the leadership effect of IT planners' role on IT planning effectiveness (See Figure 1).

The chapter is organized as follows: the first section will introduce the concept of information-enabled leadership; the second section will review IT planning and its key dimensions illustrating the impact of leadership on each; the third section will draw on the conceptual definitions in the previous section to define the construct of strategic alignment between IT planning and business planning; the fourth section will discuss the concept of the planning culture, the critical role of information-enabled leadership to establish it, and its importance in the alignment equation. Finally, the last section will complement the alignment framework by bringing in human resource issues as they relate to managing knowledge workers.

The role of information-enabled leadership will be first discussed in terms of how it is rooted in the information systems literature and how it will be used

Figure 1: Social antecedents of business process planning effectiveness

in this work. Subsequently, it will be connected to most concepts introduced in view of illustrating its central role in each.

LITERATURE REVIEW

The basic question that we will pursue throughout this chapter is how information-enabled leadership, the strategic alignment of IT with business planning within integrated business process planning, the planning culture, and the management of knowledge workers impact the effectiveness of business process planning. We will first introduce the key construct of the study, information-enabled leadership; hence, we will review the other constructs.

INFORMATION-ENABLED LEADERSHIP

One of the social antecedents to planning alignment that went ignored is the leadership style of IT planners. The rank and role of IT leaders is expected to have a determinant impact on a firm's competitive advantage. The establishment of a linkage between business objectives and IT objectives will be effective if championed by an information-enabled manager (Wysocki & DeMichiel, 1996). King and Teo (1996) identified leadership as a facilitator for the development of strategic IT applications in business firms.

IT professionals are now increasingly asked to assume entrepreneurial roles and to seed the process of IT innovation (Roepke, Agarwal, & Ferrat, 2000). A broad expectation is that, rather than wait for the business to provide requirements, IT professionals will proactively seek to create opportunities for the deployment of IT to serve business needs. In essence, IT professionals have to assume a leadership role in managing the organization's IT resources. This leadership is rather transformational than transactional. Transformational leaders engage in the creation of a vision, the mobilization of commitment to the vision, and the institutionalization of change (Tichy & Ulrich, 1984). We will refer to this leadership role as information-enabled leadership. The term was adapted from Wysocki and DeMichiel's (1996) concept of the information-enabled manager in their reference to the role played by IT managers in planning and managing IT resources in the organization. Information enablement highlights the central role of IT and information in providing IT managers with the capabilities to exercise their leadership role. Just as IT enables new forms of organizations, it also enables a new form of situational leadership. Hence, only IT-enabled leadership traits will be invoked to characterize the leader's role, unlike classical leadership studies where general leadership traits are the focus of analysis (See Ashkenas, Ulrich, Jick, & Kerr, 1998).

Information-enabled leaders are multi-skilled professionals with one discipline in IT and the other in business processes and functions. They are hence capable of understanding the strategic relationship between IT and the processes it supports. As a result, they are able to integrate IT into the organizational strategy to take advantage of the enabling role of IT in improving process efficiency and effectiveness, as well as securing a competitive advantage in the market place. They are hence expected to lead their organization's effort to exploit IT for strategic advantage. Information-enabled leadership qualities that were identified during interviews with senior IT planners included the following abilities:

- Develop effective strategies to achieve the organization's objectives;
- Align IT strategies with the human resources and business strategies;
- Establish and maintain a communication network to facilitate data sharing;
- Harness participation of knowledge workers at all levels;
- Focus on creative and innovative uses of IT;
- Emphasize the use of IS to gain a competitive advantage, which refers to the application of innovative IT for the purpose of forging ahead of the competition;
- Disseminate to other managers any relevant information on the latest technology developments and be able to help in assimilating these new technologies into the organization where appropriate; and
- Concentrate on the broader issues affecting the organization and its core business.

In addition to these abilities, information-enabled leaders should possess certain traits such as those of a facilitator, promoter, agitator, innovator, and communicator (Wysocki & DeMichiel, 1996).

The above traits and abilities are not simply technical skills; they are an embodiment of the more traditional leadership qualities identified in classic leadership studies. While they are not general traits, they do derive from these as they translate into the myriad of abilities listed above.

The role of information-enabled leaders is both reactive and proactive. In their reactive role, leaders (1) establish policies and procedures to facilitate planning objectives; (2) acquire and allocate hardware, software, services, and staff resources; and (3) ensure timely delivery of systems and services to meet corporate goals. Their proactive role includes (1) participation in the development of the organizational strategy set; (2) support of the business plan at corporate and departmental levels by bringing appropriate technology to the management team; and (3) management of integration of appropriate technologies into the way the organization functions and even into the determination of its business activity portfolio. Their proactive role is the object of this paper.

The above roles closely mirror the CIO's, hence the amalgamation between the CIO and the information-enabled leader. The IS manager who is in charge of systems development and operation has a separate set of responsibilities that are operational rather than strategic. In contrast, the CIO is the change agent for new products, services, and processes. Ashkenas et al. (1998) underscore the key role of leadership as an enabler of organizational change. His major responsibilities involve the dissemination to other managers of any relevant information on the latest technology developments and helping assimilate the new technologies into the organization.

CIOs are senior executives responsible for all aspects of their company's IT and systems. They direct the use of IT to support the company's goals. They have the knowledge of both technology and business to be able to align the IT strategy with the business strategy. CIOs oversee technology purchases, implementation and various related services provided by the IS department. In many cases, CIOs take on a leadership role in reengineering their organization's business processes and building IT infrastructures to achieve a more productive, efficient, and valuable use of information within the enterprise. Foremost, they set the premises for IT planning and provide the leadership for all planning activities, both formal and informal, to fall into the mosaic of planning efforts throughout the organization. Our focus in outlining information-enabled leadership will be mostly centered on the CIO. The information-enabled leader or CIO's role will be further examined within the context of IT planning and its key dimensions.

IT PLANNING

Definition

Boynton and Zmud (1987) define IT planning as organizational activities directed towards (1) recognizing organizational opportunities for using IT, (2) determining the resource requirements to exploit these opportunities, and (3) developing strategies and action plans for realizing these opportunities. Planning activities can take place within a rational sequential framework of decision making, or piecemeal, adaptively, and in small increments. Planning methods and approaches have evolved based on the changing nature of the organizational environment. Sullivan (1985) developed a framework describing the changing nature of planning under different conditions of IT infusion and diffusion. In the 'complex' environment (information age) characterized by high levels of information infusion and diffusion, IT planning is eclectic. Hence, no formal planning methodology is well suited to organizational needs:

As information technology becomes embedded in the firm, the process of ensuring that it is effective is no longer entrusted to mechanistic planning procedures from a bygone era. Rather, the consensus is that a company must find or develop an approach with features that match its unique information age requirements. (Sullivan, p.8)

Therefore, IT planning encompasses not only the formal method in use but process and implementation as well. Earl (1993) included these three dimensions in his study of IT planning in 27 British companies. The planning method refers to the technique, procedure, or methodology employed, e.g., Method/1, Business Systems Planning (BSP), Critical Success Factors (CSF), Strategic Set Transformation (SST). Process deals with issues of user participation, IS-user relationships, user awareness and education, and management philosophy and attitude towards planning. Finally, implementation issues relate to resources allocated to IT implementation and systems development, user resistance and management commitment.

Earl argues that method, process, and implementation are all necessary conditions for successful planning. It is in the interaction of these three elements that the fate of a particular planning approach is determined. Earl refers to an interactive and adaptive process rather than a sequential one.

An approach is not a technique per se. Nor is it necessarily an explicit study or formal, codified routine so often implied in past accounts and studies...an approach may comprise a mix of procedures, techniques, user-IS interactions, special analyses, and random discoveries. There are likely to be some formal activities and some informal behavior. (p.7)

Earl (1993) elicited five basic approaches to IT planning: business-led, method-driven, administrative, technological, and organizational. The organizational approach had the least concerns attached to it. Its underlying premise is that IT planning is a process of continuous decision-making shared by the business and the IS function. Its emphasis is on organizational learning about business problems, opportunities and IT contribution. The major stakeholders, in terms of influencing planning outcomes, are planning teams that include both systems users and IS personnel. The emphasis is on process rather than on method, and teamwork is the principal influence in IT strategy making. This approach, which differs significantly from conventional prescriptions in the literature and practice (Earl), reflects a similar change in approaching planning as the one observed in the strategic planning literature and best illustrated by Mintzberg (1983) [cited in Earl]:

[O]ften strategy is formed, rather than formulated, as actions converge into patterns and as analysis and implementation merge into a
fluid process of learning...strategy making becomes a mixture of the
formal and informal and the analytical and the emergent. (p.14)

The importance of informal planning as a key component of the organizational planning agenda was stressed by Boynton and Zmud (1987), who listed
informal planning among a set of planning behaviors that organizations ought to
develop in the information economy.

Planning does not occur only at fixed points in time, nor does it solely
involve the efforts of a planning team. To encourage a continuous, if
intermittent, planning process, an informal network of planning participants must be established and nurtured. An informal network of
planners active on an ongoing basis, constantly aware of information
technology and opportunities, is an advantageous position to take
advantage of unexpected opportunities. (p.65)

Given that the scope of informal planning cannot be mandated by rules and
procedures, it has to be spurred through informal mechanisms such as the
planning culture, which will be discussed later, and also through information-
enabled leadership both directly through formal mechanisms of organizational
design and human resource management and indirectly through the informal
system.

Philosophies & Objectives of IT Planning

A list of IT planning philosophies and objectives was compiled based on
the CIO interviews. Philosophies and objectives are very telling about the
leadership style of IT planners. We retained only items that seemed to convey
the type of leadership being studied. Objectives that showed only classical
goals of planning activities or that were not peculiar to the behavioral outcome
of information-enabled leaders are not listed here. Rather than a classical
literature review, this section draws directly from the empirical world. This is
in line with premises set forth in the introduction of the chapter and palliates the
insufficiencies of existing literature on this particular topic. A comprehensive list
of philosophies and objectives of IT planning put forth by information-enabled
leaders include:

- Focus IT on the goals of the business;
- Use IT for competitive advantage and support;
- Redesign business processes;
- Enhance IT productivity;
- Harness the creative potential of organizational members;
- Promote strategic initiative of user departments;

- Promote activities with strategic value;
- Promote a culture whereby people continuously suggest new ways of using IT in performing their work;
- Sponsor and support ideas for innovative uses of IT;
- Establish policies and procedures to facilitate planning objectives;
- Participate actively in the formation of the integrated corporate business plan;
- Support business plans at corporate and departmental levels by bringing appropriate technology to the management team;
- Manage the integration of appropriate technologies into the way the organization functions;
- Identify, recommend and implement changes that will affect the strategic direction of the organization;
- Seek additional opportunities to enhance efficiency and effectiveness of existing strategic systems;
- Propose, design, develop and implement systems that help the organization attain and sustain strategic advantage in the market place;
- Develop an IT-based strategic culture; and
- Lead the enterprise effort to exploit IT.

Information Systems Organization

Depending on the organizational structure and the sophistication of IS services, the structure of the IS function will vary from one organization to the other. In the more traditional centralized structures, a firm's information systems department is usually responsible for IS planning in conjunction with the user departments. Managers in the IS department start the planning process by reviewing their progress on the existing plan. They look at special problems such as systems approaching obsolescence. They confer with the managers in the user departments to learn about user priorities and needs for system improvements, new system requirements, and user support. In many cases, information services is a level below the more traditional business functions (e.g., Finance, Human Resources, Marketing and Sales, etc.). IT planning is formal rather than informal, hence periodical rather than continuous.

In the more decentralized IS organization where IT is more critical to the core business, the entire management philosophy is centered on empowerment and dynamic teams. This translates at the level of IS organization into a larger involvement of participants during the planning process. The leadership role played during planning does not emanate from the IT department anymore but from the CIO.

Planning Models and Methodologies

The traditional assumption of strategic planners has been that strategic planning is a rational process where an objective function can be formulated according to the wishes of top-management (Bourgeois & Brodwin, 1983). Strategists employ tools that are analytic in nature and the value of the strategy depends on the ability of the strategy makers to obtain complete and accurate information about the organization's internal capabilities and its position in the environment. This model works fine for bureaucratic organizations in stable environments or for firms with a strong competitive position and plenty of slack (Mintzberg, 1973; Fredrickson & Mitchell, 1984).

This early model of strategic planning set foot in the IT planning area through the link suggested by King (1978) whereby corporate strategy is first delineated following a top-down model and then the IT strategy is derived. This suggests that the two processes are sequential and distinct. Therefore, premises of the IT planning process are largely set by the strategy making process, and limited leverage is left for IT planners to influence positive outcomes through particular IT planning policies. For instance, deriving system objectives, constraints and design strategies from the organizational strategy set, as proposed by King, will hamper the participation of system users in IT strategy formulation. An alternative participative model was promoted as a result.

The participative model, when used effectively, overcomes some of the key limitations inherent in King's model by using participative techniques to capture information and planning-related knowledge throughout the organization. This model has a widespread use in the IS area. It has been formalized into different planning methodologies, such as IBM's BSP (IBM, 1983; Bowman, Davis, & Wetherbe, 1983) and the CSF methodology (Rockart, 1979; Boyton & Zmud, 1987; Henderson, Rockart, & Sifonis, 1987)

The basic assumption of the participative model, however, is that management allows users to participate in certain elements of planning under specified terms. Wilkof (1989) points out that:

The understanding is that participation is management's prerogative and its willingness to allow participation can be withdrawn at any time. They do not deal with a situation where consensus management is institutionalized, where the organizational culture embodies norms that preclude token or delegated participation. (p.192)

Therefore, this model preserves to some extent the subdivision of the organization into thinkers and doers and fails to draw upon the full human potential throughout the organization (Bourgeois & Brodwin, 1983; Florida & Kenney, 1991). Its basic limitations can be pinned down to two main points:

1. In a fast changing environment, information and knowledge relevant to planning might be available in different parts of the organization but remains unaccessible to planners on time because of the lack of efficient input mechanisms into the planning process. This problem is informational in nature, in the sense that planners fail to capture important planning-related information.

2. The lack of genuine participation of knowledge workers in IT plan formulation might jeopardize the implementation of IT plans. The ensuing split between thinkers and doers (Bourgeois & Brodwin, 1984) erodes doers' motivation to champion changes for which they have limited say and understanding. This problem is motivational in nature.

Empowering self-directed or autonomous teams in making planning decisions will circumvent the above two problems. Empowerment is primarily the result of a vision carried through the channel of a strong leader. It is the vesting of decision-making in knowledge workers, where, traditionally such authority was a managerial prerogative. As a vision and philosophy, empowerment means allowing self-managing teams and individuals to be in charge of making the necessary decisions to reach the organization's planning objectives. As an organizational program, empowerment means giving knowledge workers the resources to unleash, develop, and utilize their knowledge and skills to their fullest potential to resolve organizational contingencies through planning efforts (Turban, McLean, & Wetherbe 2000).

While directed at planning and re-planning IT uses in the organization on a continuous fashion, empowerment is facilitated by two major factors; one is information-enabled leadership and the other is IT itself. A CIO's leadership will set the cultural premises for knowledge workers' involvement. This is discussed in a later section. IT, on the other hand, helps provide the right information and knowledge, at the right time, at the right quality, and at the right cost. Indeed, to be fully empowered means to have control over the necessary resources to make the right decisions, and these require information and knowledge. Knowledge in particular is power and there are generally reservations about releasing it. Hence, accessibility to knowledge is generally restricted. Information-enabled leaders lift such restrictions and increase the availability of knowledge. Network-based and intelligent technologies such as Intranets and knowledge management systems provide the infrastructure for transporting knowledge wherever it is needed.

IT Planning Effectiveness

The key to IT planning effectiveness resides in harnessing the existing knowledge that is being continuously created throughout the organization by the informative effect of IT (Zuboff, 1988). This basically calls for creating appropriate conditions for users' informal planning behavior to develop.

IT planning harnesses user knowledge and allows for a learning process to take place. Users' planning behavior enhances their understanding of planning issues. De Geus (1988) argues that planning is not about making plans but about learning new ways of coping with new contingencies and developing appropriate responses. Leonard-Barton (1992) views the organizational planning process as a process of knowledge creation, collection, and control that aims at establishing a learning environment premised on egalitarianism, whereby all individuals contribute to the joint enterprise and acquire new competencies. This is in sharp contrast to earlier studies of IT planning that have mostly defined their IT planning effectiveness construct as the degree of fulfillment of IT planning objectives, improvement in performance of the IS function, and improvement in performance of the organization (Premkumar & King, 1991; Raghunathan & Raghunathan, 1991; Ramanujam, VenKatraman, & Camillus, 1986).

STRATEGIC ALIGNMENT

Most of the models of IT planning have assumed that business planning and IT planning are undertaken separately. This derives from the early link suggested by King (1978) wherein the IS strategy set is obtained from the organizational strategy set. As the strategy set transformation model, as King's model was known, became the cornerstone of IT planning research, the ensuing conventional wisdom in IT planning research and practice was that the business plan is delineated first and IT resources are subsequently planned for within the framework of IT planning. The strategic business plan hence sets the goals and agenda for the strategic IT planning effort (Henderson et al., 1988). Although subsequent research has delineated linkages between organizational planning and IT planning (Henderson et al., 1987; Bowman et al., 1983; Grover, 1991), the latter was largely considered for a while as a process distinct from overall business planning. This dichotomy between IT planning and business planning derives from the misconception about IS as technical systems rather than social systems.

The work of Brown (1991) provides an interesting point of departure in re-conceptualizing the status of IT in organizations. He presents IT as all-pervasive in the modern organization. Work in the IT-intensive organization is constructed around the technology. Therefore, tasks cannot be defined independently of their IT texture. Tasks and activities, in such an environment, are achieved through one continuous system:

The next great breakthrough of the information age will be the disappearance of discrete information technology products. Technology is finally becoming powerful enough to get out of the way. (Brown, p.104)

This view contrasts sharply with one of the main assumptions held in IT planning research that considers information systems as a collection of software, hardware, and databases used to implement chosen strategies. This assumption operates, for instance, through the popularization of some strategic planning frameworks in the IS area. Using IT for competitive advantage has come to mean the "automation" of strategic planning similar to the automation of manual data processing activities during the early adoption of IT. Porter and Millar's (1985) value chain framework considers the strategic role of IT as the exploitation of telecommunication and computing potentials of new sophisticated technical systems to improve the strategic posture of the firm. IT resources are considered as inputs into the planning process, merely as technological capabilities used for enhanced computing and telecommunications. Hence, information systems are reduced to the status of technical systems (Kling & Iacono, 1988).

It is proposed here that, because of the pervasiveness of IT use in organizations, it is no longer valid to look at information systems in a mechanistic way. They are social systems and not simply technical systems with social implications. They are unique constructions that emerge out of the use of technology in peculiar contexts. As such, they are valuable, rare, imperfectly imitable, and not substitutable (Barney, 1991). Only a social system with its informal side can have such properties. Technology as a tool is both imitable and substitutable, whereas information systems as social systems are not because they are informal and intangible.

Based on these new premises, an alternative approach to IT planning has since emerged, one that focuses on integrating IT planning with business planning within the framework of business process planning. Aligning the IT plan with the overall organizational strategies and objectives has become the first imperative of IT planning (Reich & Benbasat, 2000).

Based on the bank interviews, the level of integration between IT planning and business planning, wherever it existed, varied from reactive, where the business plan derives the IS plan to linked, where both plans are prepared simultaneously, to integrated where a unique and comprehensive plan is prepared. The latter is conceived within a new paradigm wherein business processes and the information systems that support them are inextricable. Information-enabled leaders endeavor to push a vision of the process-based organization sitting on an integrated infrastructure of information systems and delivering business products and services to both internal and external customers. Business planning boils down to IT planning itself, as information systems form the backbone of business organization and processes and do not merely provide technical support to existing business systems. It is thus incorporated into strategic business planning, operational processes, and products and services. Similarly, corporate change programs are increasingly based on the enabling power of new IT. Emerging IT has enabled new forms of business that were not feasible before. The virtual corporation is the enactment of IT as structure; it is to business organization what robots are to real beings. Less dramatic change programs immortalized through catchy acronyms such as TQM, BPR, JIT, etc., are practically meaningless without the support of IT. One of the CIOs interviewed went to the extreme of suggesting that the right question to ask in IT planning is not what IT can do for your business, but what business can you get in as a result of IT innovation. However, in today's global and digital economy (Tapscott, 1996), such an assertion is not as extreme as business leaders often look toward IT to suggest new and innovative ways in which internal and external processes might be improved. This would seem like an instance of planning IT systems before business planning, but given that IT systems cannot be implemented in isolation of the business systems they are meant to support, it still falls within the realm of strategic alignment between business and IT planning. This process is referred to as business process planning.

PLANNING CULTURE

There is no more powerful lever for an information-enabled leader to establish a learning environment conducive to planning effectiveness than the establishment of a planning culture. Be it in anthropology or in the corporate culture literature, leaders play the most critical role in forging local cultures (Schein, 1985; Kilmann, 1989). While culture is a general construct that tends to cover organization-wide activities, some have argued that subcultures could emerge intune with the overall corporate culture (Louis, 1985). One such subculture that leaders try to create is a planning culture. Cleland and King (1974) were among the first to call for developing a planning culture. They asserted that the success of long-range planning in an organization is less sensitive to the parameters of the planning techniques than it is to the overall culture within which the planning is accomplished. King and Zmud (1981) define three levels at which IT planning activities should take place: policy planning, strategic planning, and operational planning. The organizational culture can alter the organizational value system so that it becomes more receptive to strategic and operational planning. This is done during the first phase of policy planning.

> The aim of IS policy planning is to establish an appropriate organizational culture regarding information technologies. (King & Zmud, p.305)

On a more explicit note, Ciborra (1991) points to the importance of organizational culture in identifying strategic IS that are not easily imitated.

> In order to avoid easy imitation, SISs should emerge from the grass roots of the organization, out of end user hacking, computing, and tinkering. In this way the innovative SIS will be highly entrenched with the specific culture of the firm. (p.309)

The planning process he proposes is based on seven steps that can increase organizational skill in developing strategic IS.

The link between organizational culture and organizational planning has been advocated frequently. However, aside from Ciborra's seven steps and King and Zmud's (1981) three-level framework, no detailed methodology has been proposed. Moreover, little has been reported about how organizational culture impacts the informal planning behavior of users, nor are there detailed accounts about the relationship between planning and effectiveness.

In resolving these matters, we will attempt to sort out the prominent effects of information-enabled leaders as they shape the planning culture, which in return creates a favorable environment for undertaking IT planning activities. A reviews of basic concepts of organizational culture is warranted first.

Basic Concepts of Organizational Culture

There are many schools of thought related to the concept of culture. Its origin is in anthropology and it has been adapted into most fields of the social sciences, one such field being management and organizational studies (Trice & Beyer, 1983).

Definition

Kilmann (1989) and Schein's (1985) definitions illustrate the consensus on how this concept was adapted in the management literature:

> [A] pattern of basic assumptions–invented, discovered, or developed by a given group as it learns to cope with its problems of external adaptation and internal integration–that has worked well enough to be considered valid and, therefore, to be taught to new members as the correct way to perceive, think and feel in relation to those problems. (Schein, p.9)

> [T]he shared philosophies, ideologies, values, assumptions, beliefs, expectations, attitudes and norms that knit a community together. (Kilmann, p.5)

When culture develops over time into a stable ideologically based motivational frame of reference, it helps explain and legitimize collective and individual behaviors, which are hence mere manifestations of culture (Trice & Beyer, 1983). People come to share similar motivational frames of reference through processes of organizational socialization (Hackman, 1976; Schein, 1985; Trice & Beyer, 1983). Being shared and learned, culture affects the organization and accounts for organizational behavior at the levels of the individual and the group within the organization, and the organization within its environment. Smircich (1983) summarizes this relation accordingly by stating that:

> [Culture] provides a conceptual bridge between micro and macro levels of analysis, as well as a bridge between organizational behavior and strategic management interests. (p.346)

Organizational vs. Planning Culture

Louis (1985) noted that there is a variety of subcultures within a single organization. These cultures have no physical boundaries and a person may belong to several subcultures at the same time. Also, various work groups may come together on cultural grounds during specific organizational actions and diverge during others (Wilcof, 1989). Therefore, there is a dual dimension to cultures in organizations, one is their degree of pervasiveness and the other is their substance. This duality forms the essence of the planning culture, which lies at the intersection of planning (pervasive culture) and users (occupational subculture) rather than being intrinsic to users in a non-contextual fashion or to planning irrespective of local differences among participants.

Effects of Culture on Performance

The construct of culture has been put forth in the popular and scholarly literatures mainly because of its positive effects on organizational performance in ways that transcend the traditional analytical and quick fix approaches (Kilmann, 1989). It has been claimed that culture is the critical key that strategic managers might use to direct the course of their firms (Smircich, 1983), influence productivity, and help the firm cope with its external environment (Schein, 1985). In this study, the planning culture has a direct impact on business process planning effectiveness by creating an environment premised on learning and entrepreneurial behavior.

The consistent theme that emerges from existing studies is that of culture as an empowering phenomenon in an organization. Within cultures geared to empowerment, entire work operations become one large empowered team in which everyone is individually self-managing and can interact directly with everyone else in the system. Empowering cultures give workers at all levels the knowledge, confidence, and authority to use their own judgment to make important decision. Good management is described as one that works toward building corporate cultures, which grant increasing control over work processes to employees. At the task level, the motivational impact of culture transpires through aroused behavior tendencies to move towards goals, take needed action, and reinforce one's intrinsic motivation (Burke, 1992). Knowledge workers thrive within empowering cultures. Information-enabled leaders attempt to engrain empowerment within the culture itself.

MANAGING KNOWLEDGE WORKERS

There is a broad recognition in the research literature that in the new knowledge economy, the human capital of a firm, i.e., its workforce, may well represent its most important strategic asset and capability (e.g., Roepke et al., 2000; Stewart, 1997). Similarly, a recurrent theme throughout this paper has been that only an empowered workforce can rally the organization to the objective of integrating IT and business planning within an integrated process of business process planning. The premises for empowerment are determined by information-enabled leadership, both directly through formal mechanisms of delegation, participation, and other structural mechanisms or indirectly by forging a planning culture conducive to desired behavior, which positively impact planning effectiveness. However, and in order to sustain both types of intervention, leaders have to put in place supporting human resource strategies. As it has been advocated that planning participants are primarily knowledge workers, they have to be catered to as such in order to avoid the pitfalls of systems development failures that have come to characterize the IS scene. Essentially, during systems development projects, users provide information requirements–mostly data and process specifications–that are translated into information systems. While this seems to be straightforward and users should be getting the systems that mirror the requirements they have enunciated during systems analysis, recurring failures have been pinned down to a reluctance of developers to fully involve the users in systems development; that is, beyond mere procedural involvement where basic data about the business system are collected. This calls for a human resource strategy that considers users as knowledge workers and not simply as adjuncts to the systems being put in place. The real challenge for information-enabled leaders is to put in place such a strategy so that it integrates with the business process strategy outlined above.

Such a strategy will spare IT planning the miseries of systems development outcomes. It is even more vital for planning than for systems development to involve knowledge workers, as the latter represent the primary leverage through which organizations maximize the value offered to their customers. Leveraging the intellectual assets of knowledge workers should be the primary focus of planning processes. Knowledge work will require new forms of management and, implicitly a new strategy for human resource management (Collins, 1998). As a result, human resource management is increasingly trying to reinvent itself around the emerging concepts of knowledge work and core competencies (Lawler, 2000).

Firms are indeed concentrating on core competencies that depend on know-how borne by knowledge workers. Knowledge workers bear unique know-how underlying core competencies that create value for customers, sustain differentiation of the firm, and provide broad access to markets (Collins, 1998). By definition, their know-how is unique to the firm, difficult to imitate, and hard to develop. Knowledge workers are assets to retain and develop in a knowledge-based economy.

Changes in the "people" aspects of business profoundly affect HR management. Information-enabled leaders must learn to deal effectively with knowledge workers. They must learn how to define, capture, and propagate the know-how knowledge workers carry in their minds. The true meaning behind information age HR management lies in ensuring that core contributors and their know-how are understood, developed, cultivated, and retained (Wilson, 2000). It means leveraging technology that achieves these ends faster, better, and cheaper. It means ensuring the preservation and development of the firm's human and intellectual capital.

Wilson (2000) states that knowledge workers differ in key ways from the traditional employees on which conventional organizations and their HR policies and practices were developed. Some of these differences are summarized below:

1. Knowledge workers contribute the most value. They contribute the creativity that drives the organization. By creating, capturing and applying the learning of the firm, they are its institutional memory.
2. Knowledge workers are well-educated, self-motivated, and ambitious. They want work that challenges their minds and builds their know-how, which they regard as personal "intellectual capital."
3. Knowledge workers are mobile. They can move anywhere; more importantly, they can often do their work anywhere.
4. Knowledge workers want to be led, not managed. They know more about their work than a manager can ever teach them. They expect freedom to

be creative in achieving results, and guidance to point them in the direction the firm needs. They do not want traditional managers who constantly supervise them, telling them what to do and how to do it.

Managing knowledge workers implies shifting the dominant organizational paradigm from command and control to network. Traditional, multilevel hierarchies have become too bureaucratic and slow to be responsive to dynamic problem solving and harness the intellectual capabilities of knowledge workers. The network organization has proven to be a more natural habitat for knowledge workers. It has espoused some of the key characteristics of network technology itself. A marriage between the intrinsic characteristics of the technology and the structural characteristics of the organization is an ideal environment for knowledge workers:

1. *Real time*: Network technology enables real-time processing whereby processing is instantaneous. In the network organization, responsiveness to customers is coming closer to being real time as well. Empowered knowledge workers supported by online processing, shared databases and knowledge bases are able to fulfill customer requests without further hierarchical referral.

2. *Transparent*: Network technology cuts through the functional stovepipes by enabling cross-functional information systems to support processes rather than functions (Turban et al., 2000). As such, it constitutes the backbone that sustains the process-based and customer-centered organization. As a result, functional boundaries become transparent to customers, who are served fluidly through processes rather than being subjected to multiple points of contact within the same organization.

3. *Non-hierarchical*: Network technology overtook the more traditional centralized host-to-terminal architecture. It is based on resource sharing rather than resource concentration. Client-server technology, the most popular implementation of network technology, allows clients and servers to interact throughout the organization as a seamless web. The hierarchy is torn down and replaced by a network structure where control and coordination are mutual rather than top-down.

4. *Intelligent nodes*: Contrary to the old paradigm of host-to-terminal computing, network computing relies on intelligent nodes for data storage and processing. Likewise, the network organization is not longer bound by "super-thinkers" sitting on top of the hierarchy but, as argued before, is more dependent in its quest for performance on knowledge workers who form a network of intelligent nodes in the decision-making process.

CONCLUSION

Transcripts of interviews that the author had with a dozen CIOs of major banks in Bahrain were used in some sections of the chapter to illustrate the key concepts covered. However, implications of the empirical findings go far beyond what was mentioned in this chapter, as most concepts used were inductively derived from these interviews. This has not been explicitly portrayed in the developments above. For instance, the realization that information-enabled leadership was critical for IT planning effectiveness was borne out of the interviews. Invariably, there seemed to be a strong correlation between the leadership style of CIOs and the degree of strategic alignment between IT and business planning. Other key constructs that were covered in this study were not thoroughly investigated during the interviews, and a link had to be made with the relevant literature for the appropriate conceptual foundation (See list of interview questions in the Appendix).

Although this study does not make any claim to either validity or reliability of its sparse empirical findings, it could certainly serve as a launching pad for a research portfolio that will examine the social antecedents of business process planning effectiveness. The conceptual model outlined above could be operationalized into several research models examining different combinations of these antecedents. Foremost, leadership seems to have been ignored by IS researchers in determining the outcome of planning processes. A quick look at the tables of contents of MIS Quarterly, one of the leading IS journals, during the last ten years will unveil the overwhelming absence of such studies. This can be explained by the over-emphasis on the mechanics of IT planning at the expense of the social dimension. Wooldridge and Floyd (1989) observe that whenever researchers deal with planning issues, they erroneously assume that models that apply to lower level activities in the organization cease to be valid in the context of planning.

REFERENCES

Ashkenas, R., Ulrich, D. O., Jick, T., & Kerr S. (1998). *The Boundaryless Organization: Breaking the Chains of Organizational Structure*. San Francisco, CA: Jossey-Bass.

Barney, J. (1991). Firm resources and sustained competitive advantage. *Journal Of Management*, 17(1), 99-121.

Bourgeois, L. J., & Brodwin, D. R. (1984). Strategic implementation: Five approaches to an elusive phenomenon. *Strategic Management Journal*, 5, 241-264.

Bowman, B., Davis G., & Wetherbe J. (1983). Three stage model of MIS planning. *Information and Management*, June, 11-25.

Boynton, A. C., & Zmud, R. W. (1987). Information technology planning in the 1990s: Directions for practice and research. *MIS Quarterly*, March, 59-71.

Brancheau, J. C., Janz, B. D., & Wetherbe. J. C. (1996). Key issues in information systems management: 1994-95 SIM delphi results. *MIS Quarterly*, 20(2), 225-242.

Brown, J. S. (1991). Research that reinvents the corporation. *Harvard Business Review*, January-February, 102-111.

Burke, W. (1986). Leadership as empowering others. In Srivastra, S. (Ed.), *Executive Power*, 51-77. San-Francisco, CA: Jossey-Bass.

Ciborra, C. U. (1991). From thinking to tinkering: The grassroots of strategic information systems. *Proceedings of the Twelfth International Conference on Information Systems*, 283-292.

Cleland, D., & King, W. R. (1974). Developing a planning culture for more effective strategic planning. *Long Range Planning*.

Collins, D. (1998). Knowledge work or working knowledge. *Journal of Systemic Knowledge Management*, March, 10-22.

De Geus, A. P. (1988). Planning as learning. *Harvard Business Review*, March-April, 70-74.

Earl, M. J. (1993). Experiences in strategic information systems planning. *MIS Quarterly*, 17(1), 1-24.

Florida, R., & Kenney, M. (1991). Transplanted organizations: The transfer of Japanese industrial organization to the U.S. *American Sociological Review*, June, 56, 381-398.

Frederickson, J.W. & Mitchell, T.R. (1984). Strategic decision processes: Comprehensiveness and performance in an industry with an unstable environment. *Academy of Management Journal*, 27(2), 399-424.

Grover, V. (1991). Issues in corporate IS planning. *Information Resource Management Journal*, Winter, 4(1), 1-9.

Hackman, J. R. (1976). Group influences on individuals. In *Handbook of Industrial Organizational Psychology*, 1455-1526. Rand McNally.

Henderson, J., Rockart, J., & Sifonis, J. (1987). Integrating management support systems into strategic information systems planning. *Journal of Management Information Systems*, Summer, 4(1), 5-24.

Henderson, J., & Sifonis, J. (1988). The value of strategic IS planning: Understanding consistency, validity, and IS markets. *MIS Quarterly*, June, 187-200.

IBM (1984). *Business Systems Planning: Information Systems Planning Guide*, (4th Ed.). New York: IBM Press.

Kilmann, R. H. (1989). *Managing Beyond the Quick Fix: A Completely Integrated Program for Creating and Maintaining Organizational Success*. San Francisco, CA: Jossey-Bass.

Kilmann, R. H., Saxton, M. J., & Serpa, R. (1985). *Gaining Control of the Corporate Culture*. San Francisco, CA: Jossey-Bass.

King, W.R. (1978). Strategic planning for management information systems. *MIS Quarterly*, March, 27-37.

King, W. R., & Teo, T. (1996). Key dimensions of facilitators and inhibitors for the strategic use of information technology. *Journal of Management Information Systems*, 12(4), 35-19.

King, W. R., & Zmud, R. W. (1981). Managing information systems: Policy planning, strategic planning and operational planning. In *Proceedings of the Second International Conference on Information Systems*, 299-308.

Kling, R. & Iacono, S. (1989). The institutional character of computerized information systems. *Information Technology & People,* 5(1), 7-29.

Lawler III, E. E. (2000). *Rewarding Excellence*. San Francisco, CA: Jossey-Bass.

Leonard-Barton, D. (1992). The factory as a learning laboratory. *Sloan Management Review*, Fall, 23-38.

Louis, M. R. (1985). Sourcing workplace cultures: Why, when, and how. In Kilmann, R. H., Saxton, M. J., Serpa, R. and Associates. (Eds.), *Gaining Control of the Corporate Culture*, 126-136. San Francisco, CA: Jossey-Bass.

Mintzberg, H. (1973). *The Nature of Managerial Work*. New York: Harper & Row.

Mintzberg, H. (1990). The design school: Reconsidering the basic premises of strategic management. *Strategic Management Journal*, 11, 171-195.

Nelson, K. M., & Cooprider, J. G. (1996). The contribution of shared knowledge to IT group performance. *MIS Quarterly*, 20(4), 409-432.

Porter, M.E. & Millar, V.E. (1985). How information gives you competitive advantage. *Harvard Business Review,* 63(4), 149-161.

Premkumar, G., & King, W. R. (1991). Assessing strategic information systems planning. *Long Range Planning*, 24(5), 41-58.

Raghunathan, B., & Raghunathan, T. S. (1991). Information systems planning and effectiveness: An empirical analysis. *Omega*, 2(3), 125-135.

Ramanujam, V., Venkatraman, N., & Camillus, J. C. (1986). Multi-objective assessment of effectiveness of strategic planning: A discriminant analysis approach. *Academy of Management Journal*, 29(2), 347-372.

Reich, B. H., & Benbasat, I. (2000). Factors that influence the social dimension of alignment between business and information technology planning. *MIS Quarterly*, 24(1), 81-113.

Rockart, J. F. (1979). Chief executives define their own data needs. *Harvard Business Review*, 57(2), 81-93.

Rodgers, E. M. (1997). Alignment revisited. *CIO Magazine*, May, 44-45.

Roepke, R., Agarwal R., & Ferrat, T. W. (2000). Aligning the IT human resource with business vision: The leadership initiative at 3M. *MIS Quarterly*, 24(2), 327-353.

Schein, E. (1985). *Organizational Culture and Leadership*. San Francisco, CA: Jossey-Bass.

Smircich, L. (1983). Concepts of culture and organizational analysis. *Administrative Science Quarterly*, 28, 339-358.

Stewart, T. A. (1997). *Intellectual Capital: The New Wealth of Organizations*. New York: Currency.

Subramani, M. R., Henderson, J. C., & Cooprider, J. (1999). Linking IS-user partnerships to IS performance: A socio-cognitive perspective. *MISRC Working Paper WP99-01*, University of Minnesota.

Sullivan, Jr., C. H. (1985). Systems planning in the information age. *Sloan Management Review*, Winter, 3-11.

Tallon, P., & Kraemer, K. (1998). A process-oriented assessment of the alignment of information systems and business strategy: Implications for IT business value. In Hoadley, E. D. and Benbasat (Eds.), *Proceedings of the Association for Information Systems Americas Conference*, Baltimore, MD.

Tapscott, D. (1996). *The Digital Economy: Promise and Peril in the Age of Networked Intelligence*. New York: McGraw-Hill.

Tichy, N. M. and Ulrich, D. O. (1984). The leadership challenge: A call for the transformational leader. *Sloan Management Journal*, 18(7), 509-533.

Trice H. M. and Beyer, J. M. (1983). Studying organizational cultures through rites and ceremonials. *The Academy of Management Review*, 9(4), 653-670.

Turban, E., McLean, E. and Wetherbe, J. C. (2000). *Information Technology for Management: Making Connections for Strategic Advantage*. New York: Wiley.

Wilkof, M. V. (1989). Organizational culture and decision making: A case of consensus management. *R&D Management*, April, 19(2), 185-199.

Wilson, P. (2000). Clarification of the meaning of job stress in the context of sales force research. *The Jounral of Personal Selling & Sales Management*, 20(3), 51-64.

Wooldridge, B. and Floyd, S. W. (1989). Strategic process effects on consensus. *Strategic Management Journal*, 10, 295-302.

Wysocki, R. K. and DeMichiel, R. L. (1996). *Managing Information Across the Enterprise*. New York: Wiley.

Zuboff, S. (1988). *In the Age of the Smart Machine: The Future of Work and Power*. New York: Basic Books.

APPENDIX: INTERVIEW QUESTIONS FOR IT PLANNING IN BAHRAIN'S BANKING SECTOR

The interview seeks to assess the degree of integration (i.e., alignment) between business planning and information technology planning in your bank as well as the factors facilitating/inhibiting such integration.

Information technology planning consists mainly of:
- Identifying new opportunities for using information technology (IT);
- Clarifying what resources are needed to implement IT solutions; and
- Developing action plans to realize opportunities and thus to achieve important organizational goals.

1. What is your job title?
2. How many years have you worked in this bank?
3. How many years have you been in your current position?
4. What is your formal education in?
5. How many years have you been involved with IT planning?
6. What are the core competencies of your bank?
7. How is your IT function organized? (i.e., who does IT planning, who's responsible for IT infrastructure development, and who does application development)
8. Do you have a formal IT planning process?
9. What is the degree of integration between business planning and IT planning in your bank?
10. Do you use a specific planning methodology?
11. Who are the decision-makers in IT planning?
12. What are the major steps in IT planning in your bank?
13. How often do you perform IT planning?
14. What are the most important philosophies and objectives driving IT planning in your bank?
15. What are the deliverables of your IT planning?
16. What are the required skills for an IT planner?
17. Are there any special formal educational requirements for IT planners?

18. What is the nature of the triangular relationship between the CIO-IT department-user departments and how does it work practically?
19. How would you characterize the level of business awareness in the IT department?
20. How would you characterize the level of IT awareness in the user departments?
21. How would you characterize the bank's prevailing culture as it relates to IT (e.g., Does it encourage direct contacts and mutual learning between business managers and IT managers?).
22. Do you provide business training for IT managers in your bank?
23. Do you provide IT training for business managers?
24. Who carries out system development and implementation?

Chapter III

Assessing the Risks of IT-Enabled Jobs

Laura Lally
Hofstra University, USA

INTRODUCTION

This chapter provides a managerially oriented analysis of the risk factors involved as Information Technology becomes a more integral part of jobs on both an operational and managerial level. The chapter will summarize the human side risks of IT-enabled jobs, especially in organizations that have used IT to restructure more traditional jobs. Topics will include the following categories of risk.

First, the risks of using IT to create combined "case manager" jobs, recommended by reengineering advocates (Davenport & Nohria, 1994) will be examined. Employees in these positions must assume greater accountability for their work and often find their jobs more stressful and demanding than their predecessors. Another problem with combined jobs is the loss of separation of duties that arises when jobs are combined.

Secondly, the risks of using IT to reduce the numbers of levels of management will be examined. Reengineering advocates call for organizations to eliminate levels of middle management and create flatter, more efficient structures. As a result, managers in reengineered organizations are also likely to suffer from the information overload, rising job demands, and stress that operational level employees do. Internal control theory also expresses concern about the potential for managerial fraud and warns organizations to be on the lookout for "pressures and opportunities" that would drive an individual in a position of trust to do serious damage (Cushing & Romney, 1999).

The chapter will also address the human resource issues of staffing these new high-intensity jobs. The increase in the availability of job candidate information as a result of the growth of IT-based information sources makes obtaining information about candidates' medical, criminal and financial history simpler, but poses both legal and ethical issues.

This chapter will then apply this analysis to emerging trends in e-commerce. Suggestions for managers will conclude the chapter.

THEORETICAL BACKGROUND

This chapter is grounded in Normal Accident Theory and the Theory of High Reliability Organizations. These theories argue that two characteristics of an organization, the complexity of its processes and the degree to which these processes are "tightly coupled"—meaning that one process leads automatically to another, predict whether serious problems will occur in the normal course of events. This chapter will argue that reengineered organization increase in both complexity and tight coupling, resulting in both technological infrastructures and jobs that are more prone to the creation and propagation of serious problems. The analysis presented in this paper is the result of research conducted as part of the author's study, "Enumerating the Risks of Reengineering," funded by the National Science Foundation Grant #SBR-9729886.

REENGINEERING JOBS WITH INFORMATION TECHNOLOGY: PROMISING BUT RISKY

Reengineering was originally defined by Michael Hammer and James Champy in their 1993 bestseller, *Reengineering the Corporation* as "the fundamental re-thinking and radical re-design of business processes," (Hammer & Champy, 1993, p. 32). Reengineered processes are aimed at streamlining workflows, eliminating excess paperwork, downsizing the workforce, speeding up cycle time and improving organizational flexibility. Reengineering advocates propose integrating processes to create: 1) combined "case manager" jobs that integrate the functions and responsibilities of several former jobs and give employees greater decision-making autonomy, and 2) flatter organizational structures, eliminating mid-level "drone managers" (Nolan & Croson, 1995), integrating executive and operational level decision making and increasing managerial spans of control through the use of "technological intermediaries" (Nolan & Croson, 1995). The result of implementing these processes, reengineering advocates argue, should be a leaner organization that is more responsive to its customers' needs and more competitive in a global environment.

The business community has adopted the reengineering concept with great enthusiasm. However, a large percent of reengineering projects have been considered failures. In a survey of 350 executives involved with business reengineering "only 16% say they're 'fully satisfied' with their efforts. The survey also found that 68% of the executives reported that their reengineering projects had unintended side effects and created new problems instead of solving old ones" (Caldwell, 1995, p. 52). Another survey indicates the failure rate of reengineering projects to be 70% (Rock & Yu, 1994).

The reengineering of organizations is currently having a major social impact in the U.S. in terms of job security and the career paths individuals can contemplate within an organizational setting. Reengineering has caused considerable unemployment among middle managers who are often forced into lower paying temporary jobs or service jobs. Questions about the degree of loyalty organizations and their employees can expect from one another, the degree of autonomy professional and managerial decision makers have in a organizational context, and the challenges of managing and controlling "virtual" organizations have emerged with no clear answers about the best way to proceed. Before implementing processes that require radical organizational restructuring, therefore, organizational leaders need to take a sober look at the potential risks of the changes they are contemplating.

Thomas H. Davenport, author of *Process Innovation: Reengineering Work Through Information Technology,* warns that "a firm should be aware that the risks of process innovation are at least proportional to the rewards. Given this equation, organizations that can avoid such wrenching change should probably do so" (Davenport, 1993, p. 14). On the risk side of his "equation," however, Davenport only mentions that: 1) the ambitious nature of reengineering projects make their failures (and the management behind them) highly visible, 2) the cross functional nature of process innovation will greatly heighten the risk of failure, and 3) the likelihood that employees subject to losing subordinates, decision-making power, and the ability to command resources will resist the change. Likewise, Michael Hammer, in his followup book with Steven Stanton, *The Reengineering Revolution: A Handbook*, defines a reengineering failure as a project that was not completed due to political resistance:

> What happens in reengineering failure is—nothing. The reengineering army that marched to war with unfurled banners and gleaming swords is not slaughtered by the enemy. But it often gets lost in the swamp on the way to the battlefield, never to be heard from again (Hammer & Stanton, 1995, p. 252).

Both Hammer and Davenport, the two leading experts on process reengineering, therefore, see the risks of reengineered processes solely in terms of the internal political forces that can thwart a reengineering effort.

Information technology strategists Eric Clemmons and Peter Keen both focus on another aspect of reengineering risk—designing processes that are not aligned with the firm's strategic goals. Clemmons cautions against the developing of processes (supported by new expensive infrastructures) that ignore the firm's key strategic objectives or that are too limited in scope to be effective (Clemmons, 1995; Clemmons, Thatcher & Row, 1995). Keen and Knapp (1995) warns against the "Process Paradox"—creating new streamlined processes whose benefits do not impact the bottom line.

What reengineering advocates and information technology strategists alike fail to address, however, is the riskiness of the redesigned processes themselves—such as the "unintended side effects" and "new problems" reported by Caldwell (1994, p. 52). Opponents of reengineering are often characterized as irrational, turf-protecting luddites in the reengineering literature. Reengineering leaders are advised that they will have to "exorcise whatever private demons" (Hammer & Stanton, 1995, p. 130) stand the in way of reengineering efforts. The reengineering team is advised to either convert the opposition to the cause or quickly fire them to keep reengineering efforts on track – "Don't live too long with people who refuse to change their behavior, especially if their work is important to achieving your reengineering goals" (Champy, 1995, p. 109).

This limited framing of reengineering risks is not surprising. Kasperson and Stallen indicate that in risk communication the "assumption of a neutral, altruistic communicator" often fails (1990, p. 4). James F. Short comments that "risk related decisions often are embedded in organizational and institutional self interest" (Short, 1992, p. 8). Pauchant and Mitroff's study (1990) of crisis preparedness indicates that many high level managers: 1) are in a state of denial about the risks their organization face, and 2) only become convinced of the need to formally address their own risk after experiencing their own crises. This paper will argue that the risks of redesigning work processes are more fundamental than merely dealing with the political posturing of opponents or the design of strategically misaligned systems and must be addressed up front in the planning stage of organizational redesign. Reengineering "changes the relationship between management, information, technology, organizational structure and people" (Kettinger & Grover, 1995, p. 12). Reengineered processes pose radical challenges to traditional thinking about the role of information technology in designing new systems, the degree of responsibility and accountability associated with various jobs, systems theory concepts such as span of control and redundancy, and auditing principles such as the separation of duties. Until these potential risks have been fully identified and considered, organizations may be placing too much trust in the information technology that enables reengineered processes and in the employees with enhanced responsibilities who must carry them out.

Conversely, a potential reengineered process may indeed provide a less wasteful way of doing business, make organizations more responsive to their customers, and increase employee satisfaction by providing bright and motivated employees with enriched jobs and enhanced roles in their organizations. Streamlined, reengineered processes may even be less risky—transactions may be less susceptible to falling through the cracks between functional departments, or to clerical errors resulting from manual processing. A careful enumeration of the genuine risks involved in reengineered processes will leave the organizations planning reengineering well armed to combat criticism of a purely political nature and to defend worthwhile new processes.

This analysis is grounded in Charles Perrow's Normal Accident Theory (1984). Perrow's theory argues that as systems become more complex and tightly coupled, they become more accident prone. An outgrowth of Perrow's theory that also informs the analysis is Todd R. La Porte's theory of High Reliability Organizations. La Porte accepts Perrow's premise that an organization's characteristics can make it disaster prone, but focuses more attention on the characteristics of organizations that make them more robust and resilient when dealing with complexity and tight coupling. Both theoretical perspectives, as well as those of other risk analysts, will be applied to case manager jobs, and the flatter organizational structures advocated by reengineering. Based on the analysis, questions regarding the riskiness of the new integrated processes will emerge.

NORMAL ACCIDENT THEORY AND THE THEORY OF HIGH RELIABILITY ORGANIZATIONS

Normal Accident Theory argues that characteristics of a system's design make it more or less prone to accidents. Accidents are defined as "a failure in a subsystem, or the system as a whole, that damages more than one unit and in doing so disrupts the ongoing or future output of the system" (Perrow, 1984, p. 66). Perrow distinguishes between disastrous "accidents," which are system wide and seriously impact the system's overall functioning, and "incidents," which involve single failures that can be contained within a limited area and which do not compromise the system's overall functioning. Perrow argues that no system can be designed to completely avoid incidents, but that inherent qualities of the system determine how far and how fast the damage will spread. Systems that are not designed to contain the negative impact of incidents will, therefore, *be subject to accidents in the course of their normal functioning.*

The first key characteristic of accident prone systems is their complexity. Normal Accident Theory argues that as systems become more complex, they become more accident prone. Linear interactions (such as an assembly line), characterized by "dedicated," pre-defined connections between the process parts, make incidents easier to identify and less likely to propagate in unexpected ways. Linear interactions are likely to be more visible to operators, but even when the interactions are not visible, the process interactions are likely to be well understood and predictable. Operators, therefore, can respond quickly to an incident. Complex systems, in contrast, are characterized by multiple possible connections between process parts. Complex systems are also more likely to have "common-mode" connections, one part serving a number of functions. An incident involving a common mode can propagate to a number of processes that depend upon it. The unanticipated propagation of incidents is also more likely in complex systems because these systems are likely to have fewer visible interactions. Operators, therefore, become more dependent on indirect control indicators. "In complex systems, where not even the tip of the iceberg is visible, the communication must be exact, the dial correct, the switch position obvious, the reading direct and on-line" (Perrow, 1984, p. 84). Perrow also notes that the greatest source of complexity is often the external environment and that having a system interact with the external environment is likely to significantly increase its complexity.

Normal Accident Theory distinguishes a second characteristic of systems that exacerbate potential problems brought about as a result of complexity—tight coupling. Tight coupling means there is no slack time or buffering of resources between tasks; interactions happen immediately. Tight coupling, like complexity, is often more efficient from a productivity standpoint. However, incidents tend to propagate faster and their impact becomes more severe because there is no lag time during which human intervention can occur and no buffer stocks to mitigate the impact of downtime.

Perrow developed his theory while studying complex technologies such as nuclear power plants and petrochemical plants to determine the conditions under which incidents such as valve failures could lead to accidents such as meltdowns and the release of poisonous gases into populated areas. Normal Accident Theory argues that incidents need to be anticipated and controls built into the system to contain their propagation.

Researchers in High Reliability Organizations have examined organizations in which complex, tightly coupled, technologically based systems appeared to be coping successfully with the potential for disaster. High reliability theorists' studies of the Federal Aviation Administration's air traffic control system, the Pacific Gas and Electric's electric power system, including the Diablo Canyon nuclear power plant, and the peacetime flight operations of three United States Navy aircraft carriers indicate that organizations can achieve nearly error-free operation (La Porte & Consolini, 1991; Perrow, 1994; Sagan, 1993).

High reliability organization theorists identify four critical causal factors for achieving reliability:

- Political elites and organizational leaders put safety and reliability first as a goal.
- High levels of redundancy in personnel and technical safety measures.
- The development of a "high reliability culture" in decentralized and continually practiced operations, and
- Sophisticated forms of trial and error organizational learning.

The two theories have been contrasted as "pessimistic"—Perrow's contention that disaster is inevitable in badly designed systems, versus "optimistic"—La Porte's pragmatic approach to achieving greater reliability. The theories, however, are in agreement as to which characteristics of systems make them more or less accident prone.

COMBINED JOBS—RISK ANALYSIS

A common recommendation of reengineering advocates is to practice the "combination, not division, of labor" (Davenport & Nohria, 1994, p. 11). Reengineering advocates (Hammer & Champy, 1993), often recommend that a new job category—a "case manager" should be created, putting an individual in charge of an integrated process that once was handled by several people in different functional departments. In these positions, "individuals or small teams perform a series of tasks, such as the fulfillment of an order, from beginning to end, often with the help of information systems that reach through the organization" (Davenport & Nohria, 1994 p. 11). This individual will interact with all stages of the process and "needs access to all the information systems that people actually performing the process use, and the ability to contact those people with questions and requests for further assistance when necessary" (Hammer & Champy, 1993, p. 63). Employees controlling these complex tasks must also assume greater accountability for their work (Caron, Jarvenpaa

& Stoddard, 1994; Longo, 1995) and often attain greater degrees of computer literacy in order to perform their new jobs. A single bad judgment or unauthorized transaction by a case manager is, therefore, more likely to produce a "common-mode" failure with consequences propagating throughout the organization, than a single bad judgment by an individual in a functionally fragmented job.

Reengineering advocates admit that case manager jobs are far more stressful and demanding than their predecessors, and that "the broader the set of functional tasks involved and the organizations linked, the more difficult it is to find good case managers" (Davenport & Nohria, 1994, p. 16).

Case management may be far more rewarding, but is generally more demanding and stressful. It requires new personal skills, end-to-end process knowledge, and the familiarity with often complex computer systems. Moreover, the work can be isolating, involving limited interactions with other workers and demanding intense concentration (Keen & Knapp, 1995).

The high degree of computer mediation involved in these tasks may diminish the quality of the work for employees, making them feel "'chained' to the computer or the phone" (Davenport & Nohria, 1994, p. 19) and out of touch with the tangible realities about which they are making decisions. Designing frontware environments—computer user interfaces for employees handling complex, computer mediated processes—is another challenging task. "Building a frontware environment for each type of case manager in an organization could lead to a jumbled and patched-together information architecture" (Davenport & Nohria, 1994, p. 18). (For some cautionary tales due to poor interface design see Neumann, 1995; Norman, 1991; Wiener, 1993).

An alternative approach to the problem of the overburdened case manager suggested by reengineering advocates is to allow more decision making to be done by expert systems (Hammer & Champy, 1993). Expert systems are recommended to support case managers in routine decision making, limiting the degree of analysis they are required to perform, further increasing their productivity, and decreasing their cycle time. Hammer and Stanton (1995) recommend this approach, yet provide an example of how a decision that was considered routine before it was automated was actually mediated by human "shadow systems" that compensated for special circumstances. When these procedures became automated without the mediating shadow systems, the resulting systems were brittle, causing failures when special circumstances (of which there were many) occurred.

The wisdom of using expert systems in critical decision situations has been widely questioned (Littlewood & Strigini, 1992; Wiener, 1993). Expert systems, such as the programmed trading systems used by stock exchanges, are now often programmed to return control to human decision makers in critical situations. The use of expert systems may reduce decision-making autonomy and prevent the decision makers from developing their own expertise. In a crisis situation, there may no longer be an adequate number of humans who have the knowledge and experience to make the difficult decisions.

Organizations contemplating reengineering must be concerned whether, "current staff possess the expertise and credentials to perform in an increasingly technical environment" (Sears & Trotter, 1995, p. 16). Reengineering advocate Champy states, "We must hold fast to our faith in human beings; the knowledge and belief that we are all eager to learn, and capable of dedication, high spirits, and individual responsibility" (1995, p. 27). Nolan and Croson (1995) are decidedly less Emersonian and more Machiavellian in their explanation of what motivates employees to assume more responsible, stressful jobs:

> When approximately 30 percent of the workforce has be re-deployed or eliminated, it becomes crystal clear to those who remain that the downsizing initiative has passed the point of no return. The organization begins to operate in a manner that reinforces, rather than opposes, the transformation initiative. Employees interested in being on the winning side contribute by rethinking and redesigning work based upon their particular expertise (p. 64).

Reports of reengineering failures indicate, however, that either philosophy does not apply universally. "For a host of reasons, some rational and some irrational, many people don't want to adapt, change or reinvent themselves" (Sobkowiak & LeBleu, 1995, p. 41).

New job descriptions may contain tasks that are outside an employee's major area of competency or that employees feel uncomfortable performing. Hammer and Stanton (1995) give an example of field representatives not wanting to extend their responsibilities to include the entire order-fulfillment process. This new accountability took time away from their interactions with customers and would often put them in the uncomfortable position of having to tell a customer (albeit truthfully) that a product was unavailable. "The sales rep's sense of who he or she is, of his or her very identity, is under threat" (p. 127). The reps were so adverse to the new process that when the reengineering team outlined how the process would lead to substantially higher commissions they responded, "We have enough money" (p. 127).

Lower level employees may resent not being adequately compensated for their new roles. "You raised my pay $1.00 an hour and are asking me to do the work of three people. Why should I break my neck?" (Hammer & Stanton, 1995, p. 199). "Empowering" lower level workers to make decisions is recommended by advocates of reengineering and participative management (Kowal & Parsons, 1995), but employees may not welcome job enrichment. Many of the frontline workers at a telecommunication company refused to shoulder the new responsibilities that a reengineered process placed on them. They continued to operate in the old "disempowered" way, claiming that they lacked adequate training or information to perform as the new process required. They constantly sought direction from their (now far fewer) supervisors, effectively causing the process to grind to a halt (Hammer & Stanton, 1995).

Perrow's essay on complex organizations suggests that employees seek job that are in line with their abilities and ambition—their "true type." Perrow (1986) argues that if employees had wanted more challenging and responsible jobs, they would have sought them out in the first place. System theorists argue that an individual's capacity for absolute judgement cannot be expanded at will (Flood & Carson, 1988). Studies of service employees indicate that while some employees welcomed increased decision making autonomy, others preferred having a structured, algorithmic job description that allowed them to feel sure they doing what they were supposed to (Bowen & Lawler, 1995).

Keen and Knapp (1995) cite a cautionary example from a reengineering "success":

> Not mentioned in the articles and books lauding one of the first and most successful instances of case management, the Mutual Benefit insurance company, is that the stresses, uncertainties, and difficulties of learning new skills lead some employees to express their frustration by picketing their employer's head office.

> Finally, even Michael Hammer (1996) has begun to recognize the problem: It would be nice to believe that education and training will bring everyone up to the level required by process-centered jobs. Maybe it's possible, but the prospect of such dramatic improvement in the American system is very doubtful and at best would take many years. The problem of what to do with "little people" will be with us for some time.

Loss of separation of duties is another admitted source of risk from combined jobs. "Risk-averse executives will worry about including so much in one job" (Davenport, 1993, p. 21). Incompetent or dishonest employees, especially those with access to information technology, will have the potential to do greater damage. Studies of information technology risks indicate that threats arising from authorized access are less likely to be deterred by access controls and harder to detect. "High-tech insider fraud can be difficult to detect if it blends with legitimate transactions" (Neumann, 1992b, p. 154). Cases involving a single employee making an unauthorized $8.4 million transfer, or a former CEO holding a firm's mainframe computer hostage with an encoded password known only to himself, lead systems designers to worry. "At what point is it appropriate to trust a single individual in a process, as opposed to never letting one person do anything without another qualified person present?" (Morris, 1987, p. 13).

FLATTER ORGANIZATIONAL STRUCTURES— RISK ANALYSIS

Perrow (1984) argues that complex, tightly coupled systems require incidents to be anticipated and control mechanisms to be designed into the system during its development. These controls will halt the process where an incident has occurred and call for human intervention.

In stark contrast to Perrow's recommendations, however, reengineering calls for checks and controls to be reduced (Champy, 1995; Hammer & Champy, 1993; Hammer, 1995) and reconciliations minimized (Hammer & Champy, 1993). Deferred control, such as replacing immediate supervision with monthly reconciliations, is called for by Hammer and Champy as a means of reducing costs. Supervisory costs are condemned by the authors as "nonvalue-adding" because they do not contribute directly to the quality of goods and services produced. Internal auditing experts Jeff Gibbs and Patrick Keating (1995) note that:

> Control environments have been shaken and shifted as a result of downsizing, flattening and decentralization trends in business. Many of the controls on which auditors have traditionally relied, such as separation of duties and authorizations, actually tend to work at cross-purposes to the goals of the reengineered virtual corporation.

The workforce downsizing recommended by reengineering advocates extends to middle managers and the professional staff as well as to clerical and blue collar workers. Nolan and Croson (1995) declare the three-tiered organizational hierarchy "unsalvageable" and recommend "the transfer of the function of mid-level employees to a technological liaison" (p. 50). Though Nolan and Croson do not provide technical specifications for these systems, their functions are clear—to increase the span of control of upper management and to increase the degree of indirect supervision. Nolan and Croson view traditional span of control and direct supervisory practices as being "dictated by tradition" (p. 49) rather than as being based upon demonstrated limits of human cognition. Span of control to Nolan and Croson is, rather, a function of the monitoring and communications technology available—technologies that now permit changes in ratios of supervisors to workers and indirect monitoring methods. Deferring control, replacing immediate supervision with monthly reconciliations is also recommended (Hammer & Champy, 1993):

- Minimizing "nonvalue-adding" supervisory costs (Hammer & Champy, 1993)
- Reducing checks and controls, the "green eye shade crew" (Hammer & Champy, 1993)
- Minimizing reconciliations, get the work done and look after the reporting later (Keen & Knapp, 1995).

The recommendations are in complete opposition to accounting internal control theory, which advocates:

- Specific authorization by higher level managers of transactions of significant amounts
- Segregation of duties—especially those involving the authorization and recording of transactions
- Duplicate checking of calculations
- Regular reports of activities and immediate reports of exceptional activities (Cushing & Romney, 1999).

The issue of how far trust can be extended in an atmosphere of indirect supervision is a serious one, especially since reengineering efforts that involve downsizing are often accompanied by "declining morale, rising cynicism and downright hostility reported more and more frequently at all levels of an organization" (Gorman, 1997, p. xii). In the post-reengineering environment, managers are more likely to see themselves as "free agents" and feel less loyalty to their organizations (Stroh & Reilly, 1998). A Right Associates survey found that only 31 percent of employees trusted their organizations after significant downsizing (Mishra, Spreitzer, & Mishra, 1998). "Where you cannot trust, you have to become a checker once more, with all the systems of control that involves" (Handy, 1995, p. 46). Reliance on information technology-based measures of performance and monitoring to allow top managers to keep track of their subordinates actions gives rise to a number of managerial, legal and ethical concerns. Keen and Knapp (1995) concludes, "What sense does it make to presume trust in the absence of knowledge of how to build it, or for the untrustable to demand trust?" (p. 194).

Reengineering also calls for delegating decision making. James Champy in his followup book, *Reengineering Management* (1995), sees the failure to delegate more decision making as the major stumbling block preventing organizations from realizing reengineering's full benefits and calls for "a shift in authority and accountability" (p. 116). The flatter organizational structures and wider spans of control involved in many reengineered processes will make further delegation a necessity. Agency theory, which studies the difficulties of letting individuals with their own interests and agendas make decisions for an organization, suggests that concerns with delegating decisions may be justified. "The principal-agent relationship is fraught with the problems of cheating, limited information and bounded rationality in general" (Perrow, 1986, p. 224).

Employee education and training is another task reengineering advocates are delegating to information technology, via "Just-in-Time Training":

Instruction called just-in-time training is required when something goes wrong and a worker must find out how to handle it quickly. Corporate downsizing has greatly increased the need for just-in-time training. With fewer employees on staff, chances are greater that a given worker will not know how to deal with a situation that specialists might have handled before losing their jobs....rightsizing piles new responsibilities onto existing staff and requires hiring temporary staff that needs just-in-time training (Hofstetter, 1995, p. 39).

Even honest employees may fail to perform their jobs correctly due to incompetency or illness, suggesting another difficulty with combined jobs — a lack of redundancy of critical components. Redundancy is considered a key characteristic of "high-reliability" and "survivable" systems and involves the designing in of backup systems to replace critical systems if they fail (Neumann, 1992a; Sagan, 1993). Lee Clarke (1990) notes that the Exxon Valdez disaster was in part attributable to the reductions in staff that had been made to increase efficiency. Disaster planners note that reengineering "decreases the redundancy of business functions critical to company survival, making the need for a disaster plan more important" (Howard, 1994, p. 7). The use of "case teams" suggested by reengineering advocates would alleviate this problem somewhat, but at the cost of increasing still further the required knowledge and responsibilities each employee must assume.

Finding qualified individuals for case manager jobs, therefore, becomes a greater challenge. A common worry is whether "current staff possess the expertise and credentials to perform in an increasing technical environment" (Sears & Trotter, 1995, p. 16). Hiring from outside is also problematic. "The broader the set of functional tasks involved and the organizations linked, the more difficult it is to find good case managers" (Davenport & Nohria, 1994, p. 16).

Managers in reengineered organizations are also likely to suffer from the information overload, rising job demands, and stress that operational level employees do. A study conducted by Ulrich (1998) indicated that half of the "high potential" managers he interviewed planned to leave their present organization, not because of a lack of opportunity but because of enormous stress and unrealistic demands. Internal control theory also expresses concerns about the potential for managerial fraud and warns organizations to be on the lookout for "pressures and opportunities" that would drive individuals in a position of trust to do serious damage (Cushing & Romney, 1999, p. 720).

Organizations with flatter structures, therefore, face the risk of having unhappy, mistrustful, stressed out individuals in managerial roles that can have immediate major impacts on the organization's viability.

Employers are, therefore, faced with a daunting task in filling complex, stressful, yet increasingly critical and sensitive positions throughout reengineered organizations. Internal control theory counsel employers to perform extensive background checking in pre-employment screening to mitigate the risks (Cushing & Romney, 1999) but admits to limitations of this information in predicting white collar crime:

> White collar criminals tend to mirror the general public in terms of education, age, religion, marriage, length of employment and psychological makeup. In other words, there are few characteristics that can be used to distinguish white collar criminals from the general public.

Deciding which individuals possess the skills, intellect and motivation to perform the jobs, and whom the organization can trust to perform autonomously on the organizations behalf becomes a greater challenge.

ELECTRONIC COMMERCE: WHERE ARE THE WEAK LINKS?

The move to the Internet as a common platform greatly increases the potential for electronic commerce. A decade ago, electronic commerce was accomplished through closed networks that provided industry-specific value-added functions. These networks were expensive and complex and their use, therefore, was limited to larger institutions. The World Wide Web has provided a simple-to-use interface that runs on a PC platform, opening up e-commerce opportunities to a much wider range of users.

The open architecture of the Web and its distributed platform increase the complexity of the system and decrease the control individual users have over its functioning. From the human relations perspective, face-to-face interactions are replaced by interactions that are mediated through Web sites. With labor costs accounting for 80% of the budget of Web-based businesses, and venture capital drying, surviving "dot-coms" may be forced to lay off workers to cut costs. A consideration of the risk factors in further limiting face-to-face customer interactions is essential, to prevent customers losing hard-earned trust in Web-based businesses.

CONCLUSION: SUGGESTIONS FOR MANAGERS

The preceding analysis suggests that instead of viewing the redesign of jobs to achieve reengineering goals as inevitable, managers must consider the long-range impact on the organization's workforce. A number of key issues emerge:

Are the demands of the new jobs realistic for the organization's workforce? Do the jobs require greater degrees of computer literacy? If so, can the organization find and compensate people with appropriate skills? Do redesigned jobs create information overload and stress? If so, declines in employee morale and higher turnover can be expected. In addition, the potential for employee error increases.

Do the new jobs consider the issues of separation of duties and redundancy? If one individual becomes responsible for a wider range of duties, the potential for that individual to commit fraud increases. If that person should leave the organization or be unable to perform their duties, can someone else understand their job and take their place?

Do the new jobs require greater degrees of autonomy and responsibility? If so, can individuals be found who can be trusted to perform these jobs? Will there be a greater tendency on the part of managers to seek additional information, such as credit histories from potential employees?

By confronting these issues prior to job redesign, managers can design jobs that are both more efficient and realistic for a given organizational environment.

REFERENCES

Bowen, D. E., & Lawler III, E. E. (1995). Empowering service employees. *Sloan Management Review*, 36(4), 73-84.

Caldwell, B. (1994). Reengineering slip-ups. *InformationWeek*, June, 50-60.

Caldwell, B. (1995). Management's new mandate: Consultant Champy discusses what comes next after reengineering. *InformationWeek*, February, 57-58.

Caron, J. R., Javenpaa, S. L., & Stoddard, D. B. (1994) Business reengineering at CIGNA corporation: Experiences and lessons learned from the first five years. *MIS Quarterly*, September, 233-250.

Champy, J. (1995) *Reengineering Management: The Mandate for New Leadership*. New York: HarperCollins.

Clarke, L. (1990). Oil spill fantasies. *Atlantic Monthly*, November, 65.

Clemmons, E. K. (1995). Using scenario analysis to manage the strategic risks of reengineering. *Sloan Management Review*, 39(4), 39-50.

Clemmons, E. K., Thatcher, M. E., & Row, M. (1995). Identifying sources of reengineering failures: A study of behavioral factors contributing to reengineering risks. *Journal of Management Information Systems*, Fall, 12(2), 9-36.

Cushing, B. E., & Romney, M. R. (1999). *Accounting Information Systems, 6th Edition*, Reading, MA: Addision Wesley.

Davenport, T. H. (1993). *Process Innovation: Reengineering Work Through Information Technology*. Boston, MA: Harvard Business School Press.

Davenport, T. H., & Nohria, N. (1994). Case management and the integration of labor. *Sloan Management Review*, 35(2), 11-23.

Flood, R. L., & Carson, E. R. (1988). *Dealing with Complexity (2nd Ed.)*. New York: Plenum Press.

Gibbs, W. W., & Keating, P. (1994). Software's chronic crisis. *Scientific American*, September, 86-95.

Gorman, C. K. (1997). *This Isn't the Company I Joined*. New York: Van Nostrand Reinhold.

Hammer, M. (1996). *Beyond Reengineering: How the Process-Centered Organization is Changing Our Work and Our Lives*. New York: HarperCollins.

Hammer, M., & Champy, J. (1993). *Reengineering the Corporation*. New York: HarperCollins.

Hammer, M., & Stanton S.A. (1995). *The Reengineering Revolution: A Handbook*. New York: HarperCollins Publishers.

Handy, C. (1995). Trust and the virtual organization. *Harvard Business Review*, May-June, 40-48.

Hofstetter, F. (1995). *Multimedia Literacy*. New York: McGraw-Hill.

Howard, L. S. (1994). Downsizing spawns risk, expert says. *National Underwriter*, October, 98(42), 7-16.

Kasperson, R. E., & Stallen, P. J. M. (1990). Risk comunication: The evolution of attempts. In Kasperson, R. E. and Stallen, P. J. M. (Eds), *Communicating Risks to the Public, International Perspectives*. Boston, MA: Kluwer Academic Publishers.

Keen, P. G. W., & Knapp, E. M. (1995). *Every Manager's Guide to Business Processes*. Boston: Harvard Business School Press.

Kettinger, W. J., & Grover, V. (1995). Toward a theory of business process change management. *Journal of Management Information Systems*, 12(1), 9-22.

Kowal, D. C., & Parsons, R. J. (1995). Empowerment is a must if reengineering is your goal. *Journal for Quality and Participation*, 18(1), 74-76.

LaPorte, T. R., & Consolini, P. (1991). Working in practice but not in theory: Theoretical challenges of high reliability organizations. *Journal of Public Administration*, 1, 19-47.

Littlewood, B., & Strigini, L. (1992). The risks of software. *Scientific American*, November, 62-75.

Longo, S. C. (1995). After reegineering–'Dejobbing.' *CPA Journal*, 65(3), 69.

Mishra, K. E., Spreitzer, G. M., & Mishra, A. K. (1998). Preserving employees during downsizing. *Sloan Management Review*, 39(2), 83-94.

Morris, J. (1987). Another computer taken hostage. *Software Engineering Notes*, 12(3), 13.

Neumann, P. (1992a). Inside risks: Survivable systems. *Communications of the ACM*, 35(2), 130.

Neumann, P. (1992b). Inside risks: Leap-year problems. *Communications of the ACM*, 35(6), 162.

Neumann, P. (1995). *Computer-Related Risks*. New York: Addison Wesley.

Nolan, R. L., & Croson, D. C. (1995). *Creative Destruction*. Cambridge, MA: Harvard Business School Press.

Norman, D. (1991). Commentary: Human error and the design of computer systems. *Communications of the ACM*, 33(1), 4-7.

Parker, D. (1983). *Fighting Crime by Computer*. New York: Scribner.

Parnas, D. L., van Schouwen, J., & Kwan, S. P. (1990). Evaluation of safety-critical software. *Communications of the ACM*, 33(6), 636-648.

Pauchant, T., & Mitroff, I. (1992). *Transforming the Crisis Prone Organization*. San Francisco: Jossey-Bass.

Perrow, C. (1984). *Normal Accidents: Living with High Risk Technologies*. New York: Basic Books.

Perrow, C. (1986). *Complex Organizations: A Critical Essay*. New York: Random House.

Rock, D., & Yu, D. (1994). Improving business process reengineering. *AI Expert*, 9(10), 26-35.

Sagan, S. (1993). *The Limits of Safety*. Princeton, NJ: Princeton University Press.

Sears, W., & Trotter, R. (1995). Reengineering readiness test: What's your infrastructure IQ? *Industrial Engineering*, 27(1), 16-17.

Short, J. F. (1992). Defining, explaining and managing risk. *Organizations, Uncertanties and Risks*. Boulder, CO: Westview Press.

Sobkowiak, R. T., & LeBleu, R. (1995). The people cost of reengineering. *Computerworld*, 29(6), p. 41.

Stroh, L. K., & Reilly, A. H. (1998). Loyalty in an age of downsizing. *Sloan Management Review*, 38(4), 83-88.

Ulrich, D. (1998). Intellectual capital = Competence X Commitment. *Sloan Management Review*, 39(20), 15-26.

Wiener, L. (1993). *Digitial Woes: Why We Should Not Depend on Software*. Reading, MA: Addison Wesley.

Chapter IV

The Non-Technical Side of Office Technology: Managing the Clarity of the Spirit and the Appropriation of Office Technology

Huub J. M. Ruël
University of Twente, The Netherlands

INTRODUCTION

Office work plays an important role in Western economies, and the use of office technologies in this type of work is inextricably linked. People employed in office environments are confronted with an almost continuous introduction of new office technologies, as decision-makers in companies believe that the market drives them towards being very attentive to the latest developments in the field of IT. Furthermore, IT in general has become a strategic factor in doing business (e.g., e-commerce), which has further increased the need for the newest office technologies. As a result, the number of projects in organizations to develop and implement new office technologies has unarguably increased. However, office technology projects are often confronted with problems. In our view, these problematic experiences are due to a lack of attention to the non-technical side of office technology development, implementation and use. Hence, in this chapter, we present a study based on a view of office technology project that stresses the non-technical side of office technology. We introduce the concepts of *spirit of office technology* and *office technology appropriation*. By testing three hypotheses based upon this view, it is shown that this concept can be helpful in contributing to an improvement in the understanding of office technology development, implementation and use. This is scientifically interesting and relevant since the outcomes of our study say something about the value of the theoretical framework applied. It is also of practical interest, as the results of the study can help in the everyday practice of office technology projects.

This chapter is structured as follows: first, we explore the problematic aspects of office technology projects; then we present our theoretical framework and formulate the three hypotheses to test. Subsequently, we discuss the methodology, and present the results. Finally, we come to conclusions and discuss the consequences in terms of practical guidelines.

OFFICE TECHNOLOGY PROJECTS: DIFFICULT TO MANAGE

The development and implementation of new office technology in offices is, in general, managed through projects, which we can call office technology projects. We define these as: an initiative to develop, implement and use a new office technology system carried out by a temporary organization especially brought into being for the realization of this initiative.

Office technology projects are a familiar phenomenon in organizations, as shown by the results of Ewusi-Mensah and Przasnyski's study (1994). In more than 60% of the organizations that responded to the survey, over 20 IT projects had taken place in the previous five years. In a further 27% of the organizations that responded to the survey, between 1 and 20 IT projects had taken place within the same period. However, office technology projects are very often not successful. One of the main reasons for this is that the introduction of IT is often exclusively based upon the belief that the intended advantages will arise; processes to actually measure the advantages are in many cases never undertaken (Fitzgerald, 1998). So, whether the expected advantages really do occur often remains questionable–this despite the considerable impact IT projects often have on the work environment of employees, and the large amount of money invested in IT. It has become clear that to quite an extent these investments do not satisfy the objectives. A large number of office technology projects end in complete or partial failure (Doherty & King, 1998; Ewusi-Mensah & Przasnyski, 1994). However, hard evidence about the rate of project failures is not easy to find. Ewusi-Mensah and Przasnyski (1994) state that there are several studies that deal with the failure of information systems from the usage and operations viewpoint after a system has been implemented, but that the abandonment of IT projects under development has gained little attention.[1] Ewusi-Mensah and Przasnyski[2] collected data on IT projects from IT senior executives and system managers in Fortune 500 companies. The results showed that approximately one-third indicated that five or more IT projects had been abandoned in their organizations within the period 1982-1986. This is supported by a classic Dutch study on automation projects, carried out by Riesewijk and Warmerdam (1988). It showed that almost half of the projects (48.5%) ended "problematically" or ended unsuccessfully.[3]

Ewusi-Mensah and Przasnyski (1994) identified the following project management issues that "contribute" to project abandonment or failure: staffing, managerial and communicational aspects of project management, and interaction between participants and their perception of work-related issues. In an earlier study, Ewusi-Mensah and Pzrasnyski (1991) found that organizational factors are an important cause of IT project abandonment (e.g., corporate management fails to deal with behavioral, political or organizational issues, or end-users contribute to project abandonment).

Vadapalli and Mone (2000) state that human and management issues play a critical role in the ability of an organization to lead a technology project to success. Clegg et al. (1997) conclude that the context of technical change, a range of human and organizational factors, and the roles of managers and end-users, are critical areas that affect the performance of IT in organizations.

Hornsby et al. (1992) give the following reasons for IT underperformance:

- lack of guiding organizational and business strategies;
- lack of end-user participation and end-user "ownership" of systems;
- lack of attention to education, training and awareness;
- lack of organizational resources and support (concerning the "soft" infrastructure);
- lack of attention to organizational issues such as organization design, organizational culture, and management style; and
- lack of attention to psychological issues such as the design of jobs, the allocation of systems tasks, and the usability of the system.

Observing all of this, it becomes clear that a source of project failure or abandonment is the fact that, in IT projects, management, users and IT professionals have to collaborate, especially since they have different stakes. What also seems clear is that IT projects lack attention to organizational and human factors, which we consider to be a broader area than only the interaction between different parties. Organizational and human factors have to do with the organization of work and the probable changes that will occur as a result of the implementation of new IT, in our case particularly office technology.

Clegg et al. (1997) found that:

> Regarding the impact of new information technology on the way in which work is organized and upon individual job design, the majority view (of the interviewees) was that this is hugely important but largely ignored in practice. Again this was seen as a topic that is significantly under-estimated. Where it is addressed this is because the job design implications of technical change are discovered, usually relatively late in the development process. These findings demonstrate that IT projects remains technology-led. IT is not seen in an integrated way as raising sets of related business and organizational issues (p. 859).

These observations have established a belief that the lack of attention to non-technical issues is the major cause of IT project failure or abandonment.

In conclusion, it has become clear that office technology projects are not a "quick and easy fix." They often fail to meet their objectives and, as we have seen, this is often due to a lack of attention to the non-technical side of office technology projects. The question that emerges is how to contribute to improving the situation? In the literature, several theories and approaches are available that claim to provide clear answers. However, new insights seem to be necessary in order to improve our understanding of the non-technical side of office technology. To develop this non-technical side, we introduce the concepts of *spirit* and *appropriation*. These concepts are adopted from Adaptive Structuration Theory (AST) as developed by DeSanctis and Poole. AST starts from the assumption that the effects of advanced information technology are not a function of the technology itself, but of the way it is *used*. DeSanctis and Poole (1994) state that advanced information technology can be divided into *spirit* and *structural features*. Spirit concerns the *intention* of a certain technology. The structural features concern the technical "parts" of an advanced information technology. In addition, DeSanctis and Poole state that advanced information technology use must be considered as a matter of *appropriation*, which means that technology is not something from "outside" that determines user behavior, but that technology is "realized" in the actual behavior of users. In theory, office technology "carries" a certain spirit which should guide users, but this spirit can only be materialized when users work with, or appropriate, the technology. A precondition is that users have to have a clear image of this spirit. Through being involved in the development and implementation process, it is possible for users to influence this spirit and to become aware of it.

These concepts of spirit and appropriation are particularly adapted to study office technology projects, as the concepts of spirit and appropriation in our view can provide a basis for understanding the non-technical aspects of office technology. The next section presents our theoretical framework and develops the concepts of spirit and appropriation.

THEORETICAL FRAMEWORK

The social sciences, and, more specifically, organizational sciences deserve to be acknowledged in the discussion about the relationship between IT and organization, considering the number of publications on this topic. If we look at the theoretical views used in research on office technology implementation in organizations, we can observe a complex picture. The theories in use are mainly rooted in organizational theory, which is a very diverse field. Good reviews have been presented by a number of authors (e.g., Bolman and Deal, 1984; Morgan, 1986). Over the years, theories on office technology have developed in parallel with theoretical perspectives on organizations. Orlikowski (2000) notes that the following organizational theories have been "transmitted" to research on information technology: contingency theory, strategic choice models, Marxist studies, symbolic interactionist approaches, transaction-cost economics, network analyses, practice theories, structurational models, and innovation theories. All these approaches can be recognized in current research on office technology in organizations. However, if we place the discussion on office technology in organizations in a time frame, we can discern periods in which certain lines of thinking dominate.

Until the mid eighties, the discussion was characterized by basically two lines of thinking, technological determinism and technological voluntarism, which took turns in dominating this discussion. The second half of the 1980s gave birth to views that technology was dualistic in nature, meaning that technology could be both enabling and constraining. Based upon sociological theory, especially Anthony Giddens' structuration theory (1984), researchers in the field of IT and organizations tried to walk a theoretical middle line. One of the first researchers to apply structuration theory was Barley (1986). He developed a model of technology-triggered structural change, that posits that technology might "facilitate" certain social dynamics that will lead to both anticipated and unanticipated structural consequences (for example, decentralization or centralization). In Barley's view, technology is a social object. The context of use defines its meaning, however, a specific technology's physical form and function remains fixed over time and context of use. Thus, technology in Barley's view is on the one hand a social construct, but on the other hand it has a stable physical nature. He does not accept that technology can be modified physically during use (Orlikowski, 1991).

Orlikowski (1991) is of the opinion that this might be true for certain technologies (such as CT scanners, which were object of Barley's study), but not for information technologies. She argues that: "While technologies may appear to have objective forms and functions at one point, these can and do vary by different users, by different contexts of use, and by the same users over time" (p. 6).

At the start of the 1990s, Orlikowski (1991) and Orlikowski and Robey (1991) reconceptualized the relationship between technology and information technology in organizations based upon Giddens' structuration theory (1984). Orlikowksi's approach pronounces that information technology in organizations should not be considered as a stable "external" agent that impacts on organizational forms, nor as a subject of interpretation only. Information technology is itself an "agent of change" depending upon how it is used. The role of information technology is framed in terms of a mutual interaction between human agents and information technology. Information technology, in Orlikowski and Robey's view, provides certain "structures" that are brought into action by human agents and can be altered by human agents during use.

Orlikowski's reconceptualization of the relationship between information technology and the structuring of organizations is characteristic of an important line of thinking during the 1990s. This attempted to give new inputs to the discussion on this topic, by withdrawing from the traditional deterministic and voluntaristic positions in the social sciences that had influenced the discussion to date (Orlikowski & Baroudi, 1991). Others that followed this approach include Poole and DeSanctis (1989, 1990), Walsham (1993), and DeSanctis and Poole (1994). The similarity within these new models is that the focus is on information technology use. Effects of information technology cannot be predicted beyond how it is used in a certain context. In other words, effects emerge as IT is used. It is especially the approach of DeSanctis and Poole (1994), adaptive structuration theory, that will be the basis of our study.

Adaptive Structuration Theory

DeSanctis and Poole (1994) and Poole and DeSanctis (1989, 1990) were inspired by the basic ideas of structuration theory, and developed a theory initially to study groups using group decision support systems (GDSSs). However, in more recent publications, the focus has been broadened to include advanced information technologies (AIT) in general (DeSanctis & Poole, 1994). AST emphasizes that AITs have no meaning apart from their use. It is use that makes it what it is, in a given context, and gives it reality. AIT becomes meaningful as it is used through human action. As DeSanctis and Poole (1994) state: "Many researchers believe that the effects of advanced technologies are less a function of the technologies themselves than of how they are *used* by people" (p. 122).

As noted earlier, the two main concepts in AST are *spirit* and *appropriation*, and these will be explained in more detail below.

Spirit of Office Technology

One of the central elements of AST is the belief that AIT is social in nature. Hence, DeSanctis and Poole (1994) introduce the concept of spirit. They define spirit as follows: "Spirit is the general intent with regard to values and goals underlying a given set of structural features" (p. 126). According to DeSanctis and Poole, the concept of spirit concerns the "official line" that the technology presents to people regarding how to act when using the system, how to interpret its features, and how to fill in gaps in procedure that are not explicitly specified.

They explain that "the spirit of a technology provides what Giddens calls 'legitimization' to the technology by supplying a normative frame with regard to behaviors that are appropriate in the context of the technology" (p.126). The spirit can also provide "signification" to users, as it helps them to understand and interpret the meaning of the IT. Finally, the spirit can be a means of "domination," because it presents the type of influence moves to be used with the IT. Some users may be privileged by this, while it might constrain others. Therefore, in terms of structuration theory, the concept of spirit concerns the total set of possible structures that can be called upon by means of the structural features (later in this section we will discuss how to define the structural features). The concept of spirit thus suits very well what Orlikowski (1991) calls the "interpretive flexibility" of information technology. The implication of this assumption is that the realization of any object may differ between situations and that the object itself can change as people change their mode of using it.

If we project this onto the type of IT included in our study, office technology, this can be illustrated with the following example. A specific office technology may "contain" the spirit: *open organizational communication*. If we analyze this spirit into the three types of structures (based upon Giddens,

1984), it is possible to say that the spirit provides users with structures of signification by appealing to the meaning of the technology to support open organizational communication. The spirit also provides structures of domination by allowing users to send electronic messages to people higher up in the organization's hierarchy (which might not have been allowed before the implementation of the new office technology). Finally, the spirit of the new office technology may provide structures of legitimation by stating that people who use indecent words in their electronic messages are excluded from the use of the new office technology.

Appropriation

DeSanctis and Poole (1994) replace the word *use* with *appropriation* as this reflects more adequately the adaptation of AIT by its users. For the basis of the concept of appropriation, Poole and DeSanctis (1989) say they go back to Hegel and Marx. These 19th century philosophers were interested in how humanity has progressively learned to control and shape the natural world and how this, in turn, influenced and changed human society. The nature of subject-object relationships were of utmost relevance in understanding this progression. Marx stressed the productive and self-constructing nature of humanity. In his view, the concept of appropriation was the key that unlocked the nature of subject-object relationships. By appropriating an object, Marx meant that it was used constructively, incorporated into one's life, for better or worse (Ollman, 1971). People in nature make their worlds through appropriating objects, and advances in modes of appropriation are the basis for advances of human society in general.

Placing advanced (information) technology in Marx's perspective, every effect of a certain technology is dependent upon the appropriation of the technology. Appropriation of an object means that a user realizes that object (Ollman, 1971). What an object is depends on how it is used, on how it enters into human activity. The implication of this view is that the realization of any object may differ with the situation, and that the object itself can change as people change their mode of using it.

Poole and DeSanctis (1989) note that Marx's concept of appropriation, as a constructive use that shapes both user and object, needs to be elaborated further to be useful in the study of GDSS and other new technologies. Things are not as straightforward as Marx suggested, since he used the contrast between tools that are controlled by the craftsperson, and machines that control and appropriate the worker, to explain his world view. One could also observe that Marx seemed to consider people as products of their historical period, and tended to stereotype appropriation modes by class. Marx distinguished only two classes: workers and capitalists. By doing so, he ignored differences in appropriation between individuals, groups, or organizations. Despite this weakness, in the view of Poole and DeSanctis, Marx's basic concept of appropriation is a useful start for an analysis of human use of information technology.

Poole and DeSanctis are not the only researchers who adopted the concept of appropriation. Ciborra (1996) also does, but uses Heidegger's "being and time" and Dreyfus' "being-in-the-world." Ciborra considers appropriation as a form of taking care of an innovation "fallen" in its context of use (p. 11). This concept of appropriation is basically the same as Poole and DeSanctis'; information technology is a "trigger" for human behavior, but users of information technology are "active agents" and effects come from their interaction with the technology.

FORMULATING HYPOTHESES

Having discussed the concepts of spirit and appropriation, we now will formulate three hypotheses on the relationship between these concepts, inspired by AST.

According to DeSanctis and Poole (1994), some AITs presents a clear, coherent spirit, whereas others do not. A clear, coherent spirit is expected to direct AIT appropriation in a more or less predefined way, but an unclear, incoherent spirit is expected to have a less directive impact on user behavior. We would expect this relationship to be valid for office technology also and formulate the following hypothesis:

1.   **The clearer the spirit of an office technology, the higher the level of office technology appropriation**.

Although the spirit of an office technology is considered to be an important determinant of appropriation, the thought that occurs is whether there are other sources of structure that may influence the relationship between spirit and appropriation. According to AST, there are. Examples of such sources can be the tasks that users have to execute with office technology, and the internal organizational environment in which users are working (DeSanctis & Poole, 1994). We believe that in cases of office technology use in organizations, there could be two important sources of structure that might constrain or support the relationship between the spirit and appropriation: the changes in the work situation that accompanied the office technology implementation, and users' job characteristics. First, we discuss the topic of changes in the internal organizational environment.

Changes in the Internal Organizational Environment

Often the introduction of an office technology not only means a change of technology, but also a change in the work situation of users. Many researchers have elaborated on this (e.g., Hirschheim, 1985; Long, 1987). Already in 1964, Leavitt had developed a framework regarding the relationship between information technology and organization. Leavitt's framework, also called the "diamond" model, presents a dynamic view of the relationships between an organization's structure, the tasks, the people, and the technology. According to Leavitt, a change to one of the components implies changes in the other organizational components. When we project this onto our basic line of thinking about the relationship between the clarity of an office technology's spirit and the level of appropriation, it is reasonable to expect that this relationship will be more positive if the office technology implementation process includes changes in the internal organizational environment. In other words, users of an office technology will be better able to appropriate the office technology in line with its spirit if changes have taken place in the internal organizational environment in order to attain a better "fit" between the office technology and other organizational components. This leads to the second hypothesis:

2.   **The relationship between the clarity of an office technology's spirit and the level of appropriation is more positive among users of office technology who experience a high level of change in the internal organizational environment along with the office technology implementation, than among users who experience a low level of change.**

Users' Job Characteristics

Another source of structure that can intervene in the relationship between an office technology's spirit and the level of office technology appropriation is users' job characteristics. Much research has been carried out on the effects of IT on job characteristics, job content and employee well-being (e.g., Järvenpää, 1997). In general, the results of this research are inconsistent. We can identify two camps. On the one hand there is a group of researchers that concludes that IT has led to degradation of job characteristics, job content, and employee well-being (less job control, more monotonous work, etc.). On the other hand there is a group that concludes that IT has led to an upgrading of job

Figure 1: The research model

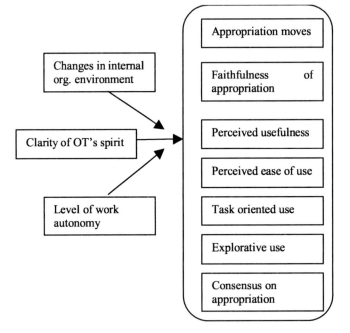

characteristics (more intellectually challenging jobs, less monotonous jobs, etc.). It is not our intention to evaluate this field of research in detail in this chapter, but we refer to this field since IT, within the context of office technology, and job characteristics are certainly related. Again, we can refer also to Leavitt's framework (1964) that supposes that changes in information technology will lead to changes in other organizational components (structure, tasks and people). In this chapter we are interested in the role of one specific job characteristic in the relationship between an office technology's spirit and the level of office technology appropriation, namely users' level of work autonomy. Reasoning from our basic theoretical line that a clear spirit of office technology will lead to a high level of office technology appropriation, we assume that the level of users' work autonomy might play an intervening role. We expect that, if the users of office technology want to appropriate office technology fully in line with its spirit, that a high level of work autonomy might support them. In other words, we expect that users who have a high level of work autonomy to be better able to work in line with an office technology's purposes and goals. In our view, having a high level of work autonomy enables employees to act more freely, which implies that the structures within the office technology may be brought into action more adequately. Therefore, a high level of work autonomy should have a positive effect on the relationship between the clarity of an office technology's spirit and the level of office technology appropriation. This leads to our third hypothesis:

3. **The relationship between the clarity of an office technology's spirit and the level of appropriation is more positive among users with a high level of work autonomy than among users with a low level of work autonomy.**

The relationships, as supposed in our hypotheses and as explained so far, are represented in a research model below (Figure 1).

The next section will elaborate on the method that was used in order to test our hypotheses.

METHODOLOGY

In order to test the hypotheses, a questionnaire was developed to assess the concepts in the research model. This is a different research strategy than that developed by DeSanctis and Poole (1994). Their micro-level coding method is quite time consuming and labor intensive. Chin, Gopal, and Salisbury (1997) are of the opinion that because of the complexity of that proposed research strategy, the frequency of its use has been low, and therefore, more applicable research methods could enhance the use of AST in AIT research. In their study, Chin et al. propose developing scales for the central constructs of AST in order to measure these more easily. We follow this approach.

For measuring the clarity of spirit, the five aspects of appropriation, changes in the internal organizational environment, and the level of work autonomy, we developed scales ourselves to an extent and partly used existing scales. The scales were measured using a 5-point response format ranging from 5 = "strongly agree" to 1 = "strongly disagree." The scales used are included in Appendix A (for descriptive statistics, see Appendix B).

In terms of office technology appropriation, a further elaboration is needed. Poole and DeSanctis (1990) initially distinguished three dimensions to modes of appropriation: *faithfulness of appropriations, attitudes towards appropriation,* and *the level of consensus on the appropriation.* However, after rethinking the theory of adaptive structuration, DeSanctis and Poole (1994) distinguished four dimensions of appropriation: *appropriation moves, faithfulness of appropriation, attitudes towards appropriation,* and *instrumental uses.* In effect, *appropriation moves* and *instrumental uses* were added and *consensus on appropriation* was removed. Because of space constraints, it is not possible to fully elaborate on this topic, but it is our belief that a combination of DeSanctis and Poole's works from 1990 and 1994 gives the best view of the concept of appropriation. Therefore, we include all the terms in our conceptualization of appropriation.

DeSanctis and Poole (1994) define *appropriation moves* as the ways in which users choose to appropriate the available technology structures. They propose four such ways. In the context of this paper we are especially interested in the level of appropriation moves, or in other words, how intensively do users appropriate AIT? *Faithfulness of appropriation* is defined as the extent to which an AIT is appropriated consistent with the spirit of the AIT. By *attitudes towards appropriation* we mean the users' assessments of the extent to which the structures within the system are useful and easy to use. Attitudes set the tone for system usage and can reinforce productive or counterproductive trends in a group's experience with the system (Poole & DeSanctis, 1990). *Instrumental uses,* another aspect of the concept of appropriation, refers to the goals and purposes for which systems are used. For example, users may use a system only for task completion, but they may also use it in an explorative way, or for individual, personal purposes. DeSanctis and Poole (1994) distinguished seven purposes for which a group decision support system could be used: the task, communication or other group processes, exerting power, for establishing or maintaining social relationships, for individual/personal purposes, for fun and/or in an exploratory way, or for moments of confusion in a group. As group decision support systems are not this chapter's focus, not all of these types are useful here. We want to apply AST to office technology use. Therefore we consider that only task-oriented use and explorative-oriented use are relevant. In line with the theoretical framework of AST, it is assumed that the clearer the spirit of AIT is to users, the more task-oriented will be their use of it. If the spirit is not clear, users will probably have a more explorative orientation. Finally, the fifth aspect of appropriation we distinguish is *consensus towards appropriation.* The definition we apply is as follows: the extent to which users of AIT agree upon how the AIT should be used. In order to achieve effective processes and the desired outcomes, it is important that a certain AIT tool is used in a similar way by all the users. Poole and DeSanctis (1989, 1990) assume that consensus on how to appropriate AIT is important, especially in groups using group decision support systems. If there is a lack of agreement, then appropriations may vary in terms of the nature and degree of conflict. We believe that a high level of consensus is necessary, not only for the use of GDSSs but for office technology use as well. If in an insurance company, employees who work with a certain office technology use it in dissimilar ways, this is unlikely to lead to effective work processes. Therefore, whether users of AIT are linked very closely with each other, or they work more as individuals, it is important that there is consensus on *how* to use AIT for the effectiveness of the work processes as a whole.

Because we are interested in the level of appropriation in the context of this chapter, we have redesigned the appropriation moves aspect. In the questionnaire, we did not focus on the types of appropriation moves, but on the level of moves (for respondents "moves" was replaced by "use"). This seems to be more in line with DeSanctis and Poole (1994), who hypothesized that it is the level of appropriation moves that is of importance with regard to the outcomes of AIT appropriation. When the number of appropriation moves is high, the desired effects can be expected, naturally taking into account the level of other aspects of appropriation.

Another point to note is that we only included scales for two types of instrumental use, namely task-oriented use and explorative use. The reason for this is that the type of AIT that was the object of our study was not suitable for all the types of instrumental uses distinguished by DeSanctis and Poole (1994). Besides, it is especially the level of task-oriented use that is affected by the clarity of the spirit. When users do not appropriate office technology in a task-oriented way, it might be because the spirit is not clear to them.

We tested the hypotheses using Pearson's product-moment correlation coefficients.

Setting

The study was carried out in four different offices in the Netherlands that had implemented new office technologies. It concerned the following types of technologies: a workflow management system, a call center support system, a health insurance support system, and a calendar management system. The offices in which these office technologies were implemented can all be typified as procedural offices (Panko, 1984). Procedural offices are those in which the main functions involve carrying out sets of explicit steps towards a specified end, such as accounting offices, insurance administration offices and income tax offices. The office technologies implemented played an important role in employees' day-to-day work. Without using these technologies, they could not carry out their tasks.

All offices included in our study were part of organizations in the service industry. The total number of employees working in the offices was 159. Of these, 114 returned the questionnaire (response rate 71.7%), 65% female and 35% male. Respondents' average age was 32.

RESULTS

Hypothesis 1

First we look at the results regarding Hypothesis 1 (Table 1).

Table 1 shows that the clarity of the spirit is:
- weakly related negatively to the level of appropriation moves (mov);
- significantly related positively to the level of faithful appropriation (faith);
- significantly related positively to the level of perceived usefulness (usef);
- significantly related positively to the level of perceived ease of use (ease);
- significantly related positively to the level of task-oriented use (task);
- not related to the level of explorative use (expl); and
- very weakly related positively to the level of consensus on appropriation (cons).

The results of testing Hypothesis 1 indicate that if the goals and intention of the office technology are clear to users, they will not really make more appropriation moves. This is not in line with our expectation, however, there is a plausible explanation. The office technologies in use played an important role in the employees' day-to-day work; without these, employees were in practice not really able to carry out their tasks. This can explain why the clarity of the spirit does not make much difference in the level of appropriation moves. Employees in reality did not have a choice; they had to work, or at least try to work, with the office technology.

The results do show that if the goals and intention of an office technology are clear to its users, they will use the office technology more in line with these goals and intention (faithful appropriation). They will also experience the office technology as more useful and easier to use. Furthermore, a clear perception of the goals and intention of office technology enables users to work with the technology in a more task-oriented way.

Somewhat disappointing is that having a clear picture of the goals and intention does not relate to the level of explorative use, and hardly leads to a higher level of consensus among users about how to work with the office

Table 1: The relationship between the clarity of the office technologies' spirit and the level of appropriation

	mov	faith	usef	ease	task	expl	cons
spirit	-.11	.26**	.39**	.42**	.26**	-.05	.13

* *= $p < 0.01$

technology. That the clarity of the spirit is not related to the level of explorative use means that users might have a clear understanding of the spirit of an office technology but may still be busy finding out how to work with it, or the other way around. One explanation for this observation is that users may have received adequate training or adequate support from system managers. By training the users or by supporting them when they experience problems, system experts teach users how to work with the system, that is, the system's structural features. In this way, users can know how to work with an office technology without really knowing its broader goals and intention.

That the clarity of the spirit is not related to the level of consensus can be explained by the existence of technical problems with the office technology in the offices included in our study. It is a well-known phenomenon that, after the implementation of new office technology, technical problems still arise. In two of the offices in our study, this was certainly the case. This makes it harder for users to "develop" a consensus on how to work with the system.

Based upon this analysis, we conclude that, overall, our first hypothesis is confirmed.

Hypothesis 2

Having discussed the results of testing Hypothesis 1, we now present the results of testing Hypothesis 2. In order to test this, we divided the respondents into two groups: one that experienced a low level of change in their internal organizational environment ("low change group"), and one that experienced a higher level of change in the internal environment ("high change group"). Respondents who gave a rating lower than 3.0 on the "level of change" scale were put into the "low change group" (n=63). Respondents who rated 3.0 or higher on this scale were put into the "high change group" (n=31). The results are shown in Table 2.

From Table 2 we can see that, in comparison with the "low change" group, the relationship between the clarity of the spirit and:

Table 2: The relationship between the clarity of the spirit and the level of appropriation in "low change" and "high change" groups of users

	mov	faith	usef	ease	task	expl	cons
low	-.16	.45**	.37**	.56**	.19	.00	.01
high	-.25	.06	.30	.15	.32	-.21	.18

** = $p < 0.01$

- the level of appropriation moves (mov) is slightly more negative in the "high change" group;
- the level of faithful appropriation is considerably less in the "high change" group;
- the level of perceived usefulness is somewhat lower in the "high change" group;
- the level of perceived ease of use is considerably lower in the "high change" group;
- the level of task-oriented use is higher in the "high change" group;
- the level of explorative use is more negative in the "high change" group; and
- the level of consensus is more positive in the "high change" group.

These observations indicate that the level of change in the internal organizational environment modifies the relationship between the clarity of an office technology's spirit and the level of appropriation. It is, however, not exactly in agreement with our second hypothesis. The overall relationship is not more positive with the "high change" group than with the "low change" group. In fact, it is the other way around!

If we limit our conclusions to the significant correlations only, the results make it clear that among users who experienced a low level of change, a clear spirit makes users work more in line with the office technology's spirit (faithful appropriation) than it does with "high change" users. Furthermore, a clear spirit leads to "low change" users perceiving the office technology as more useful and easier to use in comparison to "high change" users. Since this is not what we expected, an alternative explanation has to be sought. In our view, these results are a reason to rethink our theoretical ideas on the role of change in the internal organizational environment. Instead of assuming that this supports a better "fit" between office technology and other organizational components, perhaps a high level of change in the internal organizational environment accompanying office technology implementation disturbs this "fit." It is likely that the newly implemented office technology was developed with the current working procedures in the surveyed office in mind. The people involved in the office technology development process (office management, system developers, users) might have started (implicitly or explicitly) with the aim of developing an office technology that matched the current organizational components, such as the structure, tasks and people. That, for a number of users, the office technology implementation led to changes in the work situation (change in tasks, performance criteria, work group members) might have been an unanticipated consequence of office technology implementation.

In conclusion, our second hypothesis in not confirmed. Changes in the internal organizational environment are not supportive of the "fit" between office technology and other organizational components if these are not an anticipated consequence of the office technology development process.

Hypothesis 3

Finally, we tested our third hypothesis. In order to test this we divided the respondents into two groups: one that experiences a low level of work autonomy ("low work autonomy group"), and one that experiences a high level of work autonomy ("high work autonomy group"). Respondents who rated 3.0 or lower on the "work autonomy" scale were allocated to the "low work autonomy group" (n=49). Respondents who rated higher than 3.0 on this scale were allocated to the "high work autonomy group" (n=63). The results are shown in Table 3.

In Table 3 we observe that in comparison with the "low work autonomy group," the relationship between the clarity of the spirit and:

- the level of appropriation moves is more negative in the "high work autonomy group";
- the level of faithful appropriation is more positive in the "high work autonomy group";
- the level of perceived usefulness is more positive in the "high work autonomy group";
- the level of perceived ease of use is less positive in the "high work autonomy group";
- the level of task-oriented use is less positive in the "high work autonomy group";
- the level of explorative use is more negative in the "high work autonomy group"; and
- the level of consensus is less positive (and slightly negative) in the "high work autonomy group."

Table 3: The relationship between the clarity of the spirit and the level of appropriation among users with high and low levels of work autonomy

	mov	faith	usef	ease	task	expl	cons
low	.14	.27	.33*	.60**	.58**	.06	.25
high	-.20	.28*	.46**	.29*	.14	-.19	-.04

$* = p < 0.05; ** = p < 0.01$

To summarize, our third hypothesis is only confirmed in terms of faithful appropriation, perceived usefulness, and explorative use. It is not confirmed for the level of appropriation moves, perceived ease of use, task-oriented use, and consensus on appropriation. How can we explain this? In our view, it is likely to suppose that the office technology in use in the offices in our study was (implicitly or explicitly) developed for jobs with low autonomy. We noted earlier that all the offices in our study could be classified as procedural offices, where, in general, tasks have to be carried out in prescribed steps. The people involved in the development process probably aimed to develop a system that suited this "prescribed" way of carrying out tasks. Therefore, users with a high level of work autonomy might be clear over the spirit of the office technology, but this need not have the consequence that they work more with the office technology (a higher level of appropriation moves), work with the office technology in a more task-oriented way, and/or develop a higher level of consensus. Our explanation that the office technology in our study is better suited to "restrictive" tasks as a result of decisions taken in the office technology development process, is supported by the fact that the relationship between the clarity of the spirit and the perceived ease of use is much more positive in the "low work autonomy" group. For users with a low level of work autonomy, the office technology's spirit is a more useful "frame of reference" regarding the way to work with the office technology, than for users with a high level of work autonomy.

In conclusion, overall our third hypothesis is also not confirmed.

DISCUSSION AND CONCLUSIONS

In this chapter we shed light on some problems related to office technology projects. We have noted that they are often experienced as problematic due to the lack of attention given to the non-technical side and we introduced concepts to recognize this non-technical side: *spirit* and *appropriation*. The concept of spirit represents the underlying intention and goals of a set of technical features. Appropriation reflects the "incorporation" of an office technology into users' day-to-day activities.

Three hypotheses regarding the relationship between the clarity of an office technology's spirit and the level of appropriation were formulated and tested. The results showed that, overall, the clarity of the spirit of office technologies is positively related to the level of office technology appropriation. In other words, the more users have a clear picture of the intention of an office technology, the more they will "incorporate" the office technology into their day-to-day tasks. Unexpectedly, among users who experience a low level of change in the internal organizational environment along with an office technology implementation process, this relationship is considerably more positive than among users who experience a high level of change. Our explanation for this unexpected result is that the office technology in the offices studied might have been developed especially for the offices' existing work procedures. People involved in the office technology development process (implicitly or explicitly) did not anticipate the changes to organizational components (such as the organizational structure, tasks, and people) that resulted from the office technology implementation (such as those suggested by Leavitt's "diamond" model (1964)). That a group of users nevertheless experienced a high level of change in the internal organization was probably an unanticipated consequence.

We also found that the relationship between the clarity of the spirit of an office technology and the level of appropriation is more positive among users with a low level of work autonomy, than among users with a high level of work autonomy. As this was again not in line with our expectations, we sought an alternative explanation. In our view, this outcome is due to the fact that the office technologies in the offices surveyed were (implicitly or explicitly) developed restrictive tasks. All the offices in our study are so-called procedural offices, indicating that, in general, tasks are carried out in a prescribed way. People involved in the office technology development process may well have had this in mind, resulting in a system that is better suited to users who have a low level of work autonomy. In other words, the new office technology should "reinforce" the existing restrictive work procedures.

Having observed all of this, what do these results mean in terms of the problems office technology projects are experiencing in practice? In the first instance, people involved in office technology projects need to recognize that office technologies consist not only of physical components, but also contain a spirit. This spirit is "created" during the development and implementation process. Having observed that users who have a clear perception of this spirit appropriate the technology to a higher extent, suggests that it is of value to develop a clear and consistent spirit. It also seems beneficial to involve users so that they can contribute to the development and implementation process. This should go further than only involving users in providing information about the current situation, as is often the case in practice, and should allow users to contribute to defining the intention and goals of a new office technology.

Furthermore, the results call for more attention to changes in the internal organizational environment as a (planned or unplanned) aspect of implementating new office technology. If decision makers in office technology projects couple the implementation of new office technology with internal organizational changes, the positive effects of a clear spirit towards the level of appropriation increases. This outcome is consistent with those theories and approaches that state that the development and implementation of a new information technology always leads to changes in other organizational components (implicitly or explicitly), such as the organizational structure, tasks, and people (human resources).

Likewise the result that the relationship between the clarity of the spirit and the level of appropriation is higher among the group of users that experience a low level of work autonomy also calls for attention to be given to the organizational environment. It suggests that internal organizational components influence the extent to which users appropriate office technology in line with its spirit. For practical decision makers, the results once again emphasize that the expected effects will not automatically arise as long as the technology is technically sound.

ENDNOTES

[1] Ewusi-Mensah and Przasnyski (1994) consider IT project abandonment as different from IT failure. By IT project abandonment, they mean IT development processes that are ended before a system is implemented. By IT failure, they mean the disfunctioning of IT after its full implementation. This disfunctioning can be caused by badly designed technology or failure of usage.

[2] They sent out more than 1400 questionnaires and received 82 completed usable responses (5.6%). Ewusi-Mensah and Pzrasnyski suggest that one reason for this very low response rate might be that discussing IT project abandonment has negative connotations, and therefore is not a favored topic (besides this, it was also suggested that the length of the questionnaire [11 pages] played a role).

[3] These are projects that were supported by external automation experts. The study of Riesewijk and Warmerdam (1988) concerned a survey among 274 companies. 233 of them had carried out an automation project within the previous three years. The figures on project success or failure were collected using a written questionnaire among automation experts and managers. Since these might have had some level of responsibility for the projects, they may have been more positive than other people involved.

REFERENCES

Barley, S. R. (1986). Technology as a occasion for structuring: Evidence from observations of CT scanners and the social order of radiology departments. *Administrative Science Quarterly*, 31, 78-108.

Bolman, L., & Deal, T. (1984). *Modern Approaches to Understanding and Managing Organizations*. San Francisco: Jossey-Bass.

Chin, W., Gopal, A., & Salisbury, W. (1997). Advancing the theory of adaptive structuration: The development of a scale to measure faithfulness of appropriation. *Information Systems Research*, 8, 343-367.

Ciborra, C. (1996). Introduction: What does groupware mean for the organizations hosting it? In Ciborra, C. (Ed.), *Groupware and Teamwork*, 1-19. Chichester, NY: John Wiley & Sons.

Clegg, C., Axtell, C., Damodaran, L., Farbey, B., Hull, R., Lloyd-Jones, R., Nicholls, J., Sell, R., & Tomlinson, C. (1997). Information technology: A study of performance and the role of human and organizational factors. *Ergonomics*, 40, 851-871.

Davis, F. D. (1989). Perceived usefulness, perceived ease of use, and user acceptance of information technology. *MIS Quarterly*, 13, 319-339.

DeSanctis, G., & Poole, M. S. (1994). Capturing the complexity in advanced technology use: Adaptive structuration theory. *Organization Science*, 5, 121-147.

Doherty, N. F., & King, J. P. (1998). The consideration of organizational issues during the systems development process: An empirical analysis. *Behaviour & Information Technology*, 17, 41-51.

Ewusi-Mensah, K., & Przasnyski, Z. (1991). On information systems project abandonment: An exploratory study of organizational practices. *MIS Quarterly*, 15, 67-85.

Ewusi-Mensah, K. and Przasnyski, Z. H. (1994). Factors contributing to the abandonment of information systems development projects. *Journal of Information Technology*, 9, 185-201.

Fitzgerald, G. (1998). Evaluating information systems projects: A multidimensional approach. *Journal of Information Technology*, 13, 15-27.

Giddens, A. (1984). *The Constitution of Society: Outline of the Theory of Structure*. Berkeley, CA: University of California Press.

Hirschheim, R. A. (1985). *Office Automation: A Social and Organizational Perspective*. Chichester, NY: John Wiley & Sons.

Hornby, P., Clegg, C., Robson, J., Maclaren, C., Richardson, S., & O'Brien, P. (1992). Human and organizational issues in information systems development. *Behaviour & Information Technology*, 11, 160-174.

Järvenpää, E. (1997). Implementation of office automation and its effects on job characteristics and strain in a district court. *International Journal of Human-Computer Interaction*, 9, 425-442.

Leavitt, H. J. (1964). *Managerial Psychology*. Chicago, IL: University of Chicago Press.

Long, R. (1987). *New Office Information Technology: Human and Managerial Implications*. London: Croom Helm.

Morgan, G. (1986). *Images of Organizations*. Beverly Hills, CA: Sage Publications.

Ollman, B. (1971). *Alienation: Marx's Conception of Man in Capital Society*. Cambridge, MA: Cambridge University Press.

Orlikowski, W. (1991). *The Duality of Technology: Rethinking the Concept of Technology in Organizations*. Massachusetts Institute of Technology, *CISR Working Paper No. 219*, CISR. Sloan School of Management, Massachusetts Institute of Technology, January.

Orlikowski, W. (2000). Using technology and constituting structures: A practice lens for studying technology in organizations. *Organization Science*, 11, 404-428.

Orlikowski, W., & Baroudi, J. (1991). Studying information technology in organizations: Research approaches and assumptions. *Information Systems Research*, 2, 1-28.

Orlikowski, W., & Robey, D. (1991). *Information Technology and the Structuring of Organizations. Working Paper No. 220, CISR*. Sloan School of Management, Massachusetts Institute of Technology, March.

Panko, R. R. (1984). Office work. *Office: Technology and People*, 2, 205-238.

Poole, M. S., & DeSanctis, G. (1989). Use of group decision support systems as an appropriation process. In *Proceedings of the 22nd Annual Hawaii International Conference on System Sciences*, 149-157, New York: ACM.

Poole, M. S., & DeSanctis, G. (1990). Understanding the use of group decision support systems: The theory of adaptive structuration. In Fulk, J. and Steinfield, C. (Eds.), *Organizations and Communication Technology*, 173-193. Newbury Park/London/New Delhi: Sage Publications.

Poole, M. S., & DeSanctis, G. (1992). Micro-level structuration in computer-supported group decision making. *Human Communication Research*, 19, 5-49.

Riesewijk, B. and Warmerdam, J. (1988). *Het Slagen En Falen van Automatiseringsprojecten*. [*The Succession and Failure of Automization Projects*]. Nijmegen: ITS.

Vadapalli, A. and Mone, M. (2000). Information technology project out-
     comes: User participation structures and the impact of organization
     behavior and human resource management issues. *Journal of Engineer-
     ing and Technology Management*, 17, 127-151.
Walsham, G. (1993). *Interpreting Information Systems in Organizations*.
     Chichester, NY: John Wiley & Sons.

APPENDIX A

Scales used to measure AST concepts (translated from Dutch; the *name* of the system was inserted between the brackets)

Clarity of the Spirit of the ICT (Ruël, 1999)
(Cronbach's alpha=.87)
1.   The goals of (the system) are clear to me.
2.   The 'thoughts behind' (the system) are fairly clear to me.
3.   I know where effective use of (the system) should lead.
4.   I understand what developers of (the system) aimed for.
5.   I know in which way (the system) is used optimally, according to "(system) experts," such as the system manager.

Responses given on a 5 point Likert scale, with the following graduations: *Strongly disagree, Disagree, Neither disagree nor agree, Agree, Strongly agree.*

Extent of appropriation moves (Ruël, 1999)
1. To what extent do you use (the system)?

Faithfulness of Appropriation (Chin, et al., 1997; Ruël, 1999)
(Cronbach's alpha=.73)
1.   I use (the system) in accordance with what the manual expresses as its aims.
2.   "(system) experts" will not agree with how I use the system.
3.   I probably use (the system) in ways which are new in comparison with the initial goals of (the system).
4.   With certain features of (the system) I probably work in an unusual way.
5.   I use (the system) differently from what was intended originally.
6.   "(system) experts" will think my way of using (the system) is not the most appropriate for using the system in the best possible way.
7.   I do not succeed in using (the system) as it should be used.
8.   I do not use (the system) in the optimal way.

Attitudes towards appropriation: perceived usefulness (Davis, 1989; Ruël, 1999)
(Cronbach's alpha=.81)

Use of (the system)...
1   ....I think it is a good idea
2   ....Contributes to my effectiveness

3   ....Is not my preference, because there are better ways of working than using (this system)
4   ....Makes my job more easy
5   ....Is useful for my job

Attitudes towards appropriation: perceived ease of use (Davis, 1989; Ruël, 1999)
(Cronbach's alpha = .81)
1.   It is useful to learn to work with (the system).
2.   Most features of (the system) are easy to apply to the job.
3.   The screens of (the system) are easy to understand.
4.   I find (the system) flexible in use.
5.   I find (the system) easy to use.

Task-oriented use (Ruël, 1999)
(Cronbach's alpha = .71)
1.   I really use (the system) for tasks I can execute with it.
2.   I use (the system) a lot for my day-to-day work.
3.   I use (the system) to make progress in my job.

Explorative use (Ruël, 1999)
(Cronbach's alpha = .75)
1.   I frequently consult my colleagues about the functioning of (the system).
2.   I often use (the system)'s manual.
3.   During my work it takes me time to "discover" (the system)'s features.
4.   By trial and error I still discover new aspects of (the system).

Consensus on appropriation (Ruël, 1999)
(Cronbach's alpha = .75)
1.   Among the users of (the system) there is agreement on how (the system) should be used.
2.   I use (the system) in a similar way to my colleagues.
3.   Among the users there are considerable misunderstandings about (the system).
4.   Within the group of users of (the system) we agree on what you can do with (the system).
5.   Within the group of users of (the system) there is disagreement about how certain features of (the system) work.
6.   There are (written or tacit) rules about how to work with (the system).

Changes in the work situation (Ruël, 1999)
(Cronbach's alpha = .73)

With the implementation of (the system)…
1 …My tasks changed considerably.
2 …Changes occurred in my physical work situation.
3 …Changes occurred in the composition of the unit or group of which I am member of.
4 …The demands on the results of my work changed.

Work autonomy (Ruël, 1999)
(Cronbach's alpha = .)
1. I can determine the amount of work I execute.
2. I can schedule my work freely.
3. I can determine at what pace I execute my work.

APPENDIX B: DESCRIPTIVE STATISTICS

	N	Minimum	Maximum	Mean	Std. Deviation
The extent to which respondents know the original design intention and goals.	112	1.00	5.00	3.7942	.6620
The extent to which a respondent uses the DIS system.	113	1.00	5.00	4.1416	1.0595
The extent to which respondents use system structures consistent with the original design intent of system experts.	113	1.33	5.00	3.6685	.5596
The extent the system is perceived as useful.	113	1.80	5.00	3.7870	.7023
The extent to which the system is perceived as easy to use.	113	1.00	5.00	3.6376	.7083
The extent to which the respondents use the system in a task-oriented way.	113	2.00	5.00	3.9521	.5970
The extent to which respondents use the system in explorative ways.	113	1.00	4.75	2.5590	.8690
The extent to which respondents agree on how to use the system.	110	2.00	4.83	3.3523	.5582
The extent to which the implementation was combined with changes in the work environment.	96	1.00	5.00	2.5929	.8831
The extent to which the respondent experiences autonomy in their jobs.	112	1.00	5.00	3.2202	.9685
Valid N (listwise)	89				

Part II

Organizational Communication, Learning and Information Technology

Chapter V

Computer-Mediated Communication–The Power of Email as a Driver for Changing The Communication Paradigm

Dianne Willis
Leeds Metropolitan University, England

INTRODUCTION

Email has been with us now for a long time and is being increasingly adopted as a major communication tool in UK Higher Education (HE) establishments (colleges of Higher and Further Education and universities). As the use of email grows, the effect on communication patterns needs to be established. This chapter looks at current communication and working practices within a Higher Education institution in the UK (the author's own). A survey has been conducted to elicit people's feelings about the use of email and how they see future patterns of communication developing within the establishment. The questions that the survey set out to answer were as follows:

* Preferred methods of communication;
* Advantages and disadvantages of each of the communication methods utilized at Leeds Metropolitan University (LMU);
* Efficiency of email;

- Items not suitable for email transmission;
- Ethical considerations in using email;
- Who is contacted using email; and
- Increase or decrease of email usage in the future.

The specific focus of the survey was to elicit how staff feel about the increasing dependence on the use of email within the institution, and these findings are discussed in the results section.

The chapter will present a literature review of the area, the framework for the study, the methodology utilized, the results of the questionnaire, conclusions and future trends.

COMMUNICATION AND EMAIL

A basic theoretical model of the communication process states that messages are "sent" and "received." Confirmation of receipt and interpretation of the message indicates that it is a two-way communication process (Warner, 1996). Some major factors to be considered when choosing the communication method are as follows:

- Effectiveness–how do we measure this when using email?
- Simultaneous reception of information by recipients–what happens when people are temporarily unable to access their email due to technical problems?
- Acknowledgment of receipt–can read receipts can be used to check how quickly the message has been read?
- Speed–how quickly does the information reach the recipients?
- Cost of the process–is it cost effective?

Email can be viewed as primarily a sociotechnical system. A working definition of a sociotechnical system states that changes in one part of the system, be it technical or social, will affect the other parts and thus the system as a whole. A sociotechnical system is concerned with the interactions between the psychological and social factors and the needs and demands of the human part of the organization, and its structural and technological requirements (Mullins, 1999). Email satisfies the criteria for a sociotechnical system in that it consists of technology and the software needed to run the system, as well as operating within the social norms adopted by the organization choosing to use email as a communication tool. These social norms will help to determine the way in which email is used and the extent to which it will become a dominant communication form. The relative importance of each part of the system–the social and the technical–will vary between different institutions. When any new technology is introduced, it is important that the user population have a positive attitude towards the new technology. For it to be successful, any new technology needs to be understood and valued by the users. As can be seen from the results section, staff attitudes to the technology vary, but it can be stated that generally, the technology is readily embraced. The approach adopted in this study is to examine the extent to which staff feel happy with the use of email as a dominant communication medium.

Hirschheim (1985) argued that one of the major benefits of using email is to support communication between people who are geographically distant, as is the case in this chapter. Email can be viewed as a way of "keeping in touch" with people you are not able to see on a regular basis. In these instances, it can be supposed that email fulfills a communication need that makes it more acceptable, despite its supposed shortcomings. These findings are also supported by the work of Lucas (1998), who found that email was often judged the best mechanism for communicating regardless of distance.

Increasingly, email has become a common mode of communication for many people, though exceptions must be made for those who do not have easy and regular access to the technology required. Anderson, Bikson, Law and Mitchell (2000) considers in depth universal access to email and the personal and social benefits this can bestow. They argue that email is a mechanism providing global communication possibilities. However, the lack of access by certain sections of a society leads to the formation of an information elite, often referred to as the "information rich;" those without access being known conversely as the "information poor." The extent to which email can impact on global communications must be considered in the light of equal access for all. Anderson et al. posit that there are no fundamental technical barriers to providing universal access to email, so the responsibility for pushing forward equal access lies with society rather than the technology. Cost implications are a major consideration here. Equal access to email and hence to the communication space, would require a program of investment in access points in a variety of places, including schools, libraries and even supermarkets. The maintenance of such access points would also need to be carefully considered. While these issues are under consideration in the UK from the point of view of access to government offices, little is being considered from the viewpoint of universal access.

Email is only useful as a communication medium if the people you wish to contact also have access to email. Perhaps a system along the lines of the existing Internet cafes devoted entirely to email access may be a partial answer. Obviously, the convergence of technologies via digital TV will enable access for a large proportion of the population, but whether people would willingly embrace this type of communication medium remains to be seen. One further consideration would be the need for training in the use of email. Email came to prominence originally in both academic and business settings where people generally received training on the use of the email package chosen. Obviously, if the access is to be widened, this would require massive investment in training to enable everyone to be able to utilize the opportunities of email.

However, communications theorists argue there are problems with the use of email as the sole communication medium. Culnan and Markus (1987) suggested that a lack of face-to-face communication changes the intra- and interpersonal variables because of a lack of social context, and this will inevitably lead to problems understanding the message. They feel that communication needs extra dynamics and dimensions to be clear and easily understood. Sproull and Kiesler (1986) argued that email was devoid of social cues and this would seriously affect communication patterns. If we consider email in a work setting, we need to ask the question "Do we need social cues?" If email developed out of a memo base where social cues were always missing, is there any reason to suppose that email needs this extra dimension to be successful? Lack of social cues may lead us to a designation of "impoverished" when considering communication from a "perfect world" or theoretical perspective, but it must be acknowledged that in many organizations, it is operating effectively despite this impoverishment.

Taking the stance that email is a relatively impoverished communication style in that it provides neither audible nor visible cues to the communication process, Bavelas et al, (1999) studied "emoticons," typewritten symbols that imitate facial expressions, which could help to bring a visual dimension to email. Examples are: smiley face, ☺, [type : followed by)], and sad face, ☹, [type : followed by ( ]. However, the effectiveness of these "emoticons" is difficult to measure. The author recently received an email sporting an emoticon that was a plea for the recipients to give up time and invest energy in a new project. The extent to which these help to produce a positive response is difficult to measure; in this case, the author knows the effect this had on her, but not on the other recipients of the message. Emoticons are not widely used in the UK HE environment, where pressure and the need to concentrate on speed of response limit developments of further dimensions to email. Their effectiveness may also be a factor to be considered.

There are further problems with an email system in that it is not always possible to ensure that the recipient has received and read the message in an appropriate time frame. This may be caused by a variety of problems, both technical and human. These issues are discussed in more detail and possible solutions posited in Willis and Coakes (2000), where a separate study on attitudes to email is reported.

Further analysis of the current situation indicates that email lacks the collaborative dimension that is needed in today's world, and this lack of collaboration is an important factor. There is an element here of the need for enrichment of the communication process which is met by this collaboration. There are some email systems that allow simultaneous transmission on split screens, but these do not allow full collaboration as there is still a gap between reading the message and composing the reply (Marvin, 1999). However, in this chapter, this type of system was not considered as it was not an option in the organization surveyed. The question it poses is whether humans need "real-time" communication or whether the asynchronous mode provided by most email systems is sufficient. This aspect will be addressed in a further planned study.

Computer-Mediated Communication (CMC) is often seen as inferior to face-to-face communication. In terms of an analysis of why this is the case, Aycock and Buchignani (1995) state that in several critical ways CMC appears to stand outside the conventions of everyday orality and literacy. Baym (1995), however, argues that much CMC research is too concerned with the view that the computer itself is the sole influence on communicative outcomes, whereas it is obvious that the human element has a vital role to play, which brings us back to the earlier point about email being a sociotechnical system. Communication is always a human-to-human process; the technology can only play a facilitating role. Culnan and Markus (1987) looked at lack of social context. This raises issues about understanding of the communication process and WHEN each type of communication medium/method is most appropriate. Markus (1994) found that email was suitable for all work-related communication with the exception of confidential matters. This would tend to support the argument that previous concerns regarding the "richness" of the communication are of less concern in a workplace setting. This brings us back to the point where we need to consider to what extent the social element comes into play in the work environment. Email has previously been identified as a sociotechnical system, so the question arises, "Do people use email as primarily a 'work' tool or as a method of communicating with others and building relationships in a working environment?" This question needs to be addressed within each individual working environment as it is likely to vary between organizations.

Email is manifestly a less "rich" medium than face-to-face communication given its lack of social cues, and careful consideration must be given to whether there are conditions where it is totally inappropriate as a medium. Consideration must be given to what would happen to the social side of the system if email is used inappropriately–would this change patterns of usage or bring about new norms of social behavior? There have been several examples recently cited in the UK press where staff have been dismissed for inappropriate use of email. Recent UK legislation, The Regulation of Investigatory Powers Act 2000, gives employers the power to monitor and intercept employee email. This legislation is commonly known as the "Snooping Bill" and hotly debated in terms of the underlying concepts of privacy and freedom of speech. However, its existence has brought about a change in patterns of email communication within individual organizations.

Marvin (1999) argues that in digitized synchronous, text-based interaction, participants are forced to type quickly with less concern for spelling errors and typographical errors. Although synchronous communication was not the normal pattern of communication found in our survey, there is often pressure to respond quickly, perhaps before having thought through what to say and sometimes, leading to regret about the speed of response. Indeed, many people would contend that this inability to recall email once sent is the medium's greatest drawback. Recent UK press reports (www.silicon.com) have called for further distance between the "reply to sender" and the "reply to all" buttons on email packages to minimize the risk of sending material accidentally to the wrong people.

Lea and Spears (1992) conducted a study of paper and email messages and found that messages from strangers with a large percentage of misspelled words make a more negative impression on the recipient. Their work also found that this effect decreased when the communicators were acquaintances. They found that people have a much higher tolerance of errors between friends. This may have implications for working relationships within an organization as closer, more friendly organizations may be more positive to email as a medium.

EMAIL STYLE AND USAGE

Initial emails had a dimension that was more structured and formalized than is currently the case. Initial emails followed a "memo" structure, and people often addressed the recipient in exactly the same way they would have done with a written message. Emails now take on a variety of forms which may be regarded as innovative in that they portray informal, interpersonal communication. Walther, Anderson, and Park (1994) argue that the relative absence of formal rules enables people to use abbreviations and professional jargon to more accurately convey meaning. Questions must be posed, such as "At what point does this 'creativity' interfere with the message being communicated? How much jargon and how many errors are acceptable before some or all of the meaning is lost?"

Interestingly, contrary to the findings of previous research (Coakes and Willis, 2000), where one of the main problems with email was uncertainty over whether a message had arrived, this no longer seems to be such a large factor. This could have two possible causes. Potential recipients are unaware that they should have received something, or the technical systems have improved to the extent that it is no longer an issue. Norman (1988) discusses the principle of closure–agents performing an action require evidence, sufficient for current purposes, that they have succeeded in performing it and, in many cases, email fails to provide this closure sufficiently. Indeed, the author is uncertain whether all the intended recipients actually received the questionnaire on their desktop, so the principle still applies. Email packages should provide notification of error when there has been a problem with the delivery of an email message. However, in the author's personal experience, this is not always the case. Having replied to emails and received no notification of a technical problem, later emails have indicated the first was never received. It is interesting to speculate where all the missing email messages are! Perhaps they will eventually be delivered in years to come following the example of the UK Post Office with ordinary or "snail" mail.

Electronic mail is the most frequently used application of the Internet. A Gartner Group survey in March 2001 found that 12 billion text messages are being sent globally each month. IDC research in the same month suggests that the daily output of emails will reach 35 billion by 2005. This gives some indication of the volume and hence the importance of email as a communication tool. Perhaps further consideration is needed of exactly what is being communicated to determine the relative importance of email as a communication tool.

Advice for writing effective email may be helpful if the volume is increasing and it becomes necessary to construct messages that help rather than hinder the communication process. Such advice given at www.delta.edu is as follows:

- Always make sure to provide the proper context for your message.
- Make sure your message is clear and unambiguous.

This implies a need for training in the use of email as previously discussed.

Hirschheim (1985) built a model of possible benefits of email which is detailed in Table 1.

This table still holds true for the present, even though in technological terms, systems have moved on considerably. What people believed the system delivered and how appropriate it was for them were key factors in the survey.

Email lends itself to informal communication, ensuring interaction and conveying important information quickly. Remembering that the main advantage of email is speed, messages should be kept short and to the point to facilitate a quick response. Sherwood (2000) believes that email is a fundamen-

Table 1: Hirschheim's characteristics of email

1	To support the communications of people in the same building and on distant continents.
2	To support real-time communications, when the parties are present at their terminals at the same time (this did indeed happen on one memorable occasion when on sending a communication to a contributor in the USA, an instant response was received, as he was online at the time - this led to a discussion of the weather on the different continents), and non-real time communications with the recipient reading mail when convenient (the more normal occurrence).
3	To allow all messages to be sent when desired, stored where necessary, routed to the most appropriate destination and then easily retrieved.
4	To provide the users with facilities to prepare, edit, read, store, receive and retrieve messages easily.
5	To cater to a variety of message types such as formal letter, informal memos and brief notes (most email systems in use today do not cater to formal letters and memos).

tally different form of communication to paper-based communication, the speed of the process making it lean towards a more conversational tone. As recipients of email can quickly respond, ask questions or seek clarification, there is a tendency for emails to be not so rigorously or painstakingly constructed as letters or memos. Email also does not convey emotions nearly as well as face-to-face or telephone conversations, as it lacks the cues available in these forms of interaction. Email can therefore be seen merely as a facilitating tool for the communication process.

Kraut and Attewell (1997) found that the use of email correlated with the use of other media in that people classified as "heavy communicators" are likely to use all forms of media more often. One of the advantages of email is its relatively low cost when compared with alternative communication forms so it is often regarded as a cost-saving method in organizations. It may be the case that rather than substituting for other communication forms, email may actually stimulate new relationships within the social system, which will eventually lead to an increase in the total amount of communication taking place that may then not constitute a cost saving. However, whether this would lead to abandoning a particular communication method is a moot point. People generally have a preference in communication method. From an organizational standpoint, it is helpful when these preferences are for the most cost-effective form of communication.

Sherwood (2000) identifies one of main disadvantages of email as being that it may be used when face-to- face or written communication is more appropriate. This finding will depend on such issues as preferred communication style and appropriateness of the communication medium. Appropriateness is an interesting concept. When is it appropriate to use email? Are there any universal guidelines to determine this? One person in an organization may feel that email is an appropriate medium for the information transmitted but the recipient may not. Thus, appropriateness cannot be taken lightly as a concept. There have been instances of people rushing down corridors to take to task the sender of an email when its subject is deemed to be a matter of importance or delicacy and therefore not appropriate for transmission in this way. As a general rule, appropriateness will be determined by the culture and rules within an individual organization and by the extent to which email is used as the prime communication method. Email policies will have a major role to play, however, within academic institutions; this and previous research would indicate that confidentiality is the main determinant of appropriateness.

Email is a communication system that supports both one-to-one and one-to-many communication patterns (Harasim, Hiltz, Teles & Turgoff, 1993). This allows for asynchronous communication that can now be enriched by the addition of pictures and sounds. However, picture and sound files may lead to access problems over an individual network or between networks, and it may actually be more efficient and less frustrating to adopt a more basic format.

EMAIL IN THE WORKPLACE

Email is often seen as less disruptive than telephone and face-to-face communication, in that it does not interrupt an individual's work to the same extent. Given the quieter nature of email (even though it is possible to set up MS Outlook to deliver audible warnings that email has arrived), it can be viewed as much less disruptive than a telephone ring. In the modern work environment, there is often a requirement to finish a particular piece of work within a limited timespan. The absence of the telephone can facilitate this process, as the telephone can be very disruptive. In some cases, it may be company policy to answer the telephone within a certain number of rings, which is bound to be disruptive to whatever other work is going on at the time.

One further advantage of email is that it reduces the time and energy spent playing "telephone tag" where people leave messages because the person they wish to speak to is unavailable. When the recipient rings back, it is often the case that the instigator of the call is unavailable, necessitating further messages until the two can coincide. This is a very inefficient and frustrating way of trying to communicate.

Yet another advantage of email is that it can be left until the recipient has time to deal with it. This is an important consideration where communication is taking place across time lines, and people are working at different times. Here email can be an invaluable tool and has to a large extent replaced the fax, which was the original preferred communication tool in these circumstances. The fact that email is usually delivered to the desktop has been a positive factor in this change of preference. However, many people feel under pressure to respond quickly which leads to other problems discussed previously.

Because of its place independence, there are many possibilities for using email as a tool for student support when working with part-time or off-site students in particular, but this requires a proactive approach. Students' attitudes to email support were not covered by this study, but this is an important area. In the author's own experience, it is related to students' preferred communication styles. Those students who are happy using email to communicate generally are also happy with it as a method of distance support. Those who feel the need for face-to-face or voice contact find it less satisfactory and, in some cases, frustrating.

One of the major advantages claimed for email is that it provides a record of the communication that was not always available in face-to-face to telephone conversations. This record seems to be of increasing importance in modern academic life. One respondent in an earlier study cited this record as a useful defense against possible litigation.

Problems with email identified by Woolston and Lipschutz (1998) include:

- Non-verbal cues are limited, leading to the possible misinterpretation of the feelings associated with email;
- Discussion of confidential information is not always secure;
- Emails are context deficient—there is no simple way of determining that the sender of an email is who they claim to be; and
- Overload!

There is increasing concern about overload in the new information world, given the numbers of email messages in circulation on a daily basis. It is possible that the ease of use of the technology and the ready availability of multiple mailing lists adds to this feeling of overload.

Bjørn-Andersen [1983] says that to understand the impact of information systems on an organization it is necessary to consider five major areas. These are identified as:

1. Psychological factors;
2. Organizational structure;
3. Societal factors;

4.   Ethical and moral issues; and
5.   Epistemological aspects.
      This survey concentrates on the psychological and ethical issues and the ways in which people's perceptions of the system would influence their use of it. The ethical issues that were raised are discussed in the results section. Psychological considerations include a preference for access to the accompanying body language of a message to enhance its understanding.

FRAMEWORK FOR THE STUDY

The empirical work was conducted within Leeds Metropolitan University (LMU) in the Faculty of Information and Engineering Systems. This Faculty came together in 1987 to integrate the themes of information, engineering and systems; so that *information* (whatever the medium for storage and retrieval) is linked to *engineering* (in its broadest sense–manufacturing, software, electronics, communications engineering and media technology) through a common *systems* approach. The Faculty comprises three schools–Computing, Engineering and Information Management (www.lmu.ac.uk).

LMU is regarded by many of its staff as being "email driven" in its communication patterns. This is partly explained by the dispersed nature of the staff in the Schools of Computing, Information Management and Engineering. Staff in Computing and Information Management are located in rooms in a series of different buildings around the Beckett Park Campus, and it is difficult to physically meet to pass on information, so email is utilized to overcome this dispersal problem. Staff in the School of Engineering are located at the City Centre site some 4 miles distant, and the advantage of email for keeping staff in touch with what is happening at the campus site is obvious.

In June 1999, LMU developed a policy on the Use and Abuse of Email that was distributed to staff on 13th March 2000. As the author is a relatively new member of staff, it is not possible to say whether this was the first time this document had been circulated.

Work by Parker (1999) considers why an email policy is necessary. The findings indicate that possible abuse of the system is a real problem. Since email is so easy to send to such a large number of people, people can feel under pressure just to answer their messages. Recent publications in the UK press (The Sunday Times, 3/04/01) give an example of where staff are encouraged to have a "day off" reading email to give them time to rediscover face-to-face communication.

One issue that was not addressed by the survey was whether staff were aware of this policy and adhered to it; however, this will be addressed in some planned research to be conducted with LMU, a UK college and two institutions in Australia. The accompanying message distributed with the policy states that while email is a useful messaging system, its good features can lead to problems. Items cited include the use of wide distribution lists, using email when the telephone is more appropriate, and sending messages hurriedly. Inappropriate use of email wastes time and resources. The policy states that the content of all email stored on University servers and PCs remains the property of the university, that email is not a private or confidential medium, and that personal use is permitted. This is interesting and will be revisited in the light of the responses to the questionnaire.

In terms of use of the system at LMU, the systems administrator supplied the following information, which gives a useful indicator of the response to email messages.

Read receipts were collated from an email sent to all staff within the institution (almost exactly 2000 users, some recent leavers had not been removed and some new staff not added), and the cumulative totals are given below:

15 minutes	335
1 hour	591
end of day	1115
end of week	1399
after 1 week	1524

This indicates that over 50% of staff had responded by the end of the first day, yet after one week, the percentage had only increased to just over 75%. This response rate may well be a useful indicator to staff attitudes across the whole institution. Unfortunately, figures are not available by individual school. It may be that had the author resent the questionnaire after one week, the response rate may have been much higher, as the immediate response pattern is higher than after a period of delay.

METHODOLOGY

The methodology chosen was that of an email questionnaire with multiple responses possible. Open questions were also included to enable staff to give opinions where appropriate. An email questionnaire was deemed the most appropriate medium as the focus of the survey is email usage. Considerations about the split site nature of the Faculty also pointed towards the use of email.

The survey was sent to all academic staff within the three schools (a total of 150 people), and a total of 30 responses were received, 26 by email and 4 by internal mail. This represents a response of 20%. Two blank questionnaires were also received via the email system, which were discarded. Obviously, with such a low response rate, care must be taken with both validity and reliability of the findings and especially with the extent to which these findings can be generalized. However, all respondents had strong views–some positive and some negative–and as the object of the study was to elicit opinions, the results have value.

The timing of the questionnaire proved difficult. It was delayed until staff returned from their summer break, but coincided for many with a vast amount of email that had built up over the summer holiday; thus, many staff did not have time to respond due to email "overload." This is probably the prime reason for the low response rate, although a general negative feeling about blanket emails may also have been a contributing factor.

However, the problem that became apparent during the study was that where email was not being accessed quickly enough, the communication process is unreliable.

SURVEY RESULTS

(Please note that some questions had multiple responses and some respondents did not answer all questions.)

In terms of preferred methods of communication (Question 1), six reported a preference for email, 13 for face to face communication, and six said it would vary depending on the circumstances. No one opted for the telephone as the preferred method.

When asked for reasons why a particular method was preferred (Question 2), the most commonly cited method was face-to-face communication where people were able to pick up body language at the same time as the verbal language, which gave them a greater insight into meaning. In fact, the most common response was that staff felt they needed the accompanying body language to understand the message correctly. In terms of preference for email, a variety of reasons were given, with the speed of the transaction being the most commonly cited. Many staff seemed to feel a need for both face-to-face communication and the email.

In a couple of instances, staff reported that they would use whichever medium was most convenient or most likely to be effective in the particular circumstance.

Question 3 covered advantages of each type of communication method. The responses are given below as a series of charts.

As can be seen from Chart 1, the major advantages for email are speed and having a record of what has been said. The ability to undertake asynchronous communication was also an important factor.

Speed was also an important consideration for the telephone, along with its interactive nature. These responses far outweighed the other possible advantages, leading to the conclusion that these are the factors that are of the most benefit (Chart 2).

For face-to-face communication (Chart 3), the real advantage as previously mentioned lies in the ability to pick up the body language that goes with the communication process. It is obvious from the results that this is a very important factor for many people in terms of good communication.

For written communication, the ability to keep a permanent record was the most frequently cited response. Most people are not in the habit of keeping a written record of telephone communications though there are instances when such a record would be useful (Chart 4).

Chart 1: Advantages of email

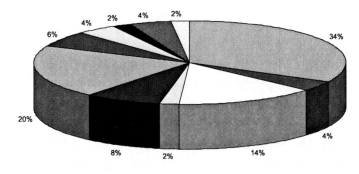

Chart 2: Advantages of the telephone

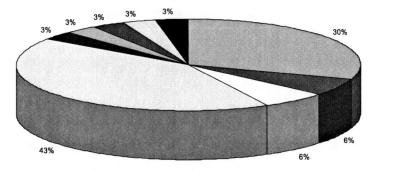

Chart 3: Advantages of face-to-face communication

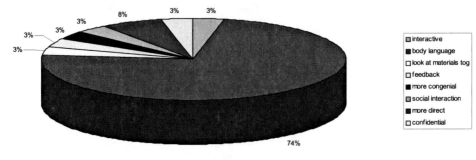

Chart 4: Advantages of written communication

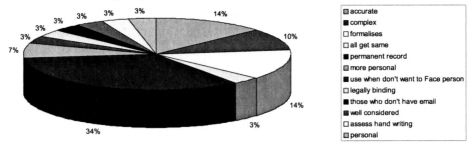

The only other communication method mentioned was the fax, and its use when transmitting diagrams and maps.

When analyzing the results of the disadvantages for each communication method, the responses were not so clear. The responses are given below in Tables 2-5.

There is a spread of reasons given in Table 2. The two responses that collected the most replies were that it could be misleading or misinterpreted and that there was excess volume. This links back to previous concerns about the volume of emails being sent and the ease with which "blanket" emails can be distributed, leading to overload. As a major disadvantage of email, one respondent pointed out that messages could not be recalled easily once they had been sent, even if the sender had occasion to think better of the response at a later date. Other responses indicated that the informality and speed of the response led to poor expression that made the message difficult to understand, often exacerbated by poor spelling, grammar and general presentation issues.

The major disadvantage of the telephone lies in both parties having to be present to complete the communication process. As previously mentioned, the absence of one party leads to playing "telephone tag" which can be very frustrating.

Table 2: Disadvantages of email

Email medium	No. of replies
Too hasty	3
Not interactive	2
Misleading/misinterpreted	8
Not easy to read on screen	1
May be overlooked	3
Poor expression	3
Unclear	1
Curt emails	1
Excess volume	9
Not read	1
Did it arrive?	1
Time consuming	4
Irrelevant	3
Impersonal	1
Impossible to recall once sent	1
Can get lost	1
Prone to technical failure	2
Limit on number saved	2
Limit on size	1
Not secure	1
Speed	1
Misused	1
Inappropriate	1

Table 3: Disadvantage of the telephone

Telephone medium	No. of replies
No record	2
Cannot see reaction	2
Need to be there	17
Being on hold	1
Canned music	2
Cold calling	1
Intrusive and antisocial	4
Less personal	1
Difficult to track	1
Cost	1
May be misunderstood	3
Cannot see person	1
Inconvenient	1

Despite the fact that face-to-face communication takes up a lot of time, it still has many advantages in terms of the clarity of the communication process and may be deliberately chosen in certain instances.

The major disadvantages quoted here surround the time it takes to compose a letter and the speed with which one can expect a response.

The survey highlighted one or two issues in the field of access to the communication space, such as the use of email to pressure staff into doing something, and one respondent felt that it could be used as a means of bullying staff. However, as the response rate to the questionnaire was low, this is likely to refer only to specific isolated incidents and not be general to the institution.

A question about efficiency of email produced the following results in Chart 5.

The majority of the respondents felt that it was very or reasonably efficient, with only one respondent classifying it as poor.

Table 4: Disadvantages of face-to-face communication

Face-to-face medium	No. of replies
Need to meet	1
Takes a long time	10
Intimidate	1
No record	4
Difficult to escape	1
Expensive	1
Time travelling	5
No access to other documents	1
No time to think about response	1
Difficult to arrange	4
Disagreeable people	3
Body language	1

A large proportion of the respondents (73%) felt that the email was the main communication method within LMU.

Answers as to what not to transmit over the email fell largely into the sensitive area (including exam papers) and personal information. In light of the university policy on privacy and email, this is unsurprising. Work by Coakes and Willis (2000) found that generally in UK universities, university staff are most concerned about sending exam results/papers over email systems because of a lack of security. Other concerns highlighted were confidential information and whether email was the most appropriate method for communicating the information.

Again the spread of answers to the question about ethical issues was very wide. One disturbing result was that eight respondents felt there were no ethical issues raised by the use of email. Less surprising in light of recent litigation where

Table 5: Disadvantages of written communication

Written medium	No. of replies
Costs more	1
Longer to produce	17
Poorly written	1
Too slow	10
Too formal	2
Handwriting hard to read	1
Annoying if make mistake	1
Impersonal	1
Needless use of paper	1
Confirmation of receipt	2
Feedback	1
Can get lost	1
Can be ignored	1
Not interactive	1

Chart 5: Efficiency of email

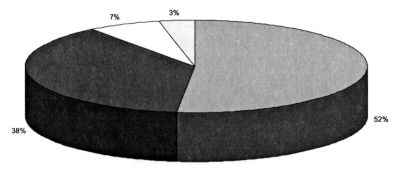

- very
- reasonably
- good
- poor

a student sued a UK university over something that was said in an email message, five respondents were concerned about possible libelous statements made in email. Table 6 gives the full range of responses.

Staff were asked who they normally contacted by email and the results are given in the chart below. This communication pattern was remarkably even in its spread. The only area showing significant deviation was the use of email to contact "others." Although university policy allows this type of communication, it was not mentioned as being used by many of the respondents. Perhaps people

Table 6: Ethical issues raised by the use of email

Ethical issues	No. of replies
None	8
Intrusive junk mail	1
Job loss for secretaries	1
Info taken out of context	1
Who owns it	1
Security	2
Monitoring by employers	3
Libellous statements	5
Easier to insult people/ harassment/bullying	3
Porn	1
Legal/formal	1
Managerial	1
Means of avoiding responsibility	1
Don't know	1
No response	2

prefer to separate their working and personal communications for security and privacy reasons.

The final question related to the incidence of the use of email and whether it would increase or decrease over time. The vast majority felt that the use of email would increase (see Chart 7). The notable exception to this rule was the Dean of the Faculty who felt there was such a high level of usage at present that it would not be possible to increase much more.

One area that highlighted the need for further clarity in the questions was where, despite the fact that the survey was aimed at discovering people's opinions about using email, one respondent referred to textbooks as the source of the answers to questions about advantages and disadvantages of the various communication forms.

It was interesting that although many staff felt the use of email was increasing, several staff made comments about overload already in terms of volume of email received. One question that may have been useful to ask was the extent to which the use of email to contact students was considered to support them in their studies. There is much interest in the university at the present time in the use of email for extra student support and to maintain a closer working environment.

Chart 6: Contacts by email

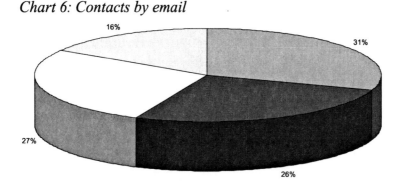

Chart 7: Use of email in the future at LMU

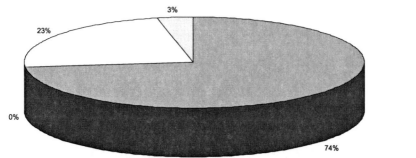

Most staff used email to contact their students, though one or two stated that this was a purely reactive response rather than a proactive one initiating a discussion.

CONCLUSIONS

Given that email is a major communication method within LMU, care must be taken that the volume of email received by each member of staff does not reach the point where it becomes impossible for them to deal with it.

Guidelines for the effective use of email include the following:

- Take care to avoid overload;
- Speed is the biggest advantage for email, make sure the culture is such that this is adhered to in communication;
- Look for ways of using email to facilitate student support;
- Use webs sites or the intranet to provide large quantities of information;
- Target the message carefully to increase efficiency;
- Think before replying;
- Use high priority sparingly; and
- Delete unwanted material to facilitate effective use and save server space.

Avoiding overload is not the easiest thing to do. Overload may lead to communication becoming less effective, and this will lead to a poorer communication environment. Unanswered emails are frustrating, even when you suspect that overload is the reason for the lack of response.

Staff generally accept that email is a favored communication method, but it can be seen that many have definite concerns about its growth in the future.

In conclusion, it can be seen that email has many advantages according to the survey results. However, care must be taken to ensure that it does not become the SOLE communication medium. Appropriateness must be the watchword or the quantity of material communicated will increase, but the quality will not.

FUTURE TRENDS

It is likely that in the near future, email will take on a greater role in terms of a mechanism for student support. This will obviously increase the load on individual lecturers who are already reaching the limit of their ability to deal with ever increasing volumes of email.

Work by Coakes and Willis (2001) suggested a web site solution with FAQs may be more effective than one which requires lecturers to respond to students on an individual basis. This will relieve pressure in terms of volume of emails and will also mean that staff can be sure all students are receiving exactly the same information, which reduces uncertainty in the communication process.

One member of staff at the author's institution is looking at a further option of using a notes facility within MS Outlook to reduce the volume of emails. The system comprises an electronic version of physical noticeboards. The idea is that people will "affix" notices to particular noticeboards and those staff who are interested in each topic will access those boards on a regular basis; e.g., research staff will access the research noticeboard daily. This can also be used as a method of keeping in touch with students who can be directed to particular noticeboards for specific information. Used correctly, this system will hopefully reduce the volume of emails which will lead to less overload.

This solution may also deal with an increasing trend among staff to delete large numbers of emails without reading them in the belief that if the message is really important and goes unanswered, it will be resent. This is not a particularly efficient way to communicate!

If, as the Dean of Faculty postulates, there is little scope for increase in the use of email, other viable communication tools must be found. It may be that in the short term, better targeting of emails will be part of the solution. In the longer term, one of the other strategies suggested may be more effective. The university will be introducing WebCT in September 2001, and it is anticipated that this new system will prove to be a factor in reducing problems of overload.

REFERENCES

Anderson, R. H., Bikson, T. K., Law, S. A., & Mitchell, B. M. (2000). Universal access to email, feasibilty and social implications, RAND.

Aycock, A., & Buchignani, N. (1995). The email murders: Reflections on dead letters. In Jones, S. G. (Ed), *Cybersociety: Computer-Mediated Communication and the Community*. London: Sage Publications.

Baym, N. (1995). The emergence of community in computer-mediated communication. In Jones, S. G. (Ed). *Cybersociety: Computer-Mediated Communication and the Community*. London: Sage Publications.

Bevalas, J.B., Hutchinson, S., Kenwood, C. and Hunt, D. (1999). Using face-to-face dialogue as a standard for other communication systems, *Canadian Journal of Information Systems,* 22(1).

Bjørn-Andersen, N. (1983). Challenge to certainty. In Bemelmans, T. (Ed.), *IFIP WG8.2 Proceedings*, August, Minneapolis, MN.

Coakes, E., & Willis, D. (2000) Computer-mediated communication universities and further education establishments–A comparison of use and utility. In Khosrowpour, M. (Ed.), *IRMA Conference Proceedings, Challenges of Information Technology Management in the 21st Century*, 202-206. Hershey, PA: Idea Group Publishing.

Coakes, E., & Willis, D. (2001). Managing large modules–Email or Web sites. In Anandarajan, M. and Simmers, C. (Eds.), *Managing Web Usage in the Workplace: A Social, Ethical and Legal Perspective*. Hershey, PA: Idea Group Publishing.

Culnan, M. J., & Markus, M. L. (1987). Information technologies. In Janlin, F. M. (Ed.), *Handbook of Organizational Communication: An Interdisciplinary Perspective*. London: Sage Publications.

Harasim, L. M., Hiltz, S., Teles, M., & Turgoff, M. (1995). *Learning Networks: A Field Guide to Teaching and Learning Online*. Cambridge, MA: MIT Press.

Hirschheim R. A. (1985). *Office Automation: Concepts, Technologies and Issues*. Boston, MA: Addison-Wesley.

Jackson, M. (1997). Assessing the structure of communication on the World Wide Web. *Journal of Computer-Mediated Communication*. Retrieved from the World Wide Web: http://www.ascu.org/jcmc/vol3/issue1/jackson.html.

Kraut, R. E., & Attewell, P. (1997). Media use in a global corporation: Electronic mail and organizational knowledge. In Keisler, S. (Ed.), *Culture of the Internet*, 321-341. Lawrence Erbaum Associates.

Lea, M., & Spears, R. (1992). Paralanguage and social perception in computer-mediated communication. *Journal of Organizational Computing*, 2(3-4), 321-341.

Lucas, W. (1998). Effects of email on the organization. *European Management Journal*, 16(1), 18-30.

Markus, M. L. (1994). Electronic mail as the medium of managerial choice. *Organization Science*, 5(4), 321-340.

Marvin, L. E. (1999). Spoof, spam, lurk and lag: The aesthetics of text-based virtual realities. *Journal of Computer-Mediated Communication*. Retrieved from the World Wide Web: http://www.ascu.org/jcmc/vol1/issue2/marvin.html.

Mullins, L. J. (1999). *Management and Organizational Behavior*, 5th Edition. London: Pitman.

Norman, D. (1988). *The Design of Everyday Things*. New York: Doubleday

Sherwood, K. D. (2000). *A Beginner's Guide to Effective Email*. Retrieved September 28, 2000 from the World Wide Web: http://www.webfoot.com/advicce/email.top.html.

Sproull, L. and Kiesler, S. (1986). Reducing social context cues: Electronic mail in organizational communication. *Management Science*, 32(11), 125-130.

The Sunday Times. (2001). Office workers told to take email holiday. March 4, London, UK.

Walther, J. B., Anderson, J. F. and Park, D. W. (1996). Interpersonal effects in computer-mediated interaction. *Communication Research*, August, 21(4), 460-487.

Warner, T. (1996) *Communication Skills for Information Systems Professionals*. London: Pitman.

Willis, D. and Coakes, E. (2000). Enabling technology for collaborative working– A sociotechnical experience. In Clarke, S. and Lehaney, B. (Eds.), *Human-Centered Methods in Information Systems: Current Research and Practice*. Hershey, PA: Idea Group Publishing.

Woolston, D. and Lipschutz, W. (1998). Using email effectively in academic advising. *Pre-conference Workshop at the 22nd Annual National Conference*, National Academic Advising Association, October.

Silicon. (2001). UK News service. Retrieved March-June, 2001, from the World Wide Web: http://www.silicon.com.

Chapter VI

Personal Information Privacy and the Internet: Issues, Challenges and Solutions

Edward J. Szewczak
Canisius College, USA

Personal information privacy is arguably the most important issue facing the growth and prosperity of the Internet, especially of e-commerce. Protecting personal information privacy has ignited a debate that pits privacy advocates against technology growth enthusiasts. This chapter explores personal information privacy on the Internet in terms of the social and legal issues surrounding it, and the technological challenges to personal information privacy facing individuals, businesses, and government regulators. Representative solutions to resolving the debate are presented, though at present the debate over personal information privacy continues and may have to be resolved by governments and the courts.

INTRODUCTION

There is a feeling of online insecurity in the community of Internet users. The results of a 1998 survey conducted by Louis Harris & Associates, Inc. revealed that worries about protecting personal information ranked as the top reason people generally are avoiding the Web (Hammonds, 1998). A 2000 telephone survey conducted by Harris Interactive found that 57% of Internet users favor laws regulating how personal information is collected and used by

Internet companies (Green, France, Stepanek & Borrus, 2000). Because of privacy concerns, the Web has been characterized by Amit Yoran, founder of security company Riptech, as "a very hostile environment" (Dornan, 2000). This feeling of insecurity appears to be worldwide. A study by Cheskin Research and Studio Archetype/Sapient found, among other things, that Internet users in the United States, Latin America and Brazil perceived threats to their personal information integrity and money from predatory individuals as well as predatory institutions (Cheskin Research, 2000). However, there is more at stake in the Internet privacy issue than simple feeling. A survey by NFO Interactive (www.nfoi.com) found that the safekeeping of online consumer personal information was the main reason people chose not to shop online. A survey by Jupiter Communications (www.jup.com) found that roughly 64% of respondents do not trust a Web site even if it has posted a privacy policy. The main concern was the handling of credit card data.

These various concerns about personal information privacy seem well-founded in light of recent events. San Francisco-based Andromedia sells software that compares a user's actions on a Web site with the actions of thousands of previous visitors to produce purchase recommendations on the fly within milliseconds ("collaborative filtering"). The software records not only a user's self-proclaimed preferences but also how long the user views a particular product and which banner ads s/he clicked. As the shopper moves through a Web store, the software combs through files of previous shoppers who have made similar choices to present attractive options each step of the way. Andromedia claims its software customers (including Chase Manhattan, E-Trade, Intuit, DaimlerChrysler and Xerox) find users stick around 75% longer, spend 33% more money, and return twice as often as before its software was used (Mchugh, 1999).

"Carders" buy and sell credit card numbers stolen from the Internet using Internet chat rooms. The carders announce a list of cards with accompanying personal information including billing address and phone number. The credit card numbers with accompanying information are usually purchased in short order (http://www.privacytimes.com/NewWebstories/oxymoron_prv_2_23.htm). A Russian teenager stole 350,000 credit card numbers from CD Universe's Web site and told CD Universe he would not post them on a Web site if the company paid him $100,000. When the company refused to pay, the teenager posted the numbers. Even before the teenager's theft, CD Universe's Web site had had several thousand visitors who had downloaded more than 25,000 credit card numbers between December 25, 1999 and January 7, 2000 (http://www.privacytimes.com/NewWebstories/carder_priv_1_27.htm). Senator Dick Durbin of Illinois was a victim of identity theft in which thousands of dollars of merchandise was purchased on credit at a Home Depot store in Denver. He believes the identity theft may have occurred on the Internet earlier in the year (Hepp, 2000).

Italian Privacy Commissioner Stefano Rodota ordered Infostrada to temporarily shut down its free ISP service because it required users to disclose their age, health status, sexual habits and political, labor and religious preferences in order to qualify for the service. Infostrada said that the information was required for marketing purposes (http://www.privacytimes.com/NewWebstories/oxymoron_prv_2_23.htm).

Failed Internet companies such as Boo.com, Toysmart.com and CraftShop.com have either sold or have tried to sell customer data that may include phone numbers, credit card numbers, home address and statistics on shopping habits, even though they had previously met Internet privacy monitor Truste's criteria for safeguarding customer information privacy. The rationale for the selling was to appease creditors (Sandoval, 2000). Walt Disney Company, a majority shareholder of Toysmart.com, has offered to buy Toysmart.com's data and "retire" it to avoid an action filed by the Federal Trade Commission (FTC) (Sapsford, 2000). The defunct political portal Voter.com has announced intentions to sell 170,000 email addresses together with party affiliations and issues of interest (Green, 2001). The Network Solutions unit of Verisign is offering to marketers its master address book for the Internet. It contains all the information that domain name registrants must provide including name, telephone number, street address and email address of a technical contact for their site (Weber, 2001).

On September 9, 1999, *Privacy Times* published the equation "Good Privacy = Good E-Commerce (& Vice Versa)." As events continued to unfold, it became increasingly clear that privacy concerns were plaguing e-commerce. Wall Street began to revalue Internet companies that accumulated customer personal information to target marketing efforts. The FTC told a Senate panel that there were more than 300 online privacy bills to limit the collection and "mining" of personal data pending before state legislatures and Capitol Hill. *Business Week* called the privacy backlash "the privacy penalty" (Stepanek, 2000b). Consumer reaction included an unwillingness to click on Web site banner ads, which in turn lead to advertisers becoming dissatisfied with Web portal effectiveness (Ginsburg, 2000). The director of IBM's Global Trust and E-commerce Services unit has been quoted as saying that privacy and security are the largest inhibitors of moving forward for e-business today (Robinson, 2000).

WHAT IS PRIVACY?

Paul and Gochenouer (1996) coined the phrase "isolation without privacy." It refers to the potential for a large percentage of the population to be alone and isolated even with (and perhaps because of) current computing and telecommunications technology–in particular, the Internet. But because of the intrusiveness of monitored electronic linkages, these individuals are not in a position to enjoy much privacy. Interconnected electronic databases make it possible to easily acquire concentrated information about individuals. Networked communications make data sharing easier than ever before. It is also easier to have digital data go astray (Kuchinskas, 2000).

But what exactly is privacy? Cate (1997) notes that the meaning of privacy is determined almost entirely by the context in which it is derived and applied:

> The demand for, and contours of, privacy differ significantly depending upon the level of development in a society. As a creation of society, therefore, it should come as no surprise that privacy is largely defined within the context of the society itself (p.22).

Gormley (1992) has identified a number of conceptions of what constitutes privacy from the literature. Privacy has been viewed as an expression of one's personality or personhood, focusing on the right of the individual to define his or her essence as a human being; as autonomy – the moral freedom of the individual to engage in his or her own thoughts, actions, and decisions; as citizens' ability to regulate information about themselves, and thus control their relationships with other human beings; and as secrecy, anonymity and solitude.

In his excellent study on privacy in the information age, Cate (1997) adopted the definition of privacy as "the claim of individuals, groups, or institutions to determine for themselves when, how, and to what extent information about them is communicated to others" from Westin (1967, p. 7). Westin/Cate's definition is interesting because it allows for flexibility in discussing privacy within the context of the Internet. Whereas many people worry about divulging personal information electronically, other people seem more than willing to give it away, trading their personal information for personal benefits such as free shipping and coupons (Kuchinskas, 2000). However, personalized service is the main benefit. A Web site can save a shopper time and money by storing and recalling a user's tastes and buying habits (Baig, Stepanek & Gross, 1999). ISPs are willing to allow Web users cheaper access to the Internet provided the users are amenable to having their online behavior tracked for marketing purposes by specialized software. The ISPs share in ad revenues (Angwin, 2000a).

It should be noted that some people choose to minimize the importance of privacy. Instead, they choose to emphasize the value in the technologies that challenge other people's privacy. For example, an overzealous approach to protecting personal information privacy by severely limiting advertising and profiling may, as Dornan (2000, p. 110) notes, "kill the golden goose that's paying for the Internet." Others see socially redeeming value in certain databases. Teir and Coy (2000) observe that databases that allow people to be found have a number of socially beneficial uses, including:

- Tracking down "deadbeat dads" who fail to pay their child support obligations;
- Locating missing children;
- Helping companies find former employees to whom pension funds are owed;
- Helping law enforcement and private investigators track down suspects;
- Helping insurance companies keep rates down by minimizing fraudulent claims; and
- Keeping online commerce safe by verifying identities quickly (p.H5).

Another interesting aspect of the Westin/Cate definition relates to children, especially to their use of the Internet both at home and at school. Since children should probably not be put in a position to determine for themselves when, how, and to what extent information about them is communicated to others, it becomes the responsibility of parents, guardians and educators to monitor children's activities on the Internet. However parents and guardians are not always informed of schools' policies. Thousands of school districts have accepted corporate handouts, signing contracts that let donor companies track children's online activities, provided the children are 13 years old or older (Dwyer, 2000). The recent Children's Internet Protection Act requires the use of monitoring software for schools and libraries that want to obtain money from the federal E-rate program that helps schools get on the Internet. N2H2 Inc.'s Web-filtering software captures students' surfing activities and produces monthly reports that detail where students are going on the Internet (Anders, 2001).

The privacy debate is very much a social issue and, as such, has easily become a political issue. In the United States, those who feel that their privacy is being invaded have turned their attention to the Congress, which is responding to events as well as issues (Borrus, 2000a) in an important election year (Borrus & Dwyer, 2000). Rhetoric aside, what constitutes privacy is often decided in courts of law.

PRIVACY AND THE LAW

In the United States, the Supreme Court has addressed privacy in terms of fundamental rights. Legal protection of privacy at the Constitutional level is possible in only two respects: 1) Constitutional rights are protected only against government actions, and 2) Constitutional rights are generally negative, i.e., they do not obligate the government to do anything, only to refrain from taking certain actions. As Cate (1997) observes:

> There is no explicit constitutional guarantee of a right to privacy. The Supreme Court, however, has interpreted many of the amendments constituting the Bill of Rights to provide some protection to a variety of elements of individual privacy against intrusive government activities. These include the First Amendment provisions for freedom of expression and association, the Third Amendment restriction on quartering soldiers in private homes, the Fourth Amendment prohibition on unreasonable searches and seizures, the due process clause and guarantee against self-incrimination in the Fifth Amendment, the Ninth and Tenth Amendment reservations of power in the people and the states, and the equal protection and due process clauses of the Fourteenth Amendment. None of these provisions refers to privacy explicitly, and the circumstances in which privacy rights are implicated are as widely varied as the constitutional sources of those rights. As a result, the Supreme Court's interpretation of constitutional protection is narrow, and the value of privacy interests is often limited when weighed against other, more explicit, constitutional rights (p.52).

In short, privacy rights outside the public sector have no support under the Constitution. Individual state constitutions are generally consistent with the Constitution. Various statutes and regulations have been created to control the collection and use of data by government, but these controls have been generally criticized as inadequate by privacy advocates because they either apply only to the government and not to the private sector or they contain significant loopholes. For example, the federal Privacy Act of 1974 obligates federal agencies to store only relevant and necessary personal information, to only collect information to the extent possible for the data subject, to maintain records with accuracy and completeness, to establish administrative and technical safeguards to protect the security of records, and to limit the disclosure of individuals' records. However, the Privacy Act also provides twelve exemptions that permit disclosure of information to other government agencies. One exemption applies to Congress; another exemption applies to data requested for "routine use" (Cate, 1997).

Within the private sector, privacy protection is provided by federal and state statutes and common law. These laws and regulations often address a specific industry or economic sectors targeting specific issues. This results in an uneven patchwork of legal protections. For example, information about an individual's video rentals is often protected by statute, whereas the same individual's medical record information may not be protected. The Employee Polygraph Protection Act of 1988 prohibits an employer's use of lie detectors but has nothing to say about the collection, storage or dissemination of personal information generally. The Family Education Rights and Privacy Act of 1974 provides that parents or students may designate that information such as name, address, telephone number, and date of birth may not be released by an educational institutional without prior consent, but does not restrict the types or sources of information that schools may gather. Nor does it limit the duration of storage of personal information contained in student files (Cate, 1997). Cavazos (1996) notes that many privacy interests are actually common law rights arising from judicial opinions and commentary with no statutory basis. Although common law is fairly consistent nationwide, there may be state differences. Because of the patchwork of at times conflicting state laws, many technology executives are reluctantly concluding that federal rules may be the only solution to the information privacy issue (Borrus, 2001).

In Europe, privacy is protected by Directive 95/46/EC of the European Parliament and of the Council on the Protection of Individuals with Regard to the Processing of Personal Data and on the Free Movement of Such Data ("The Directive") published in 1995. In keeping with the Treaty of European Union (EU) signed in 1992 in Maastricht, the Directive attempts to provide guidance to EU member states in enacting laws governing the processing of personal data. Among other things, the Directive provides guidelines about 1) disclosure to data subjects concerning intent to collect data and the obligatory or voluntary nature of a reply, 2) access to, and opportunity to correct, personal data, 3) data security against unauthorized processing, 4) requiring national registration of personal data processing activities, 5) restrictions on automated decision making, 6) establishment of supervisory authorities to protect personal data, 7) requiring civil liabilities against those conducting unlawful processing activities, and 8) restrictions on transborder data flow. The directive places privacy as a human right on par with the rights of self-determination, freedom of thought, and freedom of expression (Cate, 1997).

Much of what governs thinking about privacy in Europe includes a hidden agenda. Flaherty (1989) notes:

European data protection laws include the hidden agenda of discouraging a recurrence of the Nazi and Gestapo efforts to control the population, and so seek to prevent the reappearance of an oppressive bureaucracy that might use existing data for nefarious purposes. This concern is such a vital foundation of current legislation that it is rarely expressed in formal discussions (p.306).

The implementation of the Directive varies among European countries. Though the United Kingdom had initially indicated that it intends to adopt a minimalist approach to implementing the Directive (Cate, 1997), a Regulation of Investigatory Powers bill has been under consideration in the British Parliament that would obligate telecommunications service operators to incorporate facilities that allow the government to log and monitor all online activity. Any user who possesses encrypted material must turn it over to the police if requested, including the encryption key. Failure to do so will result in imprisonment, even if the user claims they were never in possession of the key. In France, anyone who publishes information on the Web must register their personal information with the government. Failure to do so could result in a six month jail sentence and a fine of 7000 francs (Dornan, 2000). Germany requires any company in Germany with an automated data processing unit with more than five employees to hire a data protection officer who reports to a federal commissioner. Companies cannot sell a customer database to third-party marketers unless they receive the explicit consent of each customer whose personal data is contained in the database. Companies cannot transfer data on European citizens to any country or organization that does not meet Europe's standards for data protection. Companies providing an Internet service can collect and maintain personal data necessary for billing but any additional personal data that may accumulate in a system while a user is online must be promptly deleted (Samuel, 1999).

The differences between the United States and the European Union in their approaches to personal information privacy may directly impact businesses that either are, or that aspire to be, multinational. Currently a privacy truce (known as "safe harbor") exists which specifies that any company collecting personal data must tell the individuals what information is being collected, what it will be used for and who it will be shared with. Consumers must also be able to specify whether they want their personal information to be shared with a third party. Consumers also have the right to view and correct their personal data, if necessary. Basically the truce protects United States companies from EU legal action (Weber, 2000). (For an interesting look at the issue of whether the United States should shift to the European model of privacy rights, see Smith (2001).)

Enforcement of privacy laws and statutes usually falls under the jurisdiction of various government agencies. In the United States, one such agency is the FTC. In its statement of its vision, mission and goals dated June 17, 1999 (http://www.ftc.gov/ftc/mission.htm), the FTC affirms its mission "to enhance the smooth operation of the marketplace by eliminating acts or practices that are unfair or deceptive. In general, the Commission's efforts are directed toward stopping actions that threaten consumers' opportunities to exercise informed choice." A case in point is its case against GeoCities. The FTC's complaint alleged that GeoCities violated the Federal Trade Commission Act by "impliedly or expressly misrepresenting how personal identifying information collected online would be used, and falsely or misleadingly representing that GeoCities itself was collecting and maintaining such information from children when the information in fact was collected directly by third parties hosted on GeoCities' site" (Aglion & Gidari, 1998). The FTC was concerned that GeoCities had decided not to post an online privacy policy.

A somewhat radical idea for managing the Internet privacy issue has been advanced by David Brin, an American physicist and science-fiction writer. He argues that, in order to avoid any bias between the rich and the powerful and the poor and the weak, everyone should have access to all information. Anyone should be able to access any database containing personal information at any time for any reason. This way, Brin argues, the ruled can keep an eye on the rulers. But as *The Economist* (1999, p. 23) observes, "transparency would be just as difficult to enforce legally as privacy protection is now. Indeed, the very idea of making privacy into a crime seems outlandish."

TECHNOLOGICAL CHALLENGES TO PRIVACY

Government regulators and enforcement officials have to consider a host of technological challenges to personal information privacy on the Internet. These include technologies used in corporate and government databases, email, wireless communications, clickstream tracking, CPU design, and various biometric devices.

Corporate and Government Databases

The practice of gathering personal information about customers and citizens by corporations and governments is well established. Software is available that is dedicated to analyzing data collected by company Web sites, direct-mail operations, customer service, retail stores, and field sales. Web analysis and marketing software enables Web companies to take data about customers stored in large databases and offer these customers merchandise based on past buying behavior, either actual or inferred. It also enables targeted marketing to individuals using email. The California State Auto Association uses market analysis software to extract customer information from separate databases controlled by its travel agency, emergency roadside service, insurance business, and Web site. It uses this data to give each member a "lifetime value score" which enables the Association to single out the best customers for special treatment (Hamm & Hof, 2000). Governments routinely collect personal information from official records of births, deaths, marriages, divorces, property sales, business licenses, legal proceedings, and driving records. Many of the databases containing this information are going online (Bott, 2000).

Perhaps the two most significant database areas that affect the most people are financial information databases and medical information databases.

Financial information databases. The recent deregulation of the financial services industry has made it possible for banks, insurance companies, and investment companies to begin working together to offer various financial products to consumers. Personal financial information that was kept separate before deregulation can now be aggregated. In fact the ability to mine customer data is one of the driving forces behind the creation of large financial conglomerates. Services can be offered to customers based on their information profiles. Services may also be denied based on information profiles as *Consumer Reports* (2000a) explains:

> But out of that effort to determine which customers are credit-worthy, a more insidious form of data redlining recently surfaced. Lenders profit handsomely by extending loans to subprime borrowers who diligently pay off their high-cost credit. In fact, so lucrative is this business that some creditors, including many subprime lenders and large credit-card issuers, were said by consumer groups and regulators to be withholding from the credit-reporting bureaus documentation of a borrower's good payment history that might qualify them for more-advantageous loan terms from a competitor (p.50).

Banks-finance company alliances can disseminate personal information about their customers to third parties without their permission (Consumer Reports, 2000a,c) and may even decline to alert a customer if someone is snooping in the customer's account (Schoenberger, 2000). Even though companies may choose not to sell personal information to third parties, companies within an alliance may use the data themselves to push financial products and services. For example, a financial services company may learn that a person has mutual fund accounts with another company, then call or write the person about their own funds (Sapsford, 2000).

Large credit bureaus such as Equifax and TransUnion have traditionally been a source of information about a person's credit worthiness. Their databases contain information such as a person's age, address, and occupation. Credit bureaus have begun to sell personal information to retailers and other businesses. Equifax has announced its intention to purchase the direct-marketer R.L. Polk & Company, a company that maintains records of consumer's lifestyles and purchase patterns of 105 million households. Responding to the FTC's order blocking the sale of credit bureau consumer profiles, TransUnion's PerformanceData subsidiary stated that it does not divulge confidential credit material. It also claimed that the FTC's order infringed on its commercial right of free speech (Consumer Reports, 2000a).

Online banking presents another challenge to personal information privacy. Many banks store customers' addresses and social security numbers in the same records. The information, once retrieved, can be used to reroute credit card mailings or open new accounts (Salkever, 2000).

It should be noted that large databases do not even need to be maintained by businesses and governments in many cases. The FBI and Internal Revenue Service have started to buy personal data from the private sector, notably from ChoicePoint and other commercial "lookup" services. These services specialize in culling, sorting and packaging data on individuals from scores of sources including credit bureaus, marketers and regulatory agencies–activities that the law discourages the government from conducting (Simpson, 2001b).

Medical information databases. Like personal financial information, medical information is for most people a very private matter. Despite this fact, there is a wealth of personal medical data in government and institutional databases. As Consumer Reports (2000b) notes:

> The federal government maintains electronic files of hundreds of millions of Medicare claims. And every state aggregates medical data on its inhabitants, including registries of births, deaths, immunizations, and communicable diseases. But most states go much further. Thirty-seven mandate collection of electronic records of every hospital discharge. Thirty-nine maintain registries of every newly diagnosed case of cancer. Most of these databases are available to any member of the public who asks for them and can operate the database software required to read and manipulate them (p.23).

A computer privacy researcher at Carnegie Mellon University was able to retrieve the health records of the governor of Massachusetts from an "anonymous" database of state employee health insurance claims by knowing his birth date and ZIP code. The researcher demonstrated that she could do the same for 69% of the 54,805 registered voters on the Cambridge, MA voting list (Consumer Reports, 2000b).

Although many of these government database records are stripped of information that could be used to identify individuals (such as Social Security numbers), it is still possible to link the records to private sector medical records using standard codes for diagnoses and procedures employed by the United States healthcare system. The codes are usually included on insurance claims and hospital discharge records.

The ownership of medical records is not entirely clear. When a record is present in a hospital, the hospital claims ownership. Information delivered to a pharmacy becomes the property of the pharmacy. Even written notes hand-written by doctors and nurses are being put into electronic form in the name of faster, more extensive access to needed information.

Much personal health information that is available to the public is volunteered by individuals themselves, by responding to 800 numbers, coupon offers, rebate offers and Web site registration. The information is included in commercial databases like Behavior-Bank sponsored by Experian, one of the world's largest direct-mail database companies. This information is sold to clients interested in categories of health problems, such as bladder control or high cholesterol. Drug companies are also interested in the commercial databases (Consumer Reports, 2000b).

Medical information databases are at present not available on the Internet, although many are available through private networks. However, this situation is quickly changing. Healtheon and other healthcare companies are competing to get doctors to write prescriptions over the Internet and to persuade people to place their personal health records on the Internet. Healtheon has acquired OnHealth, a consumer health information Web site that has 3.2 million visitors annually, and WebMD and Medcast, which have 100,000 registered physician users, 1.1 million registered consumers, and 2.9 million visitors monthly. It has also acquired medical transaction firms Actamed, Metis, MedE America, Envoy, CareInsite, and Kinetra. It processes an estimated 2,000,000,000 transactions a year, 96% over private data networks and 4% over the Internet (Consumer Reports, 2000b). A study by the California HealthCare Foundation found that DoubleClick sent banner ads to 8 of the 21 leading health Web sites. These sites respond to user interest by sending back to DoubleClick a URL address and information about the page visited. Though no user identification is provided directly, users are given an opportunity to register with the site by providing personally identifiable information. A California woman filed an invasion-of-privacy lawsuit against DoubleClick which she alleged collected tracking data and then cross-referenced it against personal information, despite DoubleClick's statement that it was not collecting personal and identifying data and that it gave the privacy interests of Internet users paramount importance (http://www. Privacytimes.com/New Webstories/doubleclick_priv_2_23.htm).

Email

Email accounts for 70% of all network traffic, yet only 10% of it is protected by security measures. Thus it is susceptible to tampering and snooping (Armstrong, 2000b). In many companies, employee email communications are routinely monitored. A 2000 survey of U.S. corporations by the American Management Association found that 54.1% monitored Internet connections, 38.1% monitored email, 30.8% monitored computer files, 11.5% monitored telephone conversations, and 6.8% monitored voice mail (Armstrong, 2000). The survey also revealed that, despite the fact that most companies had policies alerting employees that they were subject to monitoring, 25% surveyed had fired employees based on evidence collected during monitoring (Seglin, 2000). Hackers can also be a problem. Programs can be surreptitiously installed that monitor a user's keystrokes. The keystrokes can be sent across the Internet to a computer that logs everything that is typed for later use (Glass, 2000).

Loss of workday productivity is often cited as the major concern for businesses that monitor email. A single email message heralding a religious holiday was sent to 60,000 employees within Lockheed Martin Corporation, disabling the company's networks for more than six hours (McCarthy, 1999c). Many companies worry about possible litigation stemming from sexually charged email. *Business Week* reports that 70% of employees admit to viewing or sending adult-oriented personal email at work, and 64% sent politically incorrect or offensive personal messages. Xerox, the New York Times, Edward Jones, and First Union Bank have fired employees who sent sexually offensive messages via email. Chevron Corporation and Microsoft Corporation have settled sexual harassment lawsuits as a result of internal email that could have created hostile work environments (Conlin, 2000). Companies are also concerned with activity that may expose the company to breach of contract, trade secret, and defamation lawsuits (Armstrong, 2000).

Employee's invasion of privacy claims have not been upheld in the United States' courts which argue that, since employers own the computer equipment, they can do whatever they want with it. The 1986 Electronic Communication Privacy Act grants employers the right to review stored communications on a company's computer system. Interestingly, an attempt has been made recently to challenge the tendency of the courts to side with the employer. Using the National Labor Relations Act, a depression-era law that protects the rights of workers to communicate freely with one another about work terms and conditions, lawyers representing a Timekeeping Systems, Inc. programmer reversed his firing on the basis of an email message questioning the company's new vacation plan (McCarthy, 2000).

In an ironic turn of events, Burlington Northern Santa Fe Corporation sent company email to the screen of a former employee, who had been fired for subordination some years earlier. The email message contained an attached file containing the names, salaries and Social Security numbers of roughly 800 railroad employees. The former employee planned to publish the data on the Internet, so the company sued citing Minnesota tort law under which individuals can be found liable for "publication of private facts." The judge decided in favor of Burlington Northern Santa Fe Corporation. However the Eighth U.S. Circuit Court of Appeals set aside the ruling (Orey, 2000).

In a plan that cuts across email and database technology lines, the United States Postal Service has announced its intention to establish an email forwarding service that will be available to both people who have email and to those who do not. The plan will link email and real-world addresses in a large Postal Service database in Memphis, TN. Companies could reach consumers via Postal Service email using just a street address. Privacy advocates are concerned that, if implemented, the proposed system "would put into the hands of the U.S. government an electronic asset long regarded as the Holy Grail of digital marketing" (Angwin, 2000b).

Wireless Communications

A monitoring operation run by the U.S. National Security Agency called Echelon uses satellite technology to listen in on virtually all international and (to a limited degree) local wireless communications, including phone calls, faxes, telexes, email and all radio signals including short-wave, airline, and maritime frequencies. The operation listens for certain target words. When a target word is encountered, the transmission is sent to humans for analysis. Echelon is designed primarily for non-military targets, including governments, organizations and businesses around the globe (Port & Resch, 1999). It even has a specially adapted submarine that taps into cables on the ocean floor (Dornan, 2000). In a somewhat related development, the www.globexplorer.com Web site allows consumers to access detailed aerial and satellite photos. A user can zoom down to view neighborhoods, building and even individual homes (Clark, 2000).

Wireless advertising promises to pose a host of challenges for privacy advocates. Wireless service providers know customers' names, cell phone numbers, home and/or office addresses, and the location from where a customer is calling as well as the number a customer is calling. Each phone has a unique identifier that can be used to record where in the physical world someone travels while using the cell phone (Petersen, 2000). In 1999, Sprint admitted that its "Wireless Web" technology was revealing customer phone numbers to every site they visited (Dornan, 2000). In addition, beginning in October 2000, the Federal Communications Commission will require cell phone service providers to be able to identify the location of a caller who dials 911, the emergency number. Most likely, cell phone manufacturers will meet this requirement by embedding a Global Positioning System (GPS) chip in all cell phones. Since a cell phone service provider can track the location of a 911 call, it will also be able to track the location of any other call as well. As Klinkenborg (1999) notes:

> Already GPS is being used to monitor the movement of commercial trucks of every description. This is both a form of insight to the vehicle owners and a form of intrusion to the drivers, who find their movements visible to management in a way they never were before. GPS is also being used in experimental programs to monitor the movements of parolees. There is only a difference of emphasis between tracking a parolee with a GPS and tracking a sales representative with the same tool. We have learned all too well in the last few decades that even innocuous information can be assembled in ways that make it dangerous. Location, movement, and time are not innocuous forms of information (p.109).

Companies such as Profilium Inc. are being created to target advertising at people based on their location. Since people usually have their cell phones available most of the time, marketers see an opportunity to reach potential customers, provided the wireless service providers are willing to share their customer information with them (Petersen, 2000).

Clickstream Tracking

As with email technology, productivity and legal liability concerns are also paramount in companies' decisions to track the behavior of employees when using the Internet. *Business Week* reports that 57% of employees say that Web surfing decreases their productivity, 37% surf the Web at work for personal reasons "constantly," and 29% have been caught at work surfing non-work related sites. The most commonly visited sites at work feature pornography, though other activities also occupy workers' attention. Up to 70% of Charles Schwab & Co. customers do online trading from their office desks. Most Hallmark.com transactions occur during traditional work hours (Conlin, 2000).

Tracking employee behavior on the Internet is becoming common practice. Software programs have been specifically designed to monitor when employees use the Internet and which sites they visit. Telemate.Net can examine company network activity and produce reports identifying and ranking the company's heaviest individual Internet users. It lists the sites most visited by members of the whole company or by members of individual departments within the company and, if desired, can list sites visited by individual employees and rank them by roughly two dozen categories. Logs can reveal who went to which sites at what times (McCarthy, 1999b). Using internal programs with names like Merlin and Qwizard, Lockheed Martin Corporation tracks employee usage of step-by-step training sites on ethics and legal compliance. The monitoring programs alert managers about employees who haven't taken the required sessions (McCarthy, 1999a).

Internet companies monitor Internet user behavior by a number of means, primarily to gather data about shopping and buying preferences with a view toward developing "user profiles." These technological means include capturing and examining environment variables, cache memory, and cookies (http://www.cnil.fr/traces).

Environment variables contain data about a user's system configuration and site last visited. These variables include a user's domain name, system address, IP (Internet Protocol) address, operating system version, browser version, and URL of the last site visited. This data is transmitted with each packet of data transmitted to an Internet server, where it is extracted by a CGI (Common Gateway Interface) script (program). This capturing of data happens without the user's explicit consent. This data may be saved by the server in a file along with data about any file that the server may have sent to the user in response to the user's request.

Cache memory is a commonly available technology that was developed to enhance file download time and maximize network performance. When a user requests access to a Web site, the browser checks a directory on the user's hard drive to see if the Web page has been loaded previously. If not, it carries out the request, but when the page arrives, it records it on the user's hard disk and displays it on the screen. The next time the same request is made, the browser reads the page from the hard disk and saves network resources by not requiring an additional server transmission. The cache memory is not hidden and may be accessed by an outside observer using another computer, thereby revealing the sites that have been visited.

Cookies are text files created by a Web server and stored on a user's hard disk. A cookie is a set of fields that a user's computer and a server exchange during a transaction. The server may change or suppress the contents of a cookie it has created. Web servers work with ad placement companies that resell advertising space from popular sites. These companies maintain large databases in which are recorded details about who looks at which pages. When a user connects to a Web site, the browser checks the cookies on the hard drive. If a cookie matches the site's URL, the browser uploads the cookie to the Web site. With the information contained in the cookie, the site can run programs that personalize site offerings and/or track the user's activity while online.

Cookies have received a great deal of attention from privacy advocates. Among the concerns that have been raised are the following (http://www.anu.edu.au/people/Roger.Clarke/II/Cookies.html):

- Cookies are a surreptitious feature, and were introduced surreptitiously;
- Cookies take advantage of the user's facilities without express or even implied permission to do so;
- The Web server causes a cookie to be read without reference to any setting in the user's Web browser–Read access is ON with no opt-out mechanism;
- The Web browser settings default to writing all cookies, without asking the user what settings are desired.

The Electronic Privacy Information Center (EPIC) filed a complaint with the FTC concerning the information collection practices of DoubleClick, Inc. and its business partners. The complaint alleged that DoubleClick unlawfully tracked the online activities of Internet users through the placement of cookies. EPIC also alleged that DoubleClick combined users' Web surfing records with detailed personal profiles contained in a national database following DoubleClick's merger with Abacus Direct, the country's largest catalog database firm. Despite the controversy, DoubleClick has continued pooling transactional, geographic, and demographic data from over 275 online retailers and publishers (Nickell, 2001).

DoublesClick's use of banner ads to track online activities is the most commonly used method. But *Consumer Reports* (2000a) indicated a clandestine approach to tracking that was implemented at Web portals Lycos and Excite on behalf of DoubleClick and Matchlogic. Cookie-like Web bugs are embedded as a transparent Graphics Interchange Format (GIF) the size of a single pixel on the user's screen. Since most Web browsers do not alert users to the placement of a cookie by default, most users would be unaware that servers had planted a cookie and were tracking their movements on the Web.

It should be noted that U.S. government agencies also track the browsing and buying habits of Internet users. A congressional report released in April 2001 found that 64 federal Web sites used files that allow them to track the browsing and buying habits of Internet users. Among the agencies were the Departments of Education, Treasury, Energy, Interior and Transportation, as well as NASA and the General Services Administration (Zuckerbrod, 2001).

Microsoft Corporation plans to sell sophisticated scheduling services to users of products such as the Windows operating system and the MSN network. Programs such as Hailstorm, Passport and Smart Tags will keep track of the many details related to calendars, online shopping and user interests. Privacy advocates fear that these details will migrate to Microsoft servers, providing the company with a wealth of personal data (Carney, 2001).

Hardware and Software Watermarks

Hardware and software identifiers ("watermarks") can also be used to identify individual users.

In January 2000, Intel Corporation announced it would include a unique Processor Serial Number (PSN) in its new Pentium III microprocessor chips. The rationale for the PSN was that it was to be used for authentication purposes in e-commerce insofar as the PSN would be linked to a person's real-world identity.

Privacy advocates countered that the PSN could be read remotely by Web sites and other programs and used to link users' activities on the Internet for marketing and other purposes, such as identifying users seeking access to chat rooms. As the Big Brother Inside homepage explains (http://www.bigbrotherinside.org):

The PSN would likely be collected by many sites, indexed and accumulated in databases. Unlike cookies, which are usually different for each web site, the PSN will remain the same and cannot be deleted or easily changed. The advertising and marketing industries have been strongly advancing technical means of synchronizing cookies so that information about individual consumer behavior in cyberspace can be shared between companies. We believe that a hardware PSN used in the majority of computers would quickly be put to this purpose. The records of many different companies could be merged without the user's knowledge or consent to provide an intrusive profile of activity on the computer.

Even as a security device, the PSN was inadequate. Hackers could easily forge a PSN, thereby negating its authentication rationale. Software patches to disable the PSN have proved inadequate. In April 2000, Intel Corporation decided not to include the PSN in its forthcoming 1.5 GHz Williamette chip. However, in addition to the Pentium III machines with the PSN, there are some Pentium II and Celeron processors that have the PSN.

Every Ethernet card used in computer communications has its own Medium Access Control (MAC) address, a 48-bit number sent in the header of every message frame. As the Ethernet standard evolves into a wide-area communications protocol, this identifier may become of increasing concern to Internet users intent on protecting their privacy (Dornan, 2000).

Microsoft Corporation includes a unique numeric identifier into every copy of its Office program. When a Microsoft Office document is created, it is watermarked with this unique identifier. The creator of the Melissa virus was apprehended when he posted documents to a Web site frequented by virus makers. Authorities used the watermark found in the Melissa virus to match the watermark found in the documents (http://www.forbes.com/Forbes/99/1129/6413182s1.htm).

Biometric Devices

Various devices are available that identify people through scans of their faces, hands, fingers, eyes, or voice recognition. Biometric devices create a statistical profile by assessing a number of biological characteristics. As the equipment used to take the measurements decreases in cost, it becomes economical to scan millions of faces and other characteristics into a computer database. Digital photography adds to the growing volume of non-text data about people. Privacy advocates object to the fact that much of the measurement taking place happens without the knowledge or explicit cooperation of a subject, which can lead to abuses of the technology. A spokesperson for the Electronic Frontier Foundation has noted that a bank that has collected face scans of ATM customers could sell this information to another company for a purpose not related to banking (Stepanek, 2000a). Though not as simple as text data, biometric data can be transmitted on the Internet with little difficulty.

SOLUTIONS

There are various proposed solutions to the Internet privacy challenge. These fall into a number of categories: privacy policies; software solutions, including encryption; legal remedies; rules and guidelines; and privacy audits.

Privacy Policies

Most Web companies have published company privacy policies of various complexity and completeness. Although the FTC lacks authority to require the posting of a privacy policy, it is aware that business practices may be deceptive or unfair, whether or not the business has publicly adopted a fair information practice policy. A consent order against GeoCities in effect says that the disclosure of company practices on the online collection and use of personal identifying information is no longer optional. The FTC imposed the following standards on GeoCities:

- Notice of the personal identifying information collected and its uses;
- Choices about how their information is used;
- Access to their own information and the ability to correct errors;
- Adequate security to protect the information collected; and
- Protection of children by limiting the circumstances under which their personal identifying information can be collected and used (Aglion & Gidari, 1998).

The FTC continues to monitor Web company practice. The results of a FTC survey of major e-commerce Web sites found a nearly 90% compliance rate for posting privacy policies on the sites. Still, only 20% of the sites met FTC standards for protecting consumer privacy (Simpson, 2000). In August 2000, Amazon.com revamped its privacy policy to eliminate users' ability to block Amazon.com from sharing data about their purchases or browsing patterns with other companies (Borrus, 2000b).

Of course the FTC has no desire to stifle competition. In its statement of vision, mission and goals, it "seeks to ensure that the nation's markets function competitively, and are vigorous, efficient, and free of undue restrictions" (http://www.ftc.gov/ftc/mission.htm). In its final report on online access and security, dated May 15, 2000, the FTC Advisory Committee recommended the following security solution (http://www.ftc.gov/acoas/papers/finalreport.htm):

- Each commercial Web site should maintain a security program that applies to personal data it holds;
- The elements of the security program should be specified (e.g., risk assessment, planning and implementation, internal reviews, training, reassessment);
- The security program should be appropriate to the circumstances. This standard, which must be defined case by case, is sufficiently flexible to take into account changing security needs over time as well as the particular circumstances of the Web site – including the risks it faces, the costs of protection, and the data it must protect.

In July 2000, the five FTC commissioners voted to support a code of conduct generated by a 9-company coalition called the Network Advertising Initiative. The code of conduct called for the members of the group: 1) not to use personally identifiable information about sexual orientation, Social Security Numbers, or medical or financial data for marketing purposes; 2) to tell consumers about profiling activities; 3) to let consumers knows when cookies are placed; 4) to allow consumers to opt out of data collection; and 5) to offer "reasonable access" to the personally identifiable information that the companies had about them. However, privacy advocates argued that the agreement leaves gaps that need to be addressed. They noted that non-advertising companies are not included in the agreement, which means they can continue to place cookies and collect information. Also, Web sites that allow ad companies to place cookies without a formal contract are not bound by the group's notification rules (Schwartz & O'Harrow, 2000).

It has been argued that the "opt-out "option is rarely chosen by consumers. The reason: the privacy policies are designed to be ignored. The language of privacy policies is so difficult to understand that only highly motivated college graduates can deal with it successfully (France, 2001).

Software Solutions

Programs written to protect personal information privacy achieve their objective in different ways and with different degrees of success. The Platform for Privacy Preferences Project (P3P) allows users to define which items of personal information they are willing to divulge to a Web site. In turn, the program will alert users if a Web site asks for additional information and what the site plans to do with it. P3P will be added to certain Web browsers at no cost and users will be able to download it for free off the Web (Green, 2000). The debate over the default setting for the program continues. Microsoft wants the default setting to reject cookies from any third-party company unless that company complies with P3P and has an "opt-out" mechanism on its own site allowing users to stop placement of cookies. Privacy advocates note that this default setting places the onus on consumers to sign up for the other site's opt-out provision (Simpson, 2001a).

Different approaches to ensuring anonymity have been developed. Freedom from Zero-Knowledge Systems allow the user to open up an anonymous route, with encryption, from server to server. The target server knows merely that the user's request for service came from a server on the Freedom network (Angel, 2000). A private search engine, TopClick, powered by Google allows a user to search the Web without being bothered by banner ads, cookies or profiling. It even includes links to hundreds of online privacy sites, a privacy bookstore, news service, and links to consumer surveys and other research related to privacy (http://www.zdjournals.com/int). Anonymizer uses a proxy-server approach that allows a user to visit different sites without fear of having personal data captured and used without the user's consent (Robinson, 2000).

A security and privacy package from Symantec called Norton Internet Security 2000 provides a firewall, privacy filters, banner ad blocking, and parental controls (Armstrong, 2000a). ZoneAlarm for Windows users and Doorstop Personal for Mac users are software firewalls available on the Internet for downloading (Consumer Reports, 2000c). Using the Recreational Software Advisory Council rating system, a company can attempt to control content (language, violence, nudity, sexual content) viewing at the office using Microsoft's Content Advisor (http://www.zdjournals.com/int). Filtering programs such as SurfWatch, Cyber Patrol and Net Nanny can be used to block out violent, politically incorrect, or X-rated pages from computers used by children (Baig, 1999).

People use encryption to disguise transmitted messages against the possibility that someone other than the intended recipient receives the message. Encryption and decryption are usually programs that are available with a user's Web browser and a network's Web server. For example, Netscape Navigator currently is available in two versions–one that uses 40-bit keys and one that uses 128-bit keys. A good rule of thumb is that the larger the encryption key, the more secure the encrypted message is against hacking. Digital certificates based on the Public Key Infrastructure (PKI) are widely used to authenticate that a person sent a message and that the message has not been tampered with. Two keys are involved: a private key held by a Secure Server Certification Authority (such as Verisign) and a public key associated with a user's Web browser. The primary threat to security is that, in the process of completing a "secure" transaction, a third-party server may be involved without the user's knowledge. To date there are no publicly known instances of forged certificates resulting from successful hacking of 40- or 128-bit codes, or of issuance of compromised digital certificates. Pretty Good Privacy is a public-key cryptography system for secure email and file encryption that relies on a "web of trust." In this approach, a certification authority such as Thawte Consulting verifies that a user has given a valid email address and that no one has written back to complain that this address doesn't belong to the user. Various levels of trust can be added to the user's certificate (Richardson, 2000).

Hardware Solutions

Encryption keys that are generated by and stored in software may be compromised by viruses, inadvertent erasing, system failures and hacking. Hardware key management is a secure and dedicated method of generating, issuing, signing, storing and backing up encryption keys. Deloitte and Touche Security Services stress the following general guidelines for key protection (Baker, 2000):

- All keys must be generated in hardware;
- All keys must be stored in hardware at all times, never in software;
- All keys are backed up from hardware to hardware, never to the host hard drive;

- All digital certificates are brought to the hardware to be signed and are never passed into the host computer's memory;
- All access to the hardware is done through a trusted path, never through the host computer's keyboard;
- All hardware has Federal Information Processing Standards 140-1 Level 3 validation (p.26).

A "smart card"–a small plastic card that contains a memory chip on which data can be recorded–can be used to protect personal information such as credit card numbers. Matlack (2000) explains:

> Consider what happens when you buy online with your credit card. A secure server will probably encrypt your account number, but the merchant may store it on a vulnerable computer network...If, however, you slid a smart card into a reader on your PC and entered your password, the merchant would never get your account number–only a code authorizing the sale (p.64).

American Express' Blue Card is issued with a smart card reader. The Cherry Corporation manufacturers a keyboard that includes a biometric fingerprint reader from Identicator and a smart card reader from Gemplus (Ashbourne, 2000).

Legal Remedies

Earlier we saw that legal protection for personal information privacy is primarily at the level of individual state statutes and common law. If an individual has the resources, s/he may initiate legal action against another individual, company or government. Often various organizations such as the EPIC, Privacy International, and Junkbusters may file suit or provide free legal advice.

When the Federal Bureau of Investigation (FBI) attempted to install Carnivore (a surveillance system that tracks email and other forms of communication such as Internet chat and Web browsing) on networks of ISPs, the American Civil Liberties Union filed a Freedom of Information Act request asking the FBI to release the computer source code as well as letters, correspondence, tape recordings, notes, data, memorabilia and email con-nected with Carnivore (Wingfield, 2000).

The Securities and Exchange Commission (SEC) plans to create an automated surveillance system that would search the Internet for people who violate securities laws. The SEC wants to monitor email, public Web sites, message boards and chat rooms to develop a database of evidence that could be used in civil proceedings against people suspected of violating the law. However, PricewaterhouseCoopers LLP declined to subscribe to the system, fearing that the system might impinge on constitutional protections against unlawful search and seizure in that innocent people could end up in the database (Moss, 2000).

In December 2000, the Clinton administration issued broad new regulations to safeguard the confidentiality of medical records in the United States. These rules guarantee patients access to their health files, restrict the release of their personal information without their approval and give them greater say about how the files are used. These regulations also establish new criminal and civil penalties for health care providers and insurers that improperly use of disclose medical information. Thirty-nine healthcare organizations issued a joint letter asking the Bush administration to postpone the new privacy rules from going into effect. The biggest concern is cost: the new rules are expected to cost at least $3.8 billion over the next five years, conservatively speaking. Some put the cost at up to $38 billion (Little, 2000).

Of course, one must be circumspect about privacy organizations too. Sites can sign up with a privacy verification scheme such as TRUSTe or BBBOnline, which will certify sites to include a seal of approval in their privacy policies. However, analysts such as Forrester Research have questioned the independence of TRUSTe and BBBOnline on the grounds that their certification programs are funded by the e-commerce industry (Dornan, 2000).

Rules and Guidelines

Many publications have presented rules and guidelines for ensuring online privacy. These rules and guidelines basically offer educational advice to individuals and businesses concerned with protecting personal information privacy. Two such sets of rules and guidelines are presented below without comment or criticism.

In a *Business Week* cover story on online privacy, Green, France, Stepanek and Borrus (2000) presented a four-point plan to ensure that e-privacy and e-commerce can coexist:

1. *Display your practices.* Privacy policies should be mandatory, easy to find, and written in plain English. Companies should clearly state why they are collecting information and collect no more data than they need for that purpose. Data collected for one purpose shouldn't be used for another without consent. A simple set of icons should be developed to warn people about privacy threats.

2. *Give people a choice.* If a business wants to collect information about a consumer's health, finances, or sexual orientation, it should ask them for permission first. This allows a Web surfer to opt-in. The same rule applies if the company wants to resell personal data or share it with advertising networks. In all other situations, users should be given the option

to withhold their information by checking a prominently displayed, easy-to-understand box. This is called opt-out.

3.   *Show me the data.* Consumers must have the ability to look at and correct sensitive information, such as financial and medical data. There should also be a mechanism for double-checking a profile that combines personal information with online habits or is shared with another company. This is especially urgent when a profile triggers offensive or unwanted marketing solicitations. Web sites and marketers should share the responsibility for this.

4.   *Play fair or pay.* These rules won't enforce themselves. A broad law ensuring privacy online must be passed at a federal level. An agency, such as the FTC, would enforce and interpret the law according to the Fair Information Practices. Companies should also periodically disclose their practices in some kind of public record, such as SEC filings or trusted third-party audits. (p.87)

Keen (2000) suggests ten rules that will guide a business toward building customer trust in today's e-commerce environment:

1.   Make sure you have an explicit and formal company privacy policy in place, highlight it in all customer interactions, and make is easy to understand.

2.   Don't ask for more private information than you need.

3.   Make customers feel safe in their relationship with your company, regardless or formal–and often contradictory – legal requirements.

4.   Handle the security basics well: SET and SSL are your best friends. They don't guarantee privacy by themselves, but they sure show that your firm is responsible in its e-commerce.

5.   Associate your site with an organization, such as TrustE, BBBOnline (Better Business Bureau), or CPA WebTrust, that certifies Web sites and the business and audit processes behind them.

6.   Let customers easily opt out of allowing you to share information with other parties, but inform them that they'll probably lose convenience, service, and personalization if they do so.

7.   Don't be tempted by easy technology tricks that deceive your customers. No Web bugs (or clear GIFs), HTML email identity grabbing, or other hidden intrusions. None. These can lead to loss of trust and therefore loss of business.

8.   Take an auditor to lunch. Most breaches of privacy happen far, far away from your Web site. Access control, audit logs, and formal rules of information use are the process essentials that support or undermine what you build into the Web site.

9. Don't put all your faith in firewalls. Firewalls are only as good as the attention and expertise behind them.

10. Look on the bright side. Privacy is generally discussed in negative terms: Everyone's for it, and violating it is A Bad Thing. But in practice, it's very much a matter of common sense and ensuring informed consent. (p.132)

Privacy Audits

Businesses are hiring consultants or accounting firms to analyze how an online company collects, stores, protects and uses the personal information and purchasing records of its customers. Privacy audits reveal any business practices that violate customer privacy and if these violations are unlawful or run afoul of industry guidelines. Privacy & American Business, the nonprofit arm of the Center for Social and Legal Research, offers a training course for Corporate Privacy Officers (CPOs). IBM, American Express and AT&T, among others, have established CPO positions among their executive ranks (Robinson, 2000).

CONCLUSION

The issue of personal information privacy and the Internet continues to be debated within the community of Internet users. The concerns of privacy advocates conflict with the concerns of technology growth advocates. Clearly the challenges to personal information privacy posed by the various forms of Internet technology are not the result of the technology itself. Rather, it is the uses of the technology that poses the threat to the integrity of personal information privacy. In particular, the surreptitious monitoring of user behavior without the user's consent and the possible misuse of the collected information pose the biggest threats.

Privacy is a social issue, generally speaking. How the personal information privacy debate is ultimately resolved will be decided by the values inherent in a society. Since the position of the privacy advocates differs so markedly from the position of the technology growth advocates, and since privacy issues have been addressed in court and precedents established in state and common law, it seems likely that the personal information privacy debate will be resolved in the world's legislatures and laws produced there from enforced in the courts. As Lessig (1999) observes, resolving the debate needs the "push of law":

The law would be a kind of property right in privacy. Individuals must have both the ability to negotiate easily over privacy rights and the entitlement to privacy as a default. That is property's purpose: it says to those who want, you must negotiate before you can take...the law is the rule that says negotiation must occur. (p.160)

Assuming the privacy concerns of individuals do not bring e-commerce to its knees, Internet technology will continue to grow and be used to bolster the growth of e-commerce. Any laws that are passed must take into account the evolving nature of technology, while at the same time respect the personal information privacy values of individuals. As members of the Internet community, we can only hope that the future of e-commerce will not be embroiled in litigation, which will bring perhaps debilitating expenses to both e-business and individuals alike.

ENDNOTE

[1] The author thanks Coral R. Snodgrass for her constructive contributions to this paper.

REFERENCES

Aglion, M., & Gidari, A. (1998). Is GeoCities consent order the FTC's privacy regulation of tomorrow? *The Bureau of National Affairs, Inc. (BNA), Electronic Commerce & Law Report*, September 2. Republished as http://www.perkinscoie.com/resource/ecomm/privbna.htm.

Anders, J. (2001). Web-filter data from schools put up for sale. *The Wall Street Journal*, January 26, B1f.

Angel, J. (2000). Too many cookies are bad for you. *Network Magazine*, June, 106-112.

Angwin, J. (2000a). A plan to track Web use stirs privacy concern. *The Wall Street Journal*, May 1, B1f.

Angwin, J. (2000b). Email goes postal. *The Wall Street Journal*, July 31, B1f.

Armstrong, I. (2000). Email woes. *SC Magazine*, March, 20-24.

Armstrong, L. (2000a). Back off, hacker. *Business Week*, February 28, 160-161.

Armstrong, L. (2000b). Someone to watch over you. *Business Week*, July 10, 189-190.

Ashbourne, J. (2000). Cherry Keyboard G81-12000. *SC Magazine*, August, 44.

Baig, E. C. (1999). Shielding children from cyber perils. *Business Week*, August 16, 117.

Baig, E. C., Stepanek, M., & Gross, N. (1999). Privacy. *Business Week*, April 5, 84-90.

Baker, S. (2000). Securing vulnerable encryption keys. *SC Magazine*, August, 25-26.

Big browser is watching you! (2000). *Consumer Reports*, May, 43-50.

Borrus, A. (2000a). Internet privacy: Congress starts feeling the heat. *Business Week*, May 15, 59.

Borrus, A. (2000b). Online privacy: Congress has no time to waste. *Business Week*, September 18, 54.

Borrus, A. (2001). The stage seems set for net privacy rules this year. *Business Week*, March 5, 51.

Borrus, A., & Dwyer, P. (2000). Surprise! Bush is emerging as a fighter for privacy on the net. *Business Week*, June 5, 63.

Bott, E. (2000). We know where you live, work, shop, bank, play...and so does everyone else! *PCComputing*, March, 80-100.

Carney, D. (2001). A window into your personal life. *Business Week*, July 2, 63-64.

Cate, F. H. (1997). *Privacy in the Information Age*. Washington, D.C.: Brookings Institution Press.

Cavazos, E. A. (1996). The legal risks of setting up shop in cyberspace. *Journal of Organizational Computing and Electronic Commerce*, 6(1), 51-60.

Cheskin Research. (2000). Gaining on trust. *Business 2.0*, June 25, 165-175.

Clark, D. (2000). Now you, too, can be a spy. *The Wall Street Journal*, September 12, B1f.

Conlin, M. (2000). Workers, surf at your own risk. *Business Week*, June 12, 105-106.

Directive 95/46/EC of the European Parliament and of the council on the protection of individuals with regard to the processing of personal data and on the free movement of such data (1995). *Official Journal of the European Communities*, L281.

Dornan, A. (2000). Internet indiscretions. *Network Magazine*, June, 100-104.

Dwyer, P. (2000). The privacy debate goes to school. *Business Week*, May 1, 136-138.

Flaherty, D. H. (1989). *Protecting Privacy in Surveillance Societies: The Federal Republic of Germany, Sweden, France, Canada, and the United States*. NC: University of North Carolina Press.

France, M. (2001). Why privacy notices are a sham. *Business Week*, June 18, 82-83.

Ginsburg, J. (2000). The great portal purge. *Business Week*, June 26, 149-152.

Glass, B. (2000). Keeping your private information private. *PC Magazine*, June 6, 118-130.

Gormley, K. (1992). One hundred years of privacy. *Wisconsin Law Review*, September-October, 1337-1338.

Green, H. (2000). Privacy: Don't ask technology to do the job. *Business Week*, June 26, 52.

Green, H. (2001). Your right to privacy: Going...going.... *Business Week*, April 23, 48.

Green, H., France, M., Stepanek, M., & Borrus, A. (2000). It's time for rules in Wonderland. *Business Week*, March 20, 83-96.

Hamm, S., & Hof, R. D. (2000). An eagle eye on customers. *Business Week*, February 21, 67-76.

Hammonds, K. H. (Ed.). (1998). Online insecurity. *Business Week*, March 16, 102.

Hepp, R. (2000). The greatest theft of all. *The Buffalo News*, July 18, E7-E8.

Instant Internet. (2000). *Consumer Reports*, September, 24-27.

Keen, P. (2000). Designing privacy for your e-business. *PC Magazine*, June 6, 132-135.

Klinkenborg, V. (1999). No place to hide. *Discover*, December, 102-109.

Kuchinskas, S. (2000). One-to-(N)one. *Business 2.0*, September 12, 141-148.

Lessig, L. (1999). *Code and Other Laws of Cyberspace*. New York: Basic Books.

Little, D. (2000). Getting tangled in health care's Web. *Business Week*, December 18, 153-154.

Matlack, C. (2000). U.S. wises up to smart cards. *Business Week*, August 28, 64.

McCarthy, M. J. (1999a). How one firm tracks ethics electronically. *The Wall Street Journal*, October 21, B1f.

McCarthy, M. J. (1999b). Now the boss knows where you're clicking. *The Wall Street Journal*, October 21, B1f.

McCarthy, M. J. (1999c). Virtual morality: A new workplace quandary. *The Wall Street Journal*, October 21, B1f.

McCarthy, M. J. (2000). Your manager's policy on employee's email may have a weak spot. *The Wall Street Journal*, April 25, A1f.

McHugh, J. (1999). Mind readers. http://www.forbes.com/Forbes/99/1129/643182s4.htm.

Moss, M. (2000). SEC's plan to snoop for crime on Web sparks a debate over privacy. *The Wall Street Journal*, March 28, B1f.

Nickell, J. A. (2001). Big data's big business. *Business2.com*, February 20, 62f.

Orey, M. (2000). Burlington Northern is locked in privacy fight. *The Wall Street Journal*, May 17, B8.

Paul, M. J. and Gochenouer, J. E. (1996). Isolation without privacy. In Szewczak, E. and Khosrowpour, M. (Eds.), *The Human Side of Information Technology Management*, 318-336. Hershey, PA: Idea Group Publishing.

Petersen, A. (2000). Coming to phone screens: Pitches, privacy woes. *The Wall Street Journal*, July 24, B1f.

Port, O., & Resch, I. (1999). They're listening to your calls. *Business Week*, May 31, 110-111.

Richardson, R. (2000). Public key infrastructure. *Network Magazine*, June, 114-120.

Robinson, E. (2000). Click and cover. *Business 2.0*, September 12, 168-181.

Salkever, A. (2000). Online banking: The nightmare. *Business Week*, October 9, 166E6.

Samuel, A. (1999). German shepherds. *Business 2.0*, May, 130-132.

Sandoval, G. (2000). Sensitive data on customers being sold by failed e-retailers. *The Buffalo News*, July 1, A9.

Sapsford, J. (2000). Personalized financial Web sites spread, amid privacy concerns. *The Wall Street Journal*, July 19, C1f.

Schoenberger, C. (2000). How secret? http://www.forbes.com/Forbes99/1129/6413182s3.htm.

Schwartz, J. and O'Harrow. (2000). Trade panel backs online privacy code. *The Buffalo News*, July 28, A1f.

Seglin, J. L. (2000). Who's snooping on you? *Business 2.0*, August 8, 200-203.

Selling is getting personal. (2000). *Consumer Reports*, November, 16-20.

Simpson, G. R. (2000). FTC finds Web sites fail to guard privacy. *The Wall Street Journal*, May 11, B12.

Simpson, G. R. (2001a). The battle over Web privacy. *The Wall Street Journal*, March 21, B1f.

Simpson, G. R. (2001b). If the FBI hopes to get the goods on you, it may ask ChoicePoint. *The Wall Street Journal*, April 13, A1f.

Smith, H. J. (2001). Information privacy and marketing: What the U.S. should (and shouldn't) learn from Europe. *California Management Review*, 43(2), 8-33.

Stepanek, M. (2000a). Are they selling your face? *Business Week*, May 8, 106E6.

Stepanek, M. (2000b). None of your business. *Business Week*, June 26, 78-80.

Teir, R. and Coy, K. L. (2000). Internet privacy debate overlooks information benefits. *The Buffalo News*, June 18, H5.

The surveillance society (1999). *The Economist*, May 1, 21-23.

Weber, T. E. (2000). Europe and U.S. reach truce on net privacy, but what comes next? *The Wall Street Journal*, June 19, B1.

Weber, T. E. (2001). Network Solutions sells marketers its Web database. The Wall *Street Journal*, February 16, B1f.

Westin, A. F. (1967). *Privacy and Freedom*. New York: Atheneum.

Who knows your medical secrets. (2000). *Consumer Reports*, August, 22-26.

Wingfield, N. (2000). ACLU asks details on FBI's new plan to monitor the Web. *The Wall Street Journal*, July 17, B7.

Zuckerbrod, N. (2001). Government Web sites tracking users. *The Buffalo News*, April 17, A1f.

Chapter VII

E-communication of Interdepartmental Knowledge: An Action Research Study of Process Improvement Groups

Ned Kock
Temple University, USA

Robert J. McQueen
University of Waikato, New Zealand

ABSTRACT

This chapter presents a review of the organizational learning literature that points to process improvement (PI) groups as an appropriate tool for organizational knowledge communication. Based on this review, the impact of support provided by a class of e-communication systems, email conferencing (EC), on knowledge dissemination in organizations is examined in the context of PI groups. Data was collected through an action research project, where the researcher facilitated seven PI groups in two organizations with the support of an EC system implemented with Novell Groupwise, and using a group methodology for PI called MetaProi. The study suggests that, overall, EC support seems to have a positive impact on knowledge dissemination in organizations when used in combination with a group methodology for PI. EC support effects on PI groups can be summarized as: (a) a reduction of the influence of distance and other physical obstacles to the participation of members from different departments in PI groups, and of the disruption that group discussions are likely to cause for individual group members, particularly when these members are from different departments; (b) a reduction of interdepartmental conflict obstacles to the formation of PI groups; and (c) an increase or decrease in individual learning in PI groups, depending on the complexity of the issues being discussed and the clarity of electronic contributions by members. Organizational implications of these research findings are discussed.

INTRODUCTION

Organizations generate and deliver goods, information, or services (or a mix of these) to fulfill the needs of their customers. This is accomplished by means of business processes (often referred to simply as "processes"). Although there is some controversy over what a "process" is (Harrison, 1995), the most generally accepted definition is that of a sequence of interrelated activities carried out by organizational functions (performed by staff) with the use of tools (Davenport & Short, 1990; Harrington, 1991; Ould, 1995). Some organizational processes may be undertaken exclusively within one organizational unit (hereinafter referred to as departments), although more frequently, the participation of two or more departments in the process is required. Therefore, it is desirable that process improvement (PI) efforts targeted at processes with broad organizational importance be performed by groups comprised of staff from several departments.

The term "process improvement" has been widely used since the early 1990s, particularly due to the business process re-engineering movement (Hammer, 1990; Hammer and Stanton, 1997), to describe voluntary and purposeful organizational efforts aimed at redesigning business processes. The goal of these efforts is usually an increase in process efficiency or in the satisfaction of customers (internal or external to the organization) who use or consume process outputs. However, the idea of process-focused improvement has been long since propounded and practiced (Earl, 1994), notably in Japan since after World War II and in the US since the early 1980s, with the total quality management movement (De Cock and Hipkin, 1997; Juran, 1989; Walton, 1989).

Most PI efforts seem to share some characteristics, whether their goal is small or large-scale change. One of these is that PI is usually carried out by groups that are typically small, usually having from three to twenty members (Kock and McQueen, 1995, 1997). Two typical instances of PI groups that illustrate these common characteristics are quality circles, widely used in total quality management movement in Japan (Hutchins, 1985; Robson, 1988), and business process re-engineering groups (Hammer and Stanton, 1995).

Quality circles were originally developed in Japan in the early 1960s, as small groups of workers from the same area who, using statistical control methods, identified and developed solutions for problems affecting the quality of manufactured products. These early versions of quality circles were used as a basis for the development of other group-based organizational change approaches that have underpinned the total quality management movement in the 1980s (Deming, 1986).

Business process re-engineering groups, differently from quality circles, usually involve external consultants, key employees, and managers from different areas of the organization, and normally use non-statistical process modelling tools. These groups are usually temporary. They may, for example, be dissolved as soon as one or more processes are redesigned. Quality circles, on the other hand, have a longer lifetime and are usually composed of workers from the same organizational area. Quality circles meet typically once a week over several months or years. Finally, while business process re-engineering groups search for radical process improvement, the degree of improvement sought by quality circles is usually incremental (Davenport, 1993; Hutchins, 1985).

At least two characteristics of most contemporary organizations make it desirable to have a certain degree of departmental heterogeneity in PI groups so the effectiveness of these groups, or the likelihood that proposed process changes will lead to actual process improvements, can be maximized. First, the knowledge necessary to generate effective redesign proposals is unlikely to be possessed by a single department or manager (Hayek, 1996; Kock and McQueen, 1995; Kock, McQueen & Baker, 1996). Second, redesign proposals are likely to meet with staff resistance if they are generated without the involvement of representatives from the departments concerned.

This study examines an often hidden benefit accruing from interdepartmental PI groups to organizations, namely the communication of socio-technical knowledge between departments. This study also examines the organizational knowledge dissemination and learning that results from this sociotechnical knowledge communication. This is done with a focus on the effect that asynchronous e-communication support has on these. Asynchronous e-communication is defined as communication through a class of group support systems aimed at supporting physically distributed interaction occurring at different times (Kock & McQueen, 1997).

To narrow the scope of this study, we targeted our analysis at the effects of the use of a particular type of asynchronous e-communication technology, email conferencing (EC), on obstacles to interdepartmental communication and knowledge dissemination in organizations through PI groups. EC conferencing is a term that describes email tools used to support group communication, beyond simple one-to-one message exchanges. EC is usually found in the format popularized by the email distribution lists commonly know as "Internet listservs." Two main research questions guided us in the search for our goal:

(1)   Does EC support reduce the obstacles to desirable inter-departmental heterogeneity in PI groups?

(2)   Does EC support increase individual process-related and social learning in PI groups?

One assumption of this study is that PI groups are an effective mechanism for organizational learning and knowledge communication. This assumption is based on two previous research studies: (a) a study of PI groups (Kock & McQueen, 1995), which suggests that PI groups can foster organizational learning particularly among non-management staff; and (b) a study of 22 business processes in three organizations (Kock & Corner, 1996), which showed that the process instances carried out by PI groups had over twice the proportion of knowledge exchanges found in core and support processes. Given the assumption above, then a reduction in the obstacles to departmental heterogeneity in PI groups is likely to increase knowledge communication between departments, and consequently organizational knowledge dissemination and learning.

While this indicates the relevance of research Question (1), it is also important to assess whether the EC mediation itself is likely to increase or decrease process-related and social learning in PI groups. Given the indication that the EC medium can increase ambiguity in group communication (Daft & Lengel, 1986; Markus, 1992), it is unclear whether EC support will be detrimental or beneficial to knowledge communication in PI groups. This issue is addressed by research Question (2).

The research findings presented in this chapter provide the basis for partially answering both research questions. A further discussion about the link between PI and knowledge dissemination, which supports the assumption that the PI group is an appropriate tool for knowledge dissemination in organizations, is followed by a description of the research method used in this study and a description of the research findings. Some organizational implications are presented based on the research findings, particularly for the speed and breadth of knowledge dissemination in organizations.

PROCESS IMPROVEMENT AND KNOWLEDGE DISSEMINATION

A climate of risk-taking and experimentation has been found to be an important factor in organizational learning. While this climate may be achieved through the adoption of new management practices and paradigms, whereby organizations can move from reactive and task-oriented learning approaches to more proactive and creativity-oriented ones (Nevis, DiBella & Gould, 1995), the transferring of acquired knowledge or skills from one part of an organization to another remains a complex and problematic issue (CHE, 1995). The transfer of acquired knowledge and skills across different organizational areas is, nevertheless, one of the most important components of organizational learning (Redding & Catalanello, 1994) and competitiveness (Boland & Tenkasi, 1995).

One of the main obstacles to knowledge dissemination in organizations is functional departmentalization, that is, the grouping of functions into departments. However, functional departmentalization seems to be a necessary evil, and has probably survived into the current era of organizational design due to another contemporary phenomenon–an exponential growth in knowledge specialization (Hayek, 1996; Kock et al., 1996). Mirroring organizational models inherited from the industrial revolution, organizational departments today often tend to group together staff with similar knowledge backgrounds and skills that enable them to carry out certain activities and processes better than other non-qualified staff. For example, a marketing department will typically comprise staff with a common knowledge background in marketing, whereas an R&D department will typically involve staff with a common knowledge background in research methods and technical characteristics of products being tested and developed.

Functional departmentalization is typically reinforced by physical barriers, often in the form of office walls and physical distance between departmental offices. These add to the existing barriers to interdepartmental communication posed by knowledge specialization, and the consequent reluctance of "outsiders" to try to understand the "complexity" of the internal procedures in departments. This perceived complexity prevents staff from different departments from understanding why and how activities outside their departments are performed, which often leads to the need for expensive external coordination functions (e.g., division-level managers who coordinate the work of two or more departments). In order to reduce departmental barriers to communication and the low process efficiency and quality that can accrue from this isolation (Deming, 1986), several tools have been developed, particularly in the 1980s and 1990s. One such tool is the PI group.

The organizational learning research literature largely acknowledges two characteristics of PI groups as particularly useful for knowledge dissemination and learning in organizations. First, that literature acknowledges the effectiveness of small staff learning groups in bringing about knowledge communication between different departments and, in some cases, between different managerial levels (e.g., Revans, 1991; Casey, 1993; Peters, 1996). Second, the organizational learning literature acknowledges the need for a focus on processes, as opposed to "problems," to generate more effective types of learning–for example, moving from single-loop to double-loop learning (see e.g., Argyris, 1977, 1992). PI groups also provide both a legitimate reason and a mechanism for interdepartmental exchange of knowledge, as organizational processes almost invariably need to undergo radical or incremental redesign in order to match or surpass quality and productivity improvements in processes of rival organizations, make use of new technologies and adapt to new government regulations (Deming, 1986; Davenport & Short, 1990; Hammer & Champy, 1993).

However, it is often difficult to bring together staff from different departments to collaborate in PI group discussions. In addition to functional departmentalization and physical obstacles, some other reasons can account for this difficulty. Often different departments have their own social norms, which can be incompatible with those of other departments. For example, well-established social and behavior norms in an R&D department, such as flexible work times, casual dress and intimacy between managers and subordinates, may conflict with rigid and hierarchical norms adopted in a production department. The specialized "languages" that some departments use internally to facilitate concise exchanges of data, information and knowledge among members with similar expertise, may hamper interdepartmental communication and learning in the broader organizational context. These differences can cause communication gaps between departments that prevent the sharing of process-related knowledge and information. Our study sought to analyze the impact of EC support on these obstacles in the context of PI groups. This was done by engaging the researcher and organizational staff in collaborative business change interventions accomplished through PI groups. The following section describes the research method used to perform these interventions and collect research data.

RESEARCH METHOD

One PI group was studied over a period of one month at the School of Management Studies (SMS) of the University of Waikato, in New Zealand. Three months later, six PI groups were studied over a period of four months at MAF Quality Management (MQM), a branch of the New Zealand Ministry of Agriculture and Fisheries, with offices spread throughout the country. These six groups involved a total of forty-seven staff from eighteen different sites (known in MQM as offices and remote sites) spread over New Zealand.

All seven groups, referred to as G0-G6, were facilitated by the researcher (first author of this paper) based on a group process methodology called MetaProi (Kock, 1995, 1999). MetaProi provides a group process, guidelines and graphical tools to be used by PI groups, and comprises three main stages: (1) process definition, where the group agrees on a process (or a few processes) to be redesigned; (2) process analysis, where the selected process is modelled and related performance information is gathered and discussed by the group; and (3) process redesign, where process changes are proposed and a plan for their implementation is outlined.

Main features of the groups studied are shown in Table 1, including number of members (excluding the facilitator), duration in days, and number of organizational departments and sites involved in each group. Typically, departments were comprised of staff with shared expertise on a few related areas (e.g., academic department, animal analysis laboratory, and farm consulting department). Sites, on the other hand, were comprised of staff (often from different departments) in the same building or campus. The last column in the table shows the scope of change of the redesign proposals generated by the groups, which were classified as departmental if the redesign affected only one department; interdepartmental if it affected more than one department but not a whole business unit; and business, if it affected a whole business unit. This study involved two business units at MQM and one at SMS. These business units were characterized by their administrative autonomy and by being at the highest divisional level within their respective organizations.

Most of the interaction in the PI groups happened through an EC tool implemented using Novell Groupwise. This tool allowed group members to interact as a group by sending messages to a mailbox named "BPI" located in each organization (e.g., its address at SMS was BPI@mngt.waikato.ac.nz). The receipt of messages by the BPI mailbox triggered the execution of system macros that automated the distribution of copies of a message to all the members of a given group. The tool worked in a similar way to Internet distribution lists. The proportion of interaction time through the EC tool varied from 67 to 89 percent of the total

Table 1: Features of the PI groups studied

Group	Members	Duration (days)	Depart- ments	Sites	Change Scope
G0	7	33	2	1	Interdepartmental
G1	5	26	1	1	Departmental
G2	5	25	1	4	Interdepartmental
G3	7	14	1	6	Business
G4	11	29	4	5	Business
G5	15	28	6	10	Departmental
G6	14	10	3	8	Business

interaction time for each group, except for G3. The remainder of the interaction time involved one-to-one telephone and face-to-face interactions. In G3, the proportion of EC interaction was only 18 percent. The remaining 82 percent in G3 was spent on face-to-face meetings where all group members were present. Almost no one-to-one e-mail messages were exchanged during group discussions.

Data was collected between May 1995 and January 1996 through participant observation and unstructured interviews (12 at SMS and 32 at MQM), structured open-ended interviews (two at SMS and nine at MQM), questionnaires with open-ended questions (seven at MQM), and automatic computer generation of transcripts of electronic group discussions. All structured interview and questionnaire respondents declared having previously engaged in general work-related face-to-face groups; sixty-three percent in face-to-face PI groups. The outcomes of participant observation and unstructured interviews have been compiled as field notes. Structured interviews, typically one hour each in length, were taped and transcribed. Questionnaires were administered via email to some staff at MQM who were located in remote offices and followed up with telephone interviews.

The research was designed to improve real business processes in the participant organizations, as well as generating research data, and followed a specific action research approach (Kock, McQueen & Fernandes, 1995). This approach is based on the action research cycle proposed by Susman and Evered (1978). The data analysis combined quantitative and qualitative techniques as suggested by Miles and Huberman (1994) and led to several research findings. Part of these findings is discussed in the next section, with a focus on the two research questions stated previously.

RESEARCH FINDINGS AND DISCUSSION

Three main research findings are discussed in this section. The first finding, which was strongly supported by interview responses, is that EC support is likely to reduce physical distance and work disruption obstacles to the formation of interdepartmental PI groups. The second finding is that EC support is likely to reduce interdepartmental conflict obstacles to the formation of PI groups. The third finding is that EC support may increase or reduce individual learning in PI groups, depending on the complexity of the issues being discussed and the clarity of electronic contributions by members. Each of these findings is discussed separately next.

EC Support Effects on Physical Distance and Disruption Barriers

One of the tenets of widely practiced organizational development approaches, such as the total quality movement, is that process quality and productivity can "always" be improved (Deming, 1986; Ishikawa, 1986; Juran, 1989). If this is true, then one can have the expectation that any well-managed organization will always have a number of PI efforts under way. While our study supported the first assumption, it also indicated that the obstacles to interdepartmental PI efforts are hard to overcome. For example, whenever we approached prospective group leaders in our study, we were told by them that there were a number of problems awaiting solution. Those problems typically related to organizational processes spanning at least two departments. However, none of the staff approached was, during the first contact with the researcher, involved in any PI effort, though most of these staff declared being engaged in problem-solving efforts at the departmental level.

As shown in Table 1, all PI groups either involved staff from more than one department or generated changes that affected more than one department, except for G1. The initial interviews with prospective group leaders clearly indicated that the problems tackled by EC-supported PI groups were known to staff before the groups were begun, which indicates that EC support was perceived as particularly useful for PI groups targeting cross-departmental problems and related processes. Apparently the availability of the EC system was seen as an opportunity for staff to carry out PI groups involving different departments, which were obviously necessary given the problems reported.

The assumption above was strongly supported by responses in structured interviews. When asked whether EC support made it easier or harder for PI groups to have members from different departments, structured interview respondents' answers were distributed as shown in Table 2.

When asked to explain their answers, two main explanations were given by the respondents who were of the opinion that EC support made it easier to have members of different departments in PI groups. Those explanations were:

Table 2: Distribution of answers from 18 respondents (Question: Did EC support make it easier or harder to have members of different departments co-operating in your PI group?)

Answer	Respondents	Percentage
Made it easier	16	88
Had no effect	1	6
Do not know	1	6

(1)   that EC support enables group discussions to be carried out without affecting individual timetables (8 respondents); and

(2)   that EC support reduces the influence of distance (5 respondents).

The first explanation emphasizes the perceived reduction in the disruption of member's functional activities (i.e., routine activities) traditionally associated with face-to-face group meetings. It is likely that this perception was influenced by two underlying perceptions, aired by group members in unstructured interviews: (a) that had the PI groups been carried out only through face-to-face meetings, group members would probably have to attend three or more separate face-to-face meetings per group, owing to the perception that different group stages of the PI group discussion (i.e., process definition, analysis and redesign) would require different types of knowledge and information in order to be successfully completed; and (b) that each of these face-to-face meetings would probably be relatively long, i.e., from one to ten hours. These perceptions are supported by our previous experience facilitating face-to-face improvement groups in a similar action research study (Kock & McQueen, 1995).

The second explanation given by respondents suggests a perceived relationship between departmental heterogeneity and site heterogeneity, since the question asked concerned only departmental, not site, heterogeneity. This perception is supported by the moderately strong correlation (Pearson r = 0.70, P<0.05, 1-tailed), shown in Table 3, between the variables number of departments and number of sites in PI groups, which suggests that, as the number of departments involved in a PI groups grows, so does the number of sites involved (the other correlations shown are irrelevant for this discussion).

The findings above indicate that EC support reduces the influence of two types of obstacles to cross-departmental heterogeneity in PI groups: (a) the distance between group members from different departments; and (b) the disruption that face-to-face meetings are likely to cause for individual group members, particularly when these members are from different departments. There was not enough evidence to conclude that EC support can reduce disruption in departmental PI groups.

Table 3: Coefficients of correlation (Pearson)

	Duration	Departments	Sites
Members	-0.22	0.89*	0.84**
Duration		0.22	-0.45
Departments			0.70***

(*P<0.01, 2-tailed; **P<0.05, 2-tailed; ***P<0.05, 1-tailed)

EC Support Effects on Interdepartmental Conflict Barriers

Other than eliminating physical obstacles and reducing disruption, another type of impact EC support may have on interdepartmental communication is suggested from the analysis of two of the PI groups. Prospective members of these groups strongly indicated that the EC support makes it easier to have members from different departments in PI groups because EC support decreases the influence of previous interdepartmental conflict on staff's decision to participate in PI groups. One of the prospective members of a group involving two departments with a history of conflict stated that it would be easier to initiate the group discussion via the EC medium because:

> ...[EC] is not as formal as a face-to-face meeting is...there have been some arguments between [staff from the two departments] in the past...I don't think they would agree to face each other in a meeting room right now.

According to this prospective member, the formality of face-to-face meetings was likely to be exacerbated by the history of conflict between the two departments involved in the execution of the process(es) likely to be tackled by the PI group. Moreover, a face-to-face meeting can be interpreted by some staff as a confrontation exercise, which can lead to evasive behavior. The following comment from another group member, referring to the advantages of EC support in discussions involving conflicting departments, illustrates the increased individual safety fostered by EC support:

> You don't have to face [the staff from the other department]...it is easier to discuss unpleasant things...when you don't have to face the people you're talking to.

This perception may be explained by the EC medium being perceived as less personally threatening by prospective members, particularly because they could always "lurk" without necessarily having to actively contribute to the group discussion. Our experience suggests that this perception is accurate, as it seems exceedingly difficult for group leaders, for example, to control (i.e., increase or reduce) member participation in EC-supported PI groups. Thus, it is equally difficult to induce a member to contribute to the group discussion when he or she decided otherwise. For example, in one case a member was repeatedly asked by the leader of her PI group, over the phone and through brief face-to-face requests, to contribute to the EC group discussion. She replied to these requests by saying that she would contribute "as soon as she had some time," but posted no message to the group discussion in which she was participating as a member. Later, in an unstructured interview, that member admitted to having decided from the outset not to contribute to the group discussion, and that her apparent agreement to contribute was just an evasive tactic. In face-to-face meetings, on the contrary, that member could have been prompted to contribute by simply being asked direct questions by the group leader or any other group member.

Inter-departmental conflict often results in a situation where collaboration gives way to competition, and where departments blame each other for the lack of success in the achievement of self-set goals that disregard the other department's constraints and limitations (Goldratt & Cox, 1986). This counterproductive climate can be improved through EC-supported PI groups, for a successful PI group will solve problems by means of process redesign proposals whose implementation will typically involve collaboration among the members of the PI group. Moreover, process redesign proposals are reached through group consensus, a process that itself requires collaboration. The building of a more collaborative work environment fostered by EC-supported PI groups is illustrated by this comment from the leader of a PI group that involved two conflicting departments, made in an unstructured interview after the group was concluded:

> *[one of the members of the other department] had been avoiding greeting or talking to me...probably because of my complaints about lab problems...after this [PI] group, though, our relationship improved considerably...we work more as a team now than before.*

On the other hand, a different group member was of the opinion that EC support can cause interdepartmental conflicts to escalate, as group members are more likely to be more candid in their criticisms, often to the point of being downright blunt, when interacting through the EC medium - a phenomenon generally called "flaming" and attributed to the lack of social moderation in computer-mediated communication in general (Sproull & Kiesler, 1986, 1991). That member made the following comments about his electronic postings addressed to another member. The other member held a more senior position than he in the organization, and had recently aired critical comments about his performance in front of some of his colleagues.

> *...I told him I didn't like it, straight off...Sometimes [the other member's EC contributions] get more rough and abrupt and of course I can't reply to him face-to-face. He can put me down...I don't want to face him and he would probably want to face me to [put] me down.*

The perceptions outlined in this section indicate that EC support is likely to reduce interdepartmental conflict obstacles to the formation of PI groups. Whether this is inherently positive, though, is another matter. For example, if EC support fosters communication between conflicting departments, but that communication leads to escalation of the conflict, EC support may be doing more harm than good. Some of the evidence presented here partially supports previous research findings that indicate that computer mediation increases group conflict (Kiesler, Siege, & McGuire, 1984; Easterbrook et al., 1993). However, some of the individual experiences reported in this section indicate that interdepartmental conflicts can be solved, and the relationship between departments considerably improved, through EC-supported PI groups. This seemingly contradictory result can be explained by differences in the way individuals handle conflict, which can, in our view, be shaped by social and financial rewards, changes in the management paradigm, and staff education on how to effectively use EC to support PI group interaction.

EC Support Effects on Individual Learning

Process teams often encompass staff housed in different departments. This occurs because, as discussed previously, different staff are typically grouped according to expertise, rather than involvement in the execution of specific processes (Hammer & Champy, 1993). In this context, knowledge communication is an essential part of team learning. Without knowledge communication, it is impossible to build shared meaning within teams, and is therefore difficult to build team alignment - that is, it is difficult to enhance the team's capability of thinking and acting with a sense of unity. Team alignment requires team members to "know each other's hearts and minds" (Senge, Roberts, Ross, Smith & Kleiner, 1994, p. 352), that is, to share individual knowledge (e.g. beliefs and mental models) relevant to the effective accomplishment of their interrelated functional activities.

The empirical literature on asynchronous e-communication technologies reports a number of failures of these technologies to effectively support knowledge communication between interdepartmental groups, particularly because of the ambiguity that the electronic medium adds to the communication (Rogers, 1992), social norms and reward systems adopted by organizations that can themselves be obstacles to knowledge sharing (Orlikowski, 1992), and the disparity of benefits between those who have to do extra work because of the introduction of the e-communication system and those who do not (Grudin, 1994). Moderately positive results have been found concerning the support that asynchronous e-communication technologies can provide to the building of organizational knowledge repositories (Ackerman, 1994; Kock & McQueen, 1995).

Given the results summarized above, which suggest grim expectations regarding EC support to interdepartmental knowledge communication in the context of PI groups, interview respondent's perceptions in our study were surprisingly positive overall. When asked whether EC support increased or decreased individual socio-technical learning in PI groups, i.e., learning about processes and social norms in the organization, structured interview respondents' answers were distributed as shown in Table 4.

When asked to explain their answer, two main explanations were given by the respondents who were of the opinion that EC support increases socio-technical learning in PI groups. Those explanations were:

(1)   that EC support makes group members interact in a more sincere way, letting other group members know what their opinions are about other staff, process design, and process performance (5 respondents); and

(2)   that EC support encourages members to write more thought-out contributions because of the higher perceived ambiguity inherent in the communication medium used (5 respondents).

The main explanation for the perceived reduction in sociotechnical learning given by respondents (two respondents perceived this reduction, as shown in Table 4) was the lack of immediate feedback fostered by the almost exclusive use in most groups of EC as their communication medium. This lack of immediate feedback was perceived as increasing ambiguity, especially in the process analysis stage of PI groups where a relatively large amount of process-related knowledge and information have to be assimilated by the group members. The following comment from a senior manager regarding his PI group illustrates this point:

I think that groups dealing with complex issues will find [EC] a poor medium. For example, I could not understand what [a member of my group] meant by...nor the reply by [another member]...However, for [PI groups dealing with] simple problems, such as the lack of feedback on computer support job status, [EC] is great!

Interestingly, when asked whether the EC medium would negatively affect group risk taking, that senior manager replied negatively - i.e., that group risk taking is not directly affected by EC support. He made it clear, however, that the exclusive use of the EC medium would certainly increase ambiguity when complex issues were discussed, which could in consequence affect commitment towards process redesign proposals. This could indirectly reduce the confidence of groups to take risks. According to this senior manager, group members would not own the group outcome if they did not understand

Table 4: Distribution of answers from 18 respondents (Question: Did EC support increase or reduce your individual learning from participating in your PI group?)

Answer	Respondents	Percentage
Increased	12	67
Reduced	2	11
Had no effect	3	16
Do not know	1	6

completely the issues discussed, and therefore group agreement on risky process redesign decisions (e.g., decisions that involve high capital investment) would be compromised.

The findings above suggest that EC support influences both positively and negatively individual learning in PI groups. However, the higher proportion of respondents who thought that EC support increases, rather than decreases, individual learning suggests that the positive effects of EC support may offset the negative effects.

The main reason for the decrease in individual learning, according to the respondents, was the higher conversational ambiguity caused by the EC medium, which can be reduced by group members improving the clarity of their electronic contributions. However, a higher quality of electronic contributions was one of the reasons why respondents thought EC support increases individual learning. These two general perceptions point to message clarity as a likely moderating factor in the impact of EC support on individual learning. Our participant observation suggests that message clarity can be increased by group members following simple guidelines, such as defining unclear terms used in electronic messages in the body of those messages, avoiding ambiguous sentences, and explaining the rationale behind statements and decisions.

CONCLUSION AND IMPLICATIONS

Overall, EC support seems to have a positive impact on knowledge dissemination in organizations when used in combination with a group methodology for PI. In this study, the PI group methodology used was MetaProi (Kock, 1995), which comprises a set of activities (i.e., a process), guidelines, and a graphical tool to be used by PI groups. EC support effects on PI groups can be summarized as: (a) a reduction of the influence of distance and other physical obstacles to the participation of members from different departments in PI groups, and of the disruption that group discussions are likely to cause for individual group members, particularly when these members are from different departments; (b) a reduction of interdepartmental conflict obstacles to the formation of PI groups; and (c) an increase or decrease in individual learning in PI groups, depending on the complexity of the issues being discussed and the clarity of electronic contributions by members. EC support Effects (a) and (b) provide partial support for a positive answer to research Question (1) - Does EC support reduce the obstacles to departmental heterogeneity in PI groups? EC support Effect (c) provides partial support for a positive, but somewhat contingent, answer to research Question (2)

- Does EC support increase individual process-related and social learning in PI groups?

One of the implications of (a) is that EC support is likely to increase the number of possible interdepartmental PI groups per unit of time in organizations through the reduction of the influence of distance and physical obstacles to PI groups and of the disruption of member's functional activities. The potential increase in the number of groups per unit of time is furthered by the EC effect of making it more convenient for group members to participate in several groups at the same time. Indeed, participant observation and unstructured interviews in this study revealed that staff can effectively participate as members in at least three PI groups at a time. This, in turn, is likely to increase the speed and breadth of knowledge dissemination, which are described by Redding and Catalanello (1994, p. 27-28) as two of the three most relevant dimensions of organizational learning.

A direct implication of (b) is that EC support to PI groups can foster what Argyris (1977, 1992) christened "double-loop learning," since the EC medium increases sincerity and can thus decrease the likelihood that members will hide errors and organizational problems. On the other hand, if staff is not educated on how to effectively use the EC medium for communication (e.g., understand and use the sociological and communication characteristics of the medium in a positive way), EC support may increase conflict to a point where it may either be rejected as an appropriate communication medium for PI groups, or, worse, undermine the confidence of staff on the PI group as an appropriate tool for organizational learning and competitiveness improvement.

Two implications stem from (c). First, that EC support to knowledge dissemination can be more effective if either staff is educated on how to reduce ambiguity when interacting via the EC medium, or new EC systems that incorporate visual and sound aids for communication are used. Given that EC-mediated interaction today is mostly written, and thus very seldom relies on the use of non-verbal cues, much of the theory and techniques of written business communication can be of immediate use to reduce ambiguity in EC-mediated communication in PI groups. Second, that whenever complexity is perceived to be high in a PI group, the success of that group in disseminating knowledge will depend on the group's ability to combine face-to-face meetings with EC-supported discussion. Complexity symptoms are, for example, a high degree of perceived abstraction in the problems being discussed and a high number of misunderstandings in the initial stage of the group discussion. In groups using MetaProi or a similar group methodology, our study findings suggest that at least one stage - the analysis stage, where complexity is perceived to be high - could benefit from the use of face-to-face meetings.

ACKNOWLEDGMENTS

We would like to thank the staff at SMS and MQM who have participated in the process redesign groups described in this chapter. Special thanks are also due to Peter Grace, who reviewed and provided valuable comments to the manual that describes the methodology used by the groups - MetaProi.

REFERENCES

Ackerman, M. (1994). Augmenting the organizational memory: A field study of answer garden. In Furuta, R. and Neuwirth, C. (Eds.), *Proceedings of CSCW'94*, 243, 252. New York: The Association for Computing Machinery.

Argyris, C. (1977). Double-loop learning organizations. *Harvard Business Review*, 55(5), 115-125.

Argyris, C. (1992). *On Organizational Learning*. Cambridge, MA: Blackwell.

Boland, Jr., R. J., & Tenkasi, R. V. (1995). Perspective making and perspective taking in communities of knowing. *Organization Science*, 6(4), 350-372.

Casey, D. (1993). *Managing Learning in Organizations*. Buckingham, England: Open University Press.

CHE. (1995). The learning organization. *Chief Executive*, March, 101, 57-64.

Daft, R. L., & Lengel, R. H. (1986). Organizational information requirements, media richness and structural design. *Management Science*, 32(5), 554-571.

Davenport, T. H. (1993). *Process Innovation*. Boston, MA: Harvard Business Press.

Davenport, T. H., & Short, J. E. (1990). The new industrial engineering: Information technology and business process redesign. *Sloan Management Review*, 31(4), 11-27.

De Cock, C., & Hipkin, I. (1997). TQM and BPR: Beyond the myth. *Journal of Management Studies*, 34(5), 659-675.

Deming, W. E. (1986). Out of the crisis. *MIT*. Cambridge, MA: Center for Advanced Engineering Study.

Earl, M. J. (1994). The new and the old of business process redesign. *Journal of Strategic Information Systems*, 3(1), 5-22.

Easterbrook, S. M., Beck, E. E., Goodlet, J. S., Plowman, L., Sharples, M., & Wood, C. C. (1993). A survey of empirical studies of conflict. In Easterbrook, S. (Ed.), *CSCW: Cooperation or Conflict?* 1-68. New York: Springer-Verlag.

Goldratt, E. M., & Cox, J. (1986). *The Goal: A Process of Ongoing Improvement*. New York: North River Press.

Grudin, J. (1994). Eight challenges for developers. *Communications of the ACM*, 37(1), 93-105.

Hammer, M. (1990). Reengineering work: Don't automate, obliterate. *Harvard Business Review*, 68(4), 104-114.

Hammer, M., & Champy, J. (1993). *Reengineering the Corporation*. New York: Harper Business.

Hammer, M., & Stanton, S. A. (1995). *The Reengineering Revolution*. New York: HarperCollins.

Hammer, M., & Stanton, S. A. (1997). The reengineering revolution. *Government Executive*, 27(9), 2-8.

Harrington, H. J. (1991). *Business Process Improvement*. New York: McGraw-Hill.

Harrison, A. (1995). Business processes: Their nature and properties. In Burke, G. and Peppard, J. (Eds.), *Examining Business Process Reengineering*, 60-69. London: Kogan Page.

Hayek, F. A. (1996). The use of knowledge in society. In Myers, P. S. (Ed.), *Knowledge Management and Organizational Design*, 7-15. Boston, MA: Butterworth-Heinemann.

Hutchins, D. (1985). *Quality Circles Handbook*. London: Pitman.

Ishikawa, K. (1986). *Guide to Quality Control*. Tokyo: Asian Productivity Organisation.

Juran, J. (1989). *Juran on Leadership for Quality*. New York: The Free Press.

Kiesler, S., Siege, J. and McGuire, T. W. (1984). Social and psychological aspects of computer-mediated communication. *American Psychologist*, 39(10), 1123-1134.

Kock, N. (1995). *MetaProi: A Group Process for Business Process Improvement*, Project Report GP-G-1995-R5, Dept. of Management Systems, University of Waikato, Hamilton, New Zealand.

Kock, N. (1999). *Process Improvement and Organizational Learning: The Role of Collaboration Technologies*. Hershey, PA: Idea Group Publishing.

Kock, N., & Corner, J. L. (1996). *An Empirical Study of the Nature of Data, Information and Knowledge Exchanges in Organisations*, Research Report No. 1996-7, Dept. of Management Systems, University of Waikato, Hamilton, New Zealand.

Kock, N., & McQueen, R. J. (1995). Integrating groupware technology into a business process improvement framework. *Information Technology & People*, 8(4), 19-34.

Kock, N., & McQueen, R. J. (1997). A field study of effects of asynchronous groupware support on process improvement groups. *Journal of Information Technology*, 12(4), 245-259.

Kock, N., McQueen, R. J., & Baker, M. (1996). Learning and process improvement in knowledge organisations: A critical analysis of four contemporary myths. *The Learning Organization*, 3(1), 31-41.

Kock, N., McQueen, R. J., & Fernandes, C. T. (1995). Information systems research in organisations: An action research approach. *Brazilian Journal of Contemporary Management*, 1(4), 155-175.

Markus, M. L. (1992). Asynchronous technologies in small face-to-face groups. *Information Technology & People*, 6(1), 29-48.

Miles, M. B., & Huberman, A. M. (1994). *Qualitative Data Analysis: An Expanded Sourcebook*. London: Sage Publications..

Nevis, E. C., DiBella, A. J., & Gould, J. M. (1995). Understanding organisations as learning systems. *Sloan Management Review*, Winter, 73-85.

Orlikowski, W. J. (1992). Learning from notes: Organizational issues in groupware implementation. In Turner, J. and Kraut, R. (Eds.), *Proceedings of CSCW'92 Conference*, 362-369. New York: The Association for Computing Machinery.

Ould, M. A. (1995). *Business Processes: Modelling and Analysis for Re-engineering and Improvement*. Chichester, England: John Wiley & Sons.

Peters, J. (1996). A learning organisation's syllabus. *The Learning Organization*, 3(1), 4-10.

Redding, J. C., & Catalanello, R. F. (1994). *Strategic Readiness: The Making of the Learning Organization*. San Francisco, CA: Jossey-Bass.

Revans, R. (1991). Getting mixed up with others? In Collins, C. and Chippendale, P. (Eds.), *Proceedings of The First World Congress on Action Research*, 2, 157-194. Sunnybank Hills, Queensland, Australia: Acorn.

Robson, M. (1988). *Quality Circles: A Practical Guide*. Aldershot, UK: Gower.

Rogers, Y. (1992). Ghosts in the network: Distributed troubleshooting in a shared working environment. In Turner, J. and Kraut, R. (Eds), *Proceedings of CSCW'92 Conference*, 346-355. New York: The Association for Computing Machinery.

Senge, P. M., Roberts, C., Ross, R. B., Smith, B. J., & Kleiner, A. (1994). *The Fifth Discipline Fieldbook*. London: Nicholas Brealey.

Sproull, L., & Kiesler, S. (1986). Reducing social context cues: Electronic mail in organizational communication. *Management Science*, 32(1), 1492-1512.

Sproull, L., & Kiesler, S. (1991). Computers, networks and work. *Scientific American*, 265(3), 84-91.

Susman G. I., & Evered, R. D. (1978). An assessment of the scientific merits of action research. *Administrative Science Quarterly*, 23(4), 582-603.

Walton, M. (1989). *The Deming Management Method*. London: Mercury.

Chapter VIII

A Strategic Systems Perspective of Organizational Learning: Development of a Process Model Linking Theory and Practice

Olivia Ernst Neece
The Jet Propulsion Laboratory,
California Institute of Technology, USA

Organizational learning is an "umbrella" term that connects a variety of topics including: learning curves, organizational memory, organizational forgetting, knowledge transfer, knowledge sharing, knowledge assets, dynamic capabilities, knowledge management, and knowledge creation. This chapter will review some of these theories and extend Huber's taxonomy of organizational learning literature. Several systemic theories of learning organizations and knowledge-based organizations are discussed and then the literature is linked to a process model of learning. In conclusion, implications are evoked for further research at a variety of organizations toward a generalizable theory of innovative environments and their organizational learning practices. A short case study of the Jet Propulsion Laboratory, its organizational learning based policies, and how these policies relate to the process model is included.

The wide range of *organizational learning* literature and the related knowledge management and creation literatures offers a variety of conceptual frameworks for the study of the actual process of learning within an organization. This chapter ties these theories together via a process model of how innovative organizations learn and how knowledge becomes embedded in and integrated with the *knowledge creation* process of an organization. This innovative knowledge creation process is the key to the health and future success of organizations in a variety of technical fields (e.g., biochemical, telecommunications, technology). It is important for the academic literature to answer the questions posed by practitioners in their development of *knowledge management* processes. Important questions that can be posed include:

- How can firms develop knowledge management and learning systems that capture, develop, organize and utilize the knowledge and learning that takes place throughout the organization?
- How can firms develop a culture that encourages knowledge sharing and utilization of knowledge from a wide variety of resources?
- Since an organization is made up of individuals, what creates a culture of learning so that one can integrate individual learning into a "learning organization?"

These questions can only be understood and answered through the development of a process model of how organizations learn. Organizational learning theory traces its roots to psychological studies of individual learning curves. Learning curves helped explain the connection between improvement in efficiency within an organization and the learning that takes place over time. Learning curve studies have covered all levels of analysis. At the individual level of analysis, learning has been found during experimental studies of task completion: a reduction in errors was noted as individuals gained experience in completing tasks (Ebbinghaus, 1964, originally published in 1885; Thorndike, 1898). At the group level of analysis, learning curves were found for group performance and communication networks. (Guetzkow & Simon, 1955). At the organizational level of analysis, in determining why some firms are more productive than others, researchers have studied the measurement of learning curves in relation to organizational learning rates (Adler & Clark, 1991; Argote, Beckman, & Epple, 1990; Hayes & Clark, 1986; Ingram & Baum, 1997; Lester & McCabe, 1993; Lieberman, 1984). Unfortunately, learning curves alone cannot explain the learning process in innovative organizations. Most learning curve experiments are devoted to routine or circumscribed tasks. *Innovation*, on the other hand, relates to a more chaotic or iterative process. In fact, an orderly approach to innovation may be counterproductive. For example, in an organized approach, one may contact known resources and look for known solutions, thus missing solutions that may spring from serendipitous connections to other industries, domains, or individuals (Majchrzak, Neece, & Cooper, 2001a). By limiting access to information and knowledge through a restrictive approach, some of these unforeseen associations may be missed.

Organization memory in its earliest form was practiced by the railroads in terms of the dispersion of timetables, procedures, and rules. Later, through the practice of "scientific management," managers attempted to capture individual procedures to produce standard work practice and reporting systems that could be laid down in manuals (Taylor, 1911). These organization memory systems included both data and information. Similarity to current practice can be seen in organized training, templates, written procedures and best practices. While this type of practice may be lauded due to increased efficiency, Japanese assembly line practice and the early work of Deming (1986) found that when workers varied from these practices, they often found creative methods leading to productivity improvement.

Senge (1990) discusses the evolution of interest in organization learning as traced by Weston (1993). Weston notes that theories of organization learning commenced with Don Michael's book *On Learning to Plan—and Planning to Learn* (Michael, 1973). In actuality, early evidence of interest in organizational learning is found in Herbert Simon's work as well as that of Cyert and March (1992). The earliest mention of "organizational memory" relating to the notion of "knowledge" can be found in Herbert Simon's (1957, originally written in 1945) *Administrative Behavior, 2nd Edition.* Simon comments,

> Since an organization is not an organism the only memory it possesses, in the proper sense of the term, is the collective memory of its participants. This is insufficient for organization purposes, first, because what is in one man's mind is not necessarily available to other members of the organization, and, second, because when an individual leaves an organization the organization loses that part of its 'memory'. Hence organizations, to a far greater extent than individuals, need artificial "memories." (p.166)

Thus, Simon begins to consider the need for documents, databases and repositories where knowledge may be retained. This knowledge may be searched and accessed as needed to combine with other knowledge for knowledge creation.

Other early interest in "organization learning" is found in Cyert and March's seminal volume, *Behavioral Theory of the Firm* (1992). The firm is described as an "adaptive system" with three sub-theories of decision making; organizational goals, expectations and choice. In addition, they discuss four relational concepts: (1) quasi resolution of conflict, (2) uncertainty avoidance, (3) problemistic search, and (4) organizational learning. (p.116)

However, the "organizational learning" discussed by Cyert and March relates to a structural, decision-making construct. Rather than center upon the structural construct, the concern of this treatise is the individual's adaptation of goals, attention rules and search rules, and "organizational memory" in terms of precedents of structure and decision-making rules.

If we start with the consideration of the firm as an "adaptive organism," whose adaptation is based upon the decisions and behavior of individuals, we can delve deeper into the adaptation of the organization through team and individual decision-making and learning processes. Decision-making and learning are driven by the knowledge acquisition and knowledge creation of both individuals and teams comprised of individuals. Thus, we can discuss these varied learning and knowledge theories in conjunction with the development of a process model for how people within organizations learn. Several theoretical models of organizational behavior can be viewed from a systems perspective. The Senge (1990) model of five disciplines is a series of behavioral factors that are enablers of organizational learning. Many of Senge's five disciplines overlap with and can be compared to the enablers discussed by Von Krogh, Ichijo and Nonaka (2000), Maciariello (2000), Ghoshal and Bartlett (1997), and others. While these enablers serve to assist organizations in their strategic planning and process development, I propose a direct linkage of the organizational learning constructs to an action model.

I offer here a discussion of the taxonomy of the organizational learning literature. Several streams of this literature lead to the development of a process model of how organizations learn. I propose the linking of the literature to a theoretical model of how organizations learn. I propose that this theoretical process model of learning behavior can be linked to the strategy and structure of many innovative organizations. Theoretically, the strategy and structure of an organization will enable certain learning behaviors (Senge, 1990a; Von Krogh, Ichijo, & Nonaka, 2000). The practical implications for the successful implementation of learning enablers in the context of an innovative firm are considered. Suggestions for testing of the model are discussed in terms of future research.

LITERATURE REVIEW

Learning Theories and the Concept of Organizational Learning

An ongoing debate between researchers concerns whether *learning* should be defined in terms of changes in knowledge or changes in behavior. At the individual level, learning has been defined: as changes in individual behavior (Hilgard & Bower, 1975), changes in "behavior potentiality" as a result of prior experience (Houston, 1986), and as a change in either behavior or knowledge brought about by practice or experience (Wingfield, 1979). At the organizational level, learning has been defined both as changes in knowledge (Duncan & Weiss, 1979; Fiol & Lyles, 1985), and in terms of a "range of potential behaviors" (Huber, 1991). The definition of organizational learning adopted here is inclusive of both the knowledge and the behavioral aspects of learning. Organizational learning, in this broader context, is inclusive of a large number of concepts (Huber, 1991). According to Argote (1999):

> Agreement has not emerged about exactly what is meant by the concept of organizational learning. In my view, the concept of organizational learning is likely to remain an "umbrella" concept for many related concepts. (p.13)

Some theorists have limited the definition of organizational learning to learning that enhances organizational effectiveness (Argyris & Schon, 1978; Fiol et al., 1985). However, learning can also be of a negative nature; for example, one can "learn" bad habits or accept inaccurate information. Sometimes positive learning from one venue fails to increase organizational effectiveness in another venue. The author agrees with Huber (1991) that a broader definition of learning should be accepted including both positive and negative learning. Further, as suggested by March and Olsen (1979), learning need not be conscious or planned:

> It seems important to highlight that learning need not be conscious or intentional, as is apparent in discussions of operant conditioning in humans and other animals (Bower & Hilgard, 1981) and in case studies of organizational learning.

> It is also apparent that learning evolves through a variety of channels, both internal and external to the organization.

The term "organizational learning" has been used to discuss a multitude of theories at the organizational level of analysis and the group level of analysis. These theories include: organizational memory and organizational forgetting (Anand, Manz, & Glick, 1998; Argote, 1999; Moorman & Miner, 1998; Tuomi, 1999; Walsh & Ungson, 1991), knowledge transfer and knowledge sharing (Argote & Ingram, 2000; Bresman, Birkinshaw, & Nobel, 1999; Darr & Kurtzberg, 2000; Gilbert & Cordey-Hayes, 1996; Grant, 1996; Majchrzak, Rice, Malhotra, King, & Ba, 2000; Szulanski, 2000; Zaltman, Duncan, & Holbek, 1973). Additional theoretical concepts that are related to this line of inquiry include: knowledge management (Adler, 1988; Alavi & Leidner, 1998;

Davenport & Prusak, 1998; Hedlund, 1994; Sanchez & Mahoney, 1996), knowledge reuse (Hansen, Nohria, & Tierney, 1999; Majchrzak et al., 2001a; Markus, 2001), and knowledge creation (Alavi & Leidner, 1999; Davenport & Prusak, 1998; Grant, 1996; Hedlund, 1994; Kuwada, 1998; Matusik & Hill, 1998; Nonaka, 1994; Nonaka & Takeuchi, 1995; Von Krogh et al., 2000). The knowledge worker who is charged with acquiring, sharing, managing, reusing and creating knowledge has been the focal point many studies (Bartlett & Ghoshal, 1995; Drucker, 1979, 1999; Miller, 1977). This "knowledge worker's" productivity is often based upon how organizations utilize knowledge (Drucker, 1991; Gray & Jurison, 1995; Gregerman, 1981; Hayes & Clark, 1985; Heskett, Sasser, & Schlesinger, 1997; Iansiti & West, 1997; Jurison, 1995; Maciariello, 2000; Pfeffer, 1994; Porter, 1996).

Due to the breadth and depth of research studies, theoretical treatises, and popular press coverage continuing from 1963 to the present, we may assume that the learning organization cannot be considered a "management fad." It is one of the fundamental theories of management. Organizational learning has strategic implications for value creation, so critical for organizations in today's high-speed economy. Organizational learning, knowledge acquisition, sharing and creation are methods for firms to gain advantage through merger and acquisition activity as well as strategic alliances. Thus, firms that are able to attract, retain, and enable these learning activities can be in a better position to add value through acquisitions and alliances of all kinds.

Organizational Learning Taxonomy: Constructs, Sub-constructs and Processes

Organizing the literatures under the organizational learning "umbrella" assists in assessing their impact on various organizational activities and processes. Huber (1991), in his leading work on the literatures of organizational learning discusses four main constructs that can be linked to knowledge processes: (I) *knowledge acquisition* (acquire and capture knowledge), (II) *information distribution* (distribute knowledge), (III) *information interpretation* (analyze knowledge), and (IV) *organizational memory* (store and organize knowledge). The following is a discussion of the organizational learning literature within the context of Huber's taxonomy (Huber, 1991). I summarize here these constructs, update this literature review, and augment this taxonomy by adding a fifth construct, (V) *knowledge creation and innovation*, related to knowledge reuse (adopt and adapt) and knowledge creation (invent). It is important to keep in mind that these categories are merely representational and that the literature can often be listed in more than one category. For that matter, much of the organizational learning literature is, by its very nature, multidisciplinary. Thus, the subject of organizational learning, knowledge and innovation appear in diverse literature sources such as strategy, organizational behavior, psychology, sociology, economics, information systems, and engineering management. It has been found that papers in each discipline often do not include citations from other disciplines, thereby losing a more comprehensive view of research that relates to the subject at hand. I urge a more multidisciplinary view, gathering citations from many of these diverse literatures in order to shed light on studies that may otherwise be overlooked.

Knowledge Acquisition

The *knowledge acquisition* construct, in accordance with Huber's taxonomy, is organized around five subconstructs. The first subconstruct, *congenital learning*, includes institutionalized knowledge based on societal expectations (Meyer & Rowan, 1977) and knowledge inherited from the organization's founders (Schein, 1985; Stinchcombe, 1965). The second subconstruct is *experiential learning*, including five subprocesses:

1) *Organizational experiments* both planned (Staw, 1977; Wildavsky, 1972) and in formal analyses of "natural" experiments (Huber, Ullman, & Leifer, 1979) assist organizations in determining the results of group processes.

2) *Organizational self-appraisal,* including action research (where data about concerns and problems is collected and shared with organizational members) has been found to assist change (Argyris, 1983; Lewin, 1947).

3) *Experimenting organizations*, the process of an organization frequently, and sometimes continuously, changing structures, processes, domains, and even goals (Hedberg, Nystrom, & Starbuck, 1976; Starbuck, 1984), encourages organizational flexibility and survival in unpredictable environments (Hedberg, Nystrom, & Starbuck, 1977). Levitt and March (1988) note that this notion of experimentation–constantly changing organizational structures–may likely to lead to "random drift," and not organizational improvement (Lounamaa & March, 1987). Such constant change has been noted at Nortel Networks, where individuals may have as many as three new supervisors and positions within a year due to job rotation, transfer, and organizational restructuring (Neece, 2000). Longitudinal studies of such firms are needed to discover the long-term implications to both the organization and the people in firms employing such strategies.

4) *Unintentional or unsystematic learning* (March et al., 1979) where group learning is often found to be haphazard and multifaceted (Cangelosi & Dill, 1965).

5)   *Experience-based learning* including *learning curves*, *learning before doing* and *learning by doing*. Learning curves indicate that errors are reduced as individuals (or firms) gain experience. However, errors were found to decrease at a decreasing rate (Leavitt, 1967). Experience curves have also been utilized to measure outcomes at the organization level of analysis, for example, quality, as measured by complaints or defects per unit (Argote & McGrath, 1993) and service timeliness, as measured by late delivery of products per unit (Argote & Darr, in press). It is important to separate learning effects from the productivity gains of other factors, such as economies of scale (Argote, 1999; Rapping, 1965).

A study of *learning before doing* and *learning by doing* (Pisano, 1994) found that learning before doing (planning) had the most beneficial impact on firms in fields with a well-understood knowledge base. Learning by doing (practice, experimental approach) was found to be a more advantageous approach in an organization where the underlying knowledge base is not as well known (Eisenhardt & Tabrizi, 1995; Pisano, 1994; von Hippel & Tyre, 1995).

A third subconstruct, *vicarious learning*, includes "corporate intelligence," the study of competitor's strategies (Fuld, 1988; Porter, 1980), and diffusion theory or learning through imitation and knowledge transfer (Abrahamson & Rosenkopf, 1997; Attewell, 1992; Leonard-Barton, 1990; Rogers, 1983; Teece, 1984).

The fourth subconstruct, *grafting*, is acquiring the knowledge through hiring or through mergers and acquisitions (Ellsworth, 1999; Lyles, 1988). Matusik and Hill note,

> The relationship between organizational knowledge and competitive advantage is moderated by the firm's ability to integrate and apply knowledge... Because grafting knowledge from the outside environment does not take place automatically, a firm needs mechanisms to bring public knowledge in, to transmit this knowledge within the firm, and to fuse the new knowledge with existing stocks of knowledge. (p.685)

Another method of grafting is the use of outsourcing. It has been argued that the use of outsourcing improves knowledge flows and flexibility (Carr, 1999). Matusik and Hill (1998) note that while contingent workers can bring public knowledge in, they can also disseminate valuable private knowledge into the external environment accelerating the decay of competitive advantage. The use of contingent workers can drive down costs in a cost competitive environment, but can bleed critical knowledge from the firm and cripple the firm due to the organization's failure to build its critical competencies and stocks of knowledge.

The fifth subconstruct of knowledge acquisition is *searching & noticing.* These processes include:

1) *Scanning* is the broad sensing of the organization's external environment for non-routine cues to relevant changes (Daft & Lengel, 1986). In addition, boundary-spanning individuals may provide relevant scanning information (Davenport et al., 1998; Majchrzak, Neece, & Cooper, 2001b).

2) *Focused search* involves a deep search into both internal and external sources, focused on the narrow needs of the particular problem (Cyert & March, 1963, 1992). Search prompting signals must be from multiple sources and insistent in order to gain attention (Ansoff, 1975). It must be apparent to the searcher that the present alternatives do not satisfy the goals (Feldman & Kanter, 1965). Therefore, searching is prompted by a number of factors including the perception of a performance gap and the risk reduction requirements of a project (Majchrzak et al., 2001a).

3) *Performance monitoring* pertains to searching the organization for knowledge and cues as to specific learning situations and behavioral conditions (Mintzberg, 1975). Several researchers have analyzed when and how organizations use or do not use feedback to improve their performance (Staw & Ross, 1987; Wildavsky, 1972).

4) *Noticing* refers to the unintended acquisition of information about the internal organization or external environment (Starbuck & Milliken, 1988).

Construct II: Information Distribution

The second construct is *information distribution*, the dissemination of knowledge and information throughout the organization. According to Huber (1991), "...organizations often do not know what they know." (p. 100).

Huber (1982) and Huber and Daft (1987) studied factors relating to the probability of routing of information from the transferor to the receiver: relevance of the information, power and status, costs, workload, previous relationships, rewards or penalties. The probability of delay in the routing of the information to the receiver is related to the workload of the transferor, the number of sequential links to the receiver, and the timeliness of the information (Argyris et al., 1978; Davenport et al., 1998; Senge, 1990a). The greater the workload and the higher the degree of separation, the greater the opportunity for distortion. In addition, the probability and extent of information distortion is related to the transferor's belief that distorting the information will be in his/ her self-interest and that distortion will not cause the transferor to suffer a penalty. One may find, in some firms, exhibits of "knowledge monopolies," where the knower explicitly withholds information in order to maintain or enhance the perception of his/her own value. This knowledge-hoarding behavior has been observed in diverse firms including those involved with manufacturing, R & D, and service organizations. Add to this additional conflicts caused by the discretion in the information format and the difference between the actual information and the information desired or expected by the receiver (Huber, 1982; Huber & Daft, 1987).

Another element of distribution, not included in Huber's taxonomy is the broad field of knowledge management. Huber includes some knowledge management citations under the construct of "organizational memory," although that construct defines only a small portion of this literature. The knowledge management literature is broad and multidisciplinary. It has proliferated, in recent years, and has spread through numerous disciplines including information technology, organizational behavior, business policy and strategy, organizational management theory, economics and organizational cognition. I cover the knowledge management literature later under an additional construct.

Construct III: Information Interpretation

The third construct is *information interpretation*, defined by Daft and Weick (1984) as "the process through which information is given meaning," (p.294), as well as "the process of translating events and developing shared understandings and conceptual schemes." (p.286) However, a variety of interpretations may lead to additional learning opportunities (Huber, 1991). This interpretation of new information is affected by three subconstructs:

1)   *Cognitive maps and framing* are the beliefs, mental models or frame of reference possessed by the individual, the group and the organization. From Roger Clark's (1996) theory of language use, we know that veridicality of communication is more likely when both parties to the communication have a "common ground," defined as the knowledge, beliefs, and suppositions that both parties believe they share about the joint activity. Common ground evolves as presuppositions are created and destroyed, through interactions that include assertions, promises, questions, apologies, requests, declarations, and responses (Clark, 1996). Thus, common ground divides into three parts: initial common ground, an understanding of the current state of the joint activity, and an understanding of the events that participants presuppose have occurred that have led to the current state (Majchrzak & Beath, 2001). Interpretations of information are dependent upon the way individuals diverge and converge

in relation to the mental models of the group (Ireland, Hitt, Bettis, & DePorras, 1987; Walker, 1985). How information is framed also affects its shared meanings (Tversky & Kahneman, 1985). For example, when a proposal format has been adopted by the organization and the adherence to this format is framed as a policy to one unit and as a suggestion to a second unit, the urgency will not be understood by the second unit.

2) *Media richness* is the extent to which common ground is established during knowledge transfer (Clark, 1996; Clark & Brennan, 1993). Olson and Olson (1998) found that collaborative technologies that support conversation, work objects being linked to conversations, and the creation of shared objectives were more likely to lead to common ground. Research supports the theory that timely feedback will assist in the process (Daft & Huber, 1987; Olson et al., 1998). Some theorists argue that face-to-face interaction is superior for developing understanding (Clark, 1996; Olson et al., 1998), and that face-to-face interactions should be increased (Anand, Manz & Glick, 1998; Bresman et al., 1999). Others believe that it is necessary for groups to share tacit knowledge face-to-face prior to using other media (Davenport et al., 1998; Olivera & Argote, 2000). Virtual work can proceed effectively following these collocated meetings. Other research studies have found that face-to-face interactions actually distract the participants (Short, Williams, & Christie, 1976), and may lead to less effective outcomes (Culnan & Markus, 1987). It has also been asserted that virtual groups are actually more effective due to their dependence upon the structure and discipline of regular meetings and electronic documentation that is inclusive of all participants (Majchrzak et al., 2000). Regardless of this debate concerning the preference for face-to-face communication, the author concurs with Duarte and Snyder (1999) that:

> People who lead and work in virtual teams need to have special skills, including an understanding of human dynamics, knowledge of how to manage across functional areas and national cultures, and the ability to use communication technologies as their primary means of communicating and collaborating.

It is appropriate to note that shared interpretation is not required for groups or organizations to agree upon action (Donnellon, Gray, & Bougon, 1986; Weick, 1979). Discussion and debate will lead to decisions, preferably based upon consensus. In fact, diversity in the group may bring forth issues that would be overlooked in groups where individuals share similar attitudes and beliefs.

3) *Information overload* is the proliferation of more data than can be processed by the individual or the organization. The interpretation of information across organizational units or within the same group is less effective if the information to be processed exceeds the limits of the individual or the group's ability to process the information (Driver & Steufert, 1969; Meier, 1963). Certainly, one of the key problems facing managers and workers today is not lack of data — but too much data and a lack of systems that transform data into decision-making capabilities or strategic advantage (Jinag, 1995). When multiple people push information, important messages get lost in the noise and information overload develops. A "well-architected Intranet" is amenable to easy recovery of information when needed. Sparing use of the most critical push information will minimize information overload (Alavi et al., 1999; Telleen, 1999).

    In discussion of information overload, Simon (1973) argued that in order to reduce information overload, organizations should be designed with a minimized need for information distribution among organizational units. This "design for informational autonomy" is rejected by most theorists today, as this reduction in information sharing and transfer across units would inhibit organizational learning (Huber, 1991; Sitkin, 1992). In fact, this type of design has been discredited since it leads to "information hoarding" (Argote, 1999; Davenport et al., 1998) and "organizational silos" (Bower & Hout, 1988; Day, 1994; Drucker, 1988).

4) *Unlearning (or organizational forgetting)* is "a process through which learners discard knowledge." Hedberg (1981) stresses the discarding of "obsolete and misleading knowledge" (p.18), implying that unlearning is functional and intentional. Use of the word "unlearning" implies a decrease in the range of potential behaviors or total information. Huber (1991) is concerned with the void that is created by the "unlearning" and the subsequent search for new knowledge in the vicinity of that which was unlearned (Cyert et al., 1963, 1992) or complications attributed to unlearning that is aversive to another area. However, there may be positive implications to unlearning, as it may open the way for new learning to take place (Huber, 1991). This is analogous to the notion that for organizational change to take place, an "unfreezing" occurs prior to change and following change, a refreezing process ensures the diffusion of the change throughout the organization (Lewin, 1947; Lewin, 1951; Schein, 1985).

    Argote (1999) discusses another, more negative aspect of "organizational forgetting" or "knowledge depreciation": "...if there is forgetting, forecasts of future production based on the classic learning curve will overestimate future production. Failure to achieve expected levels of productivity can lead to large problems for organizations" (p.36).

Such problems may include late deliveries, dissatisfied customers, financial penalties, and, in extreme cases, even organizational failure. One reason for knowledge depreciation is the loss of records, such as the Steinway blueprints for a discontinued piano (Lenehan, 1982). Another reason may be the inability to access archived records, such as certain data from an early NASA mission that has been archived on obsolete electronic media or the lost blueprints from the Saturn 5 Rocket. Similarly, where the media has decayed over time such as the information stored before 1979 by Landsat, the earth surveillance program (Marshal, 1989). Further, if information has not been documented through retrospective histories, lessons learned, or detailed recording of project specifications, activities, meetings and results, the details will soon be forgotten (Markus, Majchrzak, & Gasser, 2000).

The greatest problem leading to loss of organizational memory is employee turnover (Argote, 1999) through attrition, downsizing, retirement and loss. Depreciation arises not only through the loss of knowledge generators and integrators, but also the attrition of "gatekeepers" (Allen, 1977) who occupy key positions as a bridge in social networks (Burt, 1992; Krackhardt & Hanson, 1993). Gatekeepers hold positions at a variety of levels, secretarial and administrative staff, project managers or knowledge brokers who have held key positions in a variety of projects within the firm or in other organizations.

Construct IV: Organizational Memory

Variables that influence the successfulness of organizational memory are the firm's knowledge architecture planning as well as various human factors. Huber (1991) comments,

> ...the ongoing effectiveness of organizational memory includes; (1) membership attrition, (2) information distribution and organizational interpretation of information, (3) the norms and methods for storing information, and (4) the methods for locating and retrieving stored information. (p.105)

Membership attrition has the most deleterious effect upon organizational memory. While membership attrition in terms of organizational forgetting is discussed above, the literature on this subject is extremely broad and deep and cannot be fully covered in the space allotted here. Discussion of the importance of employee retention is covered under the "knowledge creation and innovation" construct. In addition, several human resource-centered strategic theories are examined here.

Much of organizational knowledge about the methodology, operations, or processes of an organization are "stored" in the form of routines, standard operating procedures and "scripts" (Argote, 1999; Gersick & Hackman, 1990; Mintzberg, 1975; Nelson & Winter, 1982; Winter, 1995). However, the knowledge-based theory of the firm suggests that a more secure and integrated method of storing and retrieving data, information and knowledge must be addressed. Storing and retrieving information includes both documentation of these routines, as well as storage and retrieval systems for both explicit and some types of tacit knowledge that have been transferred into a codifiable format. Many organizations are developing integrated Knowledge Management Systems (KMS). Alavi (1999) defines the knowledge management process:

> Knowledge management, then, refers to a systemic and organizationally specified process for acquiring, organizing and communicating both tacit and explicit knowledge of employees so that other employees may make use of it to be more effective and productive in their work. (p. 4)
>
> He continues to define knowledge management systems (KMS) as "information systems designed specifically to facilitate codification, collection, integration, and dissemination of organizational knowledge" (p.4).

A key driver for KMS is integrative technology architecture with a variety of technological tools. A typical knowledge management system involves a data (or knowledge) base, a cataloguing system, version control, document access control, a user-friendly search and navigation capability, and a variety of advanced features for communication and messaging such as email notification or commenting (Alavi et al., 1999; Davenport, Jarvenpaa, & Beers, 1996). "The need for seamless integration of the various tools in these three areas may lead to the dominance of the Internet or internet-based KMS architectures" (Alavi et al., 1999, p. 18).

Because knowledge management systems involve the cataloguing of knowledge for later reuse, most knowledge management systems today have been developed to enhance the efficiency of a work process. As such, documents are captured and catalogued to support likely known future reuses, such as consultant services or administrative templates (Davenport et al., 1996; Majchrzak et al., 2001a).

Construct V: Knowledge Creation and Knowledge Management

Knowledge creation models have been concerned with how tacit and explicit knowledge from individuals, groups, and the entire organizational entity are combined to generate process, product and technological innovation (Kogut & Zander, 1992). Kuwada (1998) describes the process of strategic learning as an inter-organizational ecological process, integrating various levels of learning in organizations and including processes of both strategic knowledge creation and strategic knowledge distillation.

Underlying this model is the debate concerning the sharp or blurred distinction between tacit and explicit components of knowledge. Nonaka and Takeuchi (1995) and Spender (1996) separate the tacit and explicit components of knowledge. Spender also separates knowledge by individual vs. collective knowledge, yielding four "Weberian ideal types," conscious, objectified, automatic and collective (p. 51), where every firm has a mix of all types.

An alternative view of knowledge transfer has been promoted that involves transforming tacit to explicit knowledge (Hedlund, 1994; Kogut et al., 1992; Sherman & Lacey, 1999). In contrast to the model of knowledge transfer in which tacit knowledge must be made explicit, Polanyi (1966) blurs the distinction between tacit and explicit knowledge, noting that there is a tacit component to all knowledge (Kogut et al., 1992; Teece, 1981). Even articulated knowledge is based upon an unarticulated (tacit) background including social practices that are internalized and cognitive in nature (Tsoukas, 1996). In an organization, the culture, routines, stories and the "invisible assets" of the organization are common repositories for this tacit knowledge (Harris, 1994; Itami, 1987; Nelson & Winter, 1982; Ouchi, 1980). Thus, the knowledge transfer process can be one of sharing stories and interpretations (Brown & Duguid, 1998; Snowden, 2000a, 2000b, 2000c) and sharing contexts of knowledge (Majchrzak et al., 2001a; Markus, 2001), rather than making knowledge codified and explicit.

1) Knowledge creation Models: Nonaka and Takeuchi (1995) propose a four-stage knowledge creation (i.e., transfer) model:
    a) Socialization: experiencing tacit knowledge through apprenticeship or training;
    b) Externalization or articulation: linking tacit knowledge with explicit knowledge and articulating knowledge to other team members;

c) Combination of different explicit ideas in a process of standardization such as a manual or knowledge management base; and

d) Internalization: extracting tacit knowledge from the newly created knowledge base, putting new knowledge to use, developing new routines and internalizing the changes.

Von Krogh, Ichijo and Nonaka (2000) provide a systems perspective of knowledge creation in their Knowledge Enabling and Creation: 5 x 5 grid. The five enablers include: (1) Instill a vision, (2) Manage conversations, (3) Mobilize knowledge activists, (4) Create the right context, and (5) Globalize local knowledge. The five creation steps include: (1) Sharing tacit knowledge, (2) Creating concepts, (3) Justifying concepts, (4) Building a prototype, and (5) Cross-leveling knowledge.

2)   Knowledge management: Formalized communication structures and teambuilding interventions that improve the ability of team members to transfer, capture, and make tacit knowledge explicit may be a source of sustained competitive advantage (Bresman et al., 1999; Sherman et al., 1999). Various human resource processes can be embedded that will instill a knowledge creation-enabled culture.

The knowledge transfer process may be enabled using many of the techniques discussed here. However, a key to the creativity process is the ability of an organization to combine both tacit and explicit knowledge. Knowledge can be recombined from both inward and outward sources (Kogut et al., 1992). Kogut and Zander (1992) note a circular connection between exploitation (use of internal knowledge) and exploration (invention, outward search). They state,

An important limitation to the capability of developing new skills is the opportunity (or potential) in the organizing principles and technologies for further exploitation. Eventually there are decreasing returns to a given technology or method of organizing and there, consequently, results an incentive to build new, but related skills. (p. 385)

Therefore, the organizational mentors (or knowledge intermediaries) should be continuously searching outside repositories and social networks in order to encourage and inspire new ideas and technologies.

Organizational Learning From a Strategic Systems Perspective

Huber's taxonomy is indeed comprehensive; however, additional categories are needed for inclusion of more multidisciplinary theories of the firm from a systems or strategic perspective. It is important to examine some of these theories in order to grasp a view of the learning organization as a whole. Two additional literatures shed light on the complexity of the firm. These are the resource-based and knowledge-based view and the learning organization from a systems perspective.

Resource-Based View and Knowledge-Based View of Organizations

As firms struggled to succeed against foreign competition and productivity rates slowed or declined in American firms in the late 1980s, interest turned to the competitive use of firm assets. According to Argote (1999), this interest may have driven the move toward a resource-based view of the firm (Barney, 1991; Henderson & Cockburn, 1994; Lippman & Rumelt, 1982; Nelson, 1991; Prahalad & Hamel, 1990). Several researchers have expanded the resource-based view to incorporate a knowledge-based view of the firm, including knowledge as a strategic asset (Dierickx & Cool, 1989; Grant, 1996; Spender, 1996; Teece, 1990; Teece, 1998; Winter, 1995). In this view, the value of knowledge assets is inherent in leveraging those assets for the development of strategic capabilities (Due, 1995; Hayek, 1989; Teece, 1990; Winter, 1987) including both value-added product development and enhanced process effectiveness.

A few of the more prominent examples of firms that have had great success through their utilization and maximization of knowledge are; Nucor (Drucker, 1994; Maciariello, 2000; Nobles & Redpath, 1997), 3M (Brand, 1998; Ghoshal & Bartlett, 1997; Lipman-Blumen & Leavitt, 1999; Thompson, Hochwarter, & Mathys, 1997), McKinsey (Dvorak, Dean, & Singer, 1994; Foster, 1986; Ghoshal et al., 1997; Halloran, 1993; Hansen et al., 1999; McKinsey, 1998), Lincoln Electric (Drucker, 1994; Maciariello, 1997, 2000; Pfeffer, 1994), and British Petroleum (Davenport et al., 1998; Prokesch, 1997). These and other case studies underscore the necessity for instituting policies that leverage knowledge through the four major knowledge management activities: capture, develop, organize and create (Doane et al., 1999).

It has been theorized that firms that effectively transfer knowledge, while preventing competitors from tapping into their knowledge resources, are more successful than those that do not effectively manage their knowledge resources (Lippman et al., 1982; Winter, 1995; Zander & Kogut, 1995). The problem is actually more complex, as Szulanski (2000) comments, "...mere possession of potentially valuable knowledge somewhere within the organization does not necessarily mean that other parts of the organization benefit from that knowledge" (p. 31).

Internal knowledge transfer is difficult and is not a fluid process. Rather, the knowledge transfer process is inherently "sticky" (Szulanski, 1994; von

Hippel, 1994). Stickiness refers to the difficulty of transferring knowledge between or among individuals, organizations or groups. One reason for the stickiness is the notion of the distributed nature of knowledge. A firm faces the problem that knowledge is not concentrated or integrated, cannot be known by a single mind, and is disbursed into small "bits of incomplete and contradictory knowledge that all the separate individuals possess" (Hayek, 1945). Further, a firm is faced with radical uncertainty such that a firm's knowledge is inherently indeterminate. Individuals cannot know what they need to know in ex ante (Tsoukas, 1996).

In addition, the firm is embedded in a larger and continually changing environmental context (Granovetter, 1992; Spender, 1989). Thus, knowledge in the organization is constantly filtered through the activities of the firm and through the socialized role-expectations and experiences of the organization's members. The firm has some control, to a greater or lesser extent, over the normative expectations of members within the context of their work environment. However, the firm has no control over past social experiences outside the firm's boundaries (Tsoukas, 1996). The relationship between a member's role as a part of the firm and his/her role as a part of other organizations may produce internal conflict (Barnard, 1938; Griffiths, 1996; Senge, 1990a; Senge, 1990b). Inevitably, there will be tension between role-based expectations, the disposition of members, and the social interactions within and between groups of individuals. As individuals apply their unique experience and perspective to situations, creative solutions can develop if the expectation of management is that firms are involved in an emergent knowledge process (Markus et al., 2000; Senge, 1990a, 1990b).

ORGANIZATIONAL LEARNING PROCESS MODEL

Several approaches to learning in the organization and to learning of groups within the organization have taken a micro-view of the organization's purpose, values, and goals as they relate to firm structure. The structure inevitably drives the organizational policies resulting in the behaviors of groups and individuals within the firm. Many of these approaches have been presented in terms of strategic planning and human resource policies that lead to the leveraging of individual and group learning (Ghoshal et al., 1997; Heskett et al., 1997; Maciariello, 2000; Pfeffer, 1994; Senge, 1990a, 1990b). While these approaches are important for understanding the underlying strategy, structure, and behavioral cycle, I believe that there is a missing process focus. I present an organizational learning process model, an important view that assists in understanding and enabling the growth and development of knowledge assets. In the model, I link these processes to the appropriate academic literature that drives the theoretical model.

In the model's first stage, I assume that knowledge exists in a variety of forms; in the minds of individuals (Nonaka, 1991; Nonaka et al., 1995; Polanyi, 1966; Spender, 1996), and in databases, documents, electronic media and other repositories (Alavi et al., 1999; Davenport et al., 1998; Majchrzak et al., 2001). The first step in the process refers to the capture and development of knowledge in terms of databases and repositories as well as the human assets of the organization. The existence, acquisition, and capture of knowledge relates to the previously described Organizational Memory and Knowledge Acquisition literatures.

The second stage has two simultaneous activities: (1) enabling knowledge sharing and transfer between individuals or groups or through knowledge intermediaries (face-to-face, telecommunication, email), and (2) enabling direct access to knowledge (personal experience, personal viewing of a process, direct access to databases or documents). The Knowledge Acquisition literature and Information Distribution literature assist us in understanding the access, sharing and transfer of knowledge. Initiatives that will enable access or improve existing access include Knowledge Management (knowledge capture, repository design and connectivity, portal design, and mentoring). When the knowledge is held by other individuals within the firm or by individuals or in repositories of external firms (suppliers, customers, strategic alliances, academic sources, and personal relationships), the access must be through knowledge sharing or knowledge transfer. Transfer may be either voluntary, with or without assistance from another individual, or non-voluntary through research or "corporate intelligence."

The third stage is the actual knowledge acquisition process. This includes taking advantage of organization enabling of sharing and access or overcoming barriers to sharing and access.

The fourth stage is the evaluation of knowledge. This segment of the process includes one or more of the following:
1)   Knowledge is assessed (for its relevance);
2)   Knowledge is evaluated (for efficacy, usability, credibility and fit) (Szulanski, 2000); and/or
3)   Knowledge is exposed to an iterative process that involves a circular or even a more chaotic evolutionary process.

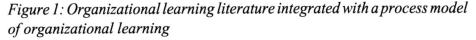

Figure 1: Organizational learning literature integrated with a process model of organizational learning

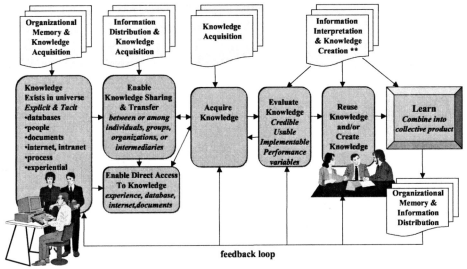

All of the literatures considered here shed light on an iterative process from assessment to reuse, creation and re-evaluation. Once acquired, the information is interpreted; the involved stages are four (evaluate knowledge), five (reuse and create knowledge), and six (learn). These processes include one or more of the following:

1)   Knowledge is reused (adopted or adapted) (Majchrzak et al., 2001a);
2)   Knowledge is utilized in a more supportive relationship to invent or create new knowledge (Nonaka et al., 1995; Von Krough, 2000); and/or
3)   Re-evaluation of knowledge and decision-making process.

The reuse process at the Jet Propulsion Laboratory (including knowledge reuse enablers and moderators) has been the subject of an exploratory study by Majchrzak, Neece and Cooper (Majchrzak et al., 2001a). This study and the enablers of organizational learning at the Jet Propulsion Laboratory will be discussed briefly later in this chapter.

It is during the evolutionary process, discussed above, that thorough documentation of the process or project, (e.g., specifications, details, and analysis) should be shared and entered into organizational documents and databases and catalogued or provided in a searchable form in order to disseminate learning throughout the organization. This portion of the sixth stage includes the continual development and augmentation of knowledge management systems that allow the capture and distribution of knowledge. Foundations for the theories related to this process may be found in the organizational memory and information distribution literatures.

The entire six-stage process is iterative and may constantly move in both directions from distribution, acquisition and interpretation and back again, until a decision has been made or an acceptable solution has been found. However, the process of transfer, sharing, learning and documentation does not take place in a vacuum. In order to enable this process, it is hypothesized that people must be trained, encouraged and motivated to accept others ideas, share their own, and provide documentation for the firm's database and document repository (Davenport et al., 1998; Majchrzak et al., 2001a).

THEORY DEVELOPMENT AND EXPLORATORY STUDY AT THE JET PROPULSION LABORATORY

The Jet Propulsion Laboratory (JPL) provides fertile ground for the study of organizational learning. Since the centralized purpose of the organization is to design, build, launch and operate spacecraft, learning is an integral part of the process. The JPL Mission (Stone & Dumas, 2000) is a blending of the NASA vision and JPL's own vision, specifically tailored to that portion of the NASA Mission that is to be fulfilled by the Jet Propulsion Laboratory. The NASA Vision is presented in the *JPL Implementation Plan*:

NASA is an investment in America's future. As explorers, pioneers, and innovators, we boldly expand frontiers in air and space to inspire and serve America and to benefit the quality of life on earth. (p.4)

The plan continues with specific directives,

Expand the frontiers of space by conducting challenging robotic space missions for NASA. Explore our solar system. Expand our knowledge of the universe. Further our understanding of Earth from the perspective of space. Pave the way for human exploration. Apply our special capabilities to technical and scientific problems of national significance. (p. 4)

JPL has provided a linked group of documents that outline all of the missions, values, goals, objectives, norms, values, organizational charts, projects, processes and procedures for the organization. The organization has developed an Implementation Plan that combines the values, implementation strategies and change goals with specific plans that fulfill all of these goals. Each of the specific goals (e.g., science, administrative, educational) is tied to a specific objective and JPL project type (e.g., flight mission project proposal, experiment package, basic research). Further, specific projects (e.g., Cassini, Kuiper) are tied back to these goals and objectives. Each of the NASA Performance Targets is tied to a specific JPL objective. Therefore, there exists a close interactive relationship between the two organizations. Since the organization is a separate entity from NASA, the Jet Propulsion Laboratory also has its own additional performance targets that it relates to specific organizational objectives such as, space and earth exploration, education, basic research, and community outreach.

The design of the Jet Propulsion Laboratory and its directives toward academic research allow us to compare the six stages in our process model of learning with the learning implementation strategies in this innovative environment.

Senge (1990a) distinguishes between detail complexity and dynamic complexity. Detail complexity includes many variables that can be understood by asking the right questions. Dynamic complexity, on the other hand is found in situations where cause and effect are subtle and where effects over time are not obvious. While other theories assist us in understanding the enablers of this learning process (Senge, 1990a; Von Krogh et al., 2000) or extend our understanding of the firm context and the behavior of individuals (Ghoshal et al., 1997; Maciariello, 2000; Pfeffer, 1997), this organizational learning model provides a process view that assists in sorting out implications for practice in an innovative environment, filled with detail complexity. The implications for each stage of the process model may be extended to practice by answering the following key questions:

Stage 1: How should firms invest their information technology resources for optimal organizational memory and improved knowledge accessibility and search capabilities?

Stage 2: What policies should organizations pursue to enable optimal direct access to knowledge as well as knowledge sharing and transfer both within and between other organizations?

Stage 3: What methods should firms use to assist in the acquisition of knowledge and the accessibility of resources for hiring appropriate experts for a project?

Stage 4: How should firms approach the problem of evaluating knowledge including the credibility, usability, implementability and fit of the knowledge to current needs?

Stage 5: What policies and organizational culture mechanisms will enable the reuse of knowledge from past projects for the development of creation of new knowledge, rather than reinvention of existing technologies?

Stage 6: What types of programs will assist the organization in capturing knowledge and ensuring the organization has a memory of past successes as well as failures?

In the following sections, some answers to these questions are provided from the Jet Propulsion Laboratory's policies, procedures, current and future knowledge-related projects.

Stage 1: How Should Firms Invest Their Information Technology Resources for Optimal Organizational Memory and Improved Knowledge Accessibility and Search Capabilities?

The current Knowledge Management architecture design and implementation project at the Jet Propulsion Laboratory has a budget that covers a wide variety of institutional information technology and people-related initiatives. In terms of availability of knowledge resources, these initiatives include such diverse projects as developing a customizable knowledge portal combined with the implementation of a search agent utilizing intelligent agents. Another aspect focuses on linking distributed databases including electronic libraries built on Xerox's Docushare system for sharing documents. Another recently completed project is a new Technical Questions Database that informs project managers of appropriate questions to ask while developing projects. JPL has developed a Web site with knowledge management Web pages and links to other NASA Centers as well as other government agencies. Further, the JPL Library maintains an excellent set of both online and "bricks and mortar" resources. Many researchers have noted the value of these types of resources. Programs oriented to individuals include recommendations for an expanded mentoring program. The method for assigning resources to each of these initiatives can be informed through greater understanding of what adds value for engineers and scientists and how the process of knowledge reuse and creation can be assisted by new technologies or programs.

Stage 2: What Policies Should Organizations Pursue to Enable Optimal Direct Access to Knowledge as Well as Knowledge Sharing and Transfer Both Within and Between Other Organizations?

Autonomy, empowerment, participative teams, training programs, skill development and cross training are enablers of the organizational learning environment (Heskett et al., 1997; Kaplan & Norton, 1996; Maciariello, 2000; Pfeffer, 1994). At the Jet Propulsion Laboratory, education, training and intellectual stretching are recognized as priorities. In addition to partial funding for academic degrees, a large number of both free and departmentally funded programs, seminars, and classes are available. Employees are encouraged to seek creative career development opportunities. The human resources department, along with various functional groups, offers resources to assist individuals in finding intellectually stimulating opportunities at JPL, at one of the other NASA centers, or at the California Institute of Technology. In addition, the projects themselves are stimulating, as scientists, engineers and technologists join together to innovate and develop new technologies that have "never been done before." One engineer, working on the current Mars Rover project at JPL said, "We're going to Mars...and I get to do this, that is motivation enough."

This attitude is not uncommon at JPL, and while some engineers, scientists and technologists could receive higher financial compensation elsewhere, the excitement about the work is an impressive motivational driver. Nonetheless, programs that encourage employees to reach a higher level of expertise and to expand into other disciplines will encourage not only motivation, but also greater innovation.

Recently, an IT Symposium was held where software, hardware and knowledge management professionals shared papers, and attended poster sessions and panel discussions. Such "Knowledge Fairs" provide an opportunity for people to find appropriate experts in the organization. Some attendees at symposiums have requested additional "free" time or networking time to meet others whose work is of interest to them. Additional assistance is being planned in the form of a "Know Who" director, however this initiative has attracted some concern from listed individuals who might expect that they could be overwhelmed with requests for assistance. Since listing is voluntary, some individuals may not be included. Other organizations, including many universities, have opted for personal Web sites listing bios, projects, journal articles, documents and books with online links to web accessible materials. Such Web sites can be individually designed for pre-formatted for ease of use. Some individuals at JPL have designed their own Web sites for internal use.

Stage 3: What Methods Should Firms Use to Assist in the Acquisition of Knowledge and the Accessibility of Resources for Hiring Appropriate Experts For a Project?

All of the above technologies and people-related programs assist in the acquisition of knowledge. However, the job is far from complete at JPL. Additional projects will need to be in place before the picture is complete.

Funding for such projects is always an issue. Further, the competition that is integral to the U.S. Government open bidding system very likely discourages a more collaborative relationship between organizations. In addition matrix organizations like JPL have inherent difficulties in the allocation of human resources between an individual's functional organization and their project groups. These conflicting demands make collaboration more difficult. Further, if another organization, NASA Center or JPL project requests knowledge, the question arises as to which organization or project will be billed for the time required for sharing and collaboration.

Considering physical facilities for knowledge acquisition, in order to accommodate virtual teams from other NASA Centers and from industry, JPL is in the process of updating and standardizing collaboration tools to share information and knowledge within JPL and across strategic alliances. Such collaborative tools will include real-time design and discussion tools as well as easier access to teleconferencing. Upgrades for conference room communication systems for virtual meetings are also underway. To facilitate knowledge acquisition and team coordination, JPL has made laptop computers and personal data assistants (PDAs, such as Palm-based devices or Windows CE-based devices) available to traveling personnel who need to stay in touch with laboratory resources while on the road.

Stage 4: How Should Firms Approach the Problem of Evaluating Knowledge, Including the Credibility, Usability, Implementability and Fit of the Knowledge to Current Needs?

Synergistic teams that combine expertise from many different disciplines and from several contexts will assist the teams in assessing the applicability of the knowledge. Team learning can be found in the knowledge sharing, openness, stretch and trust that are common elements in the conceptual models of many theorists (Ghoshal et al., 1997); Maciariello, 2000; Senge, 1990; Von Krogh, 2000]. These elements are most clearly presented in the "Management Context and Individual Behavior Model" identified by Ghoshal and Bartlett (1997) where stretch, support, trust and discipline are the contextual corner-stones eliciting the behaviors of initiative, execution, confidence, commitment, learning and collaboration. Further, it has been found that the team members must be able to query the knowledge resource whether in person or via virtual means in order to determine the credibility, usability, implementability and fit of the knowledge (Majchrzak et al., 2001a). In addition, Majchrzak, Neece and Cooper (2001b) found that it may be necessary to have frequent interaction of the knowledge generator with the team, including assistance in manipulating the knowledge (such as help in modifying a prototype).

Exploratory studies of the team learning in two projects at the Jet Propulsion Laboratory (Majchrzak et al., 2001b) have shown a culture of sharing, collaboration, and inquiry balanced with advocacy in these particular teams. Further studies would be useful to determine if this culture occurs within or between other teams at JPL or between NASA Centers. In addition, studies as to how the reward structure is tied to knowledge sharing and the knowledge management process could be helpful. It would be particularly interesting to find whether these structures translate into organization-wide norms.

Stage 5: What Policies and Organizational Culture Mechanisms Will Enable the Reuse of Knowledge From Past Projects For the Development of Creation of New Knowledge, Rather Than Reinvention of Existing Technologies?

Cultural enablers of knowledge reuse for innovation are: openness of the innovator to new knowledge and processes; a trust-based culture that assures information will not be misused; job security to prevent knowledge hoarding; commitment to excellence; and encouragement of knowledge reuse for innovation. Openness to acceptance of new ideas is a common theme found in Ghoshal and Bartlett's (1997) Renewal Process of "challenging embedded assumptions," in Lincoln Electric's participative teams, frequent information sessions and open door policy (Maciariello, 2000), and in the participation and empowerment found at NUMMI (Pfeffer, 1994). It is embedded in Von Krogh, Ichijo and Nonaka's (2000) enabler of "Managing Conversations" and is driven by their "Knowledge Activists." Several cultural mechanisms assist in this process, such as capturing the knowledge so it is accessible, a collaborative climate, and the existence of knowledge intermediaries.

JPL's espoused theory describes a culture that, "Facilitate(s) cultural change through open, candid, two-way communication." (Stone et al., 2000, p. 55)

The following values are included (Stone et al., 2000):

1. Openness: of our people and our processes. We use candid communication to ensure better results.
2. Integrity: of the individual and the institution. We value honesty and trust in the way we treat one another and in the way we meet our commitments.
3. Quality: of our products and our people. We carry out our mission with a commitment to excellence in both what we do and how we do it.

4.   Innovation: in our processes and products. We value employee creativity
      in accomplishing tasks. (p. 4)

Stage 6: What Types of Programs Will Assist the Organization in Capturing Knowledge and Ensuring the Organization Has a Memory of Past Successes as Well as Failures?

The Jet Propulsion Laboratory and Langley Research Center have made
recommendations for an upgraded NASA Lessons Learned Information
System. Goddard Space Flight Center is in the process of implementing aspects
of the JPL-designed system. JPL also has an active "storytelling program,"
where past stories are presented and shared in an informal setting. Another
project that is in its early phases is Personal Knowledge Organizers where
personal assistance will be made available to selected individuals who need to
document and catalogue their work at JPL. Another program involves a
transcription service for project meetings that would provide a map of meeting
discussion points, follow up, and decisions. Such initiatives will ensure that
knowledge is not lost when key individuals leave the organization.

Outlined here are a few of the programs, projects, policies and procedures
that have been used or are being planned at the Jet Propulsion Laboratory.
Other organizations have tried similar and also different methods of effectively
achieving these objectives. This treatise is not entirely comprehensive, but
provides a window into the program of this one organization.

CONCLUSION

Adaptive learning is about coping, and often leads us to push on symptoms
rather than sources of problems. Generative learning is about creating. Generative learning requires new ways of looking at the world, and requires seeing the
systems that control events. Leading corporations, to become successful
learning organizations, should focus on this more powerful generative learning.
Developed here is a Process Model of Organizational Learning in an Innovation
Context (Figure 1). This model and its components should assist in understanding and enabling the growth and development of organizational learning in the
organization. I have shown how this model can be adapted to assist in the
development of powerful policies, procedures and mechanisms for enabling
organizational learning through the example of the Jet Propulsion Laboratory.

The importance of a statement of purpose, direction, vision or mission is
directly related to its contextual importance in guiding the organization. The firm

must ask why do we exist and what is our direction (Drucker, 1994; Griffiths, 1996; Maciariello, 2000; Senge, 1990a)? This is a generative process that will further the learning of the organization only if systemic structures are designed to cooperate and enable this overarching purpose. When an organization builds a firm foundation that harmonizes with the organization's vision, the learning organization will be enabled. Patterns of behavior and actions that support learning will find harmony with this foundation. However, this is not an automatic process. While behaviors and events will find alignment, a personal engagement with the vision must be continually articulated and filtered down through cultural norms, policies and procedures. Without attention to detail, the vision will become an empty promise, tacked on the wall or forgotten in a drawer.

While an organization's management can express these objectives in its mission, vision, purpose, objectives, values and norms, the veridicality of converting the explicit theories into theories-in-use can only be judged by studying the actual organizational structure and behaviors. The Jet Propulsion Laboratory, as an R & D facility, is committed to being a "knowledge creating company." It is hypothesized that JPL can further improve creativity and learning by studying its processes in relationship to the theories considered here. I assert that there are far reaching implications from the appropriate allocation of resources to the development of programs that encourage knowledge sharing and knowledge reuse.

I have discussed the fact that organizational learning has been considered an "umbrella" term that covers a variety of topics including: learning curves, productivity, organizational memory, organizational forgetting, knowledge transfer, knowledge sharing, knowledge assets, dynamic capabilities, knowledge management, and knowledge creation. This chapter has linked this literature to each of the processes in the model and has proposed that the firm should consider organizational learning from a strategic systems perspective. It is suggested that a study of these models be explored at several organizations including both government-based and commercial firms involved in innovative work. These studies should assist us in assessing the efficacy of the model. The purpose is to encourage the development of organizational learning. To this end, I concur with Senge's (1990a) view, "Over the long run superior performance depends on superior learning."

Only when we take advantage of the learning and turn it into practice does it provide full value to the organization. Learning initiatives must be turned into practical applications that serve the organization.

REFERENCES

Abrahamson, E., & Rosenkopf, L. (1997). Social network effects on the extent of innovation diffusion: A computer simulation. *Organization Science*, May-June, 8(3), 289-309.

Adler, P. S. (1988). Managing flexible automation. *California Management Review*, Spring, 34-56.

Adler, P. S., & Clark, K. B. (1991). Behind the learning curve: A sketch of the learning process. *Management Science*, 37, 267-281.

Alavi, M., & Leidner, D. (1998). Knowledgement management systems: Emerging views and practices from the field. Paper presented at the *Hawaii International Conference on Systems Science*, Hawaii.

Alavi, M., & Leidner, D. (1999). Knowledge management systems: Issues, challenges, and benefits. *Communications of the Association for Information Systems*, February, 1.

Allen, T. J. (1977). *Managing the Flow of Technology: Technology Transfer and the Dissemination of Technological Information Within the R & D Organization*. Cambridge, MA: MIT Press.

Anand, V., Manz, C. C., & Glick, W. H. (1998). An organizational memory approach to information management. *Academy of Management Review*, 23(4), 796-809.

Ansoff, H. L. (1975). Managing strategic surprise by response to weak signals. *California Management Review*, 18: 21-33.

Argote, L. (1999). *Organizational Learning: Creating, Retaining, and Transferring Knowledge*. Norwell, MA: Kluwer.

Argote, L., Beckman, S. L., & Epple, D. (1990). The persistence and transfer of learning in industrial settings. *Management Science*, 36, 140-154.

Argote, L., & Darr, E. D. (In Press). Repositories of knowledge in franchise organizations: Individual, structural and technological. In Dosi, G., Nelson, R. and Winter, S. (Eds.), *Nature and Dynamics of Organizational Capabilities*.

Argote, L., & Ingram, P. (2000). Knowledge transfer: A basis for competitive advantage in firms. *Organizational Behavior and Human Decision Processes*, May, 82(1), 150-169.

Argote, L., & McGrath, J. E. (1993). Group processes in organizations: Continuity and change. *International Review of Industrial and Organizational Psychology*, 8, 333-389.

Argyris, C. (1983). Action science and intervention. *Journal of Applied Behavioral Science*, 19, 115-140.

Argyris, C., & Schon, D. A. (1978). *Organizational Learning: A Theory of Action Perspective*. Reading, MA: Addison-Wesley.

Attewell (1992). Technology diffusion and organizational learning: The case of business computing. *Organization Science*, 3(1), 1-19.

Barnard, C. I. (1938). *The Functions of the Executive* (30th Anniversary Edition ed.). Cambridge, MA: Harvard University Press.

Barney, J. (1991). Firm resources and sustained competitive advantage. *Journal of Management*, 17(1), 99-120.

Bartlett, C. A., & Ghoshal, S. (1995). Changing the top role of management; Beyond systems to people. *Harvard Business Review*, May-June.

Bower, G. H., & Hilgard, E. R. (1981). *Theories of Learning*. Englewood Cliffs, NJ: Prentice Hall.

Bower, J. L., & Hout, T., M. (1988). Fast-cycle capability for competitive power. *Harvard Business Review*, November-December, 110-118.

Brand, A. (1998). Knowledge management and innovation at 3M. *Journal of Knowledge Management*, 2(1), 17-22.

Bresman, H., Birkinshaw, J., & Nobel, R. (1999). Knowledge transfer in international acquisitions. *Journal of International Business Studies*, 30(3), 439-462.

Brown, J. S., & Duguid, P. (1998). Organizing knowledge. *California Management Review*, 40(3), 90-111.

Burt, R. S. (1992). *Structural Holes: The Social Structure of Competition*. Cambridge, MA: Harvard University Press.

Cangelosi, V. E., & Dill, W. R. (1965). Organizational learning: Observations toward a theory. *Administrative Science Quarterly*, 10, 175-203.

Carr, N. G. (1999). Being virtual: Character and the new economy. *Harvard Business Review*, May-June.

Clark, H. (1996). *Using Language*. Cambridge, England: Cambridge University Press.

Clark, H., & Brennan, S. (1993). Grounding in communication. In Baecker, R. M. (Ed.), *Groupware and Computer-Supported Cooperative Work*. San Francisco, CA: Morgan Kaufmann.

Culnan, M. J., & Markus, M. L. (1987). Information technologies. In Jablin, F., Putnam, L., Roberts, K. and Porter, L. (Eds.), *Handbook of Organizational Communication*. Beverly Hills, CA: Sage Publications.

Cyert, R. M., & March, J. G. (1992). *A Behaviorial Theory of the Firm* (2nd ed.). Cambridge MA: Blackwell Publishers.

Daft, R. L., & Huber, G. P. (1987). How organizations learn: A communication framework. *Research in the Sociology of Organizations*, 5(1-36).

Daft, R. L., & Lengel, H. R. (1986). Organizational information requirements, media richness, and structural design. *Management Science*, 32, 554-571.

Daft, R. L., & Weick, K. E. (1984). Toward a model of organizations as interpretation systems. *Academy of Management Review*, 28, 57-91.

Darr, E. D., & Kurtzberg, T. R. (2000). An investigation of partner similarity dimensions on knowledge transfer. *Organizational Behavior and Human Decision Processes*, May, 82(1), 28-44.

Davenport, T. H., Jarvenpaa, S. L., & Beers, M. C. (1996). Improving knowledge work processes. *Sloan Management Review*, Summer, 53-65.

Davenport, T. H., & Prusak, L. (1998). *Working Knowledge: How Organizations Manage What They Know*. Boston, MA: Harvard Business School Press.

Day, G. S. (1994). The capabilities of market driven organizations. *Journal of Marketing*, October.

Deming, W. E. (1986). *Out of Crisis: Quality, Productivity and Competitive Position*. Cambridge, MA: Cambridge University Press.

Dierickx, I., & Cool, K. (1989). Asset stock accumulation and sustainability of competitive advantage. *Management Science*, 35, 1504-1511.

Doane, J., Hess, S., Cooper, L. P., Holm, J., Fuhrman, D., & U'Ren, J. (1999). *A Knowledge Mangement Architecture for JPL: 161*. Pasadena, CA: Jet Propulsion Laboratory, California Institute of Technology.

Donnellon, A., Gray, B., & Bougon, M. G. (1986). Communication, meaning, and organized action. *Administrative Science Quarterly*, 31, 43-55.

Driver, M. J., & Steufert, S. (1969). Integrative complexity: An approach to individuals and groups as information processing systems. *Administrative Science Quarterly*, 14, 272-285.

Drucker, P. F. (1979). Managing the knowledge worker. *Modern Office Procedures*, 24(9).

Drucker, P. F. (1988). The coming of the new organization. *Harvard Business Review*, January-February.

Drucker, P. F. (1991). The new productivity challenge. *Harvard Business Review*, November-December, 69-79.

Drucker, P. F. (1994). The theory of the business. *Harvard Business Review*, September-October, 96-104.

Drucker, P. F. (1999). Knowledge-worker productivity: The biggest challenge. *California Management Review*, 41(2), 79-94.

Duarte, D. L., & Snyder, N. T. (1999). *Mastering Virtual Teams: Strategies, Tools, and Techniques That Succeed*. San Francisco, CA: Jossey-Bass.

Due, R. T. (1995). The knowledge economy. *Information Systems Management*, Summer, 5-8.

Duncan, R., & Weiss, A. (1979). Organizational learning: Implications for organizational design. *Research in Organizational Behavior*, 1, 75-123.

Dvorak, R., Dean, D., & Singer, M. (1994). Accelerating IT innovation (Delivering the value from IT). *McKinsey Quarterly*, Autumn, 123-136.

Ebbinghaus, H. (1964). *Memory: A Contribution to Experimental Psychology* (2nd ed.). New York: Dover (Originally published in 1885).

Eisenhardt, K. M., & Tabrizi, B. N. (1995). Accelerating adaptive processes: Product innovation in the global computer industry. *Administrative Science Quarterly*, 40, 84-110.

Ellsworth, R. R. (1999). *Creating Value through Diversification and Acquisitions*, 1-14. Claremont, CA: Peter F. Drucker School, Claremont Graduate University.

Feldman, J., & Kanter, H. E. (1965). Organizational decision making. In March, J. G. (Ed.), *Handbook of Organizations*, 614-649. Chicago, IL: Rand McNally.

Fiol, C. M., & Lyles, M. A. (1985). Organizational learning. *Academy of Management Review*, 10, 803-813.

Foster, R. (1986). *Innovation: The Attacker's Advantage*. New York: Summit Books.

Fuld, L. M. (1988). *Monitoring the Competition: Find Out What's Really Going on Over There*. Somerset, NJ: John Wiley & Sons.

Gersick, C., & Hackman, J. R. (1990). Habitual routines in task-performing groups. *Organizational Behavior and Human Decision Processes*, 47, 65-97.

Ghoshal, S., & Bartlett, C. A. (1997). *The Individualized Corporation: A Fundamentally New Approach to Management* (1st ed.). New York: HarperCollins.

Gilbert, M., & Cordey-Hayes, M. (1996). Understanding the process of knowledge transfer to achieve successful technological innovation. *Technovation*, 16, 301-312.

Granovetter, M. (1992). Problems of explanation in economic sociology. In Nohria, N. and Eccles, R. G. (Eds.), *Networks and Organizations*, 25-56. Boston, MA: Harvard Business School Press.

Grant, R. M. (1996). Toward a knowledge-based theory of the firm. *Strategic Management Journal*, 17, 109-122.

Gray, P., & Jurison, J. (1995). *Productivity in the Office and the Factory*. Danvers, MA: Boyd & Fraser.

Gregerman, I. B. (1981). Knowledge worker productivity measurement through the nominal group technique. *Industrial Management*, 23(1).

Griffiths, L. of Fforestfach. (1996). The Business of Values. Paper presented at the *The Hansen-Wessner Lecture Series*, The Peter F. Drucker Graduate Management Center of the Claremont Graduate School, Claremont, CA.

Guetzkow, H., & Simon, H. A. (1955). The impact of certain communication nets upon organization and performance in task-oriented groups. *Management Science*, 1, 233-250.

Halloran, J. P. (1993). Achieving world-class end-user computing: Making IT work and using IT effectively. *Information Systems Management*, Fall, 7-12.

Hansen, M. T., Nohria, N., & Tierney, T. (1999). What's your strategy for managing knowledge? *Harvard Business Review*, March-April, 106-116.

Harris, S. G. (1994). Organizational culture and individual sensemaking. *Organization Science*, 5, 309-321.

Hayek, F. A. (1945). The use of knowledge in society. *American Economic Review*, 35, 519-530.

Hayek, F. A. (1989). The pretense of knowledge. *American Economic Review*, 79, 3-7.

Hayes, R. H., & Clark, K. B. (1985). *Exploring Productivity Differences at the Factory Level*. New York: Wiley.

Hayes, R. H., & Clark, K. B. (1986). Why some factories are more productive than others. *Harvard Business Review*, 64(5), 66-73.

Hedberg, B. L. T., Nystrom, P. C., & Starbuck, W. H. (1976). Camping on seesaws: Prescriptions for a self-designing organization. *Administrative Science Quarterly*, 2, 39-52.

Hedberg, B. L. T., Nystrom, P. C., & Starbuck, W. H. (1977). Designing organizations to match tomorrow. In Nystrom, P. C. and Starbuck, W. H. (Eds.), *Prescriptive Models of Organizations*. Amsterdam: North Holland.

Hedlund, C. (1994). A model of knowledge management and the N-form corporation. *Strategic Management Journal*, 15, 73-90.

Henderson, R. M., & Cockburn, I. (1994). Measuring competence? Exploring firm effects in pharmaceutical research. *Strategic Management Journal*, 15, (Winter Special Issue), 63-84.

Heskett, J. L., Sasser, E. W. J., & Schlesinger, L. A. (1997). *The Service Profit Chain: How Leading Companies Link Profit and Growth to Loyalty, Satisfaction, and Value*. New York, NY: The Free Press.

Hilgard, E. R., & Bower, G. H. (1975). *Theories of Learning* (4th ed.). Englewood Cliffs, NJ: Prentice-Hall.

Houston, J. P. (1986). *Fundamentals of Learning and Memory* (3rd ed.). New York: Harcourt Brace Jovanovich.

Huber, G. P. (1982). Organizational information systems: Determinants of their performance and behavior. *Management Science*, 28, 135-155.

Huber, G. P. (1991). Organizational learning: The contributing processes and the literatures. *Organization Science*, 2, 88-115.

Huber, G. P., & Daft, R. L. (1987). The information environments of organizations. In Jablin, F., Putnam, L., Roberts, K. and Porter, L. (Eds.), *Handbook of Organizational Communication*. Beverly Hills, CA: Sage Publications.

Huber, G. P., Ullman, J., & Leifer, R. (1979). Optimum organization design: An analytic adoptive approach. *Academy of Management Review*, 4, 567-578.

Iansiti, M., & West, J. (1997). Technology integration: Turning great research into great products. *Harvard Business Review*, May-June, 75(3), 69-79.

Ingram, P., & Baum, J. A. C. (1997). Opportunity and constraint: Organizations learning from the operating and competitive experience of industries. *Strategic Management Journal*, 18(7), 75-98.

Ireland, R. D., Hitt, M. A., Bettis, R. A., & DePorras, D. A. (1987). Strategy formulation processes: Differences in perceptions of strength and weaknesses indicators and environmental uncertainty by managerial level. *Strategic Management Journal*, 8, 469-485.

Itami, H. (1987). *Mobilizing Invisible Assets*. Cambridge, MA: Harvard University Press.

Jinag, J. J. (1995). Using scanner data: IS in the consumer goods industry. *Information Systems Management*, Winter, 61-66.

Jurison, J. (1995). Defining and measuring productivity. *Productivity in the Office and the Factory*, 11-21. Danvers, MA: Boyd & Fraser.

Kaplan, R. S., & Norton, D. P. (1996). *The Balanced Scorecard: Translating Strategy into Action*. Boston: Harvard Business School Press.

Kogut, B., & Zander, U. (1992). Knowledge of the firm, combinative capabilities, and the replication of technology. *Organization Science*, 3, 383-397.

Krackhardt, D., & Hanson, J. R. (1993). Informal networks: The company behind the chart. *Harvard Business Review*, 71(4), 104-111.

Kuwada, K. (1998). Strategic learning: The continuous side of discontinuous strategic change. *Organization Science*, November-December, 9(6), 719-736.

Leavitt, H. J. (1967). Some effects of certain communication patterns on group performance. *Journal of Abnormal and Social Psychology*, 46: 38-50.

Lenehan, M. (1982). The quality of the instrument. *The Atlantic Monthly*, August, 250(2), 32-58.

Leonard-Barton, D. (1990). *Modes of Technology Transfer Within Organizations: Point-To-Point Versus Diffusion, Working Paper 90-060*. Harvard Business School.

Lester, R. K., & McCabe, M. J. (1993). The effect of industrial structure on learning by doing in nuclear power plant operation. *The Rand Journal of Economics*, 24, 418-438.

Levitt, B. & March, J.G. (1988). Organizational Learning. *Annual Review of Sociology,* 14: 319-340.

Lewin (1947). Group decision and social change. In Newcomb, T. N. and Hartley, E. L. (Eds.), *Readings in Social Psychology*. Troy, MO: Holt, Rinehart & Winston.

Lewin, K. (1951). *Field Theory in Social Science*. New York: Harper & Row.

Lieberman, M. B. (1984). The learning curve and pricing in the chemical processing industries. *The Rand Journal of Economics*, 15, 213-228.

Lipman-Blumen, J., & Leavitt, H. J. (1999). Hot groups "with attitude": A new organizational state of mind. *Organizational Dynamics*, 27(4), 63-73.

Lippman, S. A., & Rumelt, R. P. (1982). Uncertain imitability: An analysis of interfirm differences in efficiency under competition. *The Rand Journal of Economics*, 13, 418-438.

Lounamaa, P. H., & March, J. G. (1987). Adaptive coordination of a learning team. *Management Science*, 33(107-123).

Lyles, M. A. (1988). Learning among joint-venture sophisticated firms. *Management International Review*, 28, 85-98.

Maciariello, J. A. (1997). Management systems at Lincoln Electric: A century of agility. *Journal of Agility & Global Competition*, Winter, 46-61.

Maciariello, J. A. (2000). *Lasting Value: A Century of Agility at Lincoln Electric*. New York: John Wiley & Sons.

Majchrzak, A., & Beath, C. (2001). Beyond user participation: A process model of learning and negotiation during system development. In Segars, A., Sampler, J. and Zmud, R. (Eds.), *Redefining the Organizational Roles of Information Technology in the Information Age*. University of Minnesota Press.

Majchrzak, A., Neece, O. E., & Cooper, L. P. (2001a). Knowledge reuse for innovation–The missing focus in knowledge management: Results of a case analysis at the Jet Propulsion Laboratory. Paper presented at the *Academy of Management 2001*, Washington, D.C.

Majchrzak, A., Neece, O. E., & Cooper, L. P. (2001b). Knowledge reuse for innovation–The missing focus in knowledge management: Results of a case analysis. Unpublished *Journal submission* under review, University of Southern California and the Jet Propulsion Laboratory, Los Angeles, CA.

Majchrzak, A., Rice, R. E., Malhotra, A., King, N., & Ba, S. (2000). Computer-mediated inter-organizational knowledge sharing: Insights from a virtual team innovating using a collaborative tool. *Information Resources Management Journal*, 13(1), 44-59.

March, J. G., & Olsen, J. P. (1979). *Ambiguity and Choice in Organizations* (2nd ed.). Bergen: Universitets-forlaget.

Markus, M. L. (2001). Toward a theory of knowledge reuse: Types of knowledge reuse situations and factors in reuse success. *Journal of Management Information Systems*, 18(1), 57-93.

Markus, M. L., Majchrzak, A., & Gasser, L. (In press). A design theory for systems that support emergent knowledge processes. In A. Segars, JU. Sampler & R. Zmud (Eds.). *Redefining the Organizational Roles of Information Technology in the Information Age.* MIS Quarterly Monograph. University of Minnesota Press.

Marshal, E. (1989). Losing our memory. *Science*, June, 244, 1250.

Matusik, S. F., & Hill, C. W. L. (1998). The utilization of contingent work, knowledge creation, and competitive advantage. *Academy of Management Review*, 23(4), 680-697.

McKinsey. (1998). Best practice and beyond: Knowledge strategies. *McKinsey Quarterly*, 1.

Meier, R. L. (1963). Communications overload: Proposals from the study of a university library. *Administrative Science Quarterly*, 4(521-544).

Meyer, J. W., & Rowan, B. (1977). Institutionalized organizations: Formal structure as myth and ceremony. *American Journal of Sociology*, 83, 440-463.

Michael, D. N. (1973). *On Learning to Plan–and Planning to Learn.* San Francisco: Jossey-Bass.

Miller, D. B. (1977). How to improve the performance and productivity of the knowledge worker. *Organizational Dynamics*, 5(3).

Mintzberg, H. (1975). The manager's job: Folklore and fact. *Harvard Business Review*, July-August, 49-61.

Moorman, C., & Miner, A. S. (1998). Organizational improvisation and organizational memory. *Academy of Management Review*, 23(4), 698-723.

Neece, O. E. (2000). *A Systems Perspective of Virtual Team Structure and Process: A Case Study at Nortel Networks.* Unpublished Working Paper, Claremont Graduate University, Claremont, CA.

Nelson, R., & Winter, S. (1982). *An Evolutionary Theory of Economic Change.* Cambridge, MA: Belknap Press.

Nelson, R. R. (1991). Why do firms differ and what does it matter? *Journal of Strategic Management*, 12, 61-74.

Nobles, W., & Redpath, J. (1997). Market-based management™: A key to Nucor's success. *Journal of Applied Corporate Finance*, 10(3), 105-106.

Nonaka, I. (1991). The knowledge-creating company. *Harvard Business Review*, November-December.

Nonaka, I. (1994). A dynamic theory of organizational knowledge creation. *Organization Science*, 5(1), 14-37.

Nonaka, I., & Takeuchi, H. (1995). *The Knowledge-Creating Company*. New York: Oxford University Press.

Olivera, F., & Argote, L. (2000). Organizational learning and new product development: CORE processes. In Thompson, L., Messick, D. M. and Levine, J. M. (Eds.), *Shared Knowledge in Organizations*. Mahwah, NJ: Lawrence Erlbaum.

Olson, G. M., & Olson, J. S. (1998). Making sense of the findings: Common vocabulary leads to the synthesis necessary for theory building. In Finn, K., Sellen, A. and Wilbur, S. (Eds.), *Video-Mediated Communication*. Hillsdale: Erlbaum.

Ouchi, W. G. (1980). Markets, bureaucracies, and clans. *Administrative Science Quarterly*, 25, 129-141.

Pfeffer, J. (1994). *Competitive Advantage Through People: Unleashing the Power of the Work Force*. Boston, MA: Harvard Business School Press.

Pfeffer, J. (1997). The ambiguity of leadership. In Vecchio, R. P. (Ed.), *Leadership: Understanding the Dynamics of Power and Influence in Organizations*, 2, 104-112. Notre Dame, IN: University of Notre Dame Press.

Pisano, G. P. (1994). Knowledge, integration, and the locus of learning: An empirical analysis of process development. *Strategic Management Journal*, 15, 85-100.

Polanyi, M. (1966). *The Tacit Dimension*. London: Rutledge & Kegan Paul.

Porter, M. E. (1980). *Competitive Strategy: Techniques for Analyzing Industries and Competitors*. New York: The Free Press.

Porter, M. E. (1996). What is strategy? *Harvard Business Review*, November-December, 61-78.

Prahalad, C. K., & Hamel, G. (1990). The core competence of the corporation. *Harvard Business Review*, May-June, 90(3), 79-91.

Prokesch, S. E. (1997). Unleashing the power of learning: An interview with British Petroleum's John Browne. *Harvard Business Review*, September-October.

Rapping, L. (1965). Learning and World War II production functions. *Review of Economics and Statistics*, 47, 81-86.

Rogers, E. (1983). *The Diffusion of Innovation* (3rd. Ed.). New York: Free Press.

Sanchez, R., & Mahoney, J. T. (1996). Modularity, flexibility, and knowledge management in product and organization design. *Strategic Management Journal*, 17(Winter), 63-76.

Schein, E. H. (1985). *Organizational Culture and Leadership* (2nd ed.). San Francisco, CA: Jossey-Bass.

Senge, P. (1990a). *The Fifth Discipline: The Art & Practice of the Learning Organization*. New York: Currency Doubleday.

Senge, P. M. (1990b). The leader's new work: Building learning organizations. *Sloan Management Review*, Fall, 32(1), 7-23.

Sherman, W. S., & Lacey, M. Y. (1999). The role of tacit knowledge in the team building process: Explanations and interventions. Paper presented at the *Academy of Management Meeting*, Chicago.

Short, J., Williams, E., & Christie, B. (1976). *The Social Psychology of Telecommunications*. New York: John Wiley.

Sitkin (1992). Learning through failure: The strategy of small losses. In Staw, B. M. and Cummings, L. L. (Eds.), *Research in Organizational Behavior*, 14. Greenwich, CT: JAI Press.

Snowden, D. J. (2000a). The ASHEN model. *Knowledge Management*, 3(8).

Snowden, D. J. (2000b). Knowledge elicitation: Indirect knowledge discovery. *Knowledge Management*, 3(9).

Snowden, D. J. (2000c). Story circles and heuristic-based interventions. *Knowledge Management*, 3(10).

Spender, J. C. (1989). *Industry Recipes*. Oxford: Blackwell.

Spender, J. C. (1996). Making knowledge the basis of a dynamic theory of the firm. *Strategic Management Journal*, 17(Winter Special Issue), 45-62.

Starbuck, W. H. (1984). Organizations as action generators. *American Sociological Review*, 48, 91-102.

Starbuck, W. H., & Milliken, F. J. (1988). Executives perceptual filters: What they notice and how they make sense. In Hambrick, D. (Ed.), *The Executive Effect: Concepts, and Methods for Studying Top Managers*, 35-66. Greenwich, CT: JAI Press.

Staw, B. M. (1977). The experimenting organization: Problems and prospects, psychological foundations of organization behavior. *Pacific Palisades*, CA: Goodyear.

Staw, B. M., & Ross, J. (1987). Behavior in escalations situations: Antecedents, prototypes, and solutions. In Cummings, L. L. and Staw, B. M. (Eds.), *Research in Organizational Behavior*, 9, 39-78.

Stinchcombe, A. L. (1965). Social structure and organizations. In March, J. G. (Ed.), *Handbook of Organizations*. Chicago, IL: Rand McNally.

Stone, E. C., & Dumas, L. N. (2000). *The JPL Implementation Plan: Implementing NASA's Mission at the Jet Propulsion Laboratory*, 1-109. Pasadena, CA: The Jet Propulsion Laboratory.

Szulanski, G. (1994). Intra-firm transfer of best practices project: Executive summary of the findings (Report): APQC.

Szulanski, G. (2000). The process of knowledge transfer: A diachronic analysis of stickiness. *Organizational Behavior and Human Decision Processes*, May, 82(1), 9-27.

Taylor, F. (1911). The Principles of Scientific Management. New York: Harper.

Teece, D. (1990). Contributions and impediments of economic analysis to the study of strategic management. In Fredrickson, J. (Ed.), *Perspectives on Strategic Management*, 39-80. New York: Harper Business.

Teece, D. J. (1981). The market for know-how and the efficient transfer of technology. *The Annals of the American Academy of Political and Social Science*, 458, 81-96.

Teece, D. J. (1984). Economic analysis and strategic management. *California Management Review*, 26(3), 87-110.

Teece, D. J. (1998). Capturing value from knowledge assets: The new economy markets for know-how and intangible assets. *California Management Review*, 40(3), 55-79.

Telleen, S. (1999). Frequently Asked Questions. Retrieved July 21, 1999 from the World Wide Web: http://www.iorg.com/questions.html.

Thompson, K. R., Hochwarter, W. A., & Mathys, N. J. (1997). Stretch targets: What makes them effective? *Academy of Management Executive*, 11(3), 48-60.

Thorndike, E. L. (1898). Animal intelligence: An experimental study of the associative processes in animals. *The Psychological Review: Series of Monograph Supplements*, 2, 1-109.

Tsoukas, H. (1996). The firm as a distributed knowledge system: A constructionist approach. *Strategic Management Journal*, Winter, 17, 11-25.

Tuomi, I. (1999). Data is more than knowledge: Implications of the reversed knowledge hierarchy for knowledge management and organizational memory. *Journal of Management Information Systems*, Winter, 16(3), 103-117.

Tversky, A., & Kahneman, D. (1985). The framing of decisions and the psychology of choice. In Wright, G. (Ed.), *Behavioral Decision Making*. New York: Plenum Press.

von Hippel, E. (1994). "Sticky information" and the locus of problem solving: Implications for innovation. *Management Science*, 40(4), 429-439.

von Hippel, E., & Tyre, M. J. (1995). How learning by doing is done: Problem identification in novel process equipment. *Research Policy*, 24, 1-12.

Von Krogh, G., Ichijo, K., & Nonaka, I. (2000). *Enabling Knowledge Creation: How to Unlock the Mystery of Tacit Knowledge and Release the Power of Innovation.* New York: Oxford University Press.

Walker, G. (1985). Network position and cognition in a computer software firm. *Administrative Science Quarterly*, 30, 103-130.

Walsh, J. P., & Ungson, G. R. (1991). Organizational memory. *Academy of Management Review*, 16(1), 57-91.

Weick, K. E. (1979). Cognitive processes in organizations. *Research in Organizational Behavior*, 1, 41-74.

Wildavsky, A. (1972). The self-evaluating organization. *Public Administration Review*, September-October, 32(5), 502-509.

Wingfield, A. (1979). *Human Learning and Memory: An Introduction.* New York: Harper & Row.

Winter, S. G. (1987). Knowledge and competence as strategic assets. In Teece, D. (Ed.), *The Competitive Challenge*, 159-184. New York: Harper and Row.

Winter, S. G. (1995). Four Rs of profitability: Rents, resources, routines and replication. In Montgomery, C. A. (Ed.), *Resource-Based and Evolutionary Theories of the Firm: Towards a Synthesis.* Norwell, MA: Kluwer.

Zaltman, G., Duncan, R., & Holbek, J. (1973). *Innovations and Organizations.* New York: Wiley.

Zander, U., & Kogut, B. (1995). Knowledge and the speed of the transfer and limitation of organizational capabilities: An empirical test. *Organization Science*, 6, 76-92.

Part III

Organizational Groups and Information Technology

Chapter IX

GSS Facilitation: A Reflective Practitioner Perspective[1]

Pak Yoong
Victoria University of Wellington, New Zealand

Brent Gallupe
Queen's University, Canada

INTRODUCTION

GSS research recognized meeting facilitation skills, such as building rapport and relationships with participants, managing conflict, and appropriately selecting and preparing technology, as key success factors in electronic meetings (Bostrom, Clawson & Anson, 1991; Hayne, 1999; Miranda & Bostrom, 1999; Tan, Wei, & Lee-Partridge, 1999). Although these facilitation skills have been identified as important, very little is known about how electronic meeting facilitators acquire these skills. Up to now, no research has tried to examine at a detailed, theoretical level, how conventional meeting facilitators acquire the skills to become effective electronic meeting facilitators. Vogel, Nunamaker, Applegate and Konsynski (1987) alluded to this issue as early as 1987 when they commented that "while group skills are recognized as important, little systematic attention has been given to group facilitator training..." (p. 127).

Numerous researchers have raised the issue of how GSS facilitation training should be conducted (Anson, 1990; Bostrom et al., 1991; Clawson, 1992; Yoong, 1995). For example, Anson (1990) advocates that novices should concentrate first on learning to facilitate in the conventional meetings before adding the technology component. However, he recommends that if individuals were selected on their prior facilitation experience then training in the technology first (or concurrent with group dynamics training) would be equally effective. Beranek, Beise, and Niederman (1993) propose that observation and apprenticeship should probably be part of a GSS facilitation training program.

The existing literature, which focuses on descriptions of the structure and methods of specific training programs, also provides an idea of how training is conducted in these situations. Many training programs use a hands-on "experiential learning" approach with role modeling, role playing, simulation of real live meetings (mini-meetings), video taping and feedback, and group discussions. In most instances, the training programs are targeted at participants with at least some prior generic facilitation experience.

The objectives of this chapter are to describe the nature of reflective practice and the development of reflective practice in one human aspect of information technology application, namely, the facilitation of face-to face electronic meetings.

BACKGROUND TO THE STUDY

In March 1993, I[2] began a grounded theory study that investigated the question:

How do facilitators of conventional meetings make the transition to facilitating face-to-face electronic meetings?

This study aims to develop a model representing the learning processes and experiences of traditional facilitators who are undergoing training in the facilitation of computer-supported problem-solving meetings.

As I began this research journey, I reflected on my facilitation experience of both conventional and electronic meetings.[3] I know that it was not only "reading" about meeting facilitation but also "doing" meeting facilitation that has assisted my learning to be a facilitator of electronic meetings. I have also found that reflecting and talking on these facilitation experiences have made possible the links between "doing," "reading," and "making sense" of what is essentially a complex set of behaviors. This action-reflection approach to learning, which included periods of "reflective thinking" on my facilitation experiences, is the main approach that I have used, and continue to use, in my continuing learning as a facilitator of conventional and electronic meetings.

I have also found the facilitation of meetings, with its characteristic rational and irrational components, to be a complex process. Understanding my facilitation actions, intended or unintended, is possible only with attention to situational and contextual complexities (Friedman, 1989) and with the recognition that much of what I do in meetings is active, spontaneous and flexible (Anson, 1990). There is simply little time to deliberate on my actions. The facilitation literature also echoes this view (Heron, 1989; Anson, 1990; Poole, 1990; Bostrom et al., 1991; Clawson, 1992; Hirokawa and Rost, 1992; Schwarz, 1994). If this situation is also coupled with the use of electronic meeting tools, the facilitation becomes very much more complex. How then do you design a training program[4] that not only deals with this complexity in the learning situation but also equips the learners to handle this complexity in "live" situations?

One source of answers to the question is in the literature describing the use of reflection in experiential learning and professional development. For example, in *Reflection: Turning Experience into Learning*, Boud, Keogh, and Walker (1985) describe the essence of *reflection* in experiential learning as:

> reflection is a form of response of the learner to experience. In our model we have indicated two main components: the experience and the reflective activity based upon that experience ... (that is) after the experience there occurs a processing phase; this is the area of reflection. Reflection is an important human activity in which people recapture their experience, think about it, mull it over and evaluate it. (p. 18-19)

The authors also suggest that reflection should lead to action, for:

> while reflection is itself an experience it is not, of course, an end in itself. It (prepares us) for the new experience. The (results) may include a new way of doing something, the clarification of an issue, the development of a skill or the resolution of a problem. (p. 34)

Boud et al.'s description of "reflection" is similar to Schon's (1987) notion of "reflection-on-action" which is "thinking back on what we have done..." (p. 238). Schon was also concerned with what he called the "crisis of confidence in professional knowledge ... and professional education" (p. 8) and believed that this crisis was caused by the "prevailing epistemology of practice" (p. 12) in professional education institutions. He based this argument on the assumption that professional expertise and thinking should not only depend on the application of established theory on particular situations, but also on experience-based knowledge and on non-logical kinds of thinking about what is relevant and appropriate in the context of those situations.

To enhance this latter kind of professional thinking, Schon (1983) suggests a reflective approach to professional education based on the notion that "in much of the spontaneous behavior of skilled practice we reveal a kind of knowing which does not stem from a prior intellectual operation" (p. 51) but from a reflective practice process called "reflection-in-action" which is thinking about the action while one is doing it, rather than after the event. Citing his own experience of building a gate, he explains: "In the midst of action, I invented procedures to solve the problem, discovered further unpleasant surprises, and made further corrective inventions ... reflection on each trial and its results sets the stage for the next trial" (p. 27). Boud and Walker (1993) extended Schon's notion of 'reflection-in-action' which they described as "reflection which takes place during the event" (p. 76).

As I began to collect and analyze the data based on the facilitators' experience of GSS facilitation training, it soon became clear that many of the facilitators' experiences were indicative of the "action reflection" processes just described. In a later section of this paper, I describe an elaboration of Boud's model of *reflection-on-action* as well as a model of *reflection-in-action* that was inductively derived from the data collected in this study. Together, these two models are combined into the emergent model of *Active Reflection*.

A Model of Active Reflection

A Grounded Theory of Reflective Facilitation is the major theoretical framework inductively derived from this study (Yoong, 1996). It describes how facilitators of conventional meetings become facilitators of electronic meetings. The grounded theory consists of two conceptual components: *The Stages of GSS Facilitation Development* and *Reflective Practice*. *Reflective Practice* consists of two components: *Active Reflection* and *Contextual Factors* (see Figure 1). This section describes the first of these.

Active Reflection

The notion of "theoretical sensitivity" is particularly useful in the development of the model of *Active Reflection*. It is "the attribute of having insight, the ability to give meaning to data, the capacity to understand, and capability to separate the pertinent from that which isn't" (Strauss and Corbin, 1990; p. 42-43). This sensitivity can be achieved by a variety of approaches, including an extensive literature search in related fields of study and a series of reflections on personal and professional experience.

Theoretical sensitivity can also be enhanced by giving:

... careful thought to: (1) a selection of topics for study; (2) a greater openness; and (3) how to improve our powers of theoretical insight ... In particular, there are opportunities for doing cumulative/developmental work which will advance theoretical formulation without

Figure 1: The components of reflective facilitation

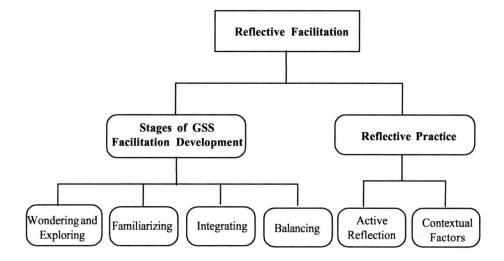

continuously checking the emergent fit of the theory against the data collected. One way of achieving this is to check theories outside the field of study ... Indeed, I would argue that we have reached a stage where we could do with less fieldwork and rather more armchair reflection (Woods, 1985; p. 56-57).

Woods (1985) introduces the notion of "Phase 1" and "Phase 2" research and theory development. "Phase 1" research and theory development are achieved by developing a descriptive "mapping" of the experiences from the field and this should "... provide a basis for the elaboration of the social context" (Cocklin, 1991; p. 4). Phase 2 emphasizes that "data gathering and analysis should be 'cumulative' ... in the sense that rather than 'discovering anew' it seeks to build upon previously 'grounded' concepts, categories and theoretical constructs derived from prior research" (ibid, p. 4).

Using "Phase 2" research and theory development, I have drawn upon the following models of learning to develop the model of *Active Reflection*: Boud et al.'s (1985) "learning from reflection" and Schon's (1987) "reflection-in-action." The analysis of data revealed that *Active Reflection*, which describes the trainees' accounts of experiential learning and action reflection processes, is an elaboration of these models.

The *Active Reflection* model only applies to a learning environment, such as this GSS facilitation training program, that is focused, intentional, deliberate, and experientially based. The trainees are aware that they are learning and that the learning is towards definite and specific goals. They also intend to retain and use what they have learned. The term *Active* is used to reinforce Boud et al.'s

(1985) assertion that reflection in learning is "pursual with intent" and "is not idle meanderings or day-dreaming, but (focused) activity directed towards a goal" (p. 11). *Active Reflection* describes the trainees' accounts of the two complementary action reflection processes, *Reflection-on-Action* and *Reflection-in-Action* (Figure 2). A detailed version of Figure 2 is given in a later section.

Three different action reflection paths are possible from the *Active Reflection* model: *Reflection-on-Action*, *Reflection-in-Action (with intuitive action)*, and *Reflection-in-Action (without intuitive action)*. The next section describes the trainees' experience of the first path, *Reflection-on-Action*.

Figure 2: A model of active reflection

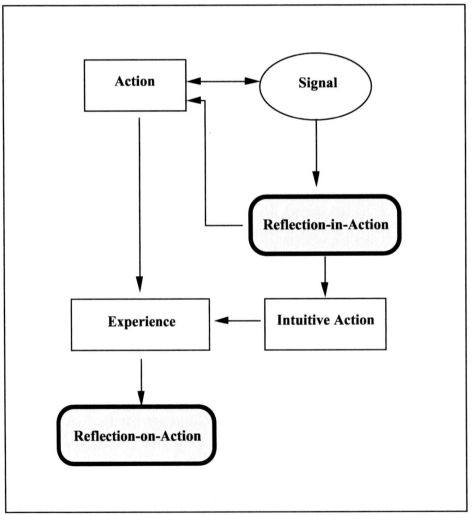

Reflection-on-Action

In the following interview excerpt, the trainee was giving an account of important learning that occurred during the facilitation of his first electronic meeting. It related to a problem in giving instructions. The interview took place two days after.

All of my practice and all of my preparation was based upon understanding the software and understanding how that works. It never occurred to me that I would have to prepare and have a fairly clear idea as to how I would communicate instructions to people. I'm naive!

...I don't know. I suspect it's possibly because I've never actually used technology with other people before—not in an interactive setting anyway and, for example, I've never demonstrated software to people.

...I got home and I started thinking about it. It was crystal clear what the problem was. I'd never thought about how I would provide those instructions. It had never crossed my mind (a) that it would be difficult and (b) that it would be something that I'd have to think about quite carefully.

...It was a real revelation. I was actually dreaming about it.

...Well I think I will still have the same level of emphasis placed upon understanding the technical side of the preparation, but I don't see there's any way of getting around that. You mustn't be stumbling around not knowing what you have to do to get from one part of the exercise to another in terms of using the software, so I think a good deal of preparation will continue on that criteria. On the other hand, I think that what I will be asking myself now almost constantly is that, okay, I've now shown that I know what's required to get from A to B, but how am I going to take other people on that journey? What approach will I take? So it's mainly that.

The analysis of the trainee's account of the learning is shown in Table 1; it illustrates the elements of the reflective process, *Reflection-on-Action*.

The above illustration is a typical example of how trainees described their *Reflection-on-Action* process. The process begins with the trainee revisiting the experience, a recollection of the salient events. Depending on the action's impact on the trainee, expressions of his feelings about the action might be included in the reflective process. Finally, the trainee re-evaluates the experience, makes connections with prior experience, and plans the appropriate

Table 1: The "reflection-on-action" process (adapted from Boud et al., 1985)

Elements	Trainee's comments	Researcher's comments
Revisiting the experience	All of my practice and all of my preparation was based upon understanding the software and understanding how that works. **It never occurred to me that I would have to prepare and have a fairly clear idea as to how I would communicate instructions to people.** I'm naive! . . . **I got home and I started thinking about it. It was crystal clear what the problem was.** I'd never thought about how I would provide those instructions. It had never crossed my mind (a) that it would be difficult and (b) that it would be something that I'd have to think about quite carefully.	The trainee started his account by describing what he did during the preparation for the electronic meeting and the action - his failure to give instructions on how to use the computers.
Expression of feelings	It never occurred to me that I would have to prepare and have a fairly clear idea as to how I would communicate instructions to people. **I'm naive!** . . . It was a real revelation. **I was actually dreaming about it.**	The trainee also expressed how he felt about the experience; considered himself to be "naïve." This had such an impact that he also "dreamt about it."
Re-evaluating the experience	I suspect it's possibly because I've never actually used technology with other people before. Not in an interactive setting anyway and for example, **I've never demonstrated software to people.** . . . Well I think I will still have the same level of emphasis placed upon understanding the technical side of the preparation, but I don't see there's any way of getting around that. You mustn't be stumbling around not knowing what you have to do to get from one part of the exercise to another in terms of using the software so I think a good deal of preparation will continue on that criteria. **On the other hand, I think that what I will be asking myself now almost constantly is that, okay, I've now shown that I know what's required to get from A to B, but how am I going to take other people on that journey? What approach will I take? So it's mainly that.**	Finally the trainee re-examined the experience, connected with prior experience, and tentatively planned to examine how he would do it differently next time.

Figure 3: A model of reflection-on-action (adapted from Boud et al., 1985)

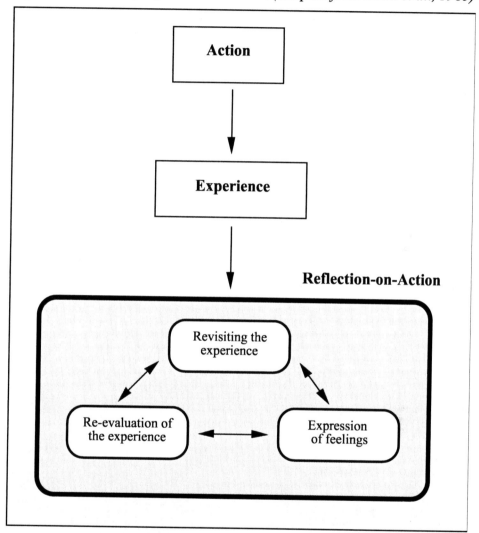

strategy to deal with similar events in the future. The *Reflection-on-Action* process is shown in Figure 3.

The next excerpt illustrates how a comment made by another person, in this case the trainer explaining the role of the technology in electronic meetings, triggered a trainee's thoughts and feelings on that action. The analysis of the excerpt is shown in Table 2.

I wrote a comment down during the session which came out of a discussion, and I think from observing yourself or a comment you made, I'm not sure - it is useful to lighten up on the technology by focusing on the group's activities rather than problems with the individuals and the technology. Don't get too serious. Work to continually communicate with the group, getting its input and approval. What I think I wrote down there is "Don't let the technology dominate." Where individuals have problems, try and focus on the needs of those individuals but without isolating them from the group but in a lighter way rather than in a heavy and serious way. Focusing on what the groups is trying to do if it's a bigger problem then just one individual, which I thought was rather interesting. Here we are up there trying to learn to use the technology and in many cases it's better not to address the issue of the technology but to address the issue of the group. There's a boundary there between group activities in relation to the technology and individual activities in relation to the technology. That's something I need to think more about.

In this example of Reflection-on-Action, the trainee reflected on someone else's comment. In this case, there was no expression of feelings during the trainee's recall and re-evaluation of the experience. Therefore, reflection from

Table 2: Example 1 of the "reflection-on-action" process

Elements	Trainee's comments	Researcher's comments
Revisiting the experience	**I wrote a comment down during the session which came out of a discussion, and I think from observing yourself or a comment you made,** I'm not sure - it is useful to lighten up on the technology by focussing on the group's activities rather than problems with the individuals and the technology. Don't get too serious. Work to continually communicate with the group getting its input and approval.	The trainee started his account by describing what took place during the event, in this case, a detailed description of the use of the technology in the meetings.
Expression of feelings		No obvious expression of feelings on the subject.
Re-evaluating the experience	**What I think I wrote down there is "Don't let the technology dominate."** Where individuals have problems, try and focus on the needs of those individuals but without isolating them from the group but in a lighter way rather than in a heavy and serious way. Focusing on what the group is trying to do if it's a bigger problem just one individual, which I thought was rather interesting . . . **That's something I need to think more about.**	Finally, the trainee re-examined the experience, made sense of it and tentatively planned to think more about it.

learning can be based on one's own or someone else's experience. In both instances, the events triggered fruitful learning. In GSS facilitation training, Anson (1990) encouraged GSS facilitators to keep a record of their own and others' performances and to "keep journals of their reflections on each of the sessions" (p. 108) and Bostrom et al. (1991) suggest that after the introduction of a new GSS tool trainees are encouraged to "acknowledge reflections about the usefulness of the product from a participant's perspective" (p. 19).

Reflection-in-Action

In this section, I will describe the second component of *Active Reflection*: *Reflection-in-Action*, which is *thinking about the action while one is doing it* (Schon, 1983) or *reflection that takes place during the event* (Boud & Walker, 1993).

In this study, the proposed model (see Figure 4) of *Reflection-in-Action* has two components: (a) *Reflection-in-Action (with intuitive action)* - intuition that led to the taking of alternative intuitive action, and (b) *Reflection-in-Action (without intuitive action)* - intuition that led to no intuitive action. Excerpts from trainees' accounts of *Reflection-in-Action* will be analyzed to illustrate the proposed model.

The next excerpt is a trainee's account of an incident during her "live" electronic meeting. It will illustrate the reflective process, *Reflection-in-Action (with intuitive action)*. The incident occurred towards the end of the meeting. At that instant, the trainee was thinking why the meeting had completed the agenda so much earlier than planned. She was wondering what to do next.

> I was asking myself all sorts of interesting questions. As it was apparent that we were getting to the end so quickly I thought, have I done something really wrong or is it just this group . . . I was sort of thinking like I wonder whether I could try one of those other things because at one point I made a comment that there are a whole lot of other tools that you can use and then I thought that was a stupid thing to do because someone could have said well let's do one.
>
> . . . Because for me, in conventional facilitation, I quite often take that approach–let's try something new, it may not work, it may work but are you willing to try it and that usually comes after I feel the group trusts me in that role but it felt exciting to do it here when really the risk is for me. The biggest risk was not for them but would I be able to make this work without having put it on the agenda which of course is what I know is the great advantage of this technology.
>
> . . . And I suppose the other thing was a feeling of caution about whether by generating more information, I would be raising expecta-

Figure 4: A model of "Reflection-in-Action" (with intuitive action)

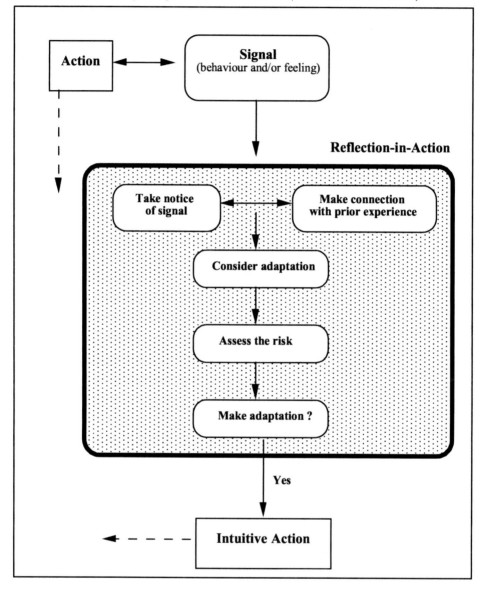

tions. By then there was only half an hour to go and would I be raising more expectations about what would come out of this. And then on balance I decided we'll go with it because we've got the time to do it and in a sense it is about something that they can take away to then do, it's not trying to resolve something here. As the discussion went around we were getting into deeper issues which did need much more focus and planned discussion.

Table 3: Example 1 of "Reflection-in-Action" (with intuitive action)

Elements	Trainee's comments	Researcher's comments
Take notice of intuitive signal	I was asking myself all sorts of interesting questions. **As it was apparent that we were getting to the end so quickly I thought, have I done something really wrong or is it just this group** . . .	The trainee noted the earlier than expected finish to the meeting (behaviour) and wondered if she has done something wrong (idea).
Make connection with prior experience	**Because for me, in conventional facilitation, I quite often take that approach** . . .	The trainee's prior experience in the facilitation of conventional meetings suggested that, under such conditions, it was worth taking the risk of doing something that was not scheduled on the agenda.
Consider adaptation	. . . **let's try something new**, it may not work, it may work but are you willing to try it and that usually comes after I feel the group trusts me in that role . . .	The trainee considered adding an agenda item that involves the use of another GSS tool.
Assess the risk	. . . **when really the risk is for me. The biggest risk was not for them** but would I be able to make this work without having put it on the agenda which of course is what I know is the great advantage of this technology . . . And I suppose the other thing was a feeling of caution about whether by generating more information, I would be raising expectations.	The trainee weighed the risks associated with the proposed adaptation.
Make adaptation?	**And then on balance I decided we'll go with it** because we've got the time to do it and in a sense it is about something that they can take away to then do, it's not trying to resolve something here.	Yes. After assessing the risks, on balance, the trainee decided to make the proposed adaptation.
Intuitive action	**As the discussion went around** we were getting into deeper issues which did need much more focus and planned discussion.	The trainee then set up another GSS tool and invited the participants to take part. As it turned out, this action helped the group identify deeper issues and engage in a more focused discussion.

In summary, during *Reflection-in-Action,* the trainee notices an intuitive signal–a behavior, an idea or a feeling–and makes a connection between that insight and prior experience. The trainee then considers an adaptation to the original action and assesses the risks associated with that adaptation. Based on her assessment of the risks, a decision is taken on whether the adaptation will be adopted as the intuitive action. If this is so, then the reflective process, *Reflection-in-Action (with intuitive action),* is executed. Clawson (1992) describes *Reflection-in-Action (with intuitive action)* as the facilitator's ability to demonstrate "flexibility." This role dimension is defined as "the facilitator thinks on feet; adapts agenda or meeting activities on the spot as needed… tries new things; is willing to do something different than originally planned" (p. 118).

I have found Vaughan's (1979) description of how intuition works most useful. She believes that intuition functions on four distinct levels: physical, emotional, mental, and spiritual. Table 4 gives a brief description of each level.

Prior experience and *intuition* are interlinked. For example, Boud et al. (1985) used the term "association" which is "the connection of the ideas and feelings which are part of the original experience and those which have occurred during reflection with existing knowledge and attitudes" (p. 31). Simon (1987, cited in Agor, 1989) asserts that "an executive can acquire by long experience an ability to seemingly instantly recognize patterns and consequences of

Table 4: Description of the different levels of intuition

Level of intuition	Descriptive "quote" (cited in Agor, 1989; p. 12-13)
Physical	Sometimes we have a strong bodily response to a person or situation when there is no apparent surface reason for doing so. We simply know something without knowing how or why. Put another way, our intuition is telling us what our body already knows to be true.
Emotional	Many of us have had the experience sometime in our lives that we instantaneously liked or disliked someone we had just met. Just feeling right or wrong about a situation or picking up visual clues about a person are good examples.
Mental	This is when mentally you see a pattern or order to seemingly unrelated facts that may not be obvious to your colleagues just yet.
Spiritual	Emphasis is on the transpersonal and underlying oneness [unity] of life. At this level, one would be conscious of how decisions today might come back to affect society in the future.

alternative actions. This is what appears to give intuition the appearance of an 'aha!' quality . . . intuition is a rational process whereby the brain evokes past memories and experiences to address the problem at hand . . . (and) this capacity is solely a product of many years of experience and training" (p. 13-14).

The trainees in this study, and especially those with many years of facilitation experience to draw on, frequently demonstrated facilitative behaviors and actions that seemingly came from nowhere and were definitely not taught during the GSS facilitation training program. The only way I could explain their response was that it was the product of their prior experience as facilitators of conventional meetings and/or as experienced computer users. Some trainees used the phrases "voices in my head," "inner voices," or "voices within" to describe those moments of intuitive insights. For them, it was like *hearing echoes from the past* when prior facilitation or computing experience helped them recognize patterns and helped them decide that alternative intuitive actions were required.

A variation of *Reflection-in-Action (with intuitive action)* was when, during the "live" electronic meeting, the trainee was so preoccupied with the technology or other matters that appropriate intuitive action that should have been taken *immediately* was not done till much later. The phrase *Leaving Instincts on Ice* was used by one trainee to describe this type of situation. In this case, the trainee was too occupied with the technology and so postponed the immediate use of the alternative actions. The following excerpt describes this situation and the analysis is given in Table 5.

Trainee: Looking at the tape . . . I'm more aware than I was at the time that some people are not contributing and that the discussion was starting to be dominated by three or four people and I'm starting to say to myself that the traditional facilitation skill here is being lost. You're forgetting that, you're too worried about the technology, you're too focused on that part of it, you should be encouraging those people to speak, the people who were being quiet. There were people who hadn't said a lot up to that point and there was a hell of a long way to go.

. . . 1.19:50 p.m. (referring to the time shown on the videotape), I finally acknowledged that one person in particular hadn't said anything and I stepped in to try to give him a bit of confidence to make a point. I gave him the opportunity to do that, which he did. And it was absolutely clear from his demeanour that he appreciated that and he felt better about participating in this experience because of that. What I'm saying to you here and now is that . . . I should have done something about it much earlier. It was very late in the piece, 1 hour and 20 minutes, to start doing that.

Researcher: And you attribute that to the focus on the technology?

Trainee: Yes, I do very definitely. My instincts, if in fact they are instincts, or whether they're acquired ways of dealing with situations - my instincts were a little left on ice there and they became shoved into the background and I just was concentrating far too much on the technology and how I was handling that, how I was giving instructions, how I was manipulating data, making sure I was pressing the right buttons and so on. In retrospect that is a big mistake. An understandable one though.

I recalled from my own experience as a facilitator of electronic meetings that there were numerous occasions when the concept *Leaving Instincts on Ice* was an accurate description of my own lack of intuitive action. Some of these occasions required a decision as to what actions were appropriate in the context of the meetings, for example, whether the actions would satisfy the meeting client or its participants. Zorn and Rosenfeld (1989) say that this dilemma often occurs when the facilitator has to decide between achieving management's goals or the group's goals: "The consultant-facilitator serves the goals of management while simultaneously serving the goals of the group, a dual role that may [suffer] from competing actions" (p. 98). There are no hard and fast rules for resolving this issue. However, when confronted with it, the facilitator has to think "on his or her feet" and weigh the consequences of the alternative actions.

The next section discusses *Reflection-in-Action (without intuitive action)* which is those situations when it was considered that, given the context of the meeting and the trainee's lack of specific GSS facilitation skills, the proposed adaptations should not be executed.

On many occasions trainees did not act on their intuition even when it would have been the right thing to do. This reflective process, *Reflection-in-Action (without intuitive action)*, was most evident when a trainee had to decide whether to take alternative action involving the use of GSS tools with which he or she was not confident. For example, one trainee described how during a meeting she sensed (*took notice of an intuitive signal*) that, by taking a vote at a particular moment in the meeting, the differences of opinion among the participants might have been resolved once and for all (*make connection with prior experience*). However, even though her intuition suggested that an Electronic Voting exercise might have been the best approach (*considered an adaptation*), her lack of confidence in using that tool deterred her from taking that alternative action–the explanation was that she did not rehearse using the

Table 5: Example 2 of "Reflection-in-Action" (with intuitive action)

Elements	Trainee's comments	Researcher's comments
Take notice of intuitive signal	**I'm more aware than I was at the time that some people are not contributing** and that the discussion was starting to be dominated by 3 or 4 people	The trainee noted some people were not contributing to the meeting (behaviour).
Make connection with prior experience	**I'm starting to say to myself that the traditional facilitation skill here is being lost. You're forgetting that, you're too worried about the technology, you're too focused on that part of it . . .**	The trainee's prior experience in the facilitation of conventional meetings suggested that he should be doing something else rather than worrying about the technology.
Consider adaptation	**. . . you should be encouraging those people to speak, the people who were being quiet . . .**	The trainee considered encouraging those non-participating people to take a more active role.
Assess the risk	**There were people who hadn't said a lot up to that point and there was a hell of a long way to go.**	The trainee weighed the risks associated with the proposed adaptation. That is, if no action was taken then these people may have felt left out for the rest of the meeting.
Make adaptation?	**I finally acknowledged that one person in particular hadn't said anything and I stepped in to try to give him a bit of confidence to make a point.**	Yes. After the assessment of the risks of not taking action, the trainee decided to make the proposed adaptation.
Intuitive action	I gave him the opportunity to do that, which he did . . . **What I'm saying to you here and now is that . . . I should have done something about it much earlier. It was very late in the piece, 1 hour and 20 minutes, to start doing that.**	The trainee finally got the person involved in the discussion. As it turned out, the trainee felt that this adaptation should have occurred earlier.

Vote tool during her preparation as it was not included in the planned agenda (*assessed the risk*). Instead, she stuck with the set agenda and continued the discussion (*decided not to make the adaptation*). Here was how another trainee described a similar dilemma.

> I will be disappointed if we don't achieve the result we want by the end of the full period. I'm more than happy to can some (agenda items) if it's necessary and change them. But the only area where I am not fully confident is if it was suggested that we redirect the whole session requiring a new input to the computer and the use of other tools. It is simply my (lack of) knowledge of the other tools and the time it takes me to think it through and set them up and the pressure of having people waiting while you do this. It tends to create opportunities for mistakes.

Other situations when the trainees stuck to the set agenda were when they had to deal with issues involving contentions, conflict, or high emotions. Even though intuitive cues signalled that alternative actions should be taken, this particular version of reflection-in-action, *Sticking to the Set Agenda*, was often made because there was insufficient time to adequately deal with the issues, or it was inappropriate for the issues to be dealt with in the meeting, or the trainees had neither the skills nor the confidence to resolve the issues. However, the trainees acknowledged to the group that these issues had surfaced and suggested that the group could deal with them at another time.

The trainees also realized that with more practice with the GSS tools and more experience in facilitating electronic meetings, a time would come when they could make intuitive choices without being constrained either by a lack of knowledge or by a lack of confidence in using those GSS tools when they were needed.

> And I trust that as I become more confident and more flexible and able to simply type in exercises in a moment or two as they arrive then that won't be an issue. But certainly it was an issue looking back on the whole session. It didn't feel like it was naturally evolving at all.

> Yes, I think there are two issues there. One is people sitting around waiting and doing nothing puts pressure on me and I don't like that, and secondly, if I was quick enough with the tools to say okay, let's drop that and we'll try something different here, I think I'll get there one (day when) I know more about other tools and when we can say yes, no, or let's try that a different way and just do it.

In summary, this section described a model of the reflective processes, *Active Reflection*, used by trainees in this study. *Active Reflection* describes the trainees' accounts of the two complementary action reflection processes

Reflection-on-Action and *Reflection-in-Action*. *Reflection-on-Action* is thinking back on what was done during the training program, while *Reflection-in-Action* is thinking about the action while one is doing it. The proposed model of *Reflection-in-Action* has two components–*Reflection-in-Action (with intuitive action)* and *Reflection-in-Action (without intuitive action)*.

IMPLICATIONS AND FUTURE TRENDS

This study has implications for GSS facilitation training in both its research and practice. Two of those implications are now considered.

First, research is required on how facilitators demonstrated "intuition" during the electronic meetings and on establishing the relationship between reflective practice and the development of intuitive and flexible facilitative behaviors. A deeper understanding of how the different levels of intuition affect facilitators' feelings and actions in an electronic meeting should provide better guidance on how facilitators can use their intuition during these meetings. We are currently pursuing this line of investigation.

Second, in the training of facilitators for both conventional and electronic meetings, more emphasis should be given to reflective practice. Training programs should include activities that promote reflective thinking and the development of less tangible facilitation attributes–for example, self-awareness of one's attitudes towards facilitation and recognition of one's beliefs in its values–because such attributes may influence the facilitators' behaviors in complex and unfamiliar situations (Heron, 1989; Poole, 1990; Bostrom et al., 1991; Hirokawa and Rost, 1992; Wynens, 1994; Schwarz, 1994). For example, Bostrom and Clawson (1991) believe that facilitators seldom question why things are done in the way they are and often accept the role model provided by their mentors or trainers without much critical thinking. Wynens (1994) further postulates that facilitators of collaborative problem-solving groups should examine closely their values and attitudes, as these will play a large part in influencing the choices of facilitative behaviors used with collaborative groups. For example, he argues that "values may influence the facilitator and the collaborative process outside the facilitator's direct awareness and ... strong value preferences may lead the facilitator to see every situation as a certain type, precluding alternative designs that might have been developed in the (planning) process" (p. 18). Heron (1989) discusses the facilitators' need for *self-awareness* in their work with groups and how awareness may help the facilitators to become more flexible. Awareness is also likely to decrease a facilitator bringing the "self" or "personal ego" into the groups' deliberations (Clawson, 1992). Hunter, Bailey & Taylor (1994) use the notion of *facilitat-*

ing oneself to describe the work that a facilitator needs to do in the understanding of self and its implications in facilitating other people. "Facilitating yourself is about self-awareness . . . Before you get involved in facilitating other people you need . . . to accept yourself . . . Facilitating yourself is about growing, developing and training yourself–but not about fixing up yourself" (p. 12-13).

In terms of future trends, advances in technology and software have increased the capabilities and complexities of the electronic meeting tools. This means that electronic meeting facilitators will need to learn about and incorporate these tools into their practices. We see this as adding to the facilitator's cognitive load during meetings and putting more stress on being able to reflect on practice while the event is occurring.

A second future trend is the increasing use of "virtual meetings." These meetings use information and communications technologies to enable dispersed group members to perform their activities. Little research has been conducted into the facilitation of virtual team meetings, and almost no research that we could find has looked at how reflective practices might influence the conduct and outcomes of these virtual meetings. Training electronic facilitators for the virtual meeting may be as challenging as training them for face-to-face electronic meetings.

CONCLUSION

Facilitating electronic meetings is a difficult and complex task. Yet, effective facilitation has been found to be a key factor in the success of these meetings. This chapter describes an approach to training electronic facilitators that focuses on the notion of reflective practice. For electronic meeting facilitation, we have found that it is not enough to simply practice a task or behavior. The trainee facilitator, and indeed the practicing facilitator, must reflect on their actions and behaviors, both during the meeting and after the meeting if the maximum amount of learning and performance is to be achieved.

In this chapter, we have described one component of our Theory of Reflective Facilitation–Reflective Practice. We have described in detail the factors and the relationships between those factors that affect Reflective Practice, and we have done so using an action learning approach with a training program for electronic meeting facilitation. We believe that incorporating reflective practices in electronic facilitator training will lead to "high performance facilitation" for high performance teams.

APPENDIX

A GSS Facilitation Training Program

Between March 1993 and June 1994, as a partial requirement for a doctoral research study, three groups of five experienced meeting facilitators participated in a GSS Facilitation Training Program. The training program consists of three modules as shown in Table 6.

The trainee facilitators (trainees) studied Modules 1 and 2 during two full-day and two half-day sessions. The practical component, "Putting It All Together," took place soon after the training. The trainees were expected to demonstrate the skills and knowledge acquired from the preceding training program. They did this by planning, managing and facilitating a "live" electronic meeting which lasted about three hours. All the meetings were videotaped and the recordings used for giving feedback to the trainees and as research data for this study.

A Typical Training Session

Experiential learning method encourages changes to a training session's agenda to accommodate the trainees' needs as they emerged during the session. For example, if the trainees thought that more time should be spent on familiarizing themselves with the GSS tools, then the agenda was changed to do just that. However, most training sessions followed this agenda:

- **Settling in**: At the beginning of each session, all trainees were encouraged to talk about what was going on in their professional, personal and family lives. Boud (1993) advocates that adult learning is a holistic process, that

Table 6: The components of a GSS Facilitation Training Program

Module Number	Title of Module	Brief Description of the Module
1	The Tools of an Electronic Meetings	This module provides the necessary hands-on skills and knowledge of the GSS product (GroupSystems V or VisionQuest).
2	Planning and Managing an Electronic Meeting	This module focuses on (a) how to plan and design an agenda for an electronic meeting, (b) how to balance human and computer interactions, and (c) the role of the facilitators in electronic meetings.
3	Putting It All Together	This practical module provides opportunities for trainees to plan and facilitate "live" electronic meetings.

has affective and cognitive features. We found that these settling-in periods allowed the trainee and peer trainees to be aware of what each was thinking and feeling. For example, during one training program, two of the trainees were feeling stressed because impending changes at work threatened them with job redundancy. Exchanging this sort of information and their responses to it resulted in increased trust among the trainees. We have used such events to learn from and have examined the implications these may have for the facilitation of "live" meetings. For example, knowledge of how some participants are feeling at the beginning of a meeting can become useful contextual cues for interpreting their behaviour during meetings.

- **Learning the GSS tools**: The learning of each GSS tool was structured as described by Bostrom et al. (1991)–"Model it, let them experience it, discuss and process it, let them experience it again. Build in structured 'playtimes'–individual time for them to play with the technology" (p. 33). A group discussion on how and when to use the tools during an electronic meeting often followed this approach. Boud's (1993) notion that learners actively construct their own experience has been found to be a useful principle. This is because "experience is not a given; it is created by learners in relation to the learning milieu and their own personal foundation of experience. Different learners will have quite different experiences within the context of the same learning event" (p. 35). The trainees found that they had to construct their learning of GSS tools differently according to a meeting's context. For example, facilitating a meeting where conflict resolution is a high priority requires a different approach to the use of GSS tools than in a meeting where the participants conduct planning scenarios. Each trainee was encouraged to think about how these shared learnings could be incorporated into his/her individual facilitation style.

- **Computer-supported group memory**: At the beginning of each training session, an electronic brainstorming tool was used to collect from the trainees any issues that were important to them. We then looked at how these issues might influence how they learned to become electronic meeting facilitators. After each session, the results were distributed and archived as the trainees' group memory. This method encourages the sharing of knowledge, skills and experience as resources for group members' learning.

- **Mini-meetings**: In addition to learning the different GSS tools, the trainees were given the opportunity to integrate them into an electronic meeting. Each trainee demonstrated the use of the tools during 15-minute structured mini-meetings with his/her peers as participants in the meeting, and in each of the meetings the topic was a current interest of the facilitator-in-practice. Immediately after the session, self- and peer feedback comments on each trainee's performance was given (see next section). It should be noted that these mini-meetings sessions were also used to increase the trainees' repertoire of facilitation skills and knowledge. The opportunity to observe each other's experience during the practice sessions served as another source of learning. This approach is in agreement with Boud's (1993) principle that "learning occurs in a socio-emotional context. Learning rarely occurs effectively in social isolation. We teach in groups, we have face-to-face contact between teachers and students, students learn much with their peer groups and when these are absent, as in distance education, we commonly accept the need to provide additional support structures for students" (p. 36).

- **Self- and peer feedback approach**: To be of most use, high-quality feedback must follow the practice of a newly-acquired skill. Feedback comments often show us if we have got that skill right. More importantly, if suggestions for changes in behaviours are given in a supportive and helpful manner, then the potential to incorporate these changes will increase (see the Appendix for a full account). As explained in the previous section, these trainees were encouraged to use the self- and peer feedback approach after each practice session.

- **"Wondering aloud" moments**: Another useful agenda item was the "wondering aloud" moments. These were periods during the training sessions when trainees were encouraged to discuss with their peers their feelings, emotions, concerns, issues and reflections on what it was like to be a facilitator of electronic meetings. "Learning is an holistic process which has affective, cognitive and connotative features. We cannot pretend, as we often do in universities, that learning is purely a cognitive process. Feelings and emotions are probably much more significant influences over what and how we learn than the ostensible cognitive content. The link with action is as necessary as it is ignored" (Boud 1993, p. 35).

The "Live" Electronic Meeting

The practical module, "Putting It All Together," took place after the training. Trainees demonstrated the skills and knowledge acquired from the preceding training program by planning, managing and facilitating a "live" electronic meeting that lasted about three hours. The participants in each meeting were told that, even though the meeting facilitator was undergoing training, they should use the meeting to deliberate on "live" issues that were important to them. In other words, they were not in a "mock" meeting. At the end of the meeting the meeting participants evaluated the trainee's performance. All the meetings were videotaped and the recordings used for giving feedback to the trainees and as research data for this study.

The Relationship between Reflective Practice and the Training Program

The features of Reflective Practice (including experiential learning methods) have informed the design and implementation of the training program. Every effort has been made to link the features of experiential learning with the action and reflection activities in the program. The following table illustrates the

Table A-1: The relationship between reflective practice and the training program

Learning activity	Features from Reflective Practice (including experiential learning)
Settling in	Share their action and reflection with others. Acknowledge that learning is an holistic process which has affective and cognitive features and occurs in a socio-emotional context.
Learning the GSS tools	Acknowledge the effects and influence of prior experience on their learning.
Computer-supported group memory	Use the knowledge, skills and experience of other group members as resources for their own learning.
Mini-meetings sessions	Gain new experiences by taking risks in testing new techniques and actions and invite group members to provide feedback, taking that feedback and implementing it, and reviewing with those members the action taken and the lessons that are learned.
Self- and peer feedback approach	Share their action and reflection with others.
"Wondering aloud" moments	Share their action and reflection with others.
"Live" electronic meeting	Work and gather data on real issues and problems associated with the facilitation of electronic meetings.

relationship between a number of the learning activities and features of experiential learning:

ENDNOTES

[1] An earlier version of this paper originally appeared in *Information Technology & People*, Vol. 12, No. 1, 1999. ©MCB University Press. Reproduced with permission.

[2] The first person singular "I" or "me" will be used to indicate the participant researcher role of the first author. "We" is used to denote the joint activities carried out by both authors. The second author provided advice and support during the study.

[3] I have 15 years experience as a facilitator of conventional meetings, four of these as a trainer of social workers in the facilitation of family conferences. Also, I have facilitated over 100 face-to-face electronic meetings for business and educational purposes.

[4] Please see the Appendix for a description of the GSS facilitation training program specifically designed and used in this study.

REFERENCES

Agor, W. (1989). *Intuition in Organizations: Leading and Managing Productively*. Newbury Park, CA: Sage Publications.

Anson, R. (1990). *Effects of Computer Support and Facilitator Support on Group Processes and Outcomes: An Experimental Assessment*. Unpublished doctoral dissertation, Indiana University.

Beranek, P., Beise, C., & Niederman, F. (1993). Facilitation and group support systems. *Proceedings of the Twenty-Sixth Annual Hawaii International Conference on Systems Sciences*, (4), 199-207.

Bostrom, R., Clawson, V., & Anson, R. (1991). *Training People to Facilitate Electronic Environments, Working Paper*, Department of Management, University of Georgia, Athens.

Boud, D. (1993). Experience as a base for earning. *Higher Education Research and Development*, 12(1), 33-44.

Boud, D., Keogh, R., & Walker, D. (1985). *Reflection: Turning Experience Into Learning*. London: Kogan Page.

Boud, D., & Walker, D. (1993). Barriers to reflection on experience. In Boud, D., Cohen, R. and Walker, D. (Eds.), *Using Experience For Learning*. Buckingham: SRHE and Open University Press.

Clawson, V. (1992). *The Role of the Facilitator in Computer-Supported Environments*. Unpublished doctoral dissertation, Walden University.

Cocklin, B. (1991). Back to school: A model of the processes of becoming an adult student. *British Journal of Sociology of Education*, 12(1), 3-21.

Friedman, P. (1989). Upstream facilitation: A proactive approach to managing problem-solving groups. *Management Communications Quarterly*, 3(1), 33-51.

Glaser, B., & Strauss, A. (1967). *The Discovery of Grounded Theory*. Chicago, IL: Aldine Publishing Co.

Glesne, C., & Peshkin, A. (1992). *Becoming Qualitative Researchers: An Introduction*. White Plaines, NY: Longman.

Hayne, S. (1999). The facilitator's perspective on meetings and implications for group support systems design. *Database for Advances in Information Systems*, 30(4), 72-91.

Heron, J. (1989). *The Facilitators' Handbook*. London: Kogan Page.

Hirokawa, R., & Rost, K. (1992). Effective group decision making in organizations: Field test of the vigilant interaction theory. *Management Communication Quarterly*, 5(3), 267-288.

Hunter, D., Bailey, A., & Taylor, B. (1994). *The Art of Facilitation*. Auckland, New Zealand: Tandem Press.

Kolb, D. A. (1984). *Experiential Learning: Experience as the Source of Learning and Development*. Englewood Cliffs, NJ: Prentice-Hall.

Miranda, S., & Bostrom, R. (1999). Meeting facilitation: Process versus content interventions. *Journal of Management Information Systems*, 15(4), 89-114.

Orlikowski, W. (1993). Case tools as organizational change: Investigating incremental and radical changes in systems development. *MIS Quarterly*, 17(3), 309-340.

Schon, D. (1983). *The Reflective Practitioner: How Professionals Think in Action*. New York: Basic Books.

Schon, D. (1987). *Educating the Reflective Practitioner: Toward a New Design for Teaching and Learning in the Professions*. San Francisco, CA: Jossey-Bass.

Schwarz, R. (1994). *The Skilled Facilitator: Practical Wisdom For Developing Effective Groups*. San Francisco, CA: Jossey-Bass.

Simon, H. (1987). Making management decisions: The role of intuition and emotion. *Academy of Management Executive*, 1(1), 57-64.

Strauss, A., & Corbin, J. (1990). *Basics of Qualitative Research: Grounded Theory Procedures and Techniques*. Newbury Park, CA: Sage Publications.

Tan, B., Wei, K., & Lee-Partridge, J. E. (1999). Effects of facilitation and leadership on meeting outcomes in a group support system environment. *European Journal of Information Systems*, 8(4), 233-246.

Vaughan, F. (1979). *A Wakening Intuition*. Garden City, NY: Anchor.

Vogel, D., Nunamaker, J., Applegate, L., & Konsynski, B. (1987). Group decision support systems: Determinants of success. In *The Proceedings of the Seventh International Conference on Decision Support Systems*, 118-128.

Woods, P. (1985). Ethnography and theory construction in educational research. In Burgess, R. (Ed.), *Field Methods in the Study of Education*, Falmer Press, Lewes.

Wynens, W. (1994). *Facilitator Values in Collaborative Problem Solving Groups*. Unpublished doctoral dissertation proposal, University of Georgia, Athens.

Yoong, P. (1995). Assessing competency in GSS skills: A pilot study in the certification of GSS facilitators. In *Proceedings of the ACM SIGCPR 1995 Conference*, 1-9. Nashville, Tennessee.

Yoong, P. (1996). *A Grounded Theory of Reflective Facilitation: Making The Transition from Traditional to GSS Facilitation*, Unpublished doctoral thesis, Victoria University of Wellington, New Zealand.

Zorn, T., & Rosenfeld, L. (1989). Between a rock and a hard place: Ethical dilemmas in problem-solving group facilitation. *Management Communication Quarterly*, 3(1), 93-106.

Chapter X

Using Action Learning in GSS Facilitation Training[1]

Pak Yoong
Victoria University of Wellington, New Zealand

Brent Gallupe
Queen's University, Canada

INTRODUCTION

Although electronic face-to-face meetings are increasingly being used by organizations to improve the productivity of their strategic planning teams, design task forces, quality circles, sales management, and other organizational groups (Alavi, 1993; Dishman & Aytes, 1996), the rate of adoption of the technologies to support these meetings appears to be slowing (Grise & Gallupe, forthcoming). A possible reason for this reduced rate of adoption may be the difficulty in training competent electronic meeting facilitators. These facilitators play a key role in electronic meetings that use computer-based group technologies or group support systems (GSS) to assist the group in tasks such as generating ideas, evaluating alternatives and developing action plans.

The purpose of this chapter is to describe how an action learning approach was used to train traditional meeting facilitators in the tools, techniques and processes of electronic meeting facilitation. This chapter begins with a description of action learning, in particular the three schools of action learning. The second section explains the nature of the "experiential" school of action learning and the GSS facilitation training program used in a research project in which 15 facilitators, already experienced in conventional meetings, were trained to become facilitators of electronic meetings. The final sections describe some lessons learned and implications for organizations training their electronic meeting facilitators.

WHAT IS ACTION LEARNING?

The term *action learning* was coined by Revans (1982) and is defined as "a means of development, intellectual, emotional or physical, that requires its subjects, through responsible involvement in some real, complex and stressful problem, to achieve intended change to improve their observable behavior henceforth in the problem field" (pp. 626-627). Revans' original concept and equation for learning–L = P + Q (i.e., Learning equals Programmed knowledge from the past plus Questioning insight)–have now been extended and applied in information systems education (Avison, 1989; Jessup & Egbert, 1995), information management (Finlay & Marples, 1998) and organizational development (Ramirez, 1983; Gregory, 1994). In these contexts, action learning is a group-learning and problem-solving process whereby group members work on real issues and problems with an emphasis on self-development and learning by doing.

Marsick and O'Neil (1999) identify three different "schools" of thought on action learning: Scientific, Experiential and Critical Reflection. Table 1 provides a summary of the theoretical background to each school of thought.

Marsick and O'Neil uncovered two themes that are common to all three schools of action learning: the group participants (a) meet on equal terms and (b) are engaged in solving unstructured problems where there is no one right solution. The group of four to six participants, known as the action learning "set," meets regularly and provides the supportive and challenging environment in which members are encouraged to learn from experience, sharing that experience with others, having other members criticize and advise, taking that advice and implementing it, and reviewing with those members the action taken and the lessons that are learned (Margerison, 1988). Many learning sets require the assistance of a "learning coach" and the role of the coach depends on (a) whether the learning set works on one project as a team or the participants work on individual projects and (b) the level of facilitation on group process (Marsick and O'Neil, 1999).

Action Learning and Action Research

Cunningham (1993) describes action research as "a spectrum of activities that focus on research, planning, theorizing, learning, and development ...a continuous process of research and learning in the researcher's long-term relationship with a problem" (p. 4). However, Carr and Kemmis (1986) emphasize the processes of "improvement" and "involvement" in action research:

Table 1: The three "schools" of action learning

School	Influenced by	Theoretical Background
Scientific	R. W. Revans (1982)	Action learning is viewed as a model of problem solving in three stages: 1. System Alpha - design of a problem-solving strategy including a situation analysis. 2. Systems Beta – the negotiation of the strategy including survey, hypothesis, experiment, audit and review. 3. System Gamma – the learning process associated with the strategy.
Experiential	D. Kolb (1984)	Based on Kolb's experiential learning cycle, proponents of this school advocate that the starting point for learning is action followed by reflection on action, preferably with the support of other group members. Any further action should focus on changing previous patterns of behaviors.
Critical Reflection	J. Mezirow (1990, 1991)	Proponents of this school see "reflection on action" as a necessary but insufficient condition for learning. They believe that participants should also go deeper and examine the assumptions and beliefs that influence their practice. Reflection at this deeper level focuses a participant's attention on the root of the problem and transforms previously held perspectives of the same problem.

(Adapted from Marsic and O'Neil, 1999; p. 161-163)

There are two essential aims of all action research: to improve and to involve. Action research aims at improvement in three areas: firstly, the improvement of a practice; secondly, the improvement of the understanding of the practice by its practitioners; and thirdly, the improvement of the situation in which the practice takes place. Those involved in the practice being considered are to be involved in the action research process... As an action research project develops, it is expected that a widening circle of those affected by the practice will become involved in the research process. (p. 165)

The use of action research in information systems research typically involves the researcher's intervention in an organization's core business process in order to both improve that process and generate new and relevant knowledge from this experience (Kock, McQueen & Scott, 1997). However, Lau's (1997) proposed IS action research framework describes the "classical" action research as having a focus on changing information systems related practice while the "emergent" version has a focus on changing social practice with a socio-technical system or a technological innovation.

Action learning is closely linked to action research. The relationship between action learning and action research is described by Zuber-Skerritt (1991) when she argues that action research is based on the "fundamental concepts of action learning, adult learning and holistic dialectical thinking..." (p. 88) and that action learning "...is a basic concept of action research" (p. 214). However, in the context of this groupware study, three differences between action learning and action research have been identified.[2] First, action learning focuses on a process in which a group of people (often from different organizations or situations) come together to help each other learn from their experience (for example, GSS facilitation). Each participant may draw different learning from his or her different experiences and organizational agenda. Therefore, the learning is unique to each participant. On the other hand, action research is a process by which a team of people, often coming from the same organization, pursues an organizational change strategy (for example, via a GSS-supported process improvement project) and the participants draw collective learning from a collective experience (Dick, 1997). Second, the researcher in an action learning project focuses on the facilitation of group members' learning, whereas, in action research, the researcher intervenes and facilitates an aspect of organizational change. Finally, both action learning and action research require participants to collect and analyze data whereas, in action research, the participants collect and analyze data in a more rigorous and formal manner (Marsick & O'Neil, 1999).

A CASE STUDY OF ACTION LEARNING AND GSS FACILITATION TRAINING

In this section, we describe the development of a GSS facilitation training program using the "experiential" school of action learning. This process was part of an intensive research study into the training of electronic meeting facilitators.

Background to the Study

This research study investigated the question: *How do facilitators of conventional meetings make the transition to facilitating face-to-face electronic meetings?* The study aimed to develop a model representing the learning processes and experiences of conventional meeting facilitators who were undergoing training in the facilitation of computer-supported problem-solving meetings (Yoong, 1995).

Between March 1993 and June 1994, I[4] trained three groups of five experienced meeting facilitators in a GSS facilitation training program. The training program consisted of three modules as shown in Table 2.

The trainee facilitators (trainees) studied Modules 1 and 2 during the two full-day and two half-day sessions. The practical component, "Putting It All Together," took place soon after the training. During this module the trainees were expected to demonstrate the skills and knowledge acquired from the preceding training program. They did this by planning, managing and facilitating a "live" electronic meeting which lasted about three hours.

The Appropriateness and Relevance of Action Learning

The facilitation of conventional meetings, with its characteristic rational and irrational components, has been found to be a complex process (Hirokawa & Rost, 1992; Schwarz, 1994). Understanding one's own facilitation actions, intended or unintended, is possible only with attention to situational and contextual complexities (Friedman, 1989) and with the recognition that much of what the facilitator does in meetings is active, spontaneous and flexible (Anson, 1990). There is simply little time to deliberate on their actions. If this situation is also coupled with the use of electronic meeting tools, the facilitation becomes very much more complex. How then do you design a training program that not only deals with this complexity in the learning situation but also equips the learners to handle this complexity in "live" situations?

To discover the personal experiences of the trainees in these complex situations, I began to search for learning approaches that would not only explicitly acknowledge my roles as researcher, facilitator and trainer but also my intimate involvement in the study.[3] This meant looking for a framework that would include me in the design of the study, in taking an active part in its implementation and in collecting, analyzing and interpreting the data. This is what Cunningham (1993)

Table 2: The components of a GSS facilitation training program

Module Number	Title of Module	Brief Description of the Module
1	The Tools of an Electronic Meetings	This module provides the necessary hands-on skills and knowledge of the GSS product (GroupSystems V or VisionQuest).
2	Planning and Managing an Electronic Meeting	This module focuses on (a) how to plan and design an agenda for an electronic meeting, (b) how to balance human and computer interactions, and (c) the role of the facilitators in electronic meetings.
3	Putting It All Together	This practical module provides opportunities for trainees to plan and facilitate "live" electronic meetings.

described as being "engaged" in the problem as it evolves. It was proposed that *action learning* would be the appropriate and relevant approach for a GSS facilitation training program to be used in the study.

Action learning provides a useful approach for a study with the intent of unravelling the nature and processes of GSS facilitation training. First, action learning focuses on tackling real "live" organizational issues and "action learning problems are always based on real work" (Marsick & O'Neil, 1999, not, p. 165). Learning to facilitate in GSS environments is real and "live" for many organizations who have or are considering installing groupware facilities (Niederman, Beise & Beranek, 1996).

Second, action learning promotes learning in collaborative groups and that group process is important to participants' learning (Marsick & O'Neil, 1999). Iacono, Vogel and Nunamaker (1990) suggest that GSS facilitation training should be conducted in groups as "this enables members to take turn practicing as facilitators and then participating as group members" (p. 5).

Third, action learning is suited to turbulent environments that are experiencing conditions of uncertainty and unpredictability (Ramirez, 1983). Electronic meetings can be turbulent environments where uncertainty and unpredictability are common phenomena. In these conditions, GSS facilitators, in consultation with meeting participants, are continually adapting the meeting agenda to accommodate to these unexpected changes (DeSanctis & Poole, 1994). In this respect, action learning is appropriate for GSS facilitation training as it encourages and promotes the practice of active flexible facilitation.

Finally, action learning meets the requirement that this training program is tailored to a group of experienced facilitators of conventional meetings who could bring their own expertise and who, by researching their own practice, would be able to improve their own facilitation practice in the electronic meeting environment.

The "Experiential" School of Action Learning

Many proponents of action learning advocate that "learning" is the main reason for their program and promote Kolb's experiential learning cycle as its theoretical base (Marsick & O'Neil, 1999). Kolb's (1984) model of experiential learning suggests that learning is a dialectic and cyclical process consisting of four action and reflection stages as shown in Figure 1 and briefly described in Table 3.

In practice, this cycle of action and reflection activity does not flow in a linear and sequential fashion. It is far more fluid and dynamic, and the learners move back and forth among the stages. The experiential learning model provides a useful guide to learning and progress through the process.

In many respects, Kolb's description of experiential learning appeals in that learning to be a facilitator of electronic meetings requires more than just "reading,"

Table 3: Kolb's model of experiential learning

Concrete experience	The learners identify their own learning activity and involve themselves fully and openly in a new experience
Reflective observation	The learners observe, analyse and reflect on the new experience
Abstract conceptualization	The learners create concepts that integrate the observations into contextually relevant models
Active experimentation	The learners apply these models in unfamiliar situations

Figure 1: Kolb's model of experiential learning

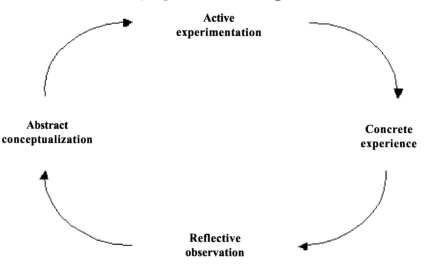

"talking" and "thinking" about it. It also requires the actual experience of "doing" it. The combined efforts of action and reflection provide the essential processes for enabling facilitators to gain the skills and insights for managing and supporting those parts of an electronic meeting that are uncertain and unpredictable. Facilitators need to know what they can or cannot do before embarking on improving or changing these facilitation behaviors. This link between what is already known - the facilitators' experience in conventional meetings - and what they want to know, change or improve - the use of the electronic meeting tools - is also a common feature of experiential learning. The process of integrating new experience with past experience through reflection is an important aspect of the trainees' learning to be facilitators of electronic meetings.

The "Experiential" School of Action Learning in Action

In this section, we will describe the use of three experiential learning activities during the a typical group training session.

Learning the GSS tools: During each training session, the trainees were encouraged to learn the GSS tools. The learning of each GSS tool was structured as described by Bostrom et al. (1991)–"Model it, let them experience it, discuss and process it, let them experience it again. Build in structured 'playtimes'–individual time for them to play with the technology" (p. 33). This approach was often followed by a group discussion on how and when to use the tools during an electronic meeting. Boud's (1993) notion that learners actively construct their own experience has been found to be a useful principle. The trainees found that they had to construct their learning of GSS tools differently according to a meeting's context. For example, facilitating a meeting where conflict resolution is a high priority requires a different approach to the use of GSS tools than in a meeting where the participants conduct planning scenarios. Each trainee was encouraged to think about how these shared learnings can be incorporated into his/her individual facilitation style.

Mini-meetings: In addition to learning the different GSS tools, the trainees were given the opportunity to integrate them into an electronic meeting. Each trainee demonstrated the use of the tools during 15-minute structured mini-meetings with his/her peers as participants in the meeting, and in each of the meetings the topic was a current interest of the facilitator-in-practice. Immediately after the session, self- and peer feedback comments on each trainee's performance was given. It should be noted that these mini-meeting sessions were also used to increase the trainees' repertoire of facilitation skills and knowledge. The opportunity to observe each other's experience during the practice sessions served as another source of learning.

The "Live" Electronic Meeting: The practical module–"Putting It All Together"–took place after the training. Trainees demonstrated the skills and knowledge acquired from the preceding training program by planning, managing and facilitating a "live" electronic meeting that lasted about three hours. The participants in each meeting were told that, even though the meeting facilitator was undergoing training, they should use the meeting to deliberate on "live" issues that were important to them. In other words, they were not in a "mock" meeting. All the meetings were videotaped and the recordings used for giving feedback to the trainees and as research data for this study.

In the next section, we will describe one of the three experiential learning activities and in particular, a trainee's attempt to learn to manage "information overload" during his "live" meeting by using Kolb's experiential learning cycle.

Kolb's Experiential Learning Cycle in Action

In a problem-solving meeting, GSS can support the generation of ideas (Gallupe & Cooper, 1993). Paradoxically, the use of this electronic brainstorming tool may also require human facilitation to help, among other things: (a) reduce the likelihood of information overload, and (b) sift the list of generated ideas into meaningful categories. Many trainees considered this aspect of GSS facilitation to be a key dimension of their facilitator's role and the "live" meetings provide an opportunity to practice the management of information overload during an electronic meeting. Table 4 provides a description of Trainee X's activities or thoughts of during his "live" meeting.

One observation that I have noted is how the notion of *managing information overload* took on its real significance only after the trainees experienced the facilitation of their first electronic meeting. For example, during the initial stage of the training sessions, the trainees said how important it was to clarify the meeting expectations - including how long a meeting might take and what could be achieved in it - with the sponsors and participants of the meetings. This was often based on their experience of conventional meetings. However, after the experience of facilitating their first electronic meeting, many trainees realized the significance of information overload from a facilitator's perspective and the time it takes to make sense of this overload during the course of a meeting. Therefore, a more realistic model of *managing information overload* in electronic meetings is now included in the trainees' strategy for electronic meetings. In this respect, the "experiential" school of action learning is useful in the development of this strategy.

LESSONS LEARNED

We believe there are a number of lessons learned from the use of the action learning approach in this situation. First, learning to use and facilitate a GSS meeting is a complex and difficult experience. Action learning provides the learner with the means to combine both experience and reflection as the learning is taking place. Having the facilitators gain concrete experience with an electronic meeting, then reflect on that experience, and then consolidate that previous experience and reflection in a new experience, seems to be a powerful means of learning in complex situations. Although action learning focused on the facilitators in this study, the action learning approach could also be used by meeting participants themselves to gain a better understanding of how the technology affects

Table 4: Kolb's experiential learning cycle during the "live" meeting

Kolb's experiential learning cycle	Trainee X's activities and/or thoughts
Concrete experience	Trainee X's goal for this experiment was to learn how to minimize participants' experience of information overload during the early stages of the electronic meeting.
Reflective observation	During the first brainstorming activity, the eight participants were asked to submit at most three ideas to the public screen. However, more than 35 ideas were submitted and many of the ideas were similar in nature. The following excerpt was reproduced from Trainee X's journal and discussed in a subsequent meeting of the learning set: "During the meeting, one person asked if he could submit more than three ideas. Instead of saying 'no' or 'hold on,' I said 'why not.' This meant I indirectly gave permission to everyone else to do the same. Therefore, I need to keep to my planned strategy in future meetings until I have more experience in GSS facilitation."
Abstract conceptualization	The following excerpt was also reproduced from Trainee X's journal: "In the future I will ask each participant to (a) submit one idea at a time, (b) then read the public screen and (c) check that the next idea to be submitted is not already shown on the screen. This approach may reduce the redundancy of ideas and therefore minimize the participants' experience of information overload.
Active experimentation	Trainee X applied the new approach in a subsequent meeting involving 11 participants. The first brainstorming exercise generated 37 ideas but many of the ideas were still similar. The following excerpt was reproduced from Trainee X's journal: "I am happy with the realistic number of ideas generated. However, I need to think a bit more about the notion of 'unique' ideas and whether asking participants to only submit ideas which are not already on the public screen may hinder the meeting's level of creativity."

the meetings they attend and how they might use the technology for even greater effect.

Second, the action learning approach enables the researcher to better understand what the learner is experiencing, and therefore better able to adapt his/her approaches to make the learning more efficient and effective. The action learning approach goes beyond some interpretative techniques in that it enables the subject to express his/her own thoughts about what is being learned and how the learning is occurring rather than being interpreted by the researcher. This "direct" link to the data is an important benefit for the researcher from the action learning approach.

Third, the action learning approach has potential beyond just GSS research. Information systems researchers, in general, might consider this approach when studying learning in complex, technology situations. For example, as end-user software becomes increasingly more complicated and difficult to navigate (as more features are added to these programs), it will be important to use action learning techniques to help those end users to learn to use the software and to aid researchers in understanding how that learning is taking place. A second example is the software developers building new e-commerce applications. Action learning techniques might help novice developers acquire the skill sets needed to build these applications in a shorter period of time and with deeper understanding. Using action research to study this approach may lead to better ways of learning in the turbulent world of web applications development.

Finally, this study examined the use of action learning in training electronic meeting facilitators in face-to-face electronic meetings. The findings from this study should provide the foundation for investigating how to train facilitators for dispersed, real-time meetings where group members are in different locations. These are more complicated facilitation situations than face-to-face electronic meetings. The experiential action learning approach should enable experienced face-to-face electronic meeting facilitators to reflect on their experiences in those situations and adapt their learning models to the dispersed situation.

CONCLUSION

It is our view that action learning, particularly "experiential" action learning, is a powerful technique in the training of electronic meeting facilitators. The action learning approach offers the potential to develop a deep understanding of what a conventional meeting facilitator goes through to become an electronic meeting facilitator. What facilitators learn and how they are trained in the facilitation of electronic meetings will remain an important issue. From a research perspective, there is much to be done to understand this area of training of GSS facilitators, as it has implications for the training of facilitators of meetings held across time and place. Avenues that require further research include the effectiveness of the action learning method, the importance of mentoring and coaching of trainee facilitators and the difference between training experienced and novice facilitators. It is hoped that this chapter, which describes the action learning approach to the training of GSS facilitators, will promote identification of and discussion about the many complex issues associated with the training of meeting facilitators for the electronic workplace.

ENDNOTES

[1] An earlier version of this paper originally appeared in *Information Technology & People*, Vol. 14, No. 1, 2001. ©MCB University Press. Reproduced with permission.

[2] Since this study focused on the learning experiences of a group of facilitators, it was decided that action learning, which focuses on participants learning from experience, has an advantage over action research as a research method. A more detailed discussion on the appropriateness and relevance of action learning is given in a later section.

[3] The first person singular "I" or "me" will be used to indicate the action learning role of the first author. "We" is used to denote the joint activities carried out by both authors. The second author provided advice and support during the study.

[4] A brief description of the role of the participant researcher is provided in the Appendix.

REFERENCES

Alavi, M. (1993). An assessment of electronic meeting systems in a corporate setting. *Information Management*, 25(4), 175-182.

Anson, R. (1990). *Effects of Computer Support and Facilitator Support on Group Processes and Outcomes: An Experimental Assessment*. Unpublished doctoral dissertation, Indiana University.

Anson, R., Bostrom, R., & Wynne, B. (1995). An experiment assessing group support system and facilitator effects on meeting outcomes. *Management Science*, 41(2), 189-208.

Avison, D. (1998). Action learning for information systems teaching. *International Journal of Information Management*, 9, 41-50.

Beranek, P., Beise, C., & Niederman, F. (1993). Facilitation and group support systems. *Proceedings of the Twenty-Sixth Annual Hawaii International Conference on Systems Sciences*, (4), 199-207.

Bostrom, R., Anson, R., & Clawson, V. (1993). Group facilitation and group support systems. In Jessup, L. and Valacich, J. (Eds.), *Group Support Systems: New Perspectives*. New York: Macmillan.

Bostrom, R., Clawson, V., & Anson, R. (1991). *Training People to Facilitate Electronic Environments*. Working Paper, Department of Management, University of Georgia, Athens.

Boud, D. (1993). Experience as a base for learning. *Higher Education Research and Development*, 12(1), 33-44.

Carr, W., & Kemmis, S. (1986). *Becoming Critical: Education, Knowledge and Action Research*. Deakin University, Geelong, Australia.

Clawson, V. (1992). *The Role of the Facilitator in Computer-Supported Environments*. Unpublished doctoral dissertation, Walden University.

Clawson, V. and Bostrom, R. (1996). Research-driven facilitation training for computer support environments. *Group Decision and Negotiation*, 5, 7-29.

Clawson, V., Bostrom, R. and Anson, R. (1993). The role of the facilitator in computer-supported meetings. *Small Group Research*, 24(4), 524-547.

Cunningham, J. (1993). *Action Research and Organizational Development*. Westport, CT: Praeger.

DeSanctis, G., & Poole, S. (1994). Capturing the complexity in advanced technology use: Adaptive structuration theory. *Organization Science*, 5(2), 121-147.

Dick, B. (1997). *Action Learning and Action Research*. Available on the World Wide Web at: http://www.scu.edu.au/schools/sawd/arr/actlearn.html.

Dishman, P., & Aytes, K. (1996). Exploring group support systems in sales management applications. *Journal of Personal Selling & Sales Management*, 16(1), 65-77.

Findlay, P., & Marples, C. (1998). Experience in using action learning sets to enhance information management and technology strategic thinking in the UK National Health Service. *Journal of Applied Management Studies*, 7(2), 165-183.

Friedman, P. (1989). Upstream facilitation: A proactive approach to managing problem-solving groups. *Management Communications Quarterly*, 3(1), 33-51.

Gallupe, B., & Cooper, W. (1993). Brainstorming electronically. *Sloan Management Review*, 35(1), 27-36.

Gans, H. (1982). The participant observer as a human being: Observations on the personal aspects of fieldwork. In Burgess, R. (Ed.), *Field Research: A Source Book and Field Manual*, London: Allen & Unwin.

Gorton, I., & Motwani, S. (1996). Issues in co-operative software engineering using globally distributed teams. *Information and Software Technology*, 38, 647-655.

Gregory, M. (1994). Accrediting work-based learning: Action learning–A model for empowerment. *Journal of Management Development*, 13(4), 41-52.

Grise, M., & Gallupe, R. B. (forthcoming). Information overload: Addressing the productivity paradox in face-to-face electronic meetings. *Journal of Management Information Systems*.

Hirokawa, R., & Rost, K. (1992). Effective group decision-making in organizations: Field test of the vigilant interaction theory. *Management Communication Quarterly*, 5(3), 267-288.

Iacono, S., Vogel, D., & Nunamaker, J. (1990). *GroupSystems Facilitation*, Working Paper, Department of MIS, University of Arizona.

Jessup, L., & Egbert, J. (1995). Active learning in business education with, through, and about technology. *Journal of Information Systems Education*, 7(3), 108-112.

Knool, K., & Jarvenpaa, S. (1995). Learning to work in distributed global teams. In *Proceedings of the 28th Annual Hawaii International Conference on Systems Sciences in Hawaii*, 92-97.

Kock, N., McQueen, R., & Scott, J. (1997). Can action research be made more rigorous in a positivist sense? The contribution of an iterative approach. *Journal of Systems and Information Technology*, 1(1), 1-24.

Kolb, D. (1984). *Experiential Learning*. Englewood, NJ: Gower Publishing.

Lau, F. (1997). A review on the use of action research in information systems studies. In Lee, A. S., Liebenau, J. and DeGross, J. I. (Eds.), *Information Systems and Qualitative Research*. London: Chapman and Hall.

MacNamara, M., & Weekes, W. (1982). The action learning model of experiential learning for developing managers. *Human Relations*, 35(10), 879-902.

Margerison, C. (1988). Action learning and excellence in management development. *Journal of Management Development*, 7(5), 43-53.

Marsick, V., & O'Neil, J. (1999). The many faces of action learning. *Management Learning*, 30(2), 159-176.

McGill, I., & Beaty, L. (1993). *Action Learning: A Practitioner's Guide*. London: Kogan Page.

McGill, I., Segal-Horn, S., Bourner, T., & Frost, P. (1989). Action learning: A vehicle for personal and group experiential learning. In Weil, S. and McGill, I. (Eds.), *Making Sense of Experiential Learning: Diversity in Theory and Practice*. Milton Keynes: Open University Press.

Niederman, F., Beise, C., & Beranek, P. (1993). Facilitation issues in distributed group support systems. In *Proceedings of the ACM SIGCPR Conference*, St. Louis, Missouri, 299-313.

Niederman, F., Beise, C., & Beranek, P. (1996). Issues and concerns about computer-supported meetings: The facilitators' perspectives. *MIS Quarterly*, 20(1), 1-22.

Nunamaker, J., Dennis, A., Valacich, J., Vogel, D., & George, J. (1991). Electronic meeting systems to support group work: Theory and practice at Arizona. *Communications of the ACM*, 34(7), 40-61.

Ramirez, R. (1983). Action learning: A strategic approach for organizations facing turbulent conditions. *Human Relations*, 36(8), 725-742.

Revans, R. (1982). *The Origins and Growth of Action Learning*. Bromley: Chartwell-Bratt.

Schwarz, R. (1994). *The Skilled Facilitator: Practical Wisdom For Developing Effective Groups*. San Francisco, CA: Jossey-Bass.

Vogel, D., Nunamaker, J., Applegate, L., & Konsynski, B. (1987). Group decision support systems: Determinants of success. In *The Proceedings of the Seventh International Conference on Decision Support Systems*, 118-128.

Yoong, P. (1995). Training facilitators for electronic meetings: A New Zealand case study. In *Proceedings of the 6th Australasian Conference in Information Systems*, 503-516. Perth, Australia.

Yoong, P. (1996). *A Grounded Theory of Reflective Facilitation: Making the Transition From Traditional to GSS Facilitation*. Unpublished doctoral thesis, Victoria University of Wellington, New Zealand.

Zuber-Skerritt, O. (1991). *Professional Development in Higher Education: A Theoretical Framework for Action Research*. Griffith University, Brisbane, Australia.

APPENDIX–THE ROLE OF THE PARTICIPANT RESEARCHER IN THIS STUDY

The role I took in this study could be described as participant researcher (Gans, 1982). Specifically, I was a participant trainer as well as a researcher. As such I was involved in the design and implementation of a training program used in this study. I was an integral part of the whole training program and the experience and learning that took place. I was also closely connected with what went on in the program which also included having a close rapport with the facilitators in the study. We were on different journeys but with the same destination.

I saw my primary goal, as researcher, as collecting, analyzing and interpreting the data. The qualitative data consists of detailed description of the facilitators, events, interactions and observed behaviors during the training programs. This included data from the facilitators' journals and memos and video recordings of actual live electronic meetings. I also collected direct quotations, via semi-structured interviews, from the facilitators about their experience, preoccupations, beliefs and attitudes on a range of subjects related to becoming facilitators of electronic meetings. This included the use of data collected in my personal journal which focused on aspects of my role during the study and my reactions to them. This source of information provided valuable insights on my role as a participant researcher.

Chapter XI

Extending Collaboration Support Systems: Making Sense in Remote Innovation

Thekla Rura-Polley and Ellen Baker
University of Technology, Sydney

This chapter first examines the role of collaboration and collective learning in regional and industry-wide innovation and how remote innovation–that is, innovation organized through electronic collaboration–could be enhanced by comprehensive computer support tools that include sensemaking aids. We look at the importance of sensemaking in collaborations and report on a study in which we analyzed sensemaking processes among students collaborating remotely. We describe a web-based computer system called *LiveNet*, that incorporates sensemaking aids to facilitate remote innovation. It brings together members within one workspace, provides them with the ability to locate needed information quickly, and supports this process with an agent-based structure that can assist members to achieve their goals. In addition, *LiveNet* supports the development of a common language and facilitates knowledge sharing, processes deemed important in the innovation and collective learning literatures. In the final section, we describe how this system can be used in remote innovation.

INTRODUCTION

Collaboration is recognized as an important organizational practice by many academics (Gray, 1989; Huxham, 1996; Pasquero, 1991; Roberts & Bradley, 1991; Wood & Gray, 1991). In particular, inter-organizational collaboration is becoming an increasingly common business practice as organizations focus on their core competencies and outsource peripheral activities in their attempts to innovate, develop emerging markets, respond to global competition or implement new technologies. Accordingly, a wide variety of new organizational forms such as networks, strategic alliances, cooperatives and joint ventures have emerged, that allow different organizations to work together (Palmer & Dunford, 1997).

The innovation literature often refers to collaboration as an important factor for enhancing innovativeness in organizations as well as in industries. For instance, Dougherty and Hardy (1996, p. 1122) suggested that mature organizations that want to develop a capacity for sustained innovation must "provide collaborative structures and processes to solve problems creatively and connect innovations with existing businesses." Similarly, Smith, Ahmed and Takanashi (1999) reported that open collaboration between different organizations represents a main driver for technological innovation in the late 20th century, while Wycoff and Snead (1999, p. 55) claimed that innovation itself was "a collaborative skill that involves actively scouting the future, generating new ideas, choosing the best ones, rapidly and effectively implementing them, and then learning the lessons from successes and failures to begin again."

As far as regional or industry-wide innovation is concerned, researchers also increasingly point to the importance of collaboration and networks. For example, Keeble, Lawson, Moore and Wilkinson (1999) as well as Asheim (1996) developed the concept of collective learning to refer to the development of the capacity of a regional innovative milieu amongst member firms. Successful collective learning is characterized by establishing a common language and by sharing technological or engineering knowledge as well as organizational knowledge across organizational boundaries (Lorenz, 1996). Establishing a common language helps to build trust between collaborating partners. Because of unanticipated events and uncertainties that often arise after formal contracts have been arranged, trust helps the partners move forward. Sharing technological or engineering knowledge often involves the detailed product design, testing and production of the innovation. Organizational knowledge may include the division of responsibilities or the choice of procedures to ensure consistent, collective decision making. In addition to these three elements, Camagni (1991) and others (e.g., Simmie, 1997) have pointed to the importance of common culture, as well as psychological and social background as facilitators of collective learning. In an empirical study of the biotechnology industry, Powell, Koput and Smith-Doerr (1996) found that collaboration within networks was an important mechanism to gain access to knowledge that was widely distributed and not necessarily produced within the boundaries of any one member of the network. Thus, there is ample evidence suggesting that collaborating with other organizations can enhance innovation. Most of this research, however, has focused on face-to-face or locally bounded rather than geographically-dispersed, remote collaboration.

Even though collaboration has received increasing attention by academics only during the last decade, as an organizing form it has been part of many industries for a long time, e.g., film production since at least the 1950s (Birkmaier, 1994; Faulkner & Anderson, 1987; Miller & Shamsie, 1996). Remote collaboration as an organizing form, however, is a phenomenon of the 1990s. Remote collaboration is an advanced form of collaboration that entails collaboration through the use of electronic networks (Mizer, 1994). While several studies have investigated remote collaboration in general, and the management of remote collaboration in particular (e.g., Baker, Geirland, Fisher, & Chandler, 1999; Palmer, Dunford, Rura-Polley, & Baker, 2001), little systematic study of managing innovation in remote collaborations exists so far.

This chapter looks at two main issues confronting the management of innovation in remote collaborations, or, as we will call it, the management of remote innovation. First, remote innovation – by definition – is managed through electronic networks and systems, but little comprehensive computer-support is available so far. A variety of group support systems exists (Huseman & Miles, 1988), but these often are not sufficiently comprehensive to support the number of processes involved in a collaboration. They may support the decision-making process or the sharing of documents, but not the development of a joint vantage point (cf. Hardy, Phillips, & Lawrence, 1997; Hardy & Phillips 1998).

Second, existing group support tools for electronic collaboration mostly address group problem solving and miss the crucial element of sensemaking (Weick & Meader 1993). This may be because, as Tenkasi (1999), among others (Lyytinen, 1987; Boland, Tenkasi, & Te'eni, 1994), argues, the prevailing technologies draw upon models from decision theory rather than upon interpretive approaches to organizations and organizational actors. Thus, they support knowledge sharing in collaborations through collating information on certain parameters, similar to collating personal preferences in electronic decision-support systems. They rely on rational actors and objectivity of information and knowledge. They support neither the situatedness nor subjectivity of knowledge nor the framing of the knowledge arenas, all of which have to be explicit before knowledge can be created and shared in remote innovation teams.

Some authors propose that reliance on decision theory has hindered the development of information technology that is capable of supporting sensemaking processes in organizations (Boland et al., 1994; Feldman & March, 1981). Also, most researchers into group support systems have favored problem definition rather than problem framing. Their research has focused on "answers rather than questions, outcomes rather than inputs, and structure rather than process" (Weick & Meader, 1993, p. 231). This leads to problems, because "in real-world practice, problems do not present themselves to the practitioners as givens. They must be constructed from the materials of problematic situations which are puzzling, troubling, and uncertain" (Weick, 1995, p. 9). In other words, problems are shaped by, and in turn shape, sensemaking, a set of activities that occurs prior to the decision-making stage.

As mentioned earlier, for Lorenz (1996) developing a shared language was as crucial for regional innovativeness as was sharing technical and organizational knowledge, while Camagni (1991) pointed to the importance of synergy effects based on common cultural, psychological and political backgrounds in successful collaborative innovation. Essentially, both authors are referring to sensemaking aids. A common language or culture helps people make sense of what somebody else means when making a request, commenting on an idea or voicing an objection. Thus, a computer system that is intended to facilitate remote innovation has to go beyond existing group support systems by incorporating devices that help with sensemaking. The next section looks at sensemaking in remote collaboration in general, before applying these insights within a web-based computer system that can be used to manage remote innovation.

SENSEMAKING IN REMOTE COLLABORATION

Generally, when individuals seek to understand phenomena that do not appear sensible, they rationalize these phenomena by using prior experiences, contextual information, or other available means. In other words, when individuals make phenomena, events, or information sensible, they engage in sensemaking (Weick, 1995). Sensemaking is a crucial organizational capacity. As Brown (1999) has observed, managers increasingly engage in making sense rather than products for their stakeholders. They interpret the market, the forces shaping the competitive landscape, and the risks and opportunities presented to their company. Thus, one essential task of managers concerns creating knowledge out of disparate data and complex information, providing guidelines for action, and understanding problems in detail so that they can be solved (Weick, 1985).

Failures in sensemaking can have disastrous consequences, as Weick's (1993) analysis of the 1949 Mann Gulch disaster showed. Thirteen fire fighters died in the process of trying to contain a fire. When the team leader, Dodge, ordered his team members to drop their tools and lie down in an area where he had lit an escape fire, no one did, because taking such extraordinary action did not make sense to them. Instead, they ran for the ridge and only two of them survived. If they had followed Dodge's directive, all would have survived.

The problem alluded to here is that individuals differ in their sensemaking. Individuals have different experiences on which they rely when making sense of phenomena and events. Thus, engaging in shared sensemaking and attaining shared meaning can be quite difficult in an organization (Weick, 1995). This difficulty is exacerbated in collaborations that are intentionally set up to bring together people with differing experiences and view points. As Hewitt and Hall (1973, p. 370) point out, "participants who differ in social class, ethnicity, religion, or other important dimensions may find common ground only with difficulty." Therefore, communication, let alone sensemaking, within such collaborations is often complicated, since effective communication relies on common language and shared meanings. In fact, Weick (1995) cited lack of shared sensemaking as a frequent cause of collaboration failures.

When it comes to sensemaking in collaborations for innovation, it is important to keep in mind that such collaborations involve not only different individuals with different prior experiences and contextual information, but also individuals who represent different functions, expertise and modes of rationality. Different functions within business often have their own languages. For instance, the language of accounting differs substantially from the language of engineering or marketing (Clegg, 1989). Moreover, each function uses its own terminology and methods of communication that may not correspond with that used by another function. Bechky (1999) showed that design engineers used different terms than assembly workers, and when the two teams used a common term, the term actually referred to different objects. The technicians, located organizationally between the design engineers and the assembly workers, brokered knowledge transfer between the teams in order to create new products successfully. These technicians made sense of, and for, the other occupations.

In face-to-face collaborations such differences in definitions of terms and resulting miscommunication will become evident very quickly in the confused looks of the participants and through other contextual cues. In electronic collaborations such cues are missing. Therefore, Weick and Meader (1993, p. 232) thought it essential for a remote collaboration "to construct moderately consensual definitions that cohere long enough for people to infer some idea of what they have, what they want, why they can't get it, and why it may not be worth getting in the first place." Moreover, electronic representations are often flawed, because the data "contain only what can be collected and processed through machines. That excludes sensory information, feelings, intuitions, and context" – all of which are important for sensemaking

(Weick, 1985, p. 51). Thus, facilitating sensemaking in remote collaborations may be a crucial process for successful innovation.

The Theory of Sensemaking

This section describes the theoretical perspectives on sensemaking that inform our thinking about a remote innovation system. The first perspective is based on Weick's (1993; 1995) approach. He (1995, p. 17) understands sensemaking as "a process that is grounded in identity construction, retrospective, enactive of sensible environments, social, ongoing, focused on and by extracted cues, and driven by plausibility rather than accuracy." He uses these characteristics "to investigate what sensemaking is, how it works and when it can fail" (Weick, 1995, p. 18). Weick (1995) views sensemaking as both an individual and a social activity by acknowledging the impact of others on the sensemaker. Through interaction with others, sensemakers can compare multiple sources of data, ponder the results and place the confusing event or information into context (Weick & Meader, 1993).

When it comes to sensemaking in organizations, shared terminology, definitions and language are important, but one should not forget that meaning is also constructed and conveyed through rites, symbols, artifacts and ceremony. As Weick (1995, p. 3) points out, organizations do not only have their own language, but also symbols "that have important effects on sensemaking." After all, sensemaking also includes "the standards and rules for perceiving, interpreting, believing, and acting that are typically used in a given cultural setting" (Sackman, 1991, p. 33). Explicit standards and rules represent underlying values of an organization. Weick's (1995, p. 28) suggestion that people need "values, priorities, and clarity about preferences to help them be clear about which projects matter" when they experience equivocality, makes sense intuitively.

Our second perspective on sensemaking comes from Boland and Tenkasi's (1995) work on perspective making and taking. They (1995, p. 356) define perspective making as a "process whereby a community of knowing develops and strengthens its own knowledge domain and practice." Perspective taking is a process where organizational knowledge emerges out of exchange, evaluation and integration of knowledge (Duncan & Weiss, 1979). It involves a range of inferential and judgmental processes, which opens the process to systematic errors and biases (Boland & Tenkasi, 1995). The usage of language and narrative is particularly important in perspective making and taking. For example, Dougherty (1992) writes that perspective taking processes in cross-functional product development teams failed because members interpreted and understood linkages between technology and marketing qualitatively differently. Different departments had different internally consistent and coherent thought worlds. Members of a cross-functional team worked from their departmental thought worlds and assumed they knew the entire story; however, each story told within the team differed substantially from one another. Successful perspective taking involves "an increased capacity for communities of knowing to take each other into account within their own language games, and to construct new language games for their interaction" (Boland & Tenkasi, 1995, p. 359).

The third perspective on sensemaking comes from Bolman and Deal's (1997) work on frames of reference and reframing. They list four frames that managers might use when making sense of organizations: the structural frame, the human resource frame, the political frame, and the symbolic frame. Individuals interpret events in different ways depending on the frames that they adopt (Morgan, 1993). In collaboration, it is important that individuals are aware of their own preferred frame as well as being capable of reframing an event. According to Bolman and Deal (1997, p. 5), "effectiveness deteriorates when managers and leaders cannot reframe." Reframing, or deliberately viewing events from different perspectives, broadens cognitive perceptions of organizational events or problems, and helps to identify appropriate courses of action (Bolman & Deal, 1997). Being capable of reframing an event is especially important in cross-functional collaborations where participants may generally prefer the frame of reference most closely related to their own professional expertise. For instance, an engineer may prefer to look at events within a structural frame while a general manager may frame everything in political terms. Reframing an event may help members to overcome such professional blind spots.

In the following section, we report some research on sensemaking processes in electronic discussions among students before describing the development of an electronic support technology for facilitating sensemaking in remote collaborations. We will report on general sensemaking processes and terminology as well as on frames of reference used by the students.

THE PRACTICE OF SENSEMAKING IN REMOTE COLLABORATION

The setting for this exploratory study was an advanced research methods class in Management. There were 15 participants whose ages ranged from 21 to 55; some of the participants actually worked as academic staff in other faculties and universities. Their backgrounds included engineering, accounting, psychology, operations management, sociology, communications studies, as well as management. Thus, the participants resembled a typical cross-functional team. The majority of the students were male (11) and came from English-speaking backgrounds (13). Some of the objectives of the class included the development and critical assessment of theories and models at different levels of analysis; generating and justifying propositions and research questions; making intelligent choices of research settings and methods; and writing a succinct and feasible proposal or publishable article.

The class met weekly for one three-hour face-to-face seminar. The seminars contained discussions of publications as well as ongoing research work of the participants. A large proportion of the class work focused on collaborative learning. For instance, participants provided detailed feedback on one another's exercises and proposals. They also participated in electronic discussions on a special Internet site. On this Internet site, electronic discussion forums were organized under six specific themes, such as *Coffee Chat*, *Exercise Extravaganza*, *Reviewing Roundrobin*, *Theorizing Team*, *Methods Meeting*, *Paper Pulp*, and *Ask Thekla*. Students were given some guidelines about appropriate topics within each discussion list to make access to and retrieval of information easier. For example, in the *Exercise Extravaganza* forum, students were encouraged to share their weekly exercises, discuss them, get feedback from others, and help one another to progress in their learning. The *Theorizing Team* represented a section where students could discuss their own theories and theorizing endeavors. All in all, 27 messages were clocked on *Coffee Chat*, six on *Exercise Extravaganza*, seven on *Reviewing Roundrobin*, 68 on *Theorizing Team*, 15 on *Methods Meeting*, 21 on *Paper Pulp,* and 18 on *Ask Thekla.*

Some students contributed 17 or 19 times, while others did not contribute at all. The contributions ranged from six words to 920 words, and on average contained 247 words. The standard deviation was 222. The length of these contributions go far beyond what we have seen in other electronic discussions among students in other management classes at this school, or at other universities. In fact, the longest contribution had to be excluded from part of our analysis, because it crashed the system every time we tried to analyze it. Students' submissions to these discussions were saved on file for analysis in this study. Sixty-seven messages from one discussion forum, the *Theorizing Team*, were chosen for analysis.

Data Analysis

The data analysis consisted of two parts. In the first part, two of the researchers carried out an informal analysis of the discussions to try to increase our understanding of sensemaking processes. All the transcripts of the *Theorizing*

Team discussions were read. We immersed ourselves in these texts in order to investigate the specific sensemaking processes that were manifest in the discussions. We looked for examples of attempts at sensemaking by the students and indications as to what these discussants found helpful in their attempts at sensemaking in this situation.

The second part of the analysis was more formal. It involved the construction and application of a dictionary to be used for computer-aided processing of electronic discussions, and was guided by the experience of Kabanoff, Waldersee and Cohen (1995), who developed a computer-aided content analysis system for categorizing organizational values from text documents. In contrast to Kabanoff et al., our analysis did not focus on organizational values, but was based on Bolman and Deal's (1997) typology of organizational analysis and their four frames of reference: the structural, human resources, political and symbolic frames. Identification of key words in their book led to a database that listed the four frames of reference and a dictionary of words that are typically associated with each of those frames. We supplemented these terms with words from lists that Palmer (1999) developed in his study of metaphor usage among managers. In addition, two researchers scanned a number of introductory management texts for the types of keywords used for organizational phenomena related to each of the four frames and added those to the dictionaries.

We extended those dictionaries by manually analyzing a small proportion of the total text database, *Methods Meeting* and *Exercise Extravaganza* discussions, searching for words that intuitively seemed to reflect one of the four frames and included terms so identified in the dictionaries. We specifically looked for words that might not be provided in an academic discourse or within academic descriptions of the frames but would be typical of the discussion style among practitioners. Examples for the structural frame included "template" and "automate"; for the human resource frame, "burnout" and "helpful"; for the political frame, "hammered" and "revolution"; and lastly, for the symbolic frame, "decode" and "connotations."

The above words and phrases were then modified so that they would be suitable for computer-aided processing. The main change was the elimination of terms that had more than one meaning. These words may be easily processed by humans who would take the context into account but at this stage would provide erroneous categorizing if carried out by computer. Another modification involved the addition of all variations of a term, for example: motivate, motivated, motivates, motivation. We then used this dictionary to analyze the 67 submissions to the *Theorizing Team* discussion forum. The total word count for each discussion item and the number of hits for each frame of reference were recorded.

Results

In their remote sensemaking, participants utilized four different vehicles. They made sense by referring to shared readings, their own and one another's disciplinary background, common popular culture, and normal day-to-day experiences to which others could readily relate. For example, one message referred to a popular children's show on TV.

> Your comments of what framework we look at things through reminds me of Play School (I have x2 kids so I have been widely exposed to the show). You know, when they say "what window will we look through today?.....aagh that's right, the arched window" and depending on what window you look through determines what you'll see. (Of course we shouldn't neglect the temporal nature of their investigations!) Kid's books are also a great source of understanding (I read to both of my children each night). There's one book that makes the proposition "suppose you had no nose." By researching the phenomena the author is able to make some statements of causal inference and theorize as to the effects of the cause of no nose, and finally examine the implications of such to children. The framework adopted is one of a functionalist. The theories are really quite generalizable to other parts of the anatomy. (Funny how the kids don't seem to enjoy my interpretations!?) By the way, my favorite's Monica - how about you?

Over time, a common popular culture frame emerged, which became the main sensemaking vehicle in the class. In the second half of the semester, references to *Star Wars and the Phantom Menace* dominated the discussions. Students even took on nicknames from the movie. Positivist researchers were classified as the "Dark Side" and their most outspoken proponent was referred to and started to sign his messages as "Darth Vader." Non-positivist, postmodern, and cultural-symbolist researchers referred to themselves as the "Light Side," their most senior proponent–a doctoral student–became "Obi-Wan," the junior–an Honors student–became "Luke." Students who were undecided about the paradigm in which to do their research did not participate much in this debate and even had to be careful where to sit during the weekly face-to-face seminar, where "Dark" and "Light" Side were clearly marked. However, using the term "Light Side" backfired, when the "Dark Side" claimed that "Light Side" stood for "light-weight" argument.

We also found that students engaged in three different sensemaking processes. The first sensemaking process involved making sense of the class itself and the tasks required from them. The second sensemaking process involved making sense of each other, and the third sensemaking process involved making sense of the collaboration process. An example of the first sensemaking process is the following statement on the discussion list:

I am just sending some of my thoughts, on the notion of theorizing with which I have and still am having great difficulty. Grappling with the distinction between typologies and theories has been of great concern especially considering that my area of interest is International Human Resource Management (IHRM). This area is inundated with typologies and frameworks such as one outlined by Samuel Bacharach in his paper "Organizational Theories: some criteria for evaluation." That is, the example he gives of the search for a goodness of fit between empirically derived categorizations of business strategy and human resource strategy (Schuler and Jackson: 1987). This is what a lot of the literature in HRM/IHRM is based on. Originally, I thought that these typologies were part of a theory. However, the past two weeks in particular have enlightened my thinking on this. I understand now how this falls in the realm of description, not theory. I too have been following this type of theorizing—the descriptive type. It is precisely the "why" and "how" questions that I am having trouble with and then contextualizing them within theories that are both internally and externally consistent to IHRM. The articles in this course are certainly moving me toward this end. However, if anyone has come across a very simplified, almost prescriptive (?) article outlining theorizing according to some basic steps I would much appreciate it. Or if anyone has any storylike or novel way of conceptualizing the practice of theorizing, I would really like to know about it as I am sure others are also having at least some difficulty with "theorizing."

Another student's reply was:

I too have been enlightened by the information provided over the past few weeks to such an extent that I am now confused. I am not familiar with any literature that provides a step-by-step process on theorizing, however there is an article by Easterby, Smith, Thorpe and Lowe entitled "What is Management Research" that gives a pretty good idea of the fit between practitioner and academic research—that is, it is what is done with the knowledge that defines the research outcome. Within this article they use some typologies by Clarke to support of their argument. I thought that this may be useful for you since it seems to me that you may be experiencing a dissonance between the practitioner and academic literature rather than difficulty with the actual theorizing process. As far as theorizing for your research, as I mentioned, I too am having difficulty. After doing the stop and thinks, readings and talking with ... I was still no closer. So I did two things. Firstly, I went back to basics. For many years I have been a person who has said "I have a theory" about many topics. For example, I have a theory, based on an observation, that the fog on the F3 freeway is always worse on the weekend. There may be several reasons for this, e.g.,: because there is less traffic to dispurse the fog at road level on the weekends; the amount of fog is actually the same on weekends and weekdays - it is actually a passageway that is created by cars during the week; there is no difference–it is less cars that create an illusion of more fog because of a greater field of vision that enables you to focus on the fog, etc. However to be sure I need to check out a few things - do some tests. Funnily enough all this fitted in some way into the stuff we've been learning.

Another student entered the discussion:

So far I have found myself just writing, much the same like ... Brainstorming and questioning their arguments in a non-structured way. Getting the ideas and coming up with a research question is one thing but theorizing and coming up with a conceptual framework, looking for constructs and then thinking about possible variables, with the limited expertise and experience in this area is something I am barely coming to grips with in the framework of the readings for this class. The current stage I am at is that I have the literature on quality in management accounting and generally readings in TQM. I have some readings in quality in the collaborative setting and have developed questions on quality strategy as to the differences between both forms of literature. The question is how does one progress from merely asking basic and encompassing questions to developing constructs and variables that fall within the parameters material given in the reading. Are there articles on the how to of conceptualizing and the relationship with constructs and variables or should I just keep reading more articles in the literature and copy them?? From brainstorming to........

The discussions on making sense of the class and the exercises also affected how they made sense of readings in other classes. One student requested that "this course should come with a warning about the effects on reading research. I read a piece this morning and found myself stopping all the way through to repeat the constructs and their relationships. It took forever to read."

The earlier description of the Star Wars metaphors and nicknames is a good example of the second sensemaking process, how the students made sense of each other, especially of one another's functional background and research epistemology.

An example of the third sensemaking process, i.e., making sense of their collaboration processes, is the following. Here, one student tried to make sense of the previous week's electronic discussion by linking it to management literatures and came to the following conclusion:

> It could be argued that the recent debate surrounding the topic "Re: social Science and Organizational Theories" (Refer "Top Class"\ "Theorizing" herein) was indeed an example of intragroup conflict. This is a valid assertion if the definition by Boulding (1963) is accepted. Boulding suggests that conflict can be considered as "perceived incompatabilities or perceptions" and that " the parties hold discrepant views." It is interesting to note, therefore, how the conflict developed from a task-related conflict into a type of interpersonal conflict. It could also be suggested that the "benefits" of this conflict diminished as the transformation took place. This demonstrates a consistency with organizational behavior theories suggesting that conflict can be interpersonal or task related and indeed destructive or beneficial depending on the circumstances and context of the group. As Jehn (1995, p.256) asserts in relation to intragroup conflict within an organization, "whether conflict is beneficial depends upon the type of conflict, the structure of the group and group norms." Wow guys! A natural experiment unfolded right before my eyes and I think that I was able to explain it from an organization behavior perspective!!! I think that this theorizing stuff has some potential! - don't you???? Now I wonder what the social psychologists would make of it .... mmmmmm.

At some other point, a different student summarized parts of the discussion that had gone on, and thereby made sense of, and constructed meaning for the other participants.

> I'm really enjoying the debate on this topic. Obviously I see it as one of the fundamental issues that need to be resolved (if that's possible) and I do believe the discussion has gone some way to resolving it for me. I won't weigh in on the various philosophical arguments except to say that there seem to be valid points in all of them. Then again, …'s cool so she must be right ;-). My thoughts on the issue to emerge from the debate are: * we need to be at least aware of the various theories and attempt to relate some of them to our work; * the best way to get a handle on these theories is to consider the "categories" or "classifications" that they are grouped in (thanks … and …); * an extensive reading exercise of each theory or category of theory can be avoided by reading overview books (thanks …) or review articles (thanks …); * we shouldn't let the use of theories stifle our creativity or get in the way of reality

(thanks ..., ... and ...). I really enjoyed ...'s listing. There are some beauties there!

His statement was rewarded with the following comment: "Thanks for your comment and summary. Have you thought of joining the diplomatic service. :)."

To a large extent, the early discussions on making sense of the class and the tasks centered on terminology and developing a shared terminology. Our analysis also indicated that the initial period of team interaction contained the more overt attempts at defining terms and explicitly talking about sensemaking. Thus, the initial start-up phase in a team may be a particularly useful period for intervention and support for sensemaking. We also noticed that it was not just the definitions but even which terms needed to be defined by the team that were a subject for argument. For example, the term "ontology" was highly relevant for some of the team who considered it crucial to their work on theorizing their own research, but considered "waffling" and "irrelevant" to theorizing by other members.

Formal analysis of the frames of reference underlying each statement led to the following indicative trends. Fifty-five messages contained one or more reference to the Human Resource Frame (average 3.6 hits per message), while 45 messages contained one or more reference to the Structural Frame (average 2.8 hits). The Power Frame was referenced in 41 messages (average 2.8 hits), while the Cultural Frame was referenced in 37 messages (average 1.7 hits). It became clear that most messages contained references to more than one frame. Our analysis also showed that no one frame emerged as the dominant frame of reference in this class; students continued to use all four frames of reference in their discussion. The moving average

Figure 1: Number of hits for each frame of reference over time

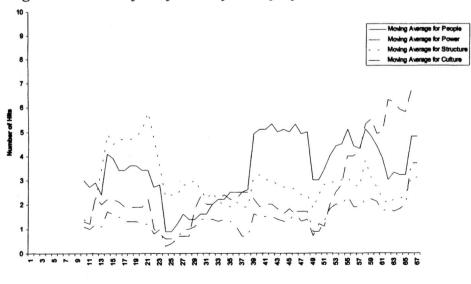

for the Power Frame, though, showed the clearest upward trend, while the moving average for Structure declined (see Figure 1).

Discussion

In this study, the students' discussions dealt with terminology and language, and their technical and organizational knowledge, and they drew upon their common experiences to clarify their communication. Thus our findings support current conceptions of collective learning. As mentioned earlier, collective learning refers to the capacity of a regional innovative milieu to facilitate innovative behavior amongst member firms (Keeble et al., 1999) and successful collective learning is characterized by developing a common language and by sharing technical and organizational knowledge (Lorenz, 1996). In addition, common cultural, psychological and social backgrounds are facilitators of successful collaborative innovation (Camagni, 1991).

Providing support mechanisms for each of these activities can facilitate cooperation and joint solutions to common problems. However, innovative firms cannot rely only on intra-firm knowledge sharing, or even on collective learning within regional clusters of firms. Research indicates that national and global innovation networks, linking the firms with selected partners outside of their geographical location, are also important (Camagni, 1991; Keeble et al., 1999). The challenge then becomes how to provide this support within a remote collaboration system. In the next section, we describe a computer system that incorporates these ideas and can be used for remote innovation.

THE PRACTICE OF SENSEMAKING IN *LIVENET*

We have developed modules for a web-based system, *LiveNet* (Hawryszkiewycz, 1998), to enhance sensemaking and, subsequently, innovation in remote collaborations. The *LiveNet* system is based on networked electronic workspaces. It is an integrated system that provides access to the team's own documents and discussions, to documents within the parent organization(s), and to agent-based tools to assist team members to carry out their tasks effectively. Users themselves create the workspaces and configure them to suit their needs. As a team continues working together, it can tailor its workspaces to suit its changing tasks and needs. There is also access within the system to sensemaking aids. A demonstration of *LiveNet* can be accessed at http://livenet.it.uts.edu.au/. In the following paragraphs we briefly describe how remote collaborators can use *LiveNet* to engage in collective learning and innovation.

As mentioned, past research identified several key elements of collective learning, such as establishing a shared language, sharing technical, engineering and organizational knowledge, and having a common cultural background. Within *LiveNet*, development of a common language is supported by a number of separate modules. One module that supports the development of shared terminology involves a database of key terms and definitions, as well as a means for discussing the database contents. This database is created through a discussion where users can ask for clarification and discuss connotations and meanings within the specific context of their team's tasks. Users are cautioned about the occurrence of similar terminology in different disciplines and suggest that collaborators set up a separate discussion in which definitions can be agreed upon and questions can be more comfortably raised about what specific words mean.

Another module assists the members to recognize different frames of reference being used within the team and encourages them to develop more flexible ways of thinking about the team's problems. This module allows participants to uncover their own latent frames of reference, as well as those of others. At any time a workspace user may request an analysis of the frames of reference to be carried out on a given portion of the electronic discussions or documents, and the analysis is conducted immediately. Thus the module provides instantaneous electronic feedback on the frames of reference being used within a particular discussion or by a specific participant. This module utilizes Bolman and Deal's (1997) work on frames of reference and reframing, in particular a dictionary of words typical of each frame of reference, as described in the earlier section on the students' remote collaborations.

Within *LiveNet*, sharing knowledge specific to the project is facilitated by threaded discussions that can draw out tacit knowledge, by easy access to individual and team-produced documents, and by links to outside expertise as well as background information from organizational databases. Initial actions in most knowledge processes involve accessing explicitly stored background and sharing experiences, typically narratives that provide understanding and meaning (Boland & Tenkasi, 1995). Such experiences and insights are shared during electronic discussions, and can be captured in discussion databases, providing a form of externalizing tacit knowledge. They then feed into the explicit output documents of the team.

Sharing of organizational knowledge is supported through customizing a team's workspace in terms of participants' roles, rules about access to information, rules about the obligations that apply to the different roles, and norms regarding project management. The team can also specify milestones for measuring its project's progress and set up agents to automatically notify members when a milestone has been reached or when inputs are required from members. Thus, much organizational knowledge can be built into the workspace's procedures by the team. Combining stored knowledge with agent systems provides improvements to collaboration processes. Two kinds of agencies have been found useful – technical agency and process agency. The technical agency primarily assists users in gathering both the information and the people needed to accomplish the workspace goal. Events within workspaces may be directed to agents that can perform a number of tasks. Process agency may be expressed by agents that facilitate workflows (Hawryszkiewycz & Debenham, 1998) through basing plans on the status of workspaces and the organizational state when events are occurring, and creating new workspaces. When combined, the technical agents provide users with a workspace that contains access to information and actions needed by the knowledge worker. The process agency then directs any outcomes from a workspace to other related workspaces.

A final factor important to facilitating collaborative innovation is the reinforcement of common cultural, psychological and social backgrounds (Camagni, 1991). In contrast to regional innovation networks, assumptions of common values or backgrounds may not be valid in remote collaboration. Thus, within *LiveNet*, we try to help members recognize differences in backgrounds, as well as to assist a team to establish its own team culture by clearly identified common workspace and membership. This helps the team develop a sense of shared identity and its members are more motivated to contribute to the achievement of the team's goals. As noted earlier, in the study of remote collaboration among students, their shared identity became increasingly framed within Star Wars metaphors, and they increasingly used Star Wars figures and images to make sense of the class events.

Remote Innovation Through *Livenet*

We now provide an example to illustrate how a remote collaboration system such as *LiveNet* could be applied to remote innovation. In Figure 2, we depict how an innovation process might be organized remotely within an organization; however, the team members could as easily come from different organizations and engage in remote innovation.

The major modeling terms of *LiveNet* are based on ideas from soft systems methodologies. They are combined as shown in Figure 2 and include activities, actors, and objects. Activities, shown as cloud-like shapes, are organizationally recognized tasks in that they produce some outputs, which are then used in other activities. Objects or outcomes are represented by rectangular boxes and actors by their names. A line from an activity to an object means that the activity may change the object. An arrow from one activity to another activity means that these two activities may affect each other and can be linked. A dashed arrow between two objects means that these objects are part of each other. Links between actors and activities mean that people who undertake these roles participate in the activity. Dashed lines between activities mean that these activities are part of a workspace network.

In this example, one team's task may be to generate innovation ideas. To facilitate this remotely, a workspace called *Idea Generation* could be set up. This team may include a large number of staff from various organizations and different levels within those organizations. It could even involve clients and customers. All members may be allowed to participate in the discussions and to make suggestions. A second workspace could be set up to review these ideas. Membership in the *Initial Screening* workspace may be limited to a select team of financial, marketing, design, production and innovation experts. Alternatively, the *Initial Screening* workspace could be read-accessible to all employees, but only write-accessible to a select team. The two teams may work in parallel or in sequence, depending on the preferences of the managers and teams involved.

When discussing ideas and screening them with respect to their potential in the marketplace, it will be important for the experts representing various functional roles

Figure 2: Organizing remote innovation

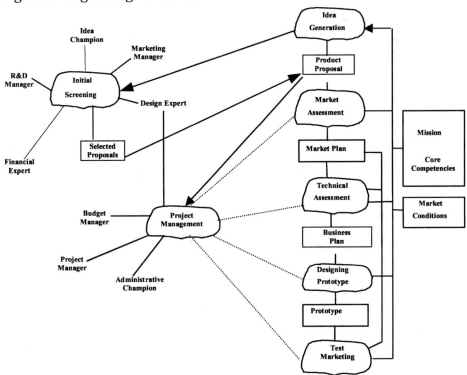

to understand each other and to make sense of one another's comments and ideas. Thus, the modules that support developing a common language and making underlying frames of reference explicit may be essential elements of this cross-functional workspace.

Without describing other activities and workspaces in detail, it may suffice to say that essentially each innovation activity could occur in a separate workspace with changing membership while still providing overall coherence through the linked tree structure of the network between the workspaces. Some people may only be a member in one workspace, while others are involved in several workspaces. The responsible senior manager may have access to the various teams' outputs, but not the discussions, if that is the agreed-upon governance structure of the workspace network.

Each workspace has access to the sensemaking modules described in the previous section. Each workspace team may have its own discussions about terms in order to develop a common language. Alternatively, the terminology database could be shared within the entire workspace network. Each workspace has access to the module that makes underlying frames of reference explicit. The sharing of knowledge can be restricted within a workspace or shared across several workspaces. Workspace members make these decisions themselves and can revisit their decisions as their team evolves.

To achieve exploration as well as exploitation of innovation ideas in the remote collaboration system, it is important that the workspace network supports both rationally planned as well as opportunely emerging processes (cf. March, 1995; Weick, 1996). Thus, *LiveNet* incorporates some preset discussions such as setting goals, setting milestones, sharing news, and discussing surprises, but also allows members to set up their own discussions.

The activity represented graphically in Figure 2 may produce some output that may be used in other activities. The way that these activities are carried out is usually collaborative in nature and often cannot be strictly predefined. The activities are dependent on each other but not necessarily sequential. The emphasis is not on sequencing but on the activities, their participants and the outputs that they produce. The sequencing relationships between activities should not be viewed as workflows, but simply as events in one activity that could initiate actions in another. In *LiveNet*, some of the coordination across workspaces can be automated through a variety of work process support tools, such as built-in project tracking support, built-in discussion tracking notification, wizards for creating a new workspace, and automated event-triggered actions within and across work spaces and teams.

CONCLUSION

In this chapter we have explored how innovation can be supported electronically in remote collaborations. Four major aspects of effective remote innovation include: (1) providing tools for establishing a common language; (2) providing a workspace for sharing technological and engineering knowledge specific to a project among members; (3) allowing sharing of organizational knowledge and developing joint organizational procedures through supporting flexible team formation and evolving structures and governance forms; and (4) facilitating the development of a common culture and identity among members. A prototype system, *LiveNet*, was described, that brings together members from different organizations within one workspace, provides them with the ability to locate needed information quickly, and supports this process with an agent-based structure that can assist members to achieve their goals. Members can re-define their tasks dynamically as they evolve, and *LiveNet* supports the building of relationships amongst the members within a workspace network. Modules within *LiveNet* assist the development of shared terminology as well as making underlying frames of reference explicit. Appropriate agents can facilitate coordination and sensemaking processes and thereby improve communication in remote innovations.

ACKNOWLEDGMENT

We are grateful to the Australian Research Council, the University of Technology, Sydney and the Organizational Researchers on Collaboration and Alliances group at UTS for financial support. We thank the 1999 students of Advanced Research Methods for permission to analyze their discussions, and numerous colleagues, in particular Prof. I. Hawryszkiewycz, for their support and feedback. Earlier versions of this chapter were presented at the 1999 Academy of Management Annual Meetings and the ACR/ANZAM Workshop on Interorganizational Collaboration, University of Melbourne, 1999.

REFERENCES

Asheim, B. (1996). Industrial districts as "learning regions": A condition for prosperity? *European Planning Studies*, 4, 379-400.

Baker, E., Geirland, J., Fisher, T., & Chandler, A. (1999). Media production: Towards creative collaboration using communication networks. *Computer-Supported Cooperative Work*, 8, 303-332.

Bechky, B. (1999). Creating shared meaning across occupational communities: An ethnographic study of a production floor. Paper presented at the *Academy of Management Meetings*, Chicago, IL.

Birkmaier, C. (1994). Through the looking glass: Re-engineering the video production process. *Videography*, 19(3), 60-70.

Boland, R. J., & Tenkasi, R. V. (1995). Perspective making and perspective taking in communities of knowing. *Organization Science*, 6, 350-372.

Boland, R. J., Tenkasi, R. V., & Te'eni, D. (1994). Designing information technology to support distributed cognition. *Organization Science*, 5, 456-475.

Bolman, L. G., & Deal, T. E. (1997). *Reframing Organizations: Artistry, Choice and Leadership* (2nd Ed.). San Francisco, CA: Jossey-Bass.

Brown, J. S. (1999). Sustaining the ecology of knowledge. *Leader to Leader*, Spring, 12, 31-36.

Camagni, R. (1991). Local milieu, uncertainty and innovation networks: Towards a new dynamic theory of economic space. In Camagni, R. (Ed.) *Innovation Networks: Spatial Perspectives*, 121-142. London: Belhaven.

Clegg, S. R. (1989). *Frameworks of Power*. Newbury Park, CA: Sage Publications.

Dougherty, D. (1992). Interpretive barriers to successful product innovation in large firms. *Organization Science*, 3, 179-202.

Dougherty, D., & Hardy, C. (1996). Sustained product innovation in large, mature organizations: Overcoming innovation-to-organization problems. *Academy of Management Journal*, 39, 1120-1153.

Duncan, R., & Weiss, A. (1979). Organizational learning: Implications for organizational design. In Cummings, L. and Staw, B. M. (Eds), *Research in Organizational Behavior*, 1. Greenwich, CT: JAI.

Faulkner, R. R., & Anderson, A. B. (1987). Short term projects and emergent careers: Evidence from Hollywood. *American Journal of Sociology*, 92: 878-909.

Feldman, M. S., & March, J. G. (1981). Information in organizations as signal and symbol. *Administrative Science Quarterly*, 26, 171-186.

Gray, B. (1989). *Collaborating: Finding Common Ground for Multiparty Problems*. San Francisco: Jossey-Bass.

Hardy, C., & Phillips, N. (1998). Strategies of engagement: Lessons from the critical examination of collaboration and conflict in an interorganizational domain. *Organization Science*, 9, 217-230.

Hardy, C., Phillips, N., & Lawrence, T. (1997). Swimming with sharks: Tensions in the Canadian HIV/AIDS domain. Paper presented at the *EGOS Colloquium*, Budapest, Hungary.

Hawryszkiewycz, I. T. (1998). Extending workspaces for knowledge sharing. In Traunmuller, R. and Csuhaj-Varju, E. (Eds.), *Proceedings of the XV. IFIP World Computer Congress, IFIP98*, 77-88. Vienna-Budapest.

Hawryszkiewycz, I. T., & Debenham, J. (1998). A workflow system based on agents. In Quirchmayr, G., Schweighofer, E. and Bench-Capon, T. (Eds). *9th International Conference on Database and Expert Systems, DEXA98*, 135-144. Vienna, Berlin: Springer-Verlag.

Hewitt, J. P., & Hall, P. M. (1973). Social problems, problematic situations, and quasi-theories. *American Sociological Review*, 38, 367-374.

Huseman, R. C., & Miles, E. W. (1988). Organizational communication in the information age. *Journal of Management*, 14, 181-204.

Huxham, C. (1996). Advantage or inertia? Making collaboration work. In Paton, R., Clark, G., Jones, G., Lewis, J. and Quinlan, P. (Eds.), *The New Management Reader*. London, New York: Routledge (in association with The Open University).

Kabanoff, B., Waldersee, R., & Cohen, M. (1995). Espoused values and organizational change themes. *Academy of Management Journal*, 38, 1075-1104.

Keeble, D., Lawson, C., Moore, B., & Wilkinson, F. (1999). Collective learning processes, networking and "institutional thickness" in the Cambridge region. *Regional Studies*, 33(4), 319-332.

Lorenz, E. (1996). *Collective Learning Processes and the Regional Labor Market*. Unpublished research note, European Network on Networks, Collective learning and RTD in regionally-clustered high technology SMEs.

Lyytinen, K. (1987). Two views of information modeling. *Information Management*, 12, 9-19.

March, J. G. (1995). Exploration and exploitation in organizational learning. In Cohen, M. D. and Sproull, L. S. (Eds). *Organizational Learning*, 101-123. Thousand Oaks, CA: Sage Publications.

Miller, D., & Shamsie, J. (1996). The resource-based view of the firm in two environments: The Hollywood film studios from 1936 to 1965. *Academy of Management Journal*, 39, 519-543.

Mizer, R. A. (1994). From post-production to the cinema of the future. *SMPTE Journal*, December, 801-804.

Morgan, G. (1993). *Imaginization: The Art of Creative Management*. Newbury Park, CA: Sage Publications.

Palmer, I. (1999). Framing managers' experiences of collaboration: A metaphor-based analysis. Under review at *Journal of Management Inquiry*.

Palmer, I., & Dunford, R. (1997). Organizing for hyper-competition: New organisational forms for a new age? *New Zealand Strategic Management*, 2(4), 38-45.

Palmer, I., Dunford, R., Rura-Polley, T., & Baker, E. (2001). Changing forms of organizing: Dualities in using remote collaboration technologies in film production. *Journal of Organizational Change Management*, 14(2), 190-212.

Pasquero, J. (1991). Supraorganizational collaboration: The Canadian environmental experiment. *Journal of Applied Behavioural Science*, 27(2), 38-64.

Powell, W. W., Koput, K. W., & Smith-Doerr, L. (1996). Interorganization collaboration and the locus of innovation: Networks of learning in biotechnology. *Administrative Science Quarterly*, 41, 116-145.

Roberts, N. C., & Bradley, R. T. (1991). Stakeholder collaboration and innovation: A study of public policy initiation at the state level. *Journal of Applied Behavioural Science*, 27(2), 209-227.

Sackman, S. A. (1991). *Cultural Knowledge in Organizations*. Newbury Park, CA: Sage Publications.

Simmie, J. (Ed.). (1997). *Innovation, Networks and Learning Regions?* London: Jessica Kingsley.

Smith, R. K., Ahmed, M. U., & Takanashi, A. (1999). International collaboration for technological change in the 21st century. *International Journal of Technology Management*, 18(3-4), 285-292.

Tenkasi, R. V. (1999). Information technology and organizational change in turbulent environments. Symposium presented at the *Academy of Management Annual Meeting*, Chicago, IL.

Weick, K. E. (1985). Cosmos vs. chaos: Sense and nonsense in electronic contexts. *Organizational Dynamics*, 14(2), 51-64.

Weick, K. E. (1993). The collapse of sensemaking in organizations: The Mann Gulch disaster. *Administrative Science Quarterly*, 38, 628-652.

Weick, K. E. (1995). *Sensemaking in Organizations*. Thousand Oaks: Sage Publications.

Weick, K. E., & Meader, D. K. (1993). Sensemaking and group support systems. In Jessup, L. M. and Valacich, J. S. (Eds.), *Group Support Systems*, 230-252. New York: Macmillan.

Weick, K. E., & Westley, F. (1996). Organizational learning: Affirming an oxymoron. In Clegg, S. R., Hardy, C. and Nord, W. R. (Eds). *Handbook of Organization Studies*, 440-458. Thousand Oaks, CA: Sage Publications.

Wood, D. J., & Gray, B. (1991). Towards a comprehensive theory of collaboration. *Journal of Applied Behavioral Science*, 27(2), 139-162.

Wycoff, J., & Snead, L. (1999). Stimulating innovation with collaboration rooms. *Journal for Quality and Participation*, 22(2), 55-57.

Part IV

Culture and Information Technology

Chapter XII

The Framework for Cross-Cultural Communication Process Efficiency and Cost in the Global Economy

Andrew Targowski and Ali Metwalli
Western Michigan University, USA

INTRODUCTION

In this millennium, global organizations will increasingly focus on the critical value of the cross-cultural communication process, efficiency, competence and the cost of doing business. In order to successfully communicate cross-culturally, knowledge and understanding of cultural factors such as values, attitudes, beliefs and behaviors should be acquired. Because culture is a powerful force that strongly influences communication behavior, culture and communication are inseparably linked.

The objective of this chapter is to define the framework for a cross-cultural communication process, efficiency, and cost of doing business in a global economy. This task is very important for the promoting of global peace through trade, since it aims at understanding how to communicate successfully among different cultures from different civilizations. This understanding should minimize conflicts, increase international trade and investment, and facilitate the development of the global economy. The research method is based on the architectural design of a cross-cultural communication process and system and their quantitative analysis. Their attributes are estimated in a normative way on a scale from 1 to 5, where 5 is the best value. The attributes for two selected cultures (Western-West and Egyptian) are estimated by expert opinions.

BACKGROUND

Worldwide, in the last 20 years, countries have experienced a phenomenal growth in international trade and foreign direct investment. Similarly, they have discovered the importance of cross-cultural communication. As a result, practitioners and scholars are paying attention to the fact that cultural dimensions influence management practices (Adler, 1983; Child, 1981; Hofstede, 1980, Laurent, 1983; Maruyama, 1984; Triandis, 1982-1983). In recent years, the empirical work in the cross-cultural arena has focused on the role of culture on employee behavior in communicating within business organizations (Tayeb, 1988). But current work on cross-cultural business communication has paid little attention to either

(a)   how to adapt these seminal works on general communication to the needs of intercultural business, or

(b)   how to create new models more relevant to cross-cultural business exchanges (Limaye & Victor, 1991, p. 283).

There are considerable and focused empirical studies on cross-cultural communication between two specific cultures (e.g., Eiler & Victor, 1988; Halpern, 1983; Varner, 1988; Victor, 1987; Victor & Danak, 1990; Zong & Hildebrandt, 1983), but the results cannot be arguable when applied across cultures. The prevailing western classical linear and process models of communication (Berlo, 1960; Shannon & Weaver 1949) neglect the complexity of cross-cultural communication. Targowski and Bowman (1988) developed a layer-based pragmatic communication process model that covered more variables than any previous models and indirectly addressed the role of cultural factors among their layer-based variables. In a similar manner, the channel ratio model for intercultural communication developed by Haworth and Savage (1989) has also failed to completely account for the multiple communication variables in cross-cultural environments.

So far there is no adequate model that can explain the cross-cultural communication process and efficiency, let alone estimate the cost of doing business with other cultures worldwide.

THE PREMISES OF THE FRAMEWORK MODEL

The developed framework based on the architectural design of a cross-cultural communication process adopts a systems approach (of which the traditional linear process and the nonlinear approach are only a part) that can be applied to managing communication between western and non-western cultures. The designed system and its quantitative analysis (based on operations research and information systems) is broad enough not only to include but to go beyond Fisher's (1988) non-linear approach to general communication (with a focus on international political negotiation). The design considers the complexities of the various cultural hierarchies and their corresponding communication climates as it influences behavioral differences and filters communication messages and intentions between business partners in different cultures. Moreover, the design offers a way to compare and quantify attributes that are culture-specific. The intention is not only to reduce the miscommunication between global business partners but also to increase the level of efficiency in cross-cultural business communication between western and non-western countries. The recent success of many countries in Asia, the Middle East, and parts of Latin America in world trade has forced, a new reality of non-linear culture patterns of communication processes, behavior and practices upon western business organizations. The universal approach in our architectural design will accurately delineate the non-western reality that exists in other cultures around the globe. This also will raise the awareness and encourage research to improve cross-cultural communication processes, efficiency and practices.

A conceptual framework is introduced to evaluate and estimate the implicit and explicit cost of cultural-specific differences in entering new foreign markets. Such valuation is undoubtedly an important addition to the study of cross-cultural communication processes and efficiency in the global economy. It enables global organizations to estimate the cost of overcoming cultural differences and allows them not only to achieve efficiency, but also effectiveness in communicating and operating across cultures.

A CONCEPT OF CULTURE

A culture is a value-guided, continuous process of developing patterned human behavior within and across cultures and civilizations. Cultures do not satisfy needs; rather, they demand values. In turn, values in their broadest sense define the member of any culture's need for rationality, meaningfulness in emotional experience, richness of imagination and depth of faith (Laszlo, 1972). Human communication, therefore, is a vehicle for cultural dissemination on the one hand, while on the other hand is itself culture-driven.

Cultures are components of a civilization that guide their behavioral patterns. For example, Western Civilization currently is composed of the following cultures:

- The Western-West, containing Western Europe and North America;
- The Western Central, embracing Poland, the Czech Republic, Slovakia, Hungary, Estonia, Latvia, Lithuania, Croatia, and Slovene;
- The Western-East, containing Greece and Israel; and
- The Western-Latin, composed of Latin America's states.

There is some opinion that since the end of the Cold War in 1989/1991, world politics is entering a new phase, and intellectuals have not hesitated to proliferate a vision of what it will be–the end of history (Fukuyama, 1989) or the clash of civilizations (Huntington, 1993). Huntington predicts that the fundamental source of conflict in this new world will not be primarily ideological or primarily economic. He perceives that the great divisions among humankind and its dominating source of conflict will be cultural.

The consequences of the clash of civilizations and cultures have already been seen in business undertakings, particularly after the Asian Crisis in 1997-99, when Islamic Malaysia accused the West of speculating too much in the Asian market, and said that Asian countries were not going to pursue the policy of Westernization. In general, those clashes take place around the following issues: security, westernization, modernization, trade, globalization, freedom, intellectual property, population control, and ecological issues.

The clashes of civilizations and cultures make a strong impact on the costs of pursuing business in international settings. There are only a few cases of businesses and countries that are making a profit in the global economy (Rodrik, 1997). Most businesses and countries, however, support the development of the global economy because, first, it is difficult to stop it, and second, perhaps one day this economy may bring some positive solutions to global problems. One of the factors that can contribute to the positive outcome of the global economy is the understanding of the cross-cultural process, efficiency and cost in the global business environment.

THE CROSS-CULTURE COMMUNICATION PROCESS

We assume that doing business in the global economy depends mostly on the partners' ability to successfully communicate in a cross-cultural environment. People pursue and communicate many common aims, including the values of pure biological survival, social collaboration, creative expression, organizational adaptability or business undertakings. From such common values one can form a hierarchy of human cultural layers:

1. Biological culture layer;
2. Personal culture layer;
3. Group culture layer;
4. Organization culture layer (ex. business enterprise);
5. Regional culture layer;
6. National culture layer; and
7. Global culture layer (including supra-national, regional ones).

    Those layers of cultures and the communication climate associated with them filter messages and intentions of business partners and determine the success of business undertakings. A model of the cross-cultural communication process is shown in Figure 1 (Targowski & Bowman, 1988).

    The model of the cross-culture communication process takes place between at least two partners who, in order to communicate, must send both a message and their intentions through several layers of cultures. For example,

Figure 1: The culture layers and communication climates in the cross-culture communication process

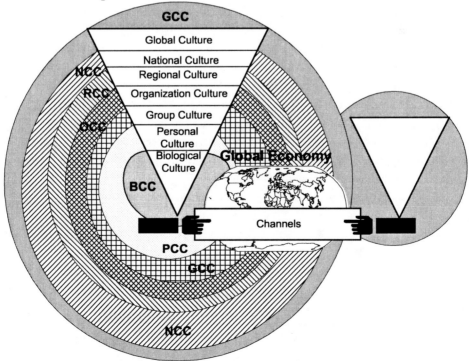

to communicate in the global economy between two different cultures each partner filters a message and intentions through seven layers of cultures (biological, personal, group, organization, regional, national, and global). Of course, to be successful, such cross-culture communication must be based upon a good understanding of rules and practices that govern each layer of culture.

Let's define components of the cross-culture communication process in the global economy.

Global Economy

The global economy is largely understood in terms of worldwide economic and political convergence around liberal market principles and the increasing real-time integration of business, technological and financial systems (World Bank, 1997). Based on an expansion and deepening of market conditions, globalization is synonymous with an irresistible process of economic, political and cultural change that is sweeping all national boundaries and protectionist tendencies before it. This pervasive neo-liberal assumption has been dubbed "hyperglobalization" (Held, Goldblatt, McGrew, & Perraton, 1997).

"Globalization" is not yet truly global – it has yet to touch a large chunk of the world's economy. Roughly half of the developing world's people have been left out of the much-discussed rise in the volume of international trade and capital flow since the early 1980s. Governments' hesitance to open up to the world economy is partly understandable. Joining the global economy, like devolving power from the center, carries risks as well as opportunities. For example, it can make countries more vulnerable to external price shocks or to large, destabilizing shifts in capital flow. But the difficulties should not be exaggerated, particularly when laid against the risks of being left out of the globalization process (World Bank 1997, p.12).

Global economic integration gives rise to combat international threats such as wars, terrorism, global warming, instability and conflict. Economic, cultural and other differences between countries, civilizations and cultures can make such cooperation difficult – even, at times, impossible. Therefore, the understanding and practice of good cross-cultural communication is so important.

The globalization process is supported by electronic communication that makes geography, borders, and time zones irrelevant to the way we conduct our business and personal lives. The "death of distance" will be the single most important economic force shaping all of society over the next half century (Cairncross, 1997). Friends, colleagues, and customers could easily be anywhere – around the corner or around the world – and new ways of communicating will effectively wipe out distance as a cost factor, indeed as a perceptible concept from our lives.

The growth of the global economy triggers the growth of a Global Information Infrastructure (GII) that improves connections among organizations and individuals. Most people on earth will eventually have access to computer networks that are all switched, interactive, and broadband with capacity to receive TV-quality motion pictures. While the Internet will continue to exist in its form, it will also be integrated into other services, such as telephone and television (Targowski, 1996).

Although the Communication Revolution has increased connections among partners through technology, it simultaneously requires a better understanding of rules and practices of cross-cultural communication, regardless of applied media.

Culture Layers

The biological culture layer is the basic layer that provides common reactions based on the same physical needs that result from a common biological makeup. This layer is common for humankind in all civilizations and cultures.

The personal culture layer is the means with which the individual survives, operates and develops within the group, organization, region, nation, and globe. The essence of an individual's personal culture is the acceptance of underlying assumptions or "theories-in-use" (Argyris, 1976; Argyris & Schon, 1974). These assumptions are, for the individual, an undebatable understanding of reality, time and space (Schein, 1985). Each individual is additionally a member of various groups, organizations, regional, national, and global cultures. Consequently, since personal culture differentiates between all individuals, all communication between two or more parties must be seen as intercultural.

The group culture layer is a managerial or an employee's tool to accomplish an organizational task or to protect the interest of group members (formal or informal). A group here may be defined as any collection of individuals united by a common relationship (e.g., work, profession or family). Group culture is the organizational equivalent of regional culture within the setting of national culture.

The organizational culture layer is a management tool that uses professional communication to influence organizational performance (Sypher, Applegate, & Sypher, 1985) and that is created (or destroyed) by its leaders (Schein, 1985). A derivative of organizational culture is a corporate culture, which is a set of broad, tacitly understood rules (policies) informing employees how to behave under a variety of circumstances. Cultural rules have an economic efficiency; they allow firms to effectively administer contracts or terms of employment with employees. Because employees and firms cannot anticipate all of the contingencies in their work relationships, broad cultural rules created by the firms act as a substitute for deciding appropriate courses of action in unanticipated situations (Camerer & Vepsalainen, 1988).

The regional culture layer contains commonalities based on the values of variables that individuals bear within a given region of a nation. Regional variables derive from two sources: 1) environmental influences (Farmerer & Richman, 1966; Terpstra & David, 1985; Borisoff & Victor, 1989), which have particular historical, political, economic, and social characteristics; and 2) traditions whose participants have similar ways of viewing space, time, things, and people (Schein, 1985; Weiss, 1988).

Regional culture may extend beyond national boundaries. In such cases, regional culture is *supranational*. For example, European culture encompasses dozens of nations with some shared values. Supranational culture can also be global (Featherstone, 1990). Regional culture may act as a subset of a particular national culture. In such cases, regional culture is *subnational*. For example, Brittany has a distinct regional culture within France but remains as a part of French national culture. Finally, regional culture may overlap with national culture. For example, Australian culture is at the same time both the culture of a nation state and that of a region (when compared to European or Latin American regions) that happens to be conterminous with a nation state.

The national culture layer is a set of common understandings, traditions, ways of thinking, feeling, behaving, and communication based on the same values of variables that influence communication through the nation. National culture is a learned behavior of its members' historical experience. For example, one can recognize an American culture, Chinese culture, Egyptian culture or Polish culture, and so forth.

The global culture layer is the new emerging layer, triggered by the developments of the global economy. At this layer, partners from different cultures and civilizations deliberately apply the same patterns of behavior in order to achieve successful communication in business (political, social, and so forth) endeavors. These patterns may not come from their own national cultures, but they are applied in order to create a level playing field among all partners (or participants). For example, partners may speak in English, which is being recognized as the global business language, or they may use the dollar or euro as a currency in business transactions.

Figure 2: The structure of a culture layer

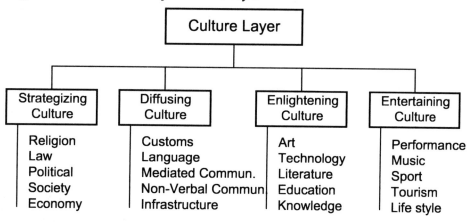

Communication Climates

Communication climate (or "atmosphere") can be defined as a set of conditions that transforms cultural behavior and information into desired (or undesired) states of a given entity (person, group, organization, region, nation, globe) through the communication process. Communication climate refers to the atmosphere or prevailing condition that exists within a specific entity. An entity's communication climate affects the degree of openness with which people communicate (Perkins & Stout, 1987). For example, within China, there are at least three communication climates: the most open communication climate exists in Hong Kong; a less open communication climate is allowed in special economic zones, such as in Shenzhen; and a closed communication climate is controlled in the remaining parts of China.

Communication climate consists of seven components: space (territory), style, time, desire for interaction (or relationship), frequency (participation), tone (receptivity or friendliness), and quality. Table 1 provides weighted attributes of communication climates for all layers of culture except the biological communication climate, which more or less is similar for all cultures.

Because the process of cross-cultural communication in the global economy is dynamic, its success depends upon the communication climate that either has been established or is actual among communicating parties. For example, the business communication climate between the US and China at the beginning of 1999 was very good; however, after the accidental bombardment of the Chinese Embassy in Belgrade in May of that year, the communication climate between both countries was at the lowest level possible.

Table 1: The weighted attributes of communication climates (A)

CC Layer	Space (Territory)	Style	Time	Relation-ship	Frequency (Participa-tion)	Tone (Friendli-ness)	Quality
Global CC	5-Personal 4-Semi-formal 3-Formal 2-Informal 1-Impersonal	5-Open 4-Semi-open 3-Semi-controlled 2-Controlled 1-Closed	5-Fixed 4-Semi-fixed 3-Inflexible 2-Semi-flexible 1-Flexible	5-V. Friendly 4-Friendly 3-Semi-friendly 2. Unfriendly 1. Hostile	5-High 4-Moderate 3-Low 2-Infrequent 1-Adhoc	5-Supporting 4-Guiding 3-Command-ing 2-Manipu-lating 1.Critiquing	5-Transcom-munication 4-Pseudocom-munication 3-Paracom-munication 2-Miscommuni-cation 1-Metacom-munication
National CC	5-Personal 4-Semi-formal 3-Formal 2-Informal 1-Impersonal	5-Democratic 4-Authori-tarian 3-Dictatorial 2-Totalitarian 1-Chaotic	5-Fixed 4-Semi-fixed 3-Inflexible 2-Semi-flexible 1-Flexible	5-V. Friendly 4-Friendly 3-Semi-friendly 2. Unfriendly 1. Hostile	5-High 4-Moderate 3-Low 2-Infrequent 1-Ad hoc	5-Supporting 4-Guiding 3-Command-ing 2-Manipu-lating 1.Critiquing	5-Transcommu-nication -Paracommuni-cation -Pseudocom-munication -Metacommu-nication -Miscommuni-cation
Regional CC	5-Personal 4-Semi-formal 3-Formal 2-Informal 1-Impersonal	5-Laissez-faire 4-Coordi-nated 3-Partnership 2-Dominance 1-Hegemonic	5-Fixed 4-Semi-fixed 3-Inflexible 2-Semi-flexible 1-Flexible	5-V. Friendly 4-Friendly 3-Semi-friendly 2. Unfriendly 1. Hostile	5-High 4-Moderate 3-Low 2-Infrequent 1-Ad hoc	5-Supporting 4-Guiding 3-Command-ing 2-Manipu-lating 1.Critiquing	5-Transcommu-nication 4-Pseudocom-munication 3-Paracommuni-cation 2-Miscommuni-cation 1-Metacommu-nication
Organiza-tional CC	5-Networks 4-System structure 3-Matrix structure 2-Flat hierarchy 1-Tall hierarchy	5-Meritocratic 4-Plutocratic 3-Techno-cratic 2-Bureau-cratic 1-Chaotic	5-Fixed 4-Semi-fixed 3-Inflexible 2-Semi-flexible 1-Flexible	5-V. Friendly 4-Friendly 3-Semi-friendly 2. Unfriendly 1. Hostile	5-High 4-Moderate 3-Low 2-Infrequent 1-Ad hoc	5-Supporting 4-Guiding 3-Command-ing 2-Manipu-lating 1.Critiquing	5-Transcommu-nication 4-Pseudocom-munication 3-Paracommu-nication 2-Miscom-munication 1-Metacom-munication
Group CC	5-Sub-networks 4-Networks 3-informal 2-Semi-Formal 1-Formal	5-Meritocratic 4-Plutocratic 3-Techno-cratic 2-Bureau-cratic 1-Chaotic	5-Fixed 4-Semi-fixed 3-Inflexible 2-Semi-flexible 1-Flexible	5-V. Friendly 4-Friendly 3-Semi-friendly 2. Unfriendly 1. Hostile	5-High 4-Moderate 3-Low 2-Infrequent 1-Ad hoc	5-Supporting 4-Guiding 3-Command-ing 2-Manipu-lating 1.Critiquing	5-Transcom-munication 4-Pseudocom-munication 3-Paracom-munication 2-Miscom-munication 1-Metacom-munication
Personal CC	5-Home 4-Social 3-Semi-social 2-Anti-social 1-Work	5-Meritocratic 4-Plutocratic 3-Techno-cratic 2-Bureau-cratic 1-Chaotic	5-Fixed 4-Semi-fixed 3-Inflexible 2-Semi-flexible 1-Flexible	5-V. Friendly 4-Friendly 3-Semi-friendly 2. Unfriendly 1. Hostile	5-High 4-Moderate 3-Low 2-Infrequent 1-Ad hoc	5-Supporting 4-Guiding 3-Command-ing 2-Manipu-lating 1.Critiquing	5-Transcom-munication 4-Pseudocom-munication 3-Paracommu-nication 2-Miscom-munication 1-Metacom-munication

Communication Channel

A communication channel is the vehicle or medium in which a message travels. Thus, channels range from light waves for nonverbal cues to radio or computers as modes for transmitting sound and visual messages. For example, the effective operation of a highly complex weapons system might hinge on adherence to formal channels of communication, while effective performance in investment banking might rely on informal as well as formal communication channels. The formal channels of communication help create and maintain authority, as well as give authenticity to messages, but they also inhibit communication; indeed, they alienate members. In the global economy, informal channels such as the Internet prevail. They create a horizontal society which exchanges messages that otherwise would not have been created.

The fact that electronic media create new interoganizational and interpersonal networks raises concerns about the individuals and groups excluded either intentionally through organizational policy and politics or accidentally through inadequate access to networking resources.

The Efficiency of Cross-Cultural Communication

To apply these attributes in cross-cultural communication, let us take an example of communication in the global economy between Western-West and Egyptian cultures. To assess the influence of each attribute in the communication process, apply weights on a scale from 1 to 5, where 5 is the highest value of the attribute. Table 2 compares those attributes of two cultures, based on the authors' expertise within both cultures.

Table 2: The comparison of richness of Western-West and Egyptian cultures

Cultural Components	West – West Culture	Islamic (Egyptian) Culture
STRATEGIZING SUB-CULTURE 25	21	20
Religion	3	5
Law	5	5
Politics	4	3
Society	4	4
Economy	5	3
DIFFUSING SUB-CULTURE 25	22	21
Customs	4	5
Language	5	5
Mediated communication	5	3
Non-verbal communication	3	5
Infrastructure	5	3
ENLIGHTENING SUB-CULTURE 25	24	16
Art	4	4
Technology	5	2
Literature	5	4
Education	5	3
Knowledge	5	3
ENTERTAINING SUB-CULTURE 25	24	18
Performance	4	4
Music	5	4
Sport	5	3
Tourism	5	4
Lifestyle	5	3
CULTURAL RICHNESS (R) $R_{max} = 100$	$R_{WW} = 91$	$R_E = 75$
CULTURAL EFFICIENCY (η)	$\eta = 91\%$	$\eta = 75\%$

The cultural difference (D_c) in attribute weights of Western-West culture richness (R_{WW}) and Egyptian culture (R_E) is:

$$D_c = R_{WW} - R_E = 91-75=16 \text{ points} \tag{1}$$

in favor of Western-West culture. It means that both cultures are not at the same developmental level to succeed in communication among both partners in the global economy, both partners must invest in their own abilities to cross-communicate successfully. We will see farther how to evaluate the cost of such investments.

The efficiency of Western-West culture in the global economy is $\eta = 91\%$, which means that only 9 times out of 100 a Western-West business person may miscommunicate, because of a lack of cultural understanding of a business partner. On the other hand, the Egyptian culture's efficiency in the global economy is $\eta = 75\%$, which means that an Egyptian business person may miscommunicate 25 times out of 100. Almost every fourth transaction will be miscommunicated because of a failure to account for cultural differences.

The role of the communication climate in cross-cultural communication is to facilitate that communication. For example, let us examine a case of communication between the Western-West and Egyptian cultures. Table 3 illustrates that comparison.

The communication climate difference (D_{CC}) between both cultures is:

$$D_{CC} = A_{WW} - A_E = 29-27 = 2 \text{ points} \tag{2}$$

in favor of Western-West culture. This means that a Western-West business person entering into a transaction with an Egyptian partner should decrease the cultural difference $(D_c) = 14$ points by $D_{CC} = 2$, calculated above. The modified culture difference of Western-West culture $(D_{MC/WW})$ after the adjustment by the communication climate difference is:

$$D_{MC/WW} = D_c - D_{CC} = 16 - 2 = 14 \text{ points} \tag{3}$$

On the other hand, the Egyptian partner has to increase the Egyptian culture difference $(D_{MC/E})$ by the same coefficient:

Table 3: The comparison of communication climate attributes (A) of western-west (A_{WW}) and Egyptian cultures (A_E) in the global economy settings

Global Comm. Climate	Western-West Culture	Egyptian Culture
Territory (Space)	3-Formal	5-Personal
Style	5-Open	4-Semi-open
Time	5-Fixed	2-Semi-flexible
Relationship	4-Friendly	5-V. Friendly
Frequency (Participation)	5-High	3-High
Tone (Friendliness)	4-Guiding	2-Commanding
Quality	3-Paracommunication	4-Paracommunication
TOTAL POINTS	$A_{WW} = 29$	$A_E = 27$

$$D_{MC/E} = D_C - D_{CC} = 16 + 2 = 18 \text{ points} \qquad (4)$$

After the adjustments, the modified culture difference (D_{MC}) between Western-West culture and Egyptian culture has increased for Egyptian culture $(D_{MC/E})$ from 14 points to 16 points and for Western-West culture $(D_{MC/WW})$ it has decreased from 14 to 12 points. The communication climate favors Western-West culture, while it disfavors the Egyptian culture. In other words, a business person from a Western-West culture has a communication advantage in the global economy, while a business person from the Egyptian culture has to work harder at the communication effort in order to succeed in the global economy.

The ability of a Western-West culture's business person (B_{WW}) to deal with a business partner from Egyptian culture is:

$$B_{WW} = R_{WW} : D_{MC/WW} = 91 : 14 = 6.5 \qquad (5)$$

The ability of the Egyptian culture's business partner (B_E) to deal with a business partner from Western-West culture is:

$$B_E = R_E : D_{MC/E} = 75 : 18 = 4.2 \qquad (6)$$

The culture's ability reflects how a given culture's strength can overcome cultural differences. The comparison of both cultures' abilities reflects a partner's cultural strength at the business table.

It also reflects his/her competitive advantage (V). Competitive advantage of a Western-West partner over an Egyptian partner can be computed in the following manner:

$$V_{WW} = B_{WW} : B_E = 6.5 : 4.2 = 1.6 \text{ or } 160\% \qquad (7)$$

In our example, B_{WW} is 1.6 (160%) times stronger than B_E. In common language, this comparison means that in a global economy of bilateral relationships, an American business person has almost twice the strength in overcoming cultural differences than does the Egyptian partner. If such knowledge is known to either partner, it can bring competitive advantage to him/her.

THE CULTURE COST FACTOR IN THE GLOBAL ECONOMY

A business entering the global economy is aware that it has to improve the understanding of foreign markets' dynamics and practices. Usually the new entry to the foreign market is associated with two types of cost:

- The explicit cost (C_E) can be anticipated, planned and quantifiable (transportation, building purchase or rental, interpreter's salary and all other overhead costs) in terms of its financial impact on doing business in a specific culture.

- The implicit cost (C_I) of cultural differences is intuitively understandable, but it is usually very difficult to predict or evaluate its structure and range. So, to guarantee success, it is very critical for a global firm to identify, examine and project the implicit costs associated with entering a foreign market.

The following conceptual framework of the implicit cost of the culture factor (C_I) will provide a definition and range of that type of cost:

$$C_I = f(GNP_C, R_C, D_{MC}, N_D, N_W) \tag{8}$$

where:

GNP - Gross National Product per capita of a given culture in terms of purchasing power parity (*ppp*);

R_C - Richness of a given culture;

D_{MC} - Adjusted modified culture difference between involved cultures;

N_D - Number of working days in another culture;

N_W - Number of workers in another culture.

Based on the variables' relationships in formula [8], one can define a formula for the culture factor cost of the culture that has a positive culture difference $(+D_{MC})$:

$$C_{I(+D)} = [(\$GNP_{C(+D)} - \$GNP_{C(-D)}) : (R_{C(+D)} + D_{MC})] \times (N_D \times N_W) \tag{9}$$

In the case of the richer culture (formula [9]), the culture difference (D_{MC}) is in favor of that culture $(R_{C(+D)})$; therefore, both variables are added to decrease the cost of overcoming the culture difference.

This formula provides a balance between economic means, expressed in a GNP level and culture richness (R). In other words, low-rich cultures (measured by a low R) with high GNPs won't communicate in the global economy at the low cost. By analogy, they may remind their associates of the behavior of a *nouveau riche,* whose manners are sometimes questionable. New millionaires from countries that are being transformed from a central planning to a market economy sometimes invade the French Riviera and behave there like a bull in a china shop. Due to a limited practice in the market economy and old attitudes, very often those *nouveau riche* prefer quick deals rather than long-term business collaboration. They are aware that their low-rich culture does not generate enough confidence in partners from a rich culture to establish long-term business relations. An additional factor plays a role too. A fresh business culture in some of those countries, very often driven by mafias, does not motivate those business persons to long-term commitments. As a result, they prefer to invest abroad rather than in their own countries. In effect, their business cultures do not develop–they misdevelop.

In the case of the less rich culture (formula [10]), the culture difference (D_{MC}) is not in favor of that culture $(R_{C(-D)})$; therefore D_{MC} is subtracted from $R_{C(+D)}$ to increase the cost of overcoming the culture difference.

$$C_{I(-D)} = [(\$GNP_{C(-D)} - \$GNP_{C(-D)}) : (R_{C(-D)} - D_{MC})] \times (N_D \times N_W) \quad (10)$$

The application of these formulas to the example of cross-cultural communication between a Western-West culture [9] and an Egyptian culture [10] for the business duration of 30 days and the involvement of one worker, provides the following results [GNP according to World Bank (1998/99)]:

$$C_{WW} = [(\$28,740 - \$2,940) : (91 + 14)] \times [30 \times 1] = \$7,400 \quad (11)$$
$$C_E = [(\$28,740 - \$2,940) : (75 - 18)] \times [30 \times 1] = \$13,600 \quad (12)$$

The richer culture (Western-West), in order to successfully communicate a business plan with the Egyptian culture, must invest only $7,400 to overcome culture differences. However, the less rich culture should spend 1.8 times more than the rich culture to overcome culture differences in 20 culture components (Table 2) and 7 culture communication climate attributes (Table 3).

This example only confirms the old truth that the comprehensive development of a rich culture takes a long time and requires many means. The paradox of this example is that the culture of Egypt is about 6,000 years old, while the Western-West culture is 1,200 years old, but has developed more comprehensively with much, much bigger means, and this is reflected in the GNP per capita of both cultures. Apparently 1 + millennium is enough time to enrich the culture of Western Civilization.

The cost of overcoming culture differences should focus on learning through education, training, and practice with all culture categories that are disadvantageous. To see the scope of that effort, one must analyze the comparison of those two cultures, provided in Table 2 and Table 3.

THE FUTURE TRENDS

Some of the future trends of the cross-culture successful communications should lead to the application of the presented framework model in calculating the factors of successful communications between numerous combinations of cultures. The science of cross-culture communications is so far based on the qualitative approach, which has to be supported by the quantitative approach. Since information technology develops more and more complex solutions in information handling and processing, it has to be accompanied by the development of communications solutions. Information and communication are not separable, and in fact create an info-communication process.

CONCLUSION

This chapter has outlined and defined a framework for a cross-cultural communication process, its efficiency and the cost of doing business in the global economy. A universal system design was developed not only to compare and quantify cultural efficiency and the attributes of communication climates through seven cultural layers (biological, personal, group, organizational, regional, national and global), but also to explain the cross cultural communication process and quantify the cultural cost in the global economy. This culture-specific design will help reduce miscommunication between partners across cultures and raise the awareness of the differences in the level of efficiency and cost in the communication process, behavior and practices between Western and non-Western cultural patterns.

Based on the presented framework, one can state that in order to be successful in cross-cultural communication in the global economy, engaged parties should be aware of the following five efficiency and cost rules:

- *Culture Richness Rule I*: **A party from a less-rich culture (lower R) will more frequently miscommunicate with a party from a richer culture (higher R).** (Formula 1).
- *Communication Climate Rule II*: **A party from a "warmer" communication climate (higher A) will be in the advantageous position with a party from a "cooler" communication climate (lower A).** (Formulas 3 and 4).
- *Communication Ability Rule III*: **When large differences exist between cultures, the party from the richer culture has the best chance to communicate his/her own message (higher R).** (Formulas 5 and 6).
- *Communication Competitive Advantage Rule IV*: **The difference in communication ability gives a measurable competitive advantage to the more skillful communicator.** (Formula 7).
- *Communication Cost Rule V*: **A party with a higher GNP and a richer culture communicates in the cross-culture setting at lower cost than a party with the opposite attributes.** (Formulas 8, 9, and 10).

The presented framework of cross-cultural communication in the global economy provides pragmatic tools about how to define a communication strategy, train representatives and conduct business talks in order to achieve success.

It is obvious that each business acts in the broader context of a given civilization's culture and, therefore, in order to pursue the best communication practice by a given company, it has to be supported by the national policies promoting the development of harmonious culture.

This framework should motivate researchers and practitioners to further production and distribution of knowledge and skills in the area of cross-culture communication.

REFERENCES

Adler, N. J. (1983). Cross-cultural management research: The ostrich and the trend. *Academy of Management Review*, 8, 226-232.

Argyris, C. (1976). *Increasing Leadership Effectiveness*. New York: Wiley-Interscience.

Argyris, C., & Schon, D. A. (1974). *Theory In Practice: Increasing Professional Effectiveness*. San Francisco: Jossey-Bass.

Beamer, L. (1992). *Learning Intercultural Communication Competence*, Journal of Business Communication, 29(3), 285-303.

Berlo, D. K. (1960). *The Process of Communication*. New York: Holt, Rinehart & Winston.

Borisoff, D., & Victor, D. A. (1989). *Conflict Management: A Communication Skills Approach*. Englewood Cliffs, NJ.: Prentice Hall.

Cairncross, F. (1997). *The Death of Distance*. Boston: Harvard Business School Press.

Camerer, C., & Vepsalainen, A. (1988). The economic efficiency of corporate culture. *Journal of Business Communication*, Fall, 24(4), 21-34.

Chaney, L., & Martin, J. (1995). *Intercultural Business Communication*. Englewood Cliffs, NJ: Prentice Hall.

Charlten, A. (1992). Breaking cultural barriers. *Quality Progress*, 25(9), 47-49.

Child, J. (1981). Culture, contingency and capitalism in the cross-national study of organizations. In Cummings, L. L. and Staw, B. M. (Eds.), *Research in Organizational Behavior*, 3, 303-356. Greenwich, CT: JAI Press.

Eiler, M. A., & Victor, D. (1988). Genre and function in the Italian and U.S. business letter. *Proceedings of the Sixth Annual Conference on Languages and Communications for World Business and the Professions*. Ann Arbor, MI.

Farmerer, R. N., & Richman, B. M. (1966). *International Business: An Operational Theory*. Homewood, IL.: Richard D. Irwin.

Featherstone, M. (1990). *Global Culture, Nationalism, Globalization And Modernity*. Newbury Park, CA: Sage Publications, Ltd.

Fisher, G. (1988). *Mindsets: The Role of Culture and Perception in International Relations*. Yarmouth, ME: Intercultural Press.

Fukuyama, F. (1989). The end of history. *The National Interest*, Summer.

Granner, B. (1980). Cross-cultural adaptation in international business. *Journal of Contemporary Business*, 9(3), 101-108.

Halpern, J. W. (1983). Business communication in China: A second perspective. *The Journal of Business Communication*, 20, 43-55.

Haworth, D. A., & Savage, G. T. (1989). A channel-ratio model of intercultural communication. *The Journal of Business Communication*, 26, 231-254.

Held, D., Goldblatt, D., McGrew, A., & Perraton, J. (1997). The globalization of economic activity. *New Political Economy*, 2(2), 257-277.

Hofstede, G. (1980). *Culture's Consequences: International Differences in Work-Related Values*. Beverly Hills, CA: Sage Publications.

Howard, E. (1998). Can business cross the cultural divide. *Communication World*, 15(9), 1-7.

Huntington, S. (1993). The clash of civilizations? *Foreign Affairs*, Summer.

Joinson, C. (1995). Cultural sensitivity adds up to good business sense. *HR Magazine*, 82-85.

Laszlo, E. (1972). *The System View of the World*. New York: George Braziller.

Laurent, A. (1983). The culture diversity of western conceptions of management. *International Studies of Management and Organization*, 13(1-2), 75-96.

Limaye, M., & Victor, D. (1991). Cross-cultural business communication research: State of the art and hypotheses for the 1990's. *Journal of Business Communication*, 28(3), 277-299.

Lindsley, S. (1999). A layered model of problematic intercultural communication in US-owned Maquiladoras in Mexico. *Communication Monographs*, 66(6).

Maruyama, M. (1984). Alternative concepts of management: Insights from Asia and Africa. *Asia Pacific Journal of Management*, 1(2), 100-111.

Moran, R., & Richard, D. (1991). Preparing technical professionals for cross-cultural interactions. *Journal of European Industrial Training*, 15(3), 17-21.

Perkins, E. A., & Stout, V. (1987). Group dynamics: Communication responsibilities of managers. *The Proceedings of the Association for Business Communication*, Atlanta, Georgia.

Richard, L. (1990). How Do You Develop Pan-European Communication? 7(8), 1-6.

Rodrik, D. (1997). Sense and nonsense in the globalization debate. *Foreign Policy*, Summer.

Schein, E. H. (1985). *Organizational Culture and Leadership*. San Francisco: Jossey-Bass.

Scott, J. (1999). Developing cultural fluency: The goal of international business communication instruction in the 21st century. *Journal of Education for Business*, 74(3), 140-143.

Sussman, L., & Johnson, D. (1993). The interpreted executive: Theory, models, and implications. *Journal of Business Communication*, 30(4), 415-434.

Sypher, B. D., Applegate, J. L., & Sypher, H. E. (1985). Culture and communication in organizational context. In Gudykunst, W. B., Stewart, L. P. and Ting-Toomey, S. (Eds.), *Communication, Culture, and Organizational Process*. Beverly Hills, CA: Sage Publications.

Targowski, A. (1996). *Global Information Infrastructure*. Hershey, PA: Idea Group Publishing.

Targowski, A. (2000). The civilization index. *The Proceedings of the East-West Conference*, Western Michigan University, Kalamazoo, MI. June 2-3.

Targowski, A., & Bowman, J. (1988). The layer-based pragmatic model of the communication process. *Journal of Business Communication*, Winter, 25(1), 5-24.

Tayeb, M. H. (1988) *Organizations and National Culture: A Comparative Analysis*. London: Sage Publications.

Terpstra, V., & David, K. (1985). *The Cultural Environment of Business* (2nd ed.). Cincinnati, Ohio: South-Western Publishing Company.

Triandis, H. C. (1982-83). Dimensions of cultural variations as parameters of organizational theories. *International Studies of Management and Organization*, 12(4), 139-169.

Varner, I., & Beamer, L. (1995). *Intercultural Communication in the Global Workplace*. Chicago, IL: Irwin.

Varner, I. I. (1988). A comparison of American and French business communication. *The Journal of Business Communication*, 25(4), 55-65.

Victor, D. A. (1987). Franco-American business communication practices: A survey. *World Communication*, 16(2), 158-175.

Victor, D. A. (in press). *International Business Communication*. New York: HarperCollins Press.

Victor, D. A., & Danak, J. (1990). Genre and function in the U.S. and Indian English-language business letter: A survey. Paper presented at the *Conference on Language and Communication for World Business and the Professions*. Ypsilanti, MI.

Weiss, J. W. (1988). *Regional Cultures, Managerial Behavior and Entrepreneurship: An International Perspective*. Westport, CT: Greenwood Press.

Williams, M. (1991). Will diversity=Equality for multicultural communicators? *Communicational World*, 8(3), 27-30.

World Bank. (1997). *The State in Changing World: The World Development Report*. Washington, D.C.

World Bank. (1998/99). *Knowledge For Development: The World Development Report*. Washington, D.C.

Zong, B., & Hildebrandt, H. W. (1983). Business communication in the People's Republic of China. *The Journal of Business Communication*, 20, 25-33.

Chapter XIII

Cultural Characteristics of IT Professionals: An Ethnographic Perspective

Robert W. Gerulat
Empire State College, USA

The basic shared norms, values, beliefs, and assumptions of an organization help define the organization's culture (Schein, 1992). Just as an organization can be comprised of different departments, functional units, groups, or occupational specialties having varying points of view, an organization's culture may also contain subcultures reflecting these differences (Frederick, 1995, p. 202; Martin, 1992; Schein, 1992, pp. 256-257; Trice, 1993). According to Trice, subcultures differentiated by occupations within an organization can also extend beyond the boundaries of the organization forming a cultural community of their own. One such occupational subculture, which can be found within many modern organizations, relates to information technology (IT) and is represented by IT professionals—the individuals responsible for the operations of modern computer information systems.

Information technology (IT), in its broadest meaning, is having a profound influence on modern society (Davis, 1992; Due, 1992; Earl, 1996). Additionally, the impact of IT is strongly felt throughout today's entire modern organization (e.g., Davis, 1992; Earl, 1996; Grover & Cheon, 1996). As articulated in Szewczak and Khosrowpour (1996), organization members, including IT professionals, have seen many changes in organizational life. These changes include the way they think about themselves, their futures, their shared norms, values, and beliefs, and what it means to contribute effectively to the well-being of their organizations. These issues constitute social and human aspects of IT that are cultural in nature. It is important that organizations understand these cultural issues because, as both Schein (1992) and Denison (1990) observed, organizational culture could have a direct impact on an organization's overall performance. But, as noted by Szewczak and Khosrowpour, organizations often pay insufficient attention to these human elements.

The purpose of this chapter is to present data and analysis from research that focused on the human side of IT. In an effort to determine the potential effects of outsourcing on the shared norms, values, beliefs, and assumptions of IT professionals, a two-part study was conducted using ethnographic research methods. Its first goal was to identify the cultural characteristics of IT professionals as an occupational group. The second goal was to determine how the cultural characteristics might potentially be affected by the phenomenon of outsourcing. The data and analysis that follow pertain to the first part of the study.

LITERATURE REVIEW AND BACKGROUND

Insufficient research information exists that accurately describes the norms of behavior, values, beliefs, or assumptions that might serve to define the culture of IT professionals. However, the research literature does provide a significant amount of theory and opinion concerning organizational culture in general terms, often offering theoretical models useful in describing specific cultures. For example, Schein (1992) defined the culture of any group as

[A] pattern of shared basic assumptions that the group learned as it solved its problems of external adaptation and internal integration that has worked well enough to be considered valued and, therefore, to be taught to new members as the correct way to perceive, think, and feel in relation to those problems. (p. 12)

He refined these concepts and applied them to a definition of organizational culture that includes the idea that the culture of an organization is comprised of levels of culture represented by artifacts, espoused values, and basic underlying assumptions (pp. 17, 46-48).

Robbins (1997) presented a slightly different view of organizational culture as a system of variables in an organization that dictates how organizational members react with each other and with the organization's external environment. He defined organizational culture as "a system of shared meanings held by members that distinguishes the organization from other organizations" (p. 237). Alternatively, O'Reilly and Chatman (1996) viewed organizational culture as a system of social controls based on "shared norms and values that set expectations about appropriate attitudes and behavior for members of the group" (p. 157). More formally, these authors defined organizational culture as "a system of shared values (that define what is important) and norms that define appropriate attitudes and behaviors for organizational members (how to feel and behave)" (p. 160).

From a similar perspective of control, Young (2000) offered a theory of Cultural Levers, or organizational processes, that managers might use to describe, maintain, or modify a culture. These included (1) strategy formulation, (2) authority and influence, (3) motivation, (4) management control, (5) conflict management, and (6) customer management. From yet another perspective, in their effort to link concepts of Total Quality Management (TQM) with a comprehensive framework for defining and measuring organizational culture, Detert, Schroeder, and Muriel (2000) offered a synthesis of prevailing theoretical models. Similar in nature to Schein's (1992) topology of cultural assumptions, their newly offered set of cultural dimensions include ideas about (1) the basis of truth and reality; (2) the nature of time and time horizon; (3) motivation; (4) stability versus change; (5) orientation to work, task, and coworkers; (6) isolation versus collaboration and cooperation; (7) control, coordination, and responsibility; and (8) orientation and focus.

According to Dessler (1980), an organization will function better when its personnel function not as individuals but as members of work groups or cohesive teams with organizational goals in mind. Normally, individualism is controlled through groups, which control individuals through the establishment of norms. However, as Dessler pointed out, norms do not apply to everyone within an organization. High status members of an organization often have more freedom to deviate from established group norms. They remain above the group norms to the extent that high status members form power relationships that allow them to form their own norms and establish their own patterns of behavior that have to be accepted by the rest of the organization, provided their power-base is sufficiently large.

Trice (1993) addressed a similar issue by discussing occupational sub-cultures in the workplace. According to Trice, in addition to core cultures, organizations can contain sub-cultures represented by informal and formal groups. These groups can be differentiated by departments, workgroups, age, sex, ethnicity, and also by occupation. They can be rich in symbolism and cultural themes that reinforce meanings and help motivate members to have beliefs that are aligned with the group's ideologies (p. 39). As articulated by Trice, "ideologies . . . are emotionalized, action-oriented beliefs held by members of an occupation about their work" (p. 48). Freidson (1973) referred to these beliefs as "the occupational principle"—a code of conduct, which holds that members of the occupation should control the main aspects of the work (pp. 19-33). Trice indicated that these sub-cultures have their own language, occupational heroes, myths, stories, and rights of passage (p. 39).

While the concept of culture within the framework of organization theory dates to Pettigrew (1979), the idea of culture, from an academic perspective, has traditionally been an essential aspect of Anthropology. This holistic discipline has been concerned, as a comparative science, with the study of humans and society. It examines culture and cultural traditions that develop over time, including customs, rituals, opinions, learned behavior, symbols, shared meanings, and patterns from a multi-level perspective (Kottak, 2000).

The various theories of organizational culture described herein are, essentially, variations within the disciplines of management and organizational behavior. They rely upon borrowed concepts of culture from anthropology that have been applied to management science (p. 8). The differences emphasize the deficiencies in attempting to define culture in organizations from a purely *business* perspective, instead of relying more on anthropological methods and concepts.

To overcome these deficiencies, this research relies upon a synthesis of ideas and methods from both business and anthropology. It combines the concepts of the various business authors mentioned, including those of Kottak (2000). For methodology, it relies upon ethnography—the primary tool of anthropology to gather and interpret data.

RESEARCH DESIGN

Research Questions

The research questions pertaining to culture that drove this study are:
1. What are the common cultural norms, values, beliefs, and assumptions that describe the culture of Information Technology professionals?
2. How are cultural norms, values, and beliefs transmitted to and reinforced by members of the IT community?

Framework

To explain the nature, dynamics, and functions of organizational culture, Schein (1992) has grouped concepts such as behavior regularities, group norms, espoused values, formal philosophy, rules, climate, embedded skills, mental models, shared meanings, and root metaphors (pp. 8-10). He further grouped these concepts into levels that include artifacts, espoused values, and basic underlying assumptions (p. 17). Using Schein's model, and the idea that organizational culture manifests itself in artifacts, espoused values, and basic underlying assumptions, along with the field techniques suggested by Kottak (2000) and Holstein and

Gubrium (1995), it is possible to explore aspects of organizational culture within organizations from an anthropological perspective.

Method

An ethnographic method of inquiry was chosen for this research because of the qualitative nature of the data that would be collected and analyzed (Agar, 1980; Denison, 1990; Fetterman, 1989; Gummesson, 1989; Hammersley, 1998; Johnson, 1990; Kottak, 2000; Schein, 1989; Schein, 1992; Stake, 1989). As a qualitative study, the methods used were justified because this study presented no initial hypotheses (Denzin & Lincoln, 1994). Rather, it was exploratory in that it sought to identify the cultural characteristics of a community of IT professionals. It was interpretive in that it sought to understand and interpret meanings from the perspective of the participants— the members of the IT cultural community (e.g., Agar, 1980; Denison, 1990; Fetterman, 1989; Gummesson, 1989; Hammersley, 1998; Johnson, 1990; Lareau & Shultz, 1996; Schein, 1989; Schein, 1992; Stake, 1995).

Placing ethnographic research methods into a contemporary perspective, Jessor, Colby, and Shweder (1996) noted that both ethnographic methods and qualitative research methods in general represent an aggregation or collection of research approaches and procedures rather than any one unique method (pp. 5-6). The ethnographic approaches used in this study included participant observation, informal and unstructured interviews, active interviews, and informal correspondence in the forms of letters and e-mail.

Population Selection. The study population was comprised of the 100 information technology professionals having functional responsibility for computer systems within the 100 largest or most significant organizations in western New York. As a cultural community, the population transcended the bounds of any one organization. Its common bond was the unique nature of the occupation in relation to other occupations that can be found within an organization, as well as the common values, assumptions, and beliefs shared by its members as articulated by Trice (1993).

Sample Selection. Sample selection was based on a purposive sampling technique. As noted by Merriam (1998), the selection of qualitative research samples is often non-random, purposeful, and small. This can be especially true in ethnographic research (Agar, 1980; Hammersley, 1998; Johnson, 1990; Schein, 1992). As articulated by Johnson (1990), the intent of purposive sampling of informants in an ethnographic study is to collect *accurate* and *reliable* information. Potential informants were defined in terms of their social roles in the organizations that employed them: (a) information technology managers or directors, (b) network or systems engineers, and (c) network or systems administrators. This distinction was made because it was anticipated there might be differences of views among the categories.

All 100 IT professionals from the study population were invited to participate. Twenty key informants were recruited and used for in-depth and on-going interviews. Additionally, five informants were recruited from the study population and used to a lesser degree to verify information.

Informal Interviews. A strategy of this research was to allow cultural themes to emerge (Agar, 1980) through informal and active interviews rather than test for their existence. Structured interviews would have been inappropriate (Fetterman, 1989). Agar referred to informal interviews as conversational yet focused in intent (see also Lareau & Scultz, 1996). Active interview techniques were used as described by Holstein and Gubrium (1995). The idea behind using the active interview technique was to ask questions pertaining to the area of study and provide an open atmosphere for undistorted communication. It was intended to "enliven the image of the subject behind the respondent," and to probe where necessary to add creativity to the interview process (p. 8).

Participant/Direct Observation. Participant and direct observation allowed this researcher to observe culture and behavior, and interpret meanings from an *emic* perspective, an important aspect of ethnographic research (Agar, 1980; Fetterman, 1989; Kirk & Miller, 1986; Merriam, 1998; Sharpe, 1997). As noted by Merriam, the key concept is "the researcher is the primary instrument for data collection and analysis" (p. 7).

Data derived from all forms of inquiry were collected and analyzed following a *cultural assumptions* topology articulated by Schein (1992, pp. 52-102). During this process, sensitivity was given to the possible emergence of data from the primary cultural forms articulated by Trice (1993) including myths, stories, rituals, taboos, rites, ceremonies, jargon, and heroes.

Data collected were recorded through the use of field notes, mail, and e-mail correspondence. Tape recordings were not used. By a written agreement to protect human subjects used in research, the identity of key informants was kept confidential.

Data Analysis. The primary goal of the data analysis function of the study was to identify patterns and interpret meanings. As articulated by Agar (1980), Fetterman (1989), Merriam (1998), and Miles and Huberman (1994), data analysis for this type of research is not a separate function to be accomplished after the data have been collected. Instead, data analysis is a function of the data collection process. Consequently, previously acquired data was continually compared to new data as they were collected in an effort to detect and match patterns using a matrix of themes as they emerged.

FINDINGS

Demographics of the Study Sample

In the study sample, the mean years of experience as an IT professional was 15.9 years (SD = 8.896). Only five of the informants (20% of the sample) were in the community for less than 11 years, indicating they were familiar with issues pertaining to the local IT community. Eleven informants (55% of the sample) had at least a Bachelor's degree, three (15% of the sample) had an Associate's degree, and six (30% of the sample) had graduated from High School (HS) and had not attended college or had graduated from HS and completed some college credits. Of the 11 informants who had at least a Bachelor degree, one also had a Master of Business Administration degree (MBA) and another had achieved a Ph.D. in biochemistry.

In terms of IT training outside of formal education, all informants (100% of the sample) indicated that their primary IT training took the form of self-study. They accomplished this through a variety of ways, including reading books, software manuals, technical material on the Internet, and taking Computer-Based Training (CBT) courses. Other common methods included On-the-Job Training (OJT) programs, attending technical institutes, attending vendor-sponsored training seminars, and classroom-based instruction in-tended to prepare them for certifications such as the Microsoft Certified System Engineer (MCSE) credential or the Novell Certified Engineer (CNE) credential.

Three of the informants (15% of the sample) were female. This was consistent with the ratio of females identified in the study population (identified females represented 11% of the population).

Norms, Values, Beliefs, and Assumptions

The primary interview questions asked, or topics introduced, pertaining to the first research question follow. It must be noted that the data derived from each interview question is a holistic interpretation of the data derived from the entire set of interview questions. It was not until after all questions were asked and answered that actual patterns emerged.

Tell me about the computer systems for which you are responsible.

Only three informants were reluctant to discuss the nature of their computer systems, citing security reasons. The remaining informants were willing to discuss their systems, often in minute detail. Since the focus of this research was not to describe or compare computer information systems, this detail will not be presented. However, it is noteworthy that the majority of informants expressed high degrees of pleasure when discussing technical or managerial aspects of their systems. It was apparent that informants took pride in their own technical knowledge and expertise, and were able to manifest this pride in the descriptions they gave.

It was also apparent that there were differences in focus among informants. The differences appeared related to the size of the IT department for which the informant was responsible. Although the informants came from the 100 largest or most prestigious organizations in western New York, there were both large and small IT operations contained within this population. There appeared to be a correlation between the number of users supported, or the nature of the data within an organization, to the number of personnel for which an IT professional was responsible. The informants who supervised greater numbers of technical computer people, having more complicated systems, tended to focus on the management aspects of their systems. Those informants supervising fewer computer people in less complicated system environments tended to focus on the minute technical details of their systems. These informants appeared to be more technical than managerial.

As an IT professional in western New York, what are the things you value most?

In terms of shared cultural value themes, 17 of the informants (85% of the sample) indicated that technical knowledge and technical skill, as a combined theme, was something that they highly valued. Twelve of the informants (60% of the sample) ranked technical knowledge and skill as something that they valued the highest. Fifteen of the informants (75% of the sample) placed a high value on general education and general knowledge. However, only six of the informants (30% of the sample) ranked general education and general knowledge as their highest value theme. Five of the informants (25% of the sample) referred to autonomy as an important value theme. They valued the ability to work independently, make decisions independently, and not have management interfere to any extent with their work. When probed, informants indicated that they had no objections to working in a team environment. Their concept of autonomy only extended to the method by which they were directly supervised. The informants indicated that autonomy of this nature was important to them because, in their opinions, their superiors were not sufficiently competent in the technical aspects of IT and should therefore stay away from day-to-day decision-making concerning IT management. As one informant stated when comparing his present-day situation to the past:

It wasn't always this way. My old boss (the former Chief Financial Officer of the company—a Certified Public Accountant) thought he knew something about computers. What an idiot! He decided we would buy clones (non-brand name computers assembled from components) to save money. I had to hire a technician just to keep them running. That fiasco cost the company a lot of money. (Confidential informant, personal communication, 2000)

The informant made it clear that he valued autonomy and resented interference in the day-to-day operations of the IT department by non-technical superiors.

Four of the informants (20% of the sample) indicated that an important value to them was a strong work ethic. It is notable that the informants who indicated this value were representative of those informants who had more management responsibility. They were referring to a trait they found valuable in the IT employees who reported to them. When probed, none of these informants indicated that a strong work ethic was the most important value. Two of the four informants who placed a strong work ethic as an important value admitted that they had supervised several IT employees who did not have a strong work ethic but were tolerated because of their exceptionally high level of technical knowledge. Informants described these individuals as brilliant within their specialty, but often unable to function well in an organizational world to the extent preferred. Informants indicated that these types of employees tended to be in their early twenties, often came to work late, did not always notify them of absence, and did not interact well with others in the organization. Of the four informants who placed importance on a strong work ethic, all considered this cultural value theme to be utopian. They valued it because they did not always find it in the employees within their charge.

Five informants (25% of the sample) placed a high value on the importance of computer system integrity and stability. They viewed one of their primary responsibilities as providing system integrity and stability to their organizations. It is interesting to note that none of the informants who placed a value on the theme of integrity viewed integrity from an ethical or moral perspective. All informants viewed integrity from a technical perspective, relating integrity to concepts of system stability or reliability.

Other value themes expressed ranged from valuing self-directed workers having generalist rather than specialist knowledge to a short commute to work. Only one informant indicated that money, as an important value theme, was high on his list. When probed, it was discovered that this informant's annual performance review had not yet taken place and was over a month past due. He was concerned that his superior was not going to adequately recognize the contribution to the organization that the informant felt he had made and was fearful that a raise would not be forthcoming or not be to his expectation. This informant also felt that his technical skills were becoming outdated and that he was losing his marketability. While only one informant referred to money as an important cultural value theme, money, in the form of salary, was a common frustration. This data will be discussed in a later section.

Do you think that these values are common values, shared by other IT professionals in western New York?
     In terms of assumptions and beliefs, 19 of the informants (95% of the sample) indicated that they believed the values they expressed were common values held by other IT professionals in western New York, or should be. The remaining informant indicated that she was simply not sure.

What is it like to be an IT professional in western New York?
     The four primary data themes that emerged from this question were (a) undervalued, (b) challenging, (c) frustrating, and (d) rewarding. The theme of *undervalued* was an extension of the theme *frustrating,* indicating that the informant was frustrated with some issue to the point of feeling undervalued. In terms of rewarding or frustrating experiences within the western New York IT community, 17 of the informants (85% of the sample) indicated some frustration. Eleven of the informants (55% of the sample) registered frustration that escalated to perceptions of being undervalued in the western New York area. The theme patterns developed relate to low pay and limited career opportunities in the western New York area, the difficulty associated with finding and keeping qualified computer people, budget restrictions, and limitations concerning available telecommunications technology in the area. As one informant noted:

> Buffalo (the major city in the western New York area and second largest in the state) is kind of a backwater town. Compared to the rest of the country, pay is way below average here and their [sic] aren't many director positions here. There are lots of low-end jobs because the companies don't want to pay for the higher-end talent. That's why it's hard to find good people. I think they all left. (Confidential informant, personal communication, 2000)

Frustrations that extended to feelings of being undervalued also included an assumption of low wages compared to other areas of the country, and a general belief on the part of informants that the economy in western New York has limited their career opportunities. However, it must be noted that while the perception of low salaries and limited opportunities in the area were among the most frequently articulated frustrations, money, as a value theme, was only mentioned by one informant.

What is it like to be an IT professional in your organization?

Identical to the previous interview question, the primary themes that emerged were (a) undervalued, (b) challenging, (c) frustrating, and (d) rewarding. While 17 informants (85% of the sample) expressed frustration with being an IT professional in western New York, only 11 informants (55% of the sample) indicated any kind of frustration with the organization for which they worked. Only six of the informants (30% of the sample) registered frustration to the extent of feeling undervalued within their organization, nearly half the rate of those who felt undervalued in the western New York area.

What is your IT mission statement, if you have one?

This question was intended to be the foundation for a request to obtain a physical copy of a mission statement, which would have represented *artifactual* evidence to support culture themes. Only one informant was able to produce an actual IT mission statement. One other informant thought that an IT mission statement existed but was unable to produce a copy.

The one mission statement made available did serve to provide some physical evidence to help substantiate cultural themes. An excerpt is as follows:

Maintain a lean (.9% of sales) internal IS department competent to support the organization both strategically and tactically, providing quick response with minimum bureaucracy. (Confidential informant, personal communication, 2000)

From this mission statement, it would appear that budgetary considerations were foremost, limiting internal information system costs to a percentage of sales. Through the use of the word *competent*, it is apparent that technical competency, in the form of technical knowledge and skill, was an espoused valued and considered to be an important element of the IT mission. The term *competent* could also be interpreted as including the value theme of *system integrity*.

Describe any rights of passage you have had to endure to get to where you are today.

All informants indicated that rights of passage associated with becoming a member of the IT community dealt with the process they went through to become accepted by others in the community and within their own organizations. Acceptance took the form of being recognized as having a high level of technical knowledge and skill. For most of the informants, they completed this process of acceptance, or performed these rights of passage, by performing their IT duties in such a manner as to show competence by articulating technical knowledge through conversation, and demonstrating technical competence by displaying technical skills to others. As one informant stated:

> I came up through the ranks. I did user support. I built PCs (personal computers). I was a network technician. I worked my way up the ladder and paid my dues like everyone else. (Confidential informant, personal communication, 2000)

Based on direct observation, this process of acceptance is ongoing and part of the cultural transference mechanism. Informants generally were eager to describe in detail the nature of their systems and articulate their technical knowledge. This aspect of the data will be discussed in more detail in a later section.

Tell me something about the users you have supported.

The central patterns that emerged from this interview theme can be described as (a) *incompetent,* (b) *demanding,* and (c) *uninformed.* Informants told stories about incompetent, demanding, and uninformed users in the organizations for which they presently worked. They described similar types of users in organizations with which they were previously associated. They also described incompetent, misinformed, and overly demanding managers, who were both users and decision-makers, and who also demonstrated some form of incompetence associated with using IT or understanding the potential use of IT.

In general, from the perspective of their individual standards, informants indicated that the many users they supported in their organizations did not possess a sufficiently high level of PC skill. Consequently, the informants tended to look down upon people who did not possess technical knowledge and skill in this context. However, within the study sample, there were variations to this theme. As one informant stated:

> We have users ranging from PC literate to nothing. The younger ones seem more knowledgeable. The older ones are harder to train. If we could improve their skills, we could cut down on the Help Desk and devote our energies elsewhere. (Confidential informant, personal communication, 2000)

Another informant viewed the users in his organization as being two-tiered. He saw the college-educated and professional users as being motivated and able to learn the PC skills necessary for their job. He observed that, in his opinion, the users who only possessed a high school education exhibited a mixture of skills and motivation. In his opinion, this latter group was more difficult to deal with and caused more support problems by requiring more frequent low-level support.

When describing the users in his organization, one informant noted: "We have three divisions [in western New York] with different customers. They (users) are generally easy to work with." However, referring to users in other organizations in which he worked in the western New York area, the informant wrote: "Users were difficult to [work] with. Unreasonably demanding and sometimes unprofessional." (Confidential informant, personal communication, 2000)

Another informant carried this theme farther stating:

Two to three years ago many of the users on our system never used a computer. Today everyone in the company has a computer on their desk with email and Faxing capabilities. And it seems that the more they have on their systems the more they want them to do and the faster they must run. After a while you come to the conclusion that you can't keep them all satisfied. (Confidential informant, personal communication, 2000)

What do you consider the most important aspects of your job?

The primary themes that developed from this question were (a) keep the system running, (b) system stability and integrity, (c) user support, and (d) planning and process. Themes such as *keep the system running* and *user support* were seen by informants as reactive activities that required high levels of technical knowledge and skill. Themes such as *stability and integrity* and *planning and process* were seen as proactive activities and more managerial in nature. The differences between a technical focus and a managerial focus will be discussed in a later section.

From an IT perspective, who do you consider your heroes, your role models, and why?

Five of the informants (20% of the sample) indicated that their heroes or role models were famous individuals in the IT field such as Bill Gates, Tim Berners-Lee, James Anderseen, and Steve Case. These individuals were heroes and role models because they were innovative and were able change the world through their technical knowledge. The informants valued what they considered to be technical *genius*. One informant strongly defended Bill Gates, a response generated by a recent antitrust lawsuit against Microsoft Corporation, by stating a hypothetical question: "Where would be today without him?"

More importantly, 14 informants (70% of the sample) referred to former co-workers, former superiors, and other ordinary IT people as their heroes and role models. The informants indicated that these individuals, at one time or another, were mentors to them and taught them technical aspects of the field.

They were heroes because they exhibited a far superior technical skill-set than others and, especially, were willing to share their knowledge with the informant. In many cases, informants formed long-lasting bonds with these mentors or formed perceptions of their technical knowledge that spanned many years. These heroes and role models were, and in some cases still are, held in awe by informants because of their IT skills and knowledge.

It seems that whenever IT professionals get together, they inevitably tell each other stories related to their profession. Without naming names or organizations, please briefly tell me your favorite IT story.
During the four months in which this ethnographic study was conducted, informants told many stories directly to this researcher. Also, this researcher observed storytelling as a common behavior between informants and other people who were members of the general IT community. Storytelling was often a primary means of communication. Stories served to make a point, convey moral messages, explain technical functions, and prove that the *story-teller* had superior IT skills and knowledge over the subject of the story.

The primary patterns that emerged from stories can be categorized as (a) incompetent users, (b) incompetent managers, and (c) incompetent IT people. Most of the stories could be classified as a type that conveyed the message: *I have greater technical knowledge than others.*

Stories about incompetent users tended to be humorous. For example, one informant told a story about a user who called the Help Desk for assistance. This incident occurred shortly after CD-ROM drives became common in commercial PCs. The user told the Help Desk support person that the cup holder in his computer had broken and asked that it be replaced.

Another story told dealt with a user who caused a computer technician to spend over one hour on the telephone attempting to solve the user's printing problem. Finally, the technician was able to determine that the user's printer was not turned on.

Stories about incompetent managers tended to be warnings to other IT people about the dangers of uninformed managers who interfered in the technical operations of IT, or tended to convey an adverse situation that was resolved through the exploits of the storyteller. For example, one informant told a story about a former CEO who had little use for technology. Being from the *old school*, as the informant put it, the CEO became irritated because the computer system had experienced a series of problems. Moreover, the CEO had just reviewed a report concerning the cost of the IT department and was displeased. In a meeting with managers, including the informant, the CEO demanded that the entire computer system be dismantled and that the company return to a *paper* environment. Not only did this decision on the part of the CEO mean an end to the informant's job, the informant *knew* that the action would have a disastrous effect on the company. The informant *heroically* solved the problems with the computer system and through the use of his *superior logic* was able to convince the CEO not to disband the IT department.

Concerning the activities of other IT people, one informant wrote the following story:

> At one particular company I worked with there were always stories flying around about the DBA (Data Base Administrator). The DBA had sole access [to] the HP (Hewlett Packard) [RS-6000 system]. No one else knew how things were set up or how to get in. Every time this DBA was out of the office or on vacation there seemed to be problems with the computer—downtime, slowness, etc. More time than not this person would need to be called in to 'save the day,' since no one else knew how or had access. The big joke among other workers was that the DBA was behind the problems to create job security. Mgt. (management) however viewed him as the savior of the computer. (Confidential informant, personal communication, 2000)

Another informant told a revealing story that places the value of technical skill and knowledge above formal education:

> My favorite IT story is about a new employee who was hired. He had a Masters degree in economics from a highly regarded university. He thought because he had an advanced degree & took a few computer courses, that he could work in I.T. His first day on the job he asked what "move spaces" meant in a Cobol program. He humiliated himself and was fired within two weeks. (Confidential informant, personal communication, 2000)

The Cobol programming language command *move spaces* is a way for a programmer to initialize a character array in a database by moving single characters to each element of the array. This is not a common term and would be known only to someone with an elite knowledge of Cobol or structured programming.

From a different perspective, one informant, when asked to tell his favorite IT story, simply stated: "Stories? IT people are kind of dull. You know, techno-geeks. The only stories you hear are about code or some stupid user."

Cultural Transference

What memberships do you maintain in local IT associations?

Twelve key informants (60% of the sample) did not belong to any local IT organizations. The remaining eight key informants did, at one time or another, belong to a local user's group. The purpose of the group was to share technical information among its members. Members met once a month, had lunch at a local restaurant, and socialized with one another while sharing information.

As a participant observer, this researcher was a guest of one informant. During the meeting, it was common for participants to share stories, technical information, help each other solve technical problems, and socialize by talking about users and their dealings with upper management.

How do you interact with other IT professionals in the local western New York IT community?

This question was intended to gather data relating to cultural transference that occurred outside of formal associations. Seventeen key informants (85% of the sample) indicated that they interacted with, or gained knowledge concerning the activities and practices of, other IT management professionals through association with vendors. In the opinion of many of these informants, vendors provide a good source of information concerning current trends in IT and what others are doing. Sixteen key informants (80% of the sample) indicated that their contact with outsourcing contractors provided them with similar information. Thirteen key informants (65% of the sample) indicated that they maintained close contact with other members of the IT community through conversations and e-mail. In some cases, this was an extension of user group contact. Eight of the key informants (40% of the sample) acknowledged that cultural themes were transferred through various training sessions they attended.

What kinds of activities are you engaged in, outside of your job, that are related to your occupation?

Only three of the informants (15% of the sample) indicated that they were engaged in any kind of activity outside of their job that was related to their occupation. Of these informants, one indicated that he did some part-time consulting work that supplemented his income. Another informant indicated that he was active in his church group and occasionally taught others, primarily senior citizens, how to use a computer. One informant taught programming at a local college in the evenings.

The remaining 17 informants (85% of the sample) indicated that they were not engaged in any extracurricular activities related to their occupations. As one informant stated: "I have to look at this stuff all day. The last thing I want to do when I get home is play with computers."

How do you keep up with the technology?

All informants indicated that the primary means by which they stayed current with technology was through some form of self-study. This included reading trade magazines and periodicals. Other common themes that emerged from this question included attending vendor-sponsored seminars and formal training courses, reading white papers published by Microsoft Corporation and other software vendors, and general interaction with other members of the local IT community. As one informant stated: "More information (in the form of free publications) comes across my desk every day than I could ever read. I just focus on a few of them."

Outsourcing

While these questions were intended to development information relating to phase two of the study, portions of the findings are presented here because they further inform the cultural aspects of the research.

1.   *Tell me about your experiences with outsourcing.*
2.   *What is your opinion about outsourcing?*
3.   *What kinds of changes are created in your organization from outsourcing?*
4.   *How does outsourcing affect the values and beliefs that you think are common among IT professionals?*

The central patterns that emerged from these interview questions related to skill-sets, the reasons why IT outsourcing was used, and information concerning informant's views of the outsourcing. The majority of the informants indicated that they used an outsourcing solution when they did not have the necessary technical skills internally. None of the informants indicated that they used outsourcing to reduce costs specifically associated with IT operations. Only one informant indicated that outsourcing was used as a means to reduce some costs, but on an organizational level, not specific to IT operations. Of the remaining informants, all considered IT outsourcing to cost more than it would to do the work internally—if they had the skills or the time. For these informants, the central issue was related to technical knowledge and skill, not money or corporate profits.

Generally, outsourcing was used in connection with a project. For example, informant 02 described how he contracted with an outside consulting company to design and build a corporate web site. The decision to outsource was made because his company wanted a professional-looking site with sophisticated functionally. Although there were programmers on staff capable of building a site, other corporate managers believed that the product they wanted required a higher level of expertise and graphical creativity. Consequently, they turned to a company that specialized in this function. When asked about his opinion concerning outsourcing, one informant indicated that outsourcing makes good sense, but only in certain circumstances. He stated:

> We're not crazy about outsourcing, only for major projects when we don't have the staff. Then it's OK. But, you have to be careful. Success really depends on the relationship you build. When the project winds down, you want your people in the loop. (Confidential informant, personal communication, 2000)

The loop to which this informant referred was the transference of technical knowledge and skill from the contractor to his IT department. He wanted his people to have this skill.

Along a similar theme, another informant indicated that his organization used outsourcing for special projects when IT personnel lacked the skills necessary. However, the informant indicated that he observed what were, in his opinion, some potentially negative effects caused by bringing new knowledge into the organization.

> To the others (the direct-hire IT employees) they were a threat in a way. They (employees of the outsourcing contractor) were new people coming in with higher skills. It places employment stability in question. (Confidential informant, personal communication, 2000)

When asked how the employees and he dealt with this problem, this informant indicated that the response was to increase their own knowledge. Upon reflection, the informant saw that the introduction of the new knowledge and skill from outsourcing enhanced technical knowledge, something that he highly valued.

Another informant had good and bad experiences with outsourcing. He indicated that the management of an outsourcing contract, from his perspective, was too time-consuming.

> There is a big learning curve. The people you bring in have to be brought up to speed. This is not always the best way. Sometimes you could get it done faster internally. But on the positive side, good things rub off. The staff sometimes takes things for granted. They hear new things from outsourcers. They learn they have it good. (Confidential informant, personal communication, 2000)

This informant was referring to aspects of cultural transference. He felt that IT outsourcing brought information in from the outside world. His employees learned that the outsourcing contractors had to work hard for their money and, as he put it, "the grass is not always greener somewhere else." (Confidential informant, personal communication, 2000)

When asked about outsourcing, one informant indicated that he would only use it when desperate. He added that outsourcing was "usually disappointing, especially for the money they charge. They get the job done but usually takes [sic] longer than planned. If [I knew] it were that easy I would have done it myself." (Confidential informant, personal communication, 2000)

Another informant reported that he had very good experience with outsourcing.

It has worked well and I would do it again. It involved outsourcing network services to former employees. [However,] if you outsource a particular function instead of a broad function or groups, you have a better chance of success. (Confidential informant, personal communication, 2000)

This informant also noted that, in his opinion, positive changes occurred as a result of outsourcing. In his opinion, the outsourcing experience brought new knowledge and methods to the table. "Outsourcing made us implement formal project management." However, he added, "If it (outsourcing) is not managed properly, IT folks have negative feelings on outsourcing. They feel IT management does not have faith in them and that they do not have the skills to do the job" (Confidential informant, personal communication). When probed concerning this issue, this informant conceded that outsourcing caused people within his department to upgrade their knowledge and skills.

Another informant noted positive effects associated with outsourcing because such relationships bring new skills into the organization. However, he also noted that outsourcing consultants are given what he termed over inflated respect. He indicated that they are viewed as the "go to person." In his opinion, this perception "can cause personality conflicts with people in the IT department who feel that *they* (emphasis added) should be the go to person."

When probed concerning this issue, the informant indicated that the negative effect on the organization was that the slighted party might look elsewhere for employment. He considered his technical knowledge as something that made him elite within his organization. Consequently, outsourcing was seen as a threat to his status.

The technical skills theme continued with another informant, who noted that outsourcing consultants bring in new technology and bring up the standards of the IT department. However, in agreement with other informants, he indicated that the introduction of the new skills and knowledge causes fear and sometimes resentment. "They (the direct-hire IT employees) automatically assume that they will lose their jobs if you go to outsourcing. They fear what the new guy knows" (Confidential informant, personal communication).

One informant articulated these perceptions perhaps better than other informants. He also recognized the potential conflicts that arise between internal IT employees, him, and outsourced contractors over who knows more about something. He noted:

> I think the conflict takes the form of resentment. It emanates from fear. But on the positive side, it streamlines systems, creates efficiencies, and improves processes. I think it actually enhances the [cultural] values (of technical skill and knowledge). It enhances the value of internal IT and can reflect on their (internal IT's) core competencies. (Confidential informant, personal communication, 2000)

One informant disagreed with this view. He felt that outsourcing was only good in those rare instances when one needed specialty skills, not necessarily limited to IT skills—such as the installation and implementation of an accounting program. From his perspective, this type of outsourcing was acceptable because the contractors were accountants and not really IT people. In his opinion, outsourcing contractors do not care about an organization's business to the same extent as internal IT people. He felt that internal IT people were the ones who "will be around for a while." As he stated: "We know our processes better than anyone else. We are the ones with a sense of urgency and (referring to quality) close isn't good enough" (Confidential informant, personal communication, 2000). In his opinion, outsourcing of this nature had a negative effect on the cultural value of quality. He believed that outsiders would somehow change things for the worse if lower quality standards were introduced.

This same sense of quality and caring was reflected in the statements made by all three of the female informants interviewed.

> We attempted to outsource a payroll while we changed software. The lack of needed reports to fit our requirements swayed us to doing parallel processing on 2 systems instead. [Consequently] we don't outsource [anymore]. If we can do it in-house it is on our time-table, and can be modified to our needs. Outsourcing, you get what is offered on someone else's schedule. (Confidential informant, personal communication, 2000)

From another female perspective, one informant noted:

I have had both good and bad experiences with outsourcing. We had one girl do some Access (Microsoft Access) programming for us that was very good. While a gentleman from another company spent months working on a project that I had to revamp when it made it in house. And the cost does not seem to be the defining factor. The girl's cost was $45 an hour while the latter's was $95 an hour. I think it's really hard to be sure just what you are going to get. The same has been true with hardware repair services. They seldom come in with a final cost that matches the quote. (Confidential informant, personal communication, 2000)

Direct and Participant Observation

Physical artifacts observed within the community took numerous forms. Patterns were detected in (a) centralized computer systems, (b) instructional and knowledge-based materials, (c) tools, (d) decorations, and (e) technology-based devices.

With only minor exceptions, the centralized computer systems observed in computer rooms were neat and orderly. They were constructed, configured, and arranged in a professional manner. It was apparent that the informants took pride in the systems for which they were responsible and in the professionalism exhibited in their physical layout.

It was observed that there existed an abundance of instructional and knowledge-based materials. These generally included technical libraries of books and manuals, technical instructions, training material, software, and other forms of technical reference. It was apparent that the informants took great pride in their training and reference collections. It was also observed that the reference and training material was easily accessed by IT employees and frequently used. It was also observed that the material was intended to be exclusively used by the IT department and not readily available to others. Reinforcing the concept of elitism, one informant, when asked if anyone in the organization could access the material, responded: "What for? They wouldn't know what it means anyway" (Confidential informant, personal communication, 2000).

Specialized tools, including workbenches and work areas, were observed at all sites visited. Common were technician tool kits that were extensive and well maintained. However, it was observed that those IT professionals whose focus was more on management than on the technical aspects of IT tended not to address tools in their tour whereas those whose focus was more on technology included tools and work areas in their discussions. Furthermore, those informants whose focus was more on technology tended to visibly carry tools and other symbols of technology on their person and appeared to show pride wearing them. Items worn also included cell phones, one or more beepers, personal computing devices, and multipurpose tools that appeared to be symbolic of their function or position within the organization.

Decorations were observed to be prolific and often took the form of posters related to technology and cartoon characters. Technology posters often included software and hardware vendors such as Microsoft Corporation, Novell, Cisco Systems, Compaq, Hewlett Packard, IBM, and general pictures of computers, printers, complicated rack-mounted computer systems, and futuristic depictions of society and technology that are often associated with computer fantasy games. Cartoon characters often included Dilbert and took the form of cartoon strips that were cut from newspapers or magazines and posted in some conspicuous place.

Technology-based devices were frequently observed. These included hand held computing devices, digital cameras, network-monitoring devices, and general technology-based gadgets. It was observed that informants took pride in displaying these state-of-the-art devices and considered them as symbolic of their occupation. Physical settings observed included both those directly associated with IT operations and those that were organizational in nature. While aspects of computer rooms were discussed above in terms of physical artifacts, the computer rooms, IT offices, and work areas were also observed in terms of physical settings. In many cases, the physical setting of the computer room was different from the physical setting of the organization. The primary difference was that the computer room conveyed the concept of technology whereas organizational settings conveyed the concept of the business in which the organization was engaged. Physical settings also conveyed the concepts of elitism and exclusion. Access to computer rooms and IT facilities were, for the most part, restricted. Restrictions ranged from signs warning that access was restricted to only authorized personnel to sophisticated, coded locking mechanisms where entry could be gained only by entering a combination or using an electronic identification card.

Throughout the study, numerous activities and interactions were observed that served to inform the research. Activities of informants within the community tended to be occupation-based and specialized. Informants, acting in their capacity as a primary IT professional answered questions, gave directions and advice, and reviewed system performance. Informants more focused on technology appeared to take great pride when answering questions or solving technical problems. Such activity appeared to give the informant observed the opportunity to exhibit technical knowledge. However, in one situation, when an informant made a recommendation to a technician to solve a problem, another technician close by indicated that the solution was inappropriate and recommended an alternative. The immediate reaction exhibited by the informant first appeared to be anger, which was quickly followed by embarrassment when he realized the alternative was correct.

Interpersonal interactions observed were numerous. The primary types of interactions observed throughout the study involved storytelling, technology discussions, and learning activities. Storytelling often reverted to stories about users who did something that exhibited some form of computer illiteracy. Stories also depicted the incompetence or misinformed actions of a boss or other individual in upper-management. As a form of interaction, technology discussions were commonplace. Often these discussions provided members of the community an opportunity to exhibit their technical knowledge.

Social interactions within the community, not focused on technology, were rare. While attending a user-group meeting at the invitation of one informant, this researcher observed that social interactions within the group appeared awkward until conversations turned to technology. Members of the group tended to congregate with other members whom they knew beforehand. Few introductions were made and few attempts were made to meet new members. While the majority if individuals attending the user-group meeting were not from within the study population, it was observed that members, in general, did not share a social bond. The common bond appeared to be related to occupation and interest in a specific computer system.

While symbolism is a separate category of observation mentioned by Merriam (1998), in this study it was found that symbolism was not so much a separate category as it was a separate dimension of the other categories articulated. For example, this researcher interpreted the majority of physical artifacts observed as symbols of technology and technical knowledge. Of the physical settings observed, restricted access was symbolic of elitism and exclusion. Activities and interactions were symbolic of technical knowledge being a primary value. Likewise, nonverbal communications appeared symbolic of the concepts of elitism and the exclusionary nature of the culture.

Nonverbal communications, as indicated above, were symbolic of elitism and exclusion. When stories were told, facial expressions, eyes being raised to the sky, hand movements, and other body language served to reinforce the message contained in the story. These forms of nonverbal communication served to reinforce the idea that the primary value of the community was technical knowledge, that anyone not well-versed in computer technology was not part of the culture, and that IT was viewed as a key factor to the success of an organization.

ANALYSIS

Norms, Values, Beliefs, and Assumptions

Following the *cultural assumptions* topology outlined by Schein (1992), an analysis and interpretation of these data are presented.

1. *Mission and strategy—the nature of the occupational community's mission and the strategies intended to achieve its mission.* While the cultural community did not have a formal mission or strategy, the common underlying mission and strategy theme was for individual members to provide quality IT skills and knowledge to the organizations in which they worked. The strategy used to accomplish this was through constant IT training, often in the form of self-study.

2. *Goals—the nature of common goals and the methods by which goals are established.* The common goal of the community was to obtain as much technical knowledge as possible and develop as many technical skills as possible.

3. *The means the occupational community has to attain its goals.* The means available to the community to meet its goals of acquiring technical knowledge and skills include IT training of both a formal and informal nature, working with computer systems, and information sharing.

4. *Performance measurement—the nature of the occupational community's measurements.* Measurements appear to be based on the individual perception of one's technical knowledge and skill-base as compared to others. Through stories and other forms of articulation, members of the community are able to inform others of the level of their expertise—thus gaining acceptance and providing measurement. Through hands-on demonstration of knowledge and skills, or through an explanation of technique, members are able to convey their knowledge and skill-levels and, at the same time, measure their perception of the knowledge and skills of others.

5. *Correction—the consensus on the appropriate remedial strategies the occupational community uses in the event goals are not met.* The correction mechanism appears to be the perceived threat of humiliation in the eyes of other members. As evidenced by the data, individual members are fearful of potential humiliation should they be perceived by others as not being technically competent. Fear of humiliation becomes a strong motivator for increasing technical knowledge and technical expertise of an applied nature.

6. *The nature of reality and truth.* Perceptions of physical reality can be described as pragmatic. Reality in this context is represented by the computer systems for which the members of the community are responsible. However,

this view of reality does not necessarily extend to the use of the systems by other organization members. Often, that is considered abstract and outside the nature of the technology. The perception of social reality can be described as that which other members of the community may possess in terms of greater technical knowledge and skill. Individual reality is also pragmatic and based on the perception that individual value is measured in terms of the extent of one's technical knowledge and skill.

Based on the data collected, truth based on tradition is rejected in that tradition is perceived as reflecting older systems, past inefficiencies, and outdated methods or technologies. Truth based on authority is similarly rejected unless the authority has been accepted as a source of technical knowledge. Truth that survives conflict and debate may be accepted, providing the conflict and debate is limited to budget, usage, selection, or scheduling and in no way involves engineering aspects associated with networking, telecommunications, or computer science. Truth as that which works—the truly pragmatic truth as established by the scientific method—is accepted with little or no hesitation.

The data presented no evidence to suggest that reality and truth was in any way based on moral or religious principles. To the contrary, informants indicated they had no problem with monitoring private e-mail correspondence, Internet usage, or user files if they felt it necessary. There was ample indication that *the end justified the means*, especially when informants dealt with non-IT people in their organizations. Likewise, informants indicated normal behavior to include stretching the truth about system costs, project completion times, and support issues. In this context, perceptions of reality and truth were relative to their own ends and agendas. Informants felt justified in these behaviors because they considered themselves to be the experts in the technology whereas those with whom they had to deal with within their organizations were not and would not understand the complexities associated with the occupation.

7.   *The nature of time—perceptions of how the concept of time influences shared assumptions.* Time is viewed as the length of time necessary to solve a technical problem or implement a system. This concept transcended a normal workday. Often, when involved in a problem, technology-minded informants paid little attention to time and worked late into the night. They became *lost* in the activity. However, in instances when held accountable to a concept of time such as reporting to work, leaving work, or completing a project, the concept of time is also viewed as restrictive to autonomy. Data suggests that informants felt that they should not be accountable for time in the same way as other organizational members. Accounting for their time was considered demeaning to their perceived organizational value.

8. *The nature of space—assumptions of how space is allocated to members of the occupational community within organizations.* Space appears to be allocated to members of the community in proportion to size and complexity of the computer system for which they are responsible, and in relation to the importance their organizations place on IT functions. Space appears to be further allocated to members in proportion to the number of people they manage.

9. *The nature of human nature—assumptions concerned with Theory X or Theory Y relative to how members perceive they are viewed and view others.* Informants who were both managerially and technically focused preferred to be viewed through the eyes of a Theory Y manager. However, managerially focused IT professionals tended to view their subordinates in this manner only if the subordinate had achieved status by possessing high levels of technical knowledge and skill. Otherwise, managerially focused IT professional tended to view employees from the perspective of Theory X. Technically focused IT professionals tended to view all their subordinates from the perspective of Theory X.

Members interact with one another in a cautious way, until such time as the interacting parties understand the levels of position and the extent of the other's knowledge and skills. Above all, the culture reflects deep individualistic rather than group assumptions.

10. *Participation and involvement—assumptions concerning the nature of perceived participation and involvement in the daily life of the occupational community and the organizations in which they work.* Members do not see participation in the community as important. They prefer to remain as individuals, yet will approach known members of the community in an effort to obtain new knowledge. Within their organizations, members of the culture tend to remain apart from the normal activity of organizational daily life.

11. *Role relationships.* Within the cultural community, role relationships appear to be neutral in that the relationship is based on a common knowledge-base and occupation where relationships can remain distant. Relationships are also particularistic in that the knowledge-base and occupational commonality is not universally applicable to other communities. Role relationships are also oriented toward achievement in that it is a highly competitive culture concerning the acquisition of technical knowledge and proficiency. Further, it is oriented toward self in that the acquisition of technical knowledge and skill is a self-fulfilling activity intended for self-benefit.

12. *High-context and low-context meanings—assumptions about what is important and what is more important than something else.* Based on the value themes that emerged from this research, the culture places a high

importance on technology, viewing IT as the most important system within their organization. High importance is placed on technical knowledge and skills. To a lesser degree, importance is also placed on general education, autonomy, work ethic, along with the quality and integrity of the systems for which the members are individually responsible.

CONCLUSIONS

The culture of IT professionals in western New York can be defined in terms of norms, values, beliefs, and assumptions. This culture can be described as elitist, valuing technical knowledge and skill above other values. It can be further described as exclusionary to the extent that it excludes from membership those individuals who do not possess a sufficiently high level of technical knowledge and skill ranging from the ability to manage IT resources to using IT resources. Furthermore, the culture views other individuals who are not members of the IT community, or others who do not possess a high level of technical skills, as uninformed. The culture tends to view others from an *etic* rather than an *emic* perspective. The culture views technical knowledge and skill as essential to achieve its informal mission of delivering stable, high-quality computer systems to organizations. It believes in a strong work ethic, tends to be pragmatic, sees the end as justifying the means, and values the ability to work and make important decisions independently.

Normative behavior for this group includes the constant acquisition of technical knowledge and skill in an effort to deliver quality and stable computer systems to the organizations that employ the individual members. Often the common strategy used to accomplish this is self-learning. Normal behavior also includes storytelling. This mode of communication is often used to articulate to others the extent to which the storyteller has mastered a level of technical knowledge and skill. Measurements of technical knowledge and skill appear to be based on the individual member's perception of his or her own knowledge and skill-base compared to others in the community, and is manifested through the constant articulation of knowledge and the visible application of skills to others. Consequently, the culture of the community is highly competitive. Individuals within and outside the community who possess high levels of technical knowledge or skill can be viewed as potential threats. This view often acts as a catalyst to learn more. Another catalyst to learn more is represented by the correction mechanism the culture uses, which is represented by the potential of humiliation in the event a member's technical knowledge or skill proves to be inadequate.

While cultural norms, values, beliefs, and assumptions are transmitted to and reinforced by members of the community in a variety of ways, through normal interaction, the data collected in this study show that two important and highly effective methods of cultural transference and reinforcement are outsourcing and storytelling. From a systems perspective (e.g., Von Bertalanffy, 1972; McLeod, 1995), IT outsourcing represents the input of new technical knowledge or skill to the organization. Since technical knowledge and skill is a primary element of the culture, the input of new technical knowledge and skill serves to enhance the cultural values.

Implications of the Research to IT Professionals

Implications of this research to the IT community relate to the necessity for increased self-awareness, increased awareness of the organization, a broader scope of knowledge, and an unexpected justification of outsourcing. The findings suggest there were differences in focus between managerially oriented IT professionals and those who were more technically focused. Those informants more focused toward the managerial tended to provide a better interface between their organizations, their subordinates, and the technology they managed. This may be due to their being more a part of the traditional management structure of their organizations than being pure technical managers. While they had technical skills and were a part of the IT community, they were also clearly part of the organization's management community to the extent that they operated within two distinct occupational subcultures. Their focus tended to closer reflect the concepts of systems theory and systems thinking than the reductionist and more positivistic views of pure IT managers who focused more on the technical. Consequently, their more holistic view of IT in relation to the organization and the organization's processes allowed them to provide a better interface. The implication is that this combination of skills, managerially based systems thinking and technical knowledge, may allow these members of the IT community to more effectively contribute to the success of IT operations and to the success of organizations that depend on the technology they provide.

For those IT professionals who are more technically focused, it is recommended that their focus be expanded to include a more holistic view of the organization. It is recommended that they become more active participants in their organizations as a whole and, especially, expand their focus to include an intimate understanding of business process. They should better understand the strategic goals of their organizations and the functional goals and processes of each department or unit within their organizations. Even if their organizations are fragmented and unfamiliar with the concepts of systems thinking, because IT touches virtually all aspects of the modern organization, their systems focus could act as a central point from which holistic thinking could emanate and spread. Consequently, they should not only support the business process by applying technology within their organizations but also become part of the business planning process.

The findings also have implications to the culture's understanding of *self*. While informants complained, to some extent, that their mission and importance to their organizations were misunderstood or undervalued, the data suggest that their elitist and exclusionary behavior was more to blame for this misunderstanding than their organizational environment. For example, misunderstandings reported may stem from poor communications or from elitist attitudes. As the findings suggest, only one actual IT mission statement was found to exist. One informant indicated that one might exist. If the mission of IT is to be understood and valued within an organization, the mission must be communicated to the organization and be a part of the overall mission of the company. However, for IT to be valued, the communication of the IT mission statement must be trusted. Elitist and exclusionary behavior, especially as indicated by and depicted in stories told, creates barriers to trust. This is because stories do not remain solely within the IT community. They become known throughout the organization and the organization's environment. While stories play an important role within the IT community as a means to display technical knowledge to others and serve to help transmit and reinforce cultural norms, values, and beliefs to new members, they are heard throughout the organization in a counterproductive way. Users *know* they are considered to be *second-class* citizens in the eyes of IT professionals and may respond accordingly. Consequently, IT professionals should be aware of the holistic effects such behavior has on their efforts to be more fully appreciated and valued.

Further implications deal with concepts of educational breadth and interpersonal interaction. Those IT management professionals who are especially focused on the technology should develop more interpersonal or *people* skills. This could be accomplished through education, beyond the technical, that would encompass a liberal studies curriculum and the development of a more open mind when dealing with users who are not part of the occupational sub-culture. Some of the fault herein lies with organizational management. IT professionals, especially whose focus is primarily or exclusively on technology, are often hired for their technical competence. Yet, they are expected to display skills in human understanding and behavior for which they were not prepared. Or, they were promoted to positions within their organizations that required these additional skills but were not provided with the proper training or educational opportunities to succeed.

Implications to Organizations

Whereas IT professionals must learn to focus more on business process, organizations must allow IT professionals to do so. This means allowing IT professionals to be proactive in the strategic and functional planning efforts of the entire organization. It also means demanding that IT professionals support organizational plans through formal IT strategic planning efforts that include or support an IT mission statement.

From the findings, there is ample evidence to suggest that IT professionals, at least within the study sample, feel unappreciated and undervalued. As previously stated, such attitudes could be caused by elitist and exclusionary behavior on the part of IT professionals. However, the cause of this problem is also shared by organizations that do not always include IT professionals in the strategic and functional planning process, value them only for technical skills, and allow elitist behavior to exist.

Other implications of this study deal with an organization's ability to understand human behavior and the human aspects of IT. While all individuals within an organization should attempt to understand human nature if they are to achieve a common goal by working together, it is especially important for all managers in an organization to understand human behavior and diversity. While diversity is often related to gender, ethnicity, and race, diversity also includes different points of view, philosophies, and the norms of behavior, beliefs, values, and assumptions of various subcultures.

REFERENCES

Agar, M. H. (1980). *The Professional Stranger*. New York: Academic Press.

Davis, E. W. (1992). Global outsourcing: Have U.S. managers thrown the baby out with the bath water? *Business Horizons*, July-August, 58-66.

Denison, D. R. (1990). *Corporate Culture and Organizational Effectiveness*. New York: John Wiley & Sons, Inc.

Denzin, N. K., & Lincoln, Y. S. (1994). *Handbook of Qualitative Research*. Thousand Oaks, CA: Sage Publications.

Dessler, G. (1980). *Organization Theory: Integrating Structure and Behavior*. Englewood Cliffs, NJ: Prentice-Hall, Inc.

Detert, J. R., Schroeder, R. G., & Muriel, J. J. (2000). A framework for linking culture and improvement initiatives in organizations. *Academy of Management Review*, 25(4), 850-878.

Due, R. T. (1992). The real costs of outsourcing. *Information Systems Management*, 9(1), 78-82.

Earl, M. J. (1996). The risks of outsourcing it. *Sloan Management Review*, 39, 26-32.

Fetterman, D. M. (1989). *Ethnography: Step by Step*. Newbury Park, CA: Sage Publications, Inc.

Frederick, W. C. (1995). *Values and Culture in the American Corporation*. New York: Oxford University Press.

Freidson, E. (1973). Professions and the occupational principle. In Freidson, E. (Ed.), *Professions and Their Prospects*. Beverly Hills, CA: Sage Publications, Inc.

Grover, V., & Cheon, M. J. (1996). The effect of service quality and partnership on the outsourcing of information systems functions. *Journal of Management Information Systems*, 12(4), 89-96.

Gummesson, E. (1988). *Qualitative Methods in Management Research: Case study Research, Participant Observation, Action Research/Action Science, and Other Qualitative Methods Used in Academic Research and Management Consultancy*. Bromley: Chartwell-Bratt.

Hammersley, M. (1998). *Reading Ethnographic Research: A Critical Guide* (2nd Ed.). New York: Addison Wesley Longman.

Holstein, J. A., & Gubrium, J. F. (1995). *The Active Interview*. Thousand Oaks, CA: Sage Publications, Inc.

Jessor, R., Colby, A., & Shweder, R. A. (Eds.). (1996). *Ethnography and Human Development*. Chicago, IL: University of Chicago Press.

Johnson, J. C. (1990). *Selecting Ethnographic Informants*. Newbury Park, CA: Sage Publications, Inc.

Kirk, J., & Miller, M. L. (1986). *Reliability and Validity in Qualitative Research*. Newbury Park, CA: Sage Publications, Inc.

Kottak, C. P. (2000). *Cultural Anthropology*. New York: McGraw-Hill, Inc.

Lareau, A., & Scultz, J. (1996). *Journeys Through Ethnography*. Boulder, CO: Westview Press.

Martin, J. (1992). *Cultures in Organizations: Three Perspectives*. New York: Oxford University Press.

McLeod, R., Jr. (1995). Systems theory and information resources management: Integrating key concepts. *Information Resources Management Journal*, 8(2), 5-14.

Merriam, S. B. (1998). *Qualitative Research and Case Study Applications in Education*. San Francisco: Jossey-Bass Publishers.

Miles, M. B., & Huberman, A. M. (1994). *Qualitative Data Analysis*. Thousand Oaks, CA: Sage Publications, Inc.

O'Reilly, C. A., & Chatman, J. A. (1996). Culture as social control: Corporations, cults, and commitment. *Research in Organizational Behavior*, 18, 157-200.

Pettigrew, A. M. (1979). On studying organizational cultures. *Administrative Science Quarterly*, 24, 570-581.

Robbins, S. P. (1997). *Essentials of Organizational Behavior*. Upper Saddle River, NJ: Prentice Hall.

Schein, E. H. (1992). *Organizational Culture and Leadership*. San Francisco: Jossey-Bass Publishers, Inc.

Schein, L. (1989). *A Manager's Guide to Corporate Culture*. New York: Conference Board, Inc.

Sharpe, M. (1997). Outsourcing, organizational competitiveness, and work. *Journal of Labor Research*, 18(4), 535-549.

Stake, R. E. (1995). *The Art of Case Study Research*. Thousand Oaks, CA: Sage Publications, Inc.

Szewczak, E., & Khosrowpour, M. (1996). *The Human Side of Information Technology Management*. Hershey, PA: Idea Group Publishing.

Trice, H. M. (1993). *Occupational Subcultures in the Workplace*, (6). Ithaca, NY: ILR Press. Cornell Studies in Institutional and Labor Relations.

Von Bertalanffy, L. (1972). *General Systems Theory: Foundations, Development, and Applications*. London: Allen Lane.

Young, D. W. (2000). The six levers for managing organizational culture. *Business Horizons*, 43(5), 19-32.

About the Authors

Edward J. Szewczak is Professor and Chair of the MCIS Department at Canisius College in Buffalo, NY. He received a Ph.D. from the University of Pittsburgh in 1985. His published research has appeared in the *Journal of MIS*, *Information & Management*, *Data Base*, the *Information Resources Management Journal*, the *European Journal of Operational Research*, the *Journal of Management Systems*, the *Journal of Microcomputer Systems Management*, *Omega*, the *Organizational Behavior Teaching Review*, *Simulation and Games* and *Logique et Analyse*. He has co-edited three books of readings published by Idea Group Publishing, including *Management Impacts of Information Technology: Perspectives on Organizational Change and Growth* (1991), *The Human Side of Information Technology* (1996), and *Measuring Information Technology Investment Payoff: Contemporary Approaches* (1999). His research interests include MIS evaluation, and information privacy and Internet technology. He is currently serving as an Associate Editor of the *Information Resources Management Journal*.

Coral R. Snodgrass (Ph.D., 1984, Katz Graduate School of Business, University of Pittsburgh) is Professor and Chair of the Management and Marketing Department at Canisius College in Buffalo, NY. She is also the Director of the International Business Programs at the College. Dr. Snodgrass has published numerous articles on the topic of strategy and international business and she has authored a number of strategy cases. She is involved with collaborative projects with colleagues in England, Ireland, France, Belgium, Germany, Sweden and Mexico. These projects include course and program development as well as student and faculty exchanges. Dr. Snodgrass is the book editor for the *Information Resources Management Journal*. She is member of such academic societies as the Strategic Management Society and the Academy of International Business. She sits on the board of a number of local organizations such as Buffalo-Niagara World Connect.

***

Ellen Baker is an Honorary Associate in the School of Management at the University of Technology, Sydney, Australia. Prior to that, she had been on the academic staff there for 20 years. Ellen holds a Ph.D. from the University of London. She has published widely on management implications of communication and information technologies. Her current research interests include virtual working, the household-workplace, and the application of collaborative technologies to innovation teams and media production work.

Walter O. Einstein specializes in management development and is Professor of Management in the Charlton College of Business at the University of Massachusetts. His numerous publications and personal consulting papers center around practical applications of theory-based management and leadership skills, as well as practical performance appraisal systems. Using diagnostic leadership models he developed, Dr. Einstein has helped managers in organizations ranging from "mom and pop" pizza restaurants to public service agencies to major employers on the Fortune 500 list. He holds a Systems Management Master's degree from the University of Southern California (1974) and a Ph.D. in Organizational Behavior from Syracuse University (1981). Dr. Einstein retired from the United States Air Force as Vice Commander of the 416th Strategic Bomb Wing at Rome, NY.

Brent Gallupe is a Professor of Information Systems and Director of the Queen's Executive Decision Centre at the School of Business, Queen's University at Kingston, Canada. His current research interests are in computer support for groups and teams, the evaluation of information systems in public sector organizations, and the history of information systems. His work has been published in such journals as *Management Science, Academy of Management Journal, Journal of Applied Psychology, and Sloan Management Review.*

Robert W. Gerulat is Asst. Professor, Business Management and Economics, SUNY-Empire State College, where he is also Director of FORUM Management Education Program. He earned a B.A. in History from SUNY-Buffalo, an M.A. in Liberal Studies at SUNY-ESC concentrating in History and Anthropology, and a Ph.D. in Management at Walden University. For over twelve years, Dr. Gerulat has been involved in the field of IT management both as a director and consultant in the insurance, computer, and health care industries. His research interests are studying the effects of information technology on organizations and cultures from an anthropological perspective.

John H. Humphreys is currently Assistant Professor of Management in the College of Business at Eastern New Mexico University. He holds a Bachelor's degree in Psychology from the University of Southern Mississippi (1988), a Master's degree in Management from Webster University (1995), and the Doctor of Business Administration degree (Management) from Nova Southeastern University (2000). His research and various publications are primarily focused on the many psychological and personality variables that impact the leader/follower dyad. Prior to joining academia, Dr. Humphreys held a leadership position with a multi-billion dollar financial services organization and has considerable experience as a corporate consultant specializing in organizational leadership, culture, change, and development.

Ned Kock is a CIGNA Research Fellow and Director of the E-Collaboration Research Center in the Fox School of Business and Management, Temple University, Philadelphia. He holds a Ph.D. in Information Systems from the School of Management Studies, University of Waikato, New Zealand. Ned has been the PI/co-PI in funded research projects totalling over US$ 500,000. He is the author/co-author of over 70 research papers and three books, including the best-selling *Process Improvement and Organizational Learning: The Role of Collaboration Technologies*.

Laura Lally is currently an Associate Professor of Business Computer Information Systems at Hofstra University. Dr. Lally received her Ph.D. in Information Systems from New York University's Stern School of Business. She has presented numerous conference papers and has published articles in *Decision Science*, the *Journal of End-User Computing*, the *Journal of Global Information Management*, the *Information Society* and the *Journal of Business Ethics*. Her current research interests include the risks of reengineering, privacy in the hiring process, and the application of the use of consumer product involvement on Web purchasing behavior.

Robert J. McQueen is Associate Professor in the Department of Management Systems, University of Waikato, New Zealand, and former Chairman of the Department of Computer Science there. He holds an M.B.A. from the Harvard Business School, and a Ph.D. in Computer Science from the University of Waikato. His previous industry experience includes positions at IBM in Toronto and DEC in Vancouver. His Harvard M.B.A. led to the founding in 1976 of McQueen Technology, a small business in Guelph, Canada, which designed and installed specialized microcomputer-based data acquisition systems for six years in the packaging industry.

Ali Metwalli is an Associate Professor of Finance at Western Michigan University. He received his Ph.D. from St. Louis University. Before joining WMU, he taught at Central Michigan University, Pacific University, and Portland State University. His teaching areas are in Finance, Management and Health Care Administration. He has published several articles and proceedings.

Olivia Ernst Neece is the Director of Operations of The Ernst Group, and EON Corporation investment groups. She has been involved in academic research at the Jet Propulsion Laboratory, Nortel Inc., and ST Inc. She has also been an Assistant Professor at California State University Northridge in the Management and Finance, Real Estate, and Insurance Departments, taught at UCLA Extension, and presented speeches and seminars nationwide for business and industry groups. Olivia is a Ph.D. candidate in Strategic Management at The Peter F. Drucker Center for Management, Claremont Graduate University. She has written numerous magazine and journal articles and received the Best Paper award for her paper in the OCIS division of the Academy of Management's 2001 meeting. Ms. Neece has held the positions of Vice President of Project Administration for Hirsch Bedner Associates, Vice President of Operations and Project Development of AIRCOA (Richfield Hotels), and President of Olivia Neece Planning and Design. She earned her B.S., Business - Finance from the University of Southern California and an M.B.A. from the University of California Los Angeles. She is a member of Beta Gamma Sigma, the Academy of Management, the Strategic Management Society, the Association for Information Systems and Institute for Operations Research and Management Sciences. Olivia is a Founder of the Performing Arts Center of Los Angeles, a member of Club 100 and has held Board and Committee posts for the L. A. Opera, Master Chorale and Philharmonic organizations.

Huub J.M. Ruël is an Assistant Professor in the Department of Human Resource Management at the University of Twente in the Netherlands. He holds an M.B.A. degree in Work and Organizational Psychology and a Bachelor's degree in Human Resource Management. In 2001, the author received his Ph.D. for his thesis on the non-technical side of office technology. Dr. Ruël is doing research on the interaction between information technology and organization and teaches courses on this topic to Business Administration and Business Information Technology undergraduates.

Thekla Rura-Polley is a Senior Lecturer in the School of Management at the University of Technology, Sydney, where she teaches organization theory and research methods. She received her Ph.D. in Business Administration from the University of Wisconsin - Madison. Her research interests cover population level learning, innovation, virtual collaboration and technology management.

Sofiane Sahraoui is an Assistant Professor of Information Systems at the American University of Sharjah in the United Arab Emirates. He received his Ph.D. in Management Information Systems from the University of Pittsburgh in the USA in 1994. His research interests are knowledge management, IT planning, enterprise modeling, and the management of IT-based change in general. He has published in the *Journal of Information Technology Management, Behaviour & Information Technology*, and the *Journal of Computer Information Systems* and had other invited papers and a book chapter. He also presented his work at numerous international conferences. His teaching interests are in the areas of business modeling with UML, IT change and strategy, and the human side of IT.

Andrew Targowski is a Professor of Computer Information Systems at Western Michigan University. He received his Ph.D. from Warsaw Polytechnic in 1969. His teaching and research interests are architectural systems development, global/national/local/enterprise information infrastructures development, and information civilization development. He is the author of numerous articles and books in the information management science discipline. He is a Vice President of Information Resource Management Association.

Dianne Willis is a Senior Lecturer in Information Management at Leeds Metropolitan University. Her research interests include sociotechnical issues surrounding the implementation of new technology in business and social environments. She is currently undertaking a Ph.D. concentrating on gender issues in the field of ICT, particularly factors influencing participation levels in both academic and practical fields. She has also published articles in journals, books and presented at conferences. As a member of the BCS Sociotechnical group, she has co-edited two books entitled *The New SocioTech: Graffiti on the Longwall* and *Knowledge Management in the Sociotechnical World: The Graffiti continues*. She is currently researching in the field of Computer-Mediated Communication.

Pak Yoong is an Associate Professor in Information Systems and Foundation Director of the Masters Programme in Information Systems at the School of Information Management, Victoria University of Wellington, New Zealand. His current research interests are computer support for groups and teams, the facilitation of distributed meetings, telework, virtual teams and end user support. His work has appeared in the *Journal of Information Technology and People*, *Informing Science*, and *Internet Research - Electronic Networking Applications and Policy.*

Index

0024